COLLINS GUIDE TO THE BUTTERFLIES OF BRITAIN AND EUROPE

RobCampbell
April 2003

D0230727

COLLINS GUIDE TO BUTTERFLIES

A photographic guide to the butterflies of Britain and Europe

Michael Chinery

with photographs by Ted Benton and Basil Yates-Smith

Photographs assembled by FLPA

HarperCollinsPublishers

HarperCollins*Publishers*
77–85 Fulham Palace Road
London
W6 8JB

First published 1998

2 4 6 8 10 9 7 5 3 1
98 00 02 03 01 99

ISBN 0 00 220059 7

Edit and page make-up by D & N Publishing, UK

Illustrations by Richard Lewington

Cartography by Carte Blanche, Basingstoke

Colour origination by United Graphic Pte., Singapore
Printed and bound by Rotolito Lombarda SpA, Milan, Italy

CONTENTS

PREFACE

The text of this book is a distillation of
information acquired during some 40 years
of wandering around the countryside of
Europe, of pulling out thousands of museum
drawers, and, of course, consulting a wide
range of other books and journals. It could
not possibly have been put together without
the help of a great many people and I am
grateful to all those authors, amateur as well
as professional, whose published work has
enabled this book to approach some degree
of comprehensiveness. Being a non-
mountaineer, I have had to rely largely on
others for information about the behaviour
of montane species and their upper limits.
The major works that I have consulted
during the preparation of the text are: *The
Moths and Butterflies of Great Britain and
Ireland* (Vol. 7, Part 1), edited by Emmet
and Heath, *The Butterflies of Scandinavia in
Nature* by Henriksen and Kreutzer, *Die
Tagfalter der Türkei* by Hesselbarth, van
Oorschot, and Wagener (in German, it
contains a wealth of information on many of
the butterflies occurring in Greece), *A Field
Guide to the Butterflies of Britain and Europe* by
Higgins and Riley, *A Field Guide to the
Butterflies and Burnets of Spain* by Manley and
Allcard, and *Tagfalter und ihre Lebensräume*
produced by Schweizerischer Bund für
Naturschutz (in German). There are still
gaps in the information on the life histories
and early stages of many butterflies. These
may be real gaps in knowledge, or merely
apparent gaps due to my failing to delve
deeply enough into the published literature.
I will be pleased to receive any information
with which to plug these gaps.

I am especially grateful to Ted Benton
and Basil Yates-Smith, who have provided
the bulk of the superb photographs that
make the book what it is, and to Richard
Lewington for most of the line drawings.
Basil was involved with the project from its
inception, willingly reading the text in its
entirety and contributing a great deal of his
knowledge and personal field observations.

Staff at The Natural History Museum and the Insect Room in the Department of Zoology at Cambridge University have kindly allowed me to examine the butterfly collections in their care over the years. The wardens of numerous nature reserves and national parks have always been helpful in pointing me in the direction of various butterflies; Mr John Coutsis of Athens suggested some remarkably rich butterfly sites in Northern Greece; and Mr Peter Jaggs, nearer home in Suffolk, kindly helped by lending literature. My wife, Jill, has been wonderfully supportive, not just during the preparation of this book but throughout the preceding 30 years when she was often left holding the babies while I chased insects across Europe.

Myles Archibald at HarperCollins has kept a firm but friendly grip on the project and guided it efficiently through its long metamorphosis from the initial idea to the printed book. But I reserve my most heartfelt thanks for my late friend John Sankey, who encouraged and honed my interest in natural history during my teenage years and who first introduced me to the joys of foreign travel and the delights of the French countryside. Over the years, we explored many areas of France together, with several particularly enjoyable trips to the slopes of Mont Ventoux ('Fabre's Mountain') where I 'interviewed' more than 50 butterfly species for the first time. I am pleased to dedicate this book to the memory of a fine teacher and a great friend.

Michael Chinery
Suffolk, 1998

INTRODUCTION

Butterflies are undoubtedly amongst the most colourful and attractive of insects and have courted more attention from amateur entomologists and naturalists than any other group of insects. With the exception of a few economically important groups and species, such as the mosquitoes and the honey bee, the butterflies have also been subjected to more intensive professional studies than any other insect. Hundreds of books have been written about them in all parts of the world, and many societies are devoted to their study and well-being. Their role as indicators of a healthy countryside adds importance to beauty. Many suggestions have been put forward to explain the origin of the word butterfly, but I believe there is no need to look further than the simple beauty of these insects for the derivation of the name. The Old English name for a butterfly was *buttor-fleoge*, and it does not require too much imagination to derive this from the Old French word *biaute* meaning beauty. In other words, butterfly may simply be a corruption or shortening of beauty-fly.

Butterflies belong to the order Lepidoptera, which they share with the moths. Lepidoptera means 'scale-wings' and refers to the dust-like scales that clothe the wings and give them their colours and patterns. The scales overlap each other like miniature roof tiles. The order contains about 165,000 known species, and many more undoubtedly await discovery. Only the beetles have more known species – over 350,000 of them. There are no butterflies or moths in Antarctica, but otherwise the group is distributed all over the world, including the Arctic tundra where the Arctic Fritillary has been seen flying at 81°N, within about 600 miles of the North Pole.

Only about 20,000 of the 165,000 or so known Lepidoptera species are butterflies. The others are all moths, so the division between butterflies and moths is a very unequal one. It is also an artificial division with no scientific basis, for the butterflies belong to just two of the 41 superfamilies into which the world's Lepidoptera is currently divided and there is no single difference between all moths on the one hand and all butterflies on the other. The figure of 41 superfamilies is that given in *The Lepidoptera*, by Malcolm Scoble (1992), although entomologists differ considerably in their opinions as to how many superfamilies – and families – there really are. Thomas Mouffet saw no fundamental difference between butterflies and moths, and in his *Theatrum Insectorum*, published in 1634, he referred to the moths simply as 'nocturnal butterflies'. Several European languages retain this simple approach: German, for example, has *tagfalter* and *nachtfalter*, while French has *papillons diurnes* and *papillons nocturnes* (or *papillons de nuit*) and Spanish has *mariposa* and *mariposa nocturna*. Hungarian has *nappali lepkék* and *éjjeli lepkék*, meaning diurnal butterflies and nocturnal butterflies respectively. But flight-time is not a reliable way of distinguishing butterflies from moths because, although all of our European butterflies fly by day, there are also many day-flying moths and many of them are just as colourful as the butterflies. In the far north, they all have to fly in daylight in the summer.

As far as the European species are concerned, the best way to distinguish the two groups is to look at the antennae: our butterflies all have swollen tips to their antennae, whereas most moths have thread-like or feathery antennae. Given this distinction, the only moths likely to be confused with butterflies are the brightly coloured burnets. These fly by day, but their antennae expand gradually towards the tip and usually end in a small point, quite unlike the antennae of most butterflies. Some skipper antennae resemble those of the burnets, but our European skippers cannot be confused with the black and red burnets. Resting positions can also be helpful in distinguishing butterflies from moths. Most moths, including the

typical clubbed antenna of butterfly

hooked antenna of skipper butterfly

feathery antenna of Emperor Moth

hair-like antenna, found in many moths

clubbed antenna of Burnet Moth

A selection of butterfly and moth antennae.

burnets, rest with their wings folded back over the body like a tent, with only the uppersides visible, but, with the exception of the very moth-like Dingy Skipper (*see* p.619), the butterflies are unable to fold their wings in this way. They may feed and bask with their wings wide open, but when truly at rest they always close their wings vertically over the body so that only the undersides are visible.

Butterfly Evolution
The fossil record shows that moths were flying at the time of the dinosaurs, some 150 million years ago. Some may have been in existence long before that, but it is impossible to tell whether the fragmentary fossils belong to moths or to caddis flies. Caddis flies, which belong to the order Trichoptera, are the closest relatives of the Lepidoptera and the two groups undoubtedly had a common ancestor, although we have no tangible evidence of such an ancestor. The earliest known butterfly fossils are only about 50 million years old, but they must have arisen a good deal earlier – probably from some kind of moth. All the major butterfly families were in existence 40 million years ago, by which time the general form of the insects was much the same as that of today's butterflies.

The Butterfly Body
In common with that of other insects, the butterfly body has three main parts: head, thorax and abdomen. The head carries the antennae or feelers, a pair of large compound eyes, and the highly characteristic nectar-sipping tongue or proboscis. The antennae, whose form has already been described, carry a wide range of sensory equipment used for detecting scent and for picking up a variety of tactile signals. Much of the head is taken up by the compound eyes, so called because each is composed of hundreds or even thousands of tiny lenses. The proboscis, about as thick as a human hair, is like a drinking straw and in some species it is as long as the body. The butterfly pushes it deep into flowers to reach the nectar. A knee-like

hinge near the middle of the proboscis allows the butterfly to probe several flowers in a cluster without continually changing its position and thereby possibly making itself more conspicuous. When not in use, the proboscis is rolled up under the butterfly's head and concealed between the palps. The latter are rather hairy, sensory appendages attached to the lower side of the head (*see* diagram below).

The two pairs of wings are carried on the thorax, with the forewings usually a little

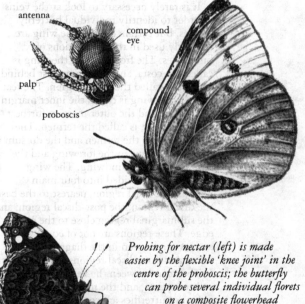

antenna

compound eye

palp

proboscis

Probing for nectar (left) is made easier by the flexible 'knee joint' in the centre of the proboscis; the butterfly can probe several individual florets on a composite flowerhead without moving its feet.

Palps and antennae are attached to the head. The palps are clothed with hairs and scales and they stick forward from the head like two short horns. They play an important role in determining the quality of food, and especially the suitability of foodplants for egg-laying. Wings and legs are attached to the thorax. The abdomen, shown ghosted through the wings above, has no limbs.

larger and more angular than the hindwings. The delicate wing-membranes are supported by a number of veins, although these are often concealed by the covering of scales. The arrangement of the veins, known as the venation, is of considerable importance in the classification of butterflies into families (*see* p.25), and even more so in the classification of moths. Although the veins have received a variety of names, entomologists now generally refer to them by number, beginning at the rear of each wing as shown in the diagram.

It is rarely necessary to look at the veins in order to identify individual butterfly species, but certain areas of the wing are regularly used in the descriptions of butterflies. The front edge of the wing is called the costa, and the region just behind it is often called the costal region. The rear edge of the wing is called the inner margin or dorsum, and the outer margin, furthest from the body, is called the termen. The angle between the termen and the dorsum is called the tornus in the forewing and the anal angle in the hindwing. The wing surface is also divided into four main regions: the basal region, nearest to the base; the discal region; the post-discal region; and the submarginal region close to the outer edge. These regions are not of equal width and, as can be seen in the diagram, the discal and post-discal regions are the largest.

The areas between the veins are called cells or spaces, and the most important one as far as butterflies are concerned is the discal cell, commonly referred to simply as 'the cell': it is large, more or less oval, and extends from near the base to about the centre of the wing. There is often a dark spot – the discal spot – at its outer end. The spaces in the outer parts of the wings are simply numbered according to the veins behind or below them. Space 2, for example (often abbreviated to S 2), lies immediately on the front of vein 2.

As already described, the wings are clothed with scales. Most of the scales

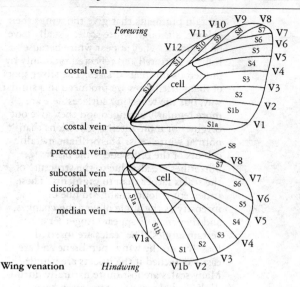

Forewing

V12 V11 V10 V9 V8 V7 V6 V5 V4 V3 V2 V1

S12 S1 S10 S9 S8 S7 S6 S5 S4 S3 S2 S1b S1a

costal vein

cell

costal vein

precostal vein

subcostal vein

discoidal vein

median vein

cell

S8 S7 V8 S6 V7 S5 V6 S4 V5

S1a

S1b

V1a V1b S1 S2 S3 V2 V3 V4

Wing venation   *Hindwing*

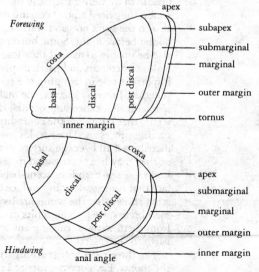

Forewing

apex

subapex

submarginal

marginal

outer margin

tornus

costa

basal   discal   post discal

inner margin

basal

costa

discal

post discal

apex

submarginal

marginal

outer margin

inner margin

Hindwing

anal angle

Wing-area notation

The butterfly wing.

contain pigments that give the wings their colours, although white scales usually have no pigment. They appear white because light is scattered and reflected randomly by numerous internal surfaces. The silver spots of many fritillaries are produced in a similar way, but the reflecting surfaces here are more regularly arranged and they give out brighter or more intense reflections than normal white cells. The brilliant metallic colours of the blues and some other butterflies are also due to the structure of the scales rather than to pigments. These iridescent colours change in hue or intensity as the angle of viewing changes, and they may disappear altogether at certain angles. The scales are inserted loosely into the wing-membrane and are easily detached if the insects are handled. Many scales are lost quite naturally during flight and older specimens often have almost transparent patches on their wings. The loss of scales appears to do no harm to some butterfly species, but others are unable to fly well if they lose too many scales: they need a good coating of scales to absorb the sun's rays and warm up their bodies before flight. Some butterflies may also be unable to mate if they lose a lot of scales, for colours and patterns play an important role in bringing the sexes together. In many species, the male bears special scales, called androconia, that release scents that stimulate the courtship and mating processes. These scales may be distributed all over the surface of the wing, or they may be concentrated in certain areas known as sex-brands or scent-bands. The fact that some scales can produce and emit scent shows that the wings are living membranes, even though bits can be torn from them without causing any apparent harm to the insects.

The three pairs of legs are all attached to the thorax. Each one consists of a number of segments and normally ends in a pair of small claws, although the front legs are reduced to brush-like structures in some families. Butterflies do not walk much and the legs are used primarily for clinging to plants. The feet, technically known as the tarsi, also possess sensory organs capable of detecting various chemicals. When a butterfly lands on a flower, it will not normally unroll its tongue unless the tarsi are stimulated by the 'taste' of sugary nectar. The tarsi are also important in reproduction: female butterflies determine the suitability of plants for egg-laying by stamping on the leaves or scratching them with their feet, and only if the right scents are released will the females begin to lay their eggs.

The abdomen is more or less cylindrical and is clothed with hairs or scales. It has no limbs, although the male has a pair of flap-like claspers right at the tip of the abdomen. These are used to hold the female during copulation, but are not normally visible at other times. Some butterflies, notably the Monarch and the Plain Tiger, have eversible tufts of long hairs at the tip of the abdomen. These tufts, known as hair-pencils, are normally concealed, but when the male goes courting he everts them and brushes them over a patch of scent-scales on each hindwing. The scent is then efficiently disseminated to the female while the male flies around her. Many moths have similar hair-pencils, either on the abdomen or on the legs.

Butterfly Feeding Habits

Although nectar is the main source of food for butterflies, many woodland species, such as the Speckled Wood and the Purple Hairstreak, rely largely on the sugary honeydew dropped by aphids. Over-ripe fruit and the sap oozing from wounded trees also attract many butterflies, and several species sip the putrid fluids surrounding carrion and dung. In the drier parts of Europe, clouds of blues can be seen drinking from wet ground, especially in the vicinity of animal dung and urine. Several skippers and fritillaries also indulge in this habit, and they are often joined by the Black-veined White. The butterflies in these drinking parties are nearly all males and recent research indicates that they are replenishing their supplies of mineral salts, especially sodium, which is needed for the proper formation of the sperm packages that are passed on to the females during mating. The drinking habit is not confined to dry regions, but it is most obvious there because of the way in which the insects congregate at the scattered damp patches. In damper regions there is rarely any need for the butterflies to congregate in any one spot to drink.

The Butterfly Life-cycle   Courtship among the butterflies is usually initiated by visual signals, most often with the male making the first move and flying towards anything of about the right size and colour. If it turns out to be a receptive female of the same species, scents or pheromones take over and courtship becomes more serious. The females emit one or more scents from glands in the abdomen, while the males release scent from specialized scales on their wings, as described on p.14. Courting males often flutter their wings in what looks like a visual display, but it is really a way of wafting the scent from their wings to the female antennae. In some species, including many skippers and the much-studied grayling, the female has to brush her

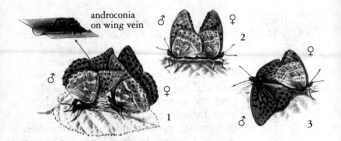

androconia on wing vein

The final stages of courtship and mating in the Silver-washed Fritillary (after Magnus). Attracted initially by the female's pattern, the male dances around her until she settles and then lands in front of her. He rubs his wings against her antennae (1), and in doing so transfers stimulating pheromones from the androconia (scent scales) on his wing veins. Copulation soon follows (2). During copulation, the male often sits with his wings open (3): by absorbing the sun's heat in this way, he is ready for a quick take-off in any emergency.

antennae on the male's wings in order to get enough pheromone to trigger the next stage of courtship. If she is not sufficiently stimulated, she will break off the affair and not waste further time and effort on a less than vigorous suitor who might not be able to fertilize her eggs efficiently.

If all the right signals are given and accepted, courtship ends in mating. The butterflies face in the same direction at first and the male caresses the female's abdomen with his own rear end, but when the genitalia link up the male usually turns to face the opposite way. The pair may remain coupled like this – 'in cop', to use the entomologist's jargon – for several hours. They usually rest on the ground or vegetation, but a copulating pair can fly if necessary. Because they are linked tail-to-tail, one individual has to take the lead and carry the other. In some species it is the male and in others it is the female. The 'carrier' may sit with wings wide open while mating, thus ensuring that the body is warm enough for take-off should it become necessary.

After mating, the female flies off to lay her eggs. Some grass-feeding species, including the marbled whites, merely scatter their eggs as they fly, but the majority of butterflies fix their eggs securely to the appropriate foodplants, after testing their suitability with feet and antennae (*see* p.15). The eggs are laid singly or in batches, according to the species, and their appearance ranges from flattened and button-like, through barrel-shaped to skittle-shaped. A range of butterfly eggs is illustrated here. When examined under a microscope, or even a strong lens, many can be seen to have exquisitely sculptured surfaces, which Edward Newman described more than a century ago as 'a thousand times more delicate and fine than any human hand could execute'.

Although some butterfly species pass the winter in the egg stage, the majority of eggs hatch within days of being laid. They usually darken shortly before hatching and the young caterpillars can sometimes be

White Admiral

Silver-spotted Skipper

Brown Hairstreak

Large White

Peacock

A selection of butterfly eggs, showing something of the wide variation in shape.

seen through the shells. After biting their way out, the caterpillars or larvae often eat the shells before starting to nibble the leaves of the foodplant. The youngest larvae sometimes simply scrape the surface layers of the leaves and indicate their presence by producing translucent 'windows'. Older caterpillars usually attack the leaf-margins and carve out larger and larger chunks as they nibble in towards the mid-ribs.

The butterfly caterpillar has a tough head-capsule carrying the jaws and a cluster of simple eyes – usually six on each side. There are also two bristle-like antennae, but these are very small and, being on the underside of the head, they are rarely seen. The body is typically cylindrical – although many of the blues and coppers and their relatives in the family Lycaenidae have flattened, slug-like bodies – and divided into a number of segments. There are three pairs of true legs at the front and five pairs of fleshy or stumpy prolegs on the rear half of the body. The final pair of legs are called claspers. Moth caterpillars are built on exactly the same plan, although they often lack some of the prolegs. The body is often clothed with hairs and spines, some of which are highly decorative as well as protective. The caterpillars of the fritillaries and some of their relatives are especially well endowed in this respect.

The caterpillar is a remarkable eating machine and rapidly puts on weight. It is soon ready to change its outer skin. This skin, known as the cuticle, is made of a tough material called chitin, which is secreted by the underlying cells of the epidermis. It is not a living tissue and, although it is slightly elastic, it cannot grow with the caterpillar, so it has to be changed for a larger one every now and then. The skin-changing process is called moulting or ecdysis and it takes place four or five times during the life of most caterpillars. The stage between any two moults is called an instar. A caterpillar just out of its egg is in its first instar: it becomes a second instar caterpillar after its first moult, and so on.

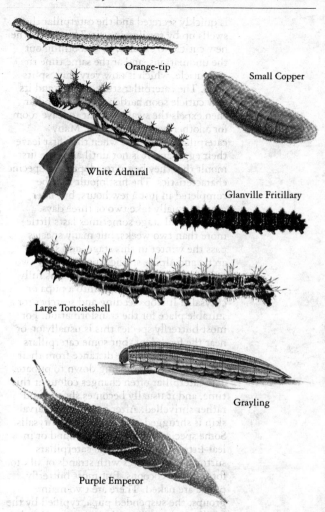

Orange-tip

Small Copper

White Admiral

Glanville Fritillary

Large Tortoiseshell

Grayling

Purple Emperor

A selection of butterfly caterpillars showing something of the wide range of form, from smooth and velvety to extremely spiky.

A caterpillar about to moult becomes quiescent, and the cuticle becomes separated from the epidermis by a layer of fluid – the moulting fluid. This fluid slowly dissolves the inner layer of the cuticle, and while this is going on the epidermal cells multiply rapidly and cause the whole epidermis to become wavy or undulating. A new cuticle is quickly secreted and the caterpillar then swells up by swallowing air. This causes the new cuticle to expand, by smoothing out the undulations, and at the same time the old cuticle, which is now very thin, splits open. The caterpillar struggles out and its new cuticle soon hardens. The caterpillar then expels the swallowed air to leave room for another period of growth. Many caterpillars look alike when they first leave their eggs, and it is not until after the first moult that they begin to adopt their specific characteristics. The first moult may be completed in just a few hours, but later moults usually take two or three days.

The larval stage sometimes lasts little more than two weeks, but many species pass the winter in this stage, and some arctic and alpine species spend almost two years as larvae. When a caterpillar is fully grown it prepares to turn into a pupa or chrysalis. It stops feeding and searches for a suitable place for the transformation. For most butterfly species this is usually on or near the foodplant, but some caterpillars wander a considerable distance from their foodplants before settling down to pupate. The caterpillar often changes colour at this time, and it usually becomes shorter and rather shrivelled. After a while, the larval skin is shrugged off to reveal the chrysalis. Some species pupate on the ground or in leaf-litter, and some of the caterpillars surround themselves with strands of silk to form flimsy cocoons. But most butterfly pupae are naked. There are two main groups: the suspended pupa, typified by the fritillaries and their relatives, hangs head-down from a silken pad produced by the caterpillar; the succinct pupa, characteristic of the whites and swallowtails, is normally fixed head-up on the foodplant or other support. Its tail end is attached to a silken pad, and a silken girdle around its middle keeps it upright. Some species that pupate in leaf-litter also attach themselves to dead leaves by means of silken girdles.

Pupae that are formed on the ground or in leaf-litter are usually quite smooth and

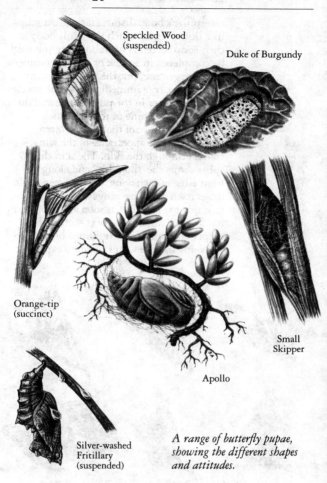

Speckled Wood
(suspended)

Duke of Burgundy

Orange-tip
(succinct)

Small
Skipper

Apollo

Silver-washed
Fritillary
(suspended)

*A range of butterfly pupae,
showing the different shapes
and attitudes.*

dull in colour, but suspended and succinct
pupae are often markedly angular. Many are
adorned with sharp spikes and they usually
blend in well with their surroundings. The
pupae of many fritillaries bear metallic
spots that are easily mistaken for drops of
water on shrivelled leaves.

The outlines of the adult wings, legs, and
antennae are clearly visible on the surface of
a chrysalis as soon as the larval skin is
shrugged off; big changes are already
taking place inside the body by this time.
The tissues that once made up the

caterpillar's body disintegrate into a soup-like liquid, from which the adult body is then constructed. This rebuilding job may be completed in a week or so, depending on the temperature, but the adult butterfly may not emerge immediately. Some species pass the winter in the pupal stage and do not emerge for nine or ten months.

The emergence of the adult is often heralded by the appearance of the wing colours through the skin. The skin then splits across the 'shoulders' and along the front edge of each wing, and the new adult drags itself out. The wings are soft and crumpled at first, but as soon as the butterfly has found a suitable support – often the empty chrysalis case – it pumps blood into the veins and the wings begin to expand.

Stages in the emergence of the Pale Clouded Yellow from its chrysalis. The wing colour becomes visible through the skin shortly before emergence, and the skin then splits behind the head and along the front edge of the wing. The head emerges first, quickly followed by the front legs. Gripping whatever support is available, the legs gradually heave the rest of the body from the chrysalis skin. The wings are small and soft at this stage, but they expand quite quickly as blood is pumped into their veins, and within an hour or two they are firm enough to carry the butterfly away on its first flight.

They usually reach their full size in half an hour or so, but they may need another hour or two to harden sufficiently for flight. During the later stages of drying a butterfly may bask with its wings wide open, and this is an ideal time to photograph them.

Male butterflies usually emerge from their pupae a few days earlier than females in the same area. They feed well and build up their pheromone stocks so that they are ready to mate as soon as the females emerge. The earlier emergence of the males also enables them to spread themselves around the habitat before mating, thereby reducing the likelihood of inbreeding with their sisters. Females can mate within an hour or two of emergence, and some don't even wait that long: they are 'raped' by the males before their wings are dry. Early mating is important for the females because most of them will live for only a few days and they must get on with egg-laying as soon as possible. Male butterflies will mate several times if the opportunity arises, but most females probably mate only once and then concentrate on egg-laying. Some are known to release anti-male pheromones once they have mated. The female Apollo is prevented from mating more than once because the male fits her with a 'chastity belt' when he has finished with her. Technically known as a sphragis, it is a horny structure that plugs the female's genital opening and also forms a pouch under her abdomen (see p.247).

Sphragis on a female Small Apollo.

Adult butterflies have many enemies in the form of birds, lizards, spiders, hornets, and other small animals; but, even if they avoid being captured, the majority do not live very long. Two or three weeks is a good adult life for most species, although those that hibernate in the adult state obviously live very much longer. Single-brooded species, such as the Brimstone and the Peacock, regularly survive for about a year. Adult hibernation is not common in butterflies, however, and only 13 of the 400 or so species regularly found in Europe pass the winter in this way. With the exception of the brimstones and the Nettle-tree Butterfly, they all belong to the Nymphalidae. In common with other hibernating stages, they all contain 'anti-freeze' that enables them to withstand sub-zero temperatures but, unlike hibernating caterpillars, they often wake up on sunny days, even in the depths of winter. They may fly around for a few hours before settling down to sleep again.

Hollow trees, caves, buildings, and dense vegetation are all used by hibernating butterflies. Good camouflage is clearly essential if the sleeping butterflies are to avoid detection, and the undersides of all the hibernating species display superb cryptic coloration. The Brimstone's leaf-like wings are very difficult to spot in a clump of ivy or some other broad-leaved evergreen shrub, while the Comma and the Nettle-tree Butterfly both display an uncanny resemblance to dead leaves. Peacocks and tortoiseshells choose dark cavities, including lofts, for their winter sleep and their dark undersides render them almost invisible in such places. The Queen of Spain Fritillary usually passes the winter as a caterpillar, but in some parts of southern Europe it survives as an adult. It is active on warm days, but sleeps through the cooler weather. The large, mirror-like spots on its underside are surprisingly effective at camouflaging the insect amongst the dead grasses on rough ground.

Migration Many butterfly species that are resident in southern Europe throughout the year fly northwards in spring. Some of them get as far as Iceland and the North Cape and, as long as they find suitable habitats, they can give rise to a new generation of butterflies in the summer. Examples of such migrants that reach central and northern Europe during the summer include the Queen of Spain Fritillary, the Clouded Yellow and the Bath White. The Painted Lady travels even further. It seems unable to survive the winter anywhere in Europe and it repopulates the continent from North Africa each spring. The Red Admiral, generally the commonest summer visitor to the British Isles, is hardier than the others. It is a permanent resident of both southern and central Europe, probably to about 50°N, and some individuals are known to survive the winter in sheltered spots in Britain and other northern areas. Nevertheless, the butterfly's existence in Britain and northern Europe is due almost entirely to immigration in spring and early summer.

The numbers of migrants reaching Britain and northern Europe depend on favourable breeding conditions further south and also on favourable winds, and they fluctuate markedly from year to year. Most of these migrants and their offspring die in the autumn and contribute nothing to the gene pool for future generations, but there is a certain amount of southward migration at that time and some of the butterflies undoubtedly reach areas in which they can survive the winter. In Europe, southward migration in the autumn is well known in the Painted Lady and the Red Admiral – although there is nothing on the scale of the Monarch migrations that take place in North America – and several more of our summer visitors have recently been shown to attempt the return trip. There is no reason why these migrants should not one day evolve cold-hardy strains able to withstand the northern winter, and thus become permanent residents in the more northerly parts of their ranges. If global warming is a reality, some of the migrants may be able to settle down in their more northerly haunts even without genetic change, and many non-migratory species will also be able to extend their ranges.

Classification The world's butterflies are grouped into two superfamilies: the Hesperioidea and the Papilionoidea. The Hesperioidea contains a single family, the Hesperiidae, which includes all the skippers (*see* p.598). The Papilionoidea contains all the other butterflies. Traditionally, this latter superfamily is divided into about 15 families, although not all of them occur in Europe. Recent schemes of classification have tended to reduce the number of families and Scoble (1992) lists only four families within the Papilionoidea, but, in order to avoid undue confusion with other popular books, the present work follows the traditional scheme and recognizes nine European families. The names of the families, like those of all other families in the animal kingdom, end in '-idae'.

Each family is divided into a number of genera, and each genus (the singular of genera) contains one or more species, each of which is an individual kind of butterfly. The members of one species are all more or less alike and they can interbreed to produce more of the same kind. The different species contained in a given genus are all closely related and often quite similar in appearance, although they do not resemble each other as closely as do the individuals within a species. Each species has a scientific name which is made up of its generic name (given first) and the specific name (which follows it). The Brimstone, for example, is scientifically known as *Gonepteryx rhamni* and the Cleopatra is *Gonepteryx cleopatra*. These names immediately reveal that the butterflies both belong to the genus *Gonepteryx* and are thus closely related. The scientific name is a unique combination that cannot be given to any other species, although the specific name or epithet can be used with more than one generic name.

From the foregoing, it might be expected that the scientific names are permanent and immutable. Unfortunately, the classification of butterflies has not yet reached this desirable state and names change with alarming frequency as the specialists delve ever more deeply into the relationships between species. Such detailed investigations, often involving microscopical and biochemical studies that were unthinkable when the insects were originally named, may reveal significant differences between species that were once thought to be closely related and therefore placed in the same genus. Taxonomists must then decide whether the differences are sufficient for the original genus to be split into two or more separate genera. But this will always be a matter of opinion: there will always be 'lumpers', who favour large genera, and 'splitters', who prefer to divide the species among a lot of smaller genera. There is a tendency at the moment to favour reducing the number of genera. The European coppers, for example, were, until recently, arranged in five genera, but the most recent classification schemes place them all in the genus *Lycaena*.

Specific names also have to be changed if it is discovered that two or more names have been given to the same species. This often happened in the past because communication between biologists in different countries was nothing like as good as it is today. A name and description may have been published in one country and then buried in the literature without being seen by many people. The same species could then have received a different name at a later date or in another country. If the earlier name comes to light again, usually through the researches of specialists, the rules of zoological nomenclature dictate that it has precedence over any others and should be adopted, even if this means abandoning a long-used and familiar name. But the specialists must be quite sure that the two names *do* refer to the same species, and this means a lot of painstaking work to check the original descriptions – and the original specimens if possible. Names also have to be changed if it is discovered that two or more species have been given the same name.

In scientific literature, the name of the first person to describe a species is given after the scientific name, together with the date of the first published description. This helps zoologists to eliminate confusion and to know exactly which species is being referred to.

Geographical Races and other Variations

Although each butterfly species has its own characteristic shape and colour, the pattern is not immutably fixed, and many species exhibit a good deal of variation around the norm. Much of this variation has a genetic basis, but abnormalities can also be caused by environmental factors, such as extreme heat or cold. Any specimen deviating appreciably from the norm used to be called a variety, but this term, covering several different kinds of variation, is rather vague and is no longer used in scientific literature.

Butterflies with wide geographical ranges often become split into isolated populations by mountain ranges and other natural barriers, and the separate populations often evolve along slightly different pathways. Influenced by local climates and other factors, they may develop small, but distinct differences. As long as they can still interbreed if they meet, the separate populations can be regarded as geographical races or subspecies. Islands commonly have their own subspecies, and so do many mountain ranges. If separation continues, the differences between the subspecies may increase to the point where they cannot interbreed even if brought together. Two or more separate species are thus created, but only if sufficient genetic changes occur in the separated populations. Some species seem to have a much more stable genetic make-up than others and exhibit far less variation even when they exist in fragmented and widely separated colonies. Strong-flying species, such as the Peacock and the Red Admiral, that roam over wide areas show little variation because their mobility ensures that no population remains isolated from any other for very long: their genes become well mixed and the genetic make-up remains more or less constant throughout the range.

There is a tendency for modern entomologists to establish new species on the basis of visible differences, regardless of the ability of the insects to interbreed. The Scarce Swallowtail of southwest Europe and North Africa, for example, is very white and, although it almost certainly interbreeds with the yellower race typical of other parts of Europe where they overlap, the two races are sometimes treated as separate species. This seems an unnecessary proliferation of species when we are happy for *Homo sapiens* to embrace all of the world's human population, regardless of physical differences.

Total isolation is not always necessary for the development of subspecies. A species with an extensive distribution may experience totally different conditions at the two ends of its range, and consequently evolve some very different features which lead to the development of true subspecies, although they may well be linked by intermediates in the central part of the range. Gene exchange may take place between neighbouring parts of the population, but sheer distance prevents any real mingling of the genes from the two extremes, and thus the identity of the two subspecies is maintained. Such a series exhibiting gradual change is called a cline and is well shown by the Speckled Wood butterfly, which has cream spots in the north and east of its range but orange ones in the south and west (*see* p.589).

Subspecies have an extra part added to their scientific names to form a trinomial. For example, the two subspecies of the Speckled Wood are *Pararge aegeria aegeria* – the 'typical', orange-spotted race from which the species was originally described – and the cream-spotted *P. a. tircis*.

Forms are varieties that occur on a regular basis within a population of normal insects and make up a fairly constant proportion of that population. The Silver-washed Fritillary (*see* p.441) provides a good example: the butterfly normally has a bright-orange ground colour, but in certain areas, notably England's New Forest, 10 to 15 per cent of the females have an olive-green ground colour and are known as f. *valezina* (f. denotes form). The existence of two or more forms within a species is called polymorphism and it is maintained by a mixture of genetic and environmental factors. The Clouded Yellow and some of its relatives also exhibit polymorphism (*see* p.293), with a proportion of the females having pale-cream wings instead of golden yellow.

Several double-brooded species exhibit marked seasonal differences between the two broods. Because one brood gives rise to the other, there can be no real genetic differences between them and the two variants cannot be regarded as subspecies; they are therefore known as forms. The best example among European butterflies is undoubtedly the Map Butterfly (*see* p.438), whose two broods are so different that they were originally thought to be different species. The spring form (f. *levana*) resembles a small fritillary and the summer form (f. *prorsa*) resembles a small White Admiral. This kind of variation is known as seasonal polyphenism.

Forms and subspecies occur on a regular basis, but there are other variations that are of very infrequent and irregular occurrence – sometimes known from just one specimen. These freaks are brought about by changes in the nature or arrangement of the genes during the formation of eggs or sperm, or during the development of the embryos. Known as aberrations, these unusual specimens have always been much sought after by collectors, who have been prepared to pay large sums of money for them. Some of the commoner aberrations have been given names. *Limenitis camilla* ab. *obliterae*, for example, is an aberration of the White Admiral in which the white markings are almost obliterated. Whole books have been devoted to butterfly aberrations, and there is even a complete book on the aberrations of just one species, the Chalk-hill Blue, which seems particularly inclined to throw up abnormal individuals.

Although genetically produced aberrations can theoretically be passed on to the following generation, this rarely happens for the aberrant butterflies are often deficient in other ways as well. They may be captured by predators before they get a chance to mate, and even if they avoid capture their abnormal colours and patterns may make it difficult for them to attract mates. The aberrations crop up again only if the particular genetic 'mistake' recurs.

Gynandromorphs are freaks in which part of the body is male and part is female. The most common condition is that in which the dividing line is right down the centre, with one sex on the left and the other on the right. Such insects are called bilateral gynandromorphs. They are most obvious in those species, such as the blues, in which the sexes have different colours, but they have been found in nearly all butterfly species and they are not uncommon. Bilateral gynandromorphs arise through a fault in the first division of the fertilized egg, causing all the cells derived from one side to have male characteristics and all the cells derived from the other side to have female characteristics. As well as differing in colour, the two sides of the insect may differ in the size of the wings and the length of the antennae. The genitalia are also half male and half female, so the insects are unable to mate. Genetic slip-ups occurring during the later stages of development can result in the appearance of small patches of male colour on a female wing and vice-versa.

Some aberrations can be produced by extremes of temperature, especially during the pupal period when temperature changes are known to alter the distribution and formation of pigments in the wings.

How to Use this Guide

This book describes almost all of the 400 or so butterfly species occurring in Europe. The only absentees are some recently discovered species from Greece, where a lot of work is currently being carried out on the browns and the blues, and a number of essentially Asiatic species that creep into the southeastern corner of Europe. Most species are illustrated by one or more photographs covering the major geographical races and other variations as well as any marked differences between the sexes. Underside and upperside are illustrated for most species, although some groups, notably the clouded yellows and some of the heaths, habitually rest with their wings closed and only the undersides of these butterflies are normally seen.

The species are arranged on a family by family basis, and because the European families have fairly distinctive shapes and colours they are also arranged roughly by shape and colour. Typical members of each family are illustrated on pp.37–9, and their outlines are repeated as thumb-tabs on the relevant colour plates to help you track down the butterflies that you see. On finding a specimen, look at the shape of the wings and the resting attitude as well as the colour and pattern, and then look for the thumb-tab most like it; this will narrow down your search for the name of the butterfly. At the beginning of each family within the colour plates there is a further page describing the various sub-divisions within the family, which will enable you to track down a species even more easily.

The sex of the butterfly is given only if the two sexes are significantly different. The butterflies are pictured as close to life-size as possible, but some of the smaller ones have been enlarged and the largest species have obviously been reduced. Each picture is also accompanied by the page number of the relevant text entry.

The text for each family begins with a general introduction to the family, accompanied by line-drawings showing the typical form of eggs, larvae, and pupae. Each species within the family is then described in detail.

The text for each species begins with the location of the relevant photographs, its common or English name, and its scientific name. The English and scientific names are, in general, those given by Tolman and Lewington in *Butterflies of Britain and Europe* (Collins Field Guide, 1997), but not all entomologists follow the same system and, as explained on pp.26–7, scientific names may change for one reason or another. The scientific names given in one book are therefore not always the same as those appearing in another book.

There then follows a complete profile of the species, arranged as follows:

Description: The description of each species begins with the size. Given in millimetres and inches, this is the length of the forewing. This is more accurate than giving wingspans because wingspans vary with the angle at which the wings are held, and also because many butterflies rest with their wings closed and the span cannot be assessed. The size given is generally close to the maximum, but a range is given for species that are particularly variable. Specimens reared in captivity are frequently much smaller than wild specimens because their larval food is not always fresh or of good quality. Similarly, butterflies emerging in the autumn are often smaller than spring and summer specimens because they grow up on older and less nutritious vegetation.

The basic or ground colour of the wings is described, together with all significant markings and any significant features of the shape. The upperside is described first and then the underside. The male is usually described in full, and then differences between it and the female are pointed out, although where the two sexes are noticeably different the female may be described in full as well.

Similar species: This paragraph contains brief notes on distinguishing the butterfly from all other superficially similar European species, not just those with a similar range. This will help in the identification of specimens in collections as well as butterflies in the wild.

Flight: This paragraph gives the months during which the butterfly can be seen in flight and indicates whether there are two or more broods or generations in a year. If no figure is given, the species is single-brooded. The dates given cover the whole of the insect's range in Europe and the insect will not necessarily be seen throughout the period in any one place. Most of the widely distributed species fly earlier in southern Europe than in the north, and also go on later because they often have two or three broods. Flight-times vary a lot with the weather and also with altitude, but are unlikely to lie outside the periods given. Flight characteristics are given where these are of assistance in identifying the insect.

Habitat: This paragraph lists the preferred environment or surroundings of the species, and also gives some idea of the altitude range of the species. Larval foodplants are also listed here. Scientific names of plants are given only where no published English name exists. English names are those used in *The Illustrated Flora of Britain and Northern Europe*, *Mediterranean Wild Flowers*, and *Alpine Flowers of Britain and Europe*, all by Marjorie Blamey and Christopher Grey-Wilson.

Life-cycle: These paragraphs provide a brief description of the egg, caterpillar and chrysalis, although these details are still unknown for many species. The stage in which the species spends the winter is also stated here if it is known.

Range: The range or distribution given for each species indicates the area in which it is known to occur. Individual countries are listed for some species with restricted

The area covered by this book (white). The dotted lines indicate the borders of northern, central and southern Europe as used here.

distributions, but more general areas are given for others. In this context, northern Europe is the region north of latitude 55°N, including Denmark, but not Scotland. The far north or Arctic region is the area beyond the Arctic Circle. Central Europe extends southwards from 55°N, which approximates to the southern edge of the Baltic, to 45°N, but for the purposes of this book it also includes the whole of the British Isles. Southern Europe is the area south of 45°N, which approximates to a line from Bordeaux through Turin to the Danube Delta.

The small-scale maps accompanying the text can give no more than a rough

indication of the range of each species.
Bear in mind that ranges are not
accurately known for all species, so it is
quite possible for a butterfly to occur
outside its indicated range. Many species
are likely to spread northwards in the
foreseeable future if global warming
continues (*see* p.25). Remember also that a
species will not normally occur everywhere
in its range: it can exist only in areas
where the habitat is suitable and supports
the right foodplants.

At the end of a species' entry there may be
some notes on geographical and other
variations, together with miscellaneous
ecological information including recent
changes in range and abundance.

**Papilionidae
p.41**

Swallowtails pp.42–3

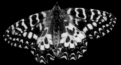

Festoons pp.44–5

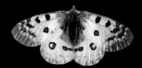

Apollos pp.46–7

**Pieridae
p.49**

Whites pp.50–60

Orange-tips pp.61–3

Clouded yellows pp.64–9

Brimstones p.69

Lycaenidae
p.71

Hairstreaks pp.72–5

Coppers pp.76–83

Blues pp.84–125

Riodinidae,
Libytheidae
and Danaidae
p.127

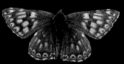

Duke of Burgundy p.128

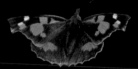

Nettle-tree Butterfly p.128

Monarchs p.129

Nymphalidae
p.131

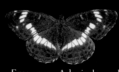

Emperors, Admirals, and Gliders pp.132–9

Nymphalidae p.131

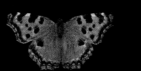

Vanessids pp.140–6

Fritillaries pp.147–71

Satyridae p.173

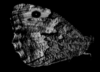

Marbled whites pp.174–7

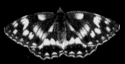

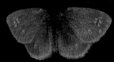

Graylings, ringlets, meadow browns, gatekeepers, walls, and lattice browns pp.178–215 and 220–3

Heaths pp.215–19

Hesperiidae p.225

Grizzled and marbled skippers pp.226–39

Golden skippers pp.240–3

 Swallowtails pp.42–3

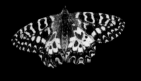 Festoons pp.44–5

 Apollos pp.46–7

Papilionidae

 The inner margin of the hindwing is
noticeably concave in this family and the
abdomen is clearly visible from the side
when the butterfly is perched with its
wings closed. All six legs are fully
developed in both sexes. The European
species, which have wingspans ranging
from about 45 mm to 100 mm
(1.8–4.0 in), fall into three groups.

Swallowtails are essentially yellow or
cream with black markings and they
have a conspicuous 'tail' on each hindwing.

Festoons are basically yellow or cream
and heavily spotted with black and red.
The hindwings have a slightly scalloped
appearance and there may be a short 'tail'.

Apollos are essentially white with black
spots and often red ones as well. There is
usually an irregular dusting of black scales,
but the scaling is fairly thin and the wings
are commonly quite translucent.

Swallowtail *Papilio machaon* p.249 1. upperside
spring brood; 2. upperside summer brood; 3. underside

Corsican Swallowtail *Papilio hospiton* p.250
1. upperside; 2. underside

Southern Swallowtail *Papilio alexanor* p.251
upperside

Scarce Swallowtail *Iphiclides podalirius* p.252
upperside

Southern Festoon *Zerynthia polyxena* p.255
1. upperside; 2. underside, mating pair

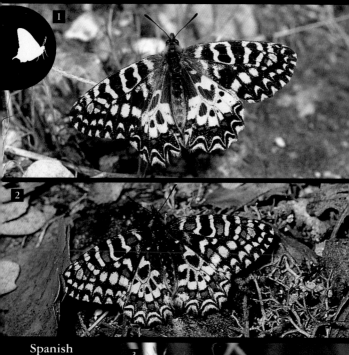

Spanish
Festoon
*Zerynthia
rumina*
p.254
1. upperside;
2. upperside,
f. *medesicaste*
3. underside

Eastern Festoon *Zerynthia cerisyi* p.257
1. male upperside; 2. female upperside;
3. male underside

Apollo
Parnassius apollo p.258
1. upperside;
2. upperside,
P. a. hispanicus;
3. underside

False Apollo *Archon apollinus* p.257
female upperside

Small Apollo *Parnassius phoebus* p.260
upperside

Clouded Apollo *Parnassius mnemosyne* p.261
upperside

Whites pp.50–60

Orange-tips pp.61–3

Clouded yellows pp.64–9

Brimstones p.69

Pieridae

The European members of this family are
basically white or yellow. The inner margin
of the hindwing is convex or straight and
the abdomen is completely concealed when
the insect is at rest with its wings closed.
All six legs are fully developed. There are
often colour differences between the sexes.
The European species, whose wingspans
range from about 20 to 80 mm
(0.8–3.1 in), fall into four main groups.

Whites usually have black wingtips, but
never complete black borders. The
undersides are often yellowish or heavily
mottled with green. The wood whites are
not closely related to the others.

Orange-tip males are either white or
yellow with orange wingtips. Females
generally lack the orange patches and look
very like some of the whites.

Clouded yellows are yellow or cream with
black borders to all wings on the upperside.
The undersides are mainly yellow, usually
with a few dark spots.

Brimstone males are bright yellow with no
black markings. Females are greenish
white. Both sexes have pointed wingtips
and are very leaf-like at rest.

Wood White *Leptidea sinapis* p.263
1. underside, courting pair; 2. underside

Eastern Wood White *Leptidea duponcheli* p.265
1. underside, 1st brood; 2. underside, 2nd brood

Black-veined White *Aporia crataegi* p.267
1. male upperside; 2. male underside

Large White *Pieris brassicae* p.269
1. male upperside; 2. female upperside; 3. female underside

Small White *Pieris rapae* p.271
1. male upperside; 2. male underside;
3. female upperside; 4. female underside

Mountain Small White *Pieris ergane* p.273
1. male upperside; 2. female upperside

Green-veined White
Pieris napi p.275
1. male upperside;
2. female upperside;
3. underside, 1st brood;
4. underside, 2nd brood;
5. female upperside, *P. n. bryoniae*

Southern Small White *Pieris mannii* p.272
1. male upper- and undersides; 2. female upperside

Krueper's Small White *Pieris krueperi* p.274
underside

Bath White *Pontia daplidice* p.277
1. male upperside; 2. female upperside; 3. female underside

Small Bath White *Pontia chloridice* p.279
1. male upperside; 2. female underside

Peak White *Pontia callidice* p.279
1. female upper- and underside; 2. female underside

Dappled White
Euchloe ausonia
p.280
1. upperside;
2. males in flight,
female perched;
3. underside

Mountain Dappled White *Euchloe simplonia*
p.282 1. upperside; 2. underside

Portuguese Dappled White *Euchloe tagis* p.283
upper- and underside

Green-striped White *Euchloe belemia* p.284
1. upperside; 2. underside

Greenish Black-tip *Elphinstonia charlonia* p.290
E. c. penia: 1. upperside; 2. underside; 3. underside

Orange-tip
Anthocharis
cardamines
p.285
1. male upper- and
underside;
2. male
underside at rest;
3. female upper-
and underside

Moroccan Orange-tip
Anthocharis belia p.286
1. male upper- and underside;
2. male upperside;
3. male underside;
4. female upperside;
5. female underside

Eastern Orange-tip
Anthocharis damone
p.287
1. male upperside;
2. male underside;
3. female underside

Gruner's Orange-tip
Anthocharis gruneri p.288
1. male upperside;
2. male upper- and underside;
3. female upper- and underside

1

2

Mountain Clouded Yellow
Colias phicomone
p.297
1. male upperside;
2. underside

Pale Arctic Clouded Yellow *Colias nastes* p.298
1. underside

**Moorland
Clouded Yellow
Colias palaeno
p.299**
male underside

**Greek
Clouded Yellow
Colias aurorina
(*above*) p.293**
1. male underside;
2. female underside

**Danube
Clouded Yellow
Colias myrmidone
p.294** underside

Clouded Yellow
Colias croceus
p.291
1. male upper-
and underside;
2. underside;
3. female underside,
f. *helice*

**Balkan
Clouded Yellow
Colias caucasica
p.294**
1. male upperside;
2. male underside;
3. female underside,
pale form

Northern Clouded Yellow *Colias hecla* p.296
1. male upperside; 2. male underside; 3. female upperside

Pale Clouded Yellow *Colias hyale* p.300
female underside

Berger's Clouded Yellow *Colias alfacariensis* p.301
1. female upperside; 2. male underside; 3. female underside

**Eastern Pale
Clouded Yellow**
Colias erate
p.303
female underside

Brimstone *Gonepteryx rhamni* p.303
1. male underside; 2. female underside

Cleopatra
Gonepteryx cleopatra
p.305 male underside

Powdered Brimstone
Gonepteryx farinosa
p.306 female underside

Hairstreaks pp.72–5

Coppers pp.76–83

Blues pp.84–125

Lycaenidae

These are all relatively small butterflies, the European species having wingspans ranging from about 15 to 40 mm (0.6–1.6 in). The hindwings often bear slender 'tails' at the rear. All six legs are fully developed and are used for walking. There are three major groups.

Hairstreaks are named for the pale, hair-like streaks on the undersides of most species. Most hairstreaks also have short 'tails'. The uppersides are usually dull brown, although they are not often displayed.

Coppers are mostly bright orange or copper-coloured, often with black spots and a brilliant metallic lustre on the uppersides. The undersides are usually grey and orange with white-ringed black spots.

Blues are named for the predominantly blue uppersides of the males, although the males of some species are entirely brown. Most females are also brown, with a variable amount of blue at the wing-base, and often with orange spots around the wing margins. The undersides are mainly grey with white-ringed black spots and often with red spots around the margins. All blue butterflies in Europe belong to this group.

Brown Hairstreak *Thecla betulae* p.309
1. female upperside;
2. female underside

Purple Hairstreak *Quercusia quercus* p.310
1. male upperside; 2. female upperside; 3. underside

Spanish Purple Hairstreak *Laeosopis roboris* p.311
1. male upperside; 2. male underside

Sloe Hairstreak *Satyrium acaciae* p.312

Ilex Hairstreak
Satyrium ilicis
p.313
underside

**False Ilex
Hairstreak**
*Satyrium esculi
(left)* p.314
female underside

Blue-spot Hairstreak
Satyrium spini
p.315 underside

White-letter Hairstreak
Satyrium w-album
p.316 underside

Black Hairstreak
Satyrium pruni
p.317 underside

Green Hairstreak
Callophrys rubi
(left) p.318
underside

Chapman's
Green Hairstreak
Callophrys avis p.319
underside

Provence Hairstreak
Tomares ballus p.320
underside

Violet Copper *Lycaena helle* p.321
1. male upperside; 2. female upperside; 3. female underside

Small Copper *Lycaena phlaeas* p.322 1. upperside;
2. upperside; 3. underside; 4. upper- and underside, mating pair

Large Copper
Lycaena dispar
p.323
1. male upperside,
L. d. batavus;
2. female upperside,
L. d. batavus;
3. female upperside
L. d. rutilus;
4. female underside,
L. d. batavus

Scarce Copper *Lycaena virgaureae* p.324
1. male upperside; 2. male upperside, *L. v. montanus*;
3. female upperside; 4. underside, mating pair

Grecian Copper *Lycaena ottomana* p.326
1. male upperside; 2. male upper- and underside; 3. female
upperside; 4. female underside

Sooty Copper *Lycaena tityrus* p.327
1. male upperside; 2. male underside; 3. female upperside

Purple-shot Copper *Lycaena alciphron* p.328
1. male upperside, *L. a. gordius*; 2. male upperside,
L. a. alciphron; 3. female upperside, *L. a. gordius*; 4. female
upperside, *L. a. alciphron*; 5. female underside, *L. a. alciphron*

**Lesser Fiery
Copper**
*Lycaena
thersamon*
p.329
1. male upperside;
2. underside;
3. female upperside

Fiery Copper
Lycaena thetis
p.330
1. male upperside;
2. male underside;
3. female upper- and
underside

Purple-edged Copper
Lycaena hippothoë
p.331
1. male upperside,
L. h. hippothoë;
2. female upperside,
L. h. eurydame;
3. underside,
L. h. eurydame;
4. underside,
L. h. hippothoë

Long-tailed Blue *Lampides boeticus* p.332
1. male upperside; 2. female upperside; 3. underside

Geranium Bronze *Cacyreus marshalli* p.335
underside

Lang's Short-tailed Blue *Leptotes pirithous* p.334
1. male upperside; 2. female upperside;
3. female underside

Common Tiger Blue *Tarucus theophrastus* p.336
1. male upperside; 2. female upperside; 3. female underside

Little Tiger Blue *Tarucus balkanicus* p.336
underside

African Grass Blue *Zizeeria knysna* p.337
1. male upperside; 2. male underside; 3. female upperside

Short-tailed Blue *Everes argiades* p.338
1. male upperside; 2. female upperside

Eastern Short-tailed Blue *Everes decoloratus* p.339
male underside

Provençal Short-tailed Blue *Everes alcetas* p.340
1. male upperside; 2. female underside

Holly Blue
Celastrina argiolus
p.343
1. male upperside;
2. male underside;
3. female upperside

Little Blue *Cupido minimus* p.341
1. male upperside; 2. underside

Osiris Blue *Cupido osiris* p.342
1. male upperside; 2. underside

Lorquin's Blue *Cupido lorquinii* p.343
1, male upperside; 2, male underside

Green-underside Blue *Glaucopsyche alexis* p.345
1. female upperside; 2. underside, mating pair (female on right)

Black-eyed Blue
Glaucopsyche melanops
p.346
1. male upperside;
2. male upper- and underside

Odd-spot Blue *Turanana endymion* p.346
1. male upperside; 2. underside

Alcon Blue *Maculinea alcon* p.347
1. male upperside; 2. female upperside; 3. underside

Large Blue *Maculinea arion* p.348
1. male upperside; 2. female upper- and underside; 3. underside

Scarce Large Blue
Maculinea telejus
p.351
1. female upper- and underside;
2. female underside

Dusky Large Blue *Maculinea nausithous* p.352
1. male upperside; 2. underside

Baton Blue
Pseudophilotesbaton p.354
1. male upperside;
2. female upperside;
3. underside, mating pair

False Baton Blue *Pseudophilotes abencerragus*
p.355 1. female upperside; 2. underside

Panoptes Blue *Pseudophilotes panoptes* p.356
1. male upperside; 2. male underside

Bavius Blue *Pseudophilotes bavius* p.357
1. male upper- and underside; 2. underside;
3. female upperside

Chequered Blue *Scolitantides orion* p.357
1. male upperside; 2. female upperside; 3. female upperside;
4. female underside

Grass Jewel *Chilades trochylus* p.358
Upper- and underside

Iolas Blue *Iolana iolas* p.353
1. male upperside; 2. female upper- and underside;
3. female underside

Zephyr Blue *Plebejus pylaon* p.359 1. male upper-
and underside; 2. male underside; 3. female upperside

Silver-studded Blue *Plebejus argus* p.360
1, male upperside; 2, male underside; 3, female upperside

Idas Blue *Plebejus idas* p.362
1. male upperside; 2. male underside; 3. female upperside

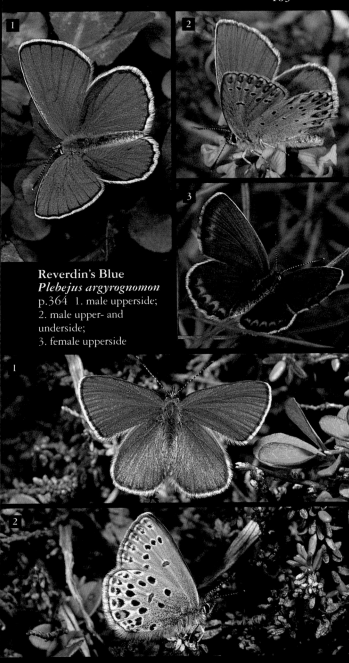

Reverdin's Blue
Plebejus argyrognomon
p.364 1. male upperside;
2. male upper- and
underside;
3. female upperside

Cranberry Blue *Vacciniina optilete* p.365
1. male upperside; 2. male underside

Brown Argus
Aricia agestis
p.368
1. female upperside;
2. male underside

Mountain Argus
Aricia artaxerxes
(below) p.369
1. upperside,
Scottish race;
2. underside,
Scottish race

Spanish Argus
Aricia morronensis
(above) p.371
1. upperside;
2. underside

Blue Argus
Ultraaricia
anteros
p.371
1. male upperside;
2. male upper- and
underside

Silvery Argus *Pseudaricia nicias* p.372
1. & 2. male upperside; 3. & 4. male underside

Alpine Argus
Albulina orbitulus p.373
1. male upperside;
2. male under- and upperside

Geranium Argus *Eumedonia eumedon* p.367
1. male upperside; 2. male underside

Glandon Blue
Agriades glandon
p.374
1. male upperside;
2. female upperside;
3. underside;
4. underside;

Arctic Blue *Agriades aquilo* p.375
1. male upperside; 2. female underside

Gavarnie Blue *Agriades pyrenaicus* p.376

Mazarine Blue
*Cyaniris
semiargus* p.377
1. male upperside;
2. male upper-
and underside;
3. female upperside

Greek Mazarine Blue *Cyaniris helena* p.378
1. male upperside; 2. male underside

Damon Blue *Agrodiaetus damon* p.379
1. male upperside; 2. male underside

Chelmos Blue *Agrodiaetus iphigenia* p.380
1. male upperside; 2. male underside

Furry Blue *Agrodiaetus dolus* p.381
1. male upperside; 2. male underside;
3. female upperside; 4. female underside

Anomalous Blue
Agrodiaetus
admetus p.382
1. male upper- and
underside;
2. male underside;
3. female underside

1

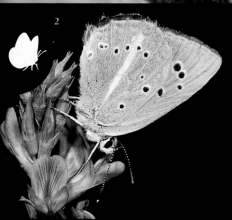

2

Ripart's Anomalous Blue *Agrodiaetus ripartii* p.383
1. male upperside, *A. r. pelop*;
2. female underside, *A. r. pelop*

Grecian Anomalous Blue *Agrodiaetus aroaniensis* p.384 underside

Piedmont
Anomalous Blue
*Agrodiaetus
humedasae*
p.386
underside

Escher's Blue *Agrodiaetus escheri* p.387
1. male upperside; 2. female upperside; 3. male underside

Amanda's Blue
*Agrodiaetus
amanda* p.388
1. male upperside;
2. female underside;
3. female underside

Chapman's Blue
*Agrodiaetus
thersites* p.389
1. male upperside;
2. female upperside;
3. male underside

Pontic Blue *Neolysandra coelestina* p.390
1 male upperside; 2 male underside

Turquoise Blue *Plebicula dorylas* p.391
1. male upperside; 2. female upperside; 3. female underside

Nevada Blue
Plebicula golgus
p.392
1. male upper- and
underside;
2. male underside

**Mother-of-pearl
Blue**
Plebicula nivescens
p.393
1. male upper- and
underside;
2. male underside

Meleager's Blue *Meleageria daphnis* p.393
1. male upperside; 2. female upperside; 3. female underside

Chalk-hill Blue *Lysandra coridon* p.394
1. male upperside; 2. female upper- and underside;
3. female underside; 4. male underside

**Provençal
Chalk-hill Blue**
*Lysandra
hispana* p.396
1. male upperside;
2. female upperside

**Macedonian
Chalk-hill Blue**
*Lysandra
philippi* p.397
male upper- and
underside

**Spanish
Chalk-hill Blue**
*Lysandra
albicans* p.397
male upper- and
underside

Adonis Blue *Lysandra bellargus* p.398
1 male upperside; 2 female upperside; 3 mating pair

Common Blue *Polyommatus icarus* p.400
1. male upperside; 2. female upperside; 3. female underside

Eros Blue
*Polyommatus
eros* p.402
1. male upperside;
2. male upper- and
underside

False Eros Blue
*Polyommatus
eroides* p.403
male underside

 Duke of Burgundy p.128

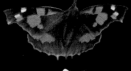 Nettle-tree Butterfly p.128

 Monarchs p.129

Riodinidae

There is just one European member of this family: the Duke of Burgundy. Although superficially like a fritillary, it is smaller and browner than most fritillaries. The male's front legs are much reduced and are useless for walking.

Libytheidae

There is just one European species in this family – the Nettle-tree Butterfly, which is easily recognized by its long palps and the prominent triangular beak-shaped projection near the tip of the forewing. The female's front legs are fully formed, but those of the male are too short for walking.

Danaidae

The two members of this family occurring in Europe, the Monarch and the Plain Tiger, are easily recognized by their large size and their vivid black and orange colours. The front legs are very small and are useless for walking.

Duke of Burgundy
Hamearis lucina
p.404
1. female upperside;
2. male upperside;
3. underside

Nettle-tree Butterfly
Libythea celtis
p.406
1. upperside;
2. underside

Monarch
Danaus plexippus
p.409
1. upperside;
2. underside

Plain Tiger
Danaus chrysippus
p.411
1. upperside;
2. underside

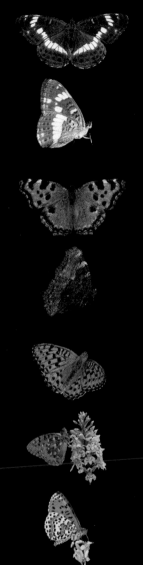

Emperors, Admirals, and
Gliders pp.132–9

Vanessids pp.140–6

Fritillaries pp.147–71

Nymphalidae

This is a large and quite varied family, whose European members have wingspans ranging from about 30 to 85 mm 1.2–3.3 in). The front legs of both sexes are very small and often brush-like, and are quite useless for walking. There are three main groups in the family.

Emperors, Admirals, and Gliders are fairly large butterflies with dark brown or black uppersides crossed by white stripes or bands.

Vanessids are mostly large butterflies whose wing margins are somewhat irregular and often jagged. Their uppersides are mostly orange with large black spots, although some are largely black. Their undersides are generally dark brown.

Fritillaries are mostly large or medium-sized butterflies whose bright orange uppersides are heavily patterned with dark brown or black. The undersides are also largely orange, with black spots on the forewings and cream or silvery spots on the hindwings.

Two-tailed Pasha *Charaxes jasius* p.413
1. upperside; 2. underside

Purple Emperor *Apatura iris* p.414
1. male upperside; 2. female upperside; 3. male underside

Lesser Purple Emperor
Apatura ilia p.416
1. male upperside;
2. male upperside;
f. *clytie*; 3. male underside

Freyer's Purple Emperor *Apatura metis* p.417
1. male upperside; 2. female upperside; 3. female underside

Poplar Admiral *Limenitis populi* p.418
1. male upperside; 2. male underside

White Admiral *Limenitis camilla* p.419
1. upperside; 2. underside

Southern White Admiral *Limenitis reducta* p.421
1. upperside; 2. underside

Common Glider *Neptis sappho* p.422
1. female upperside; 2. underside

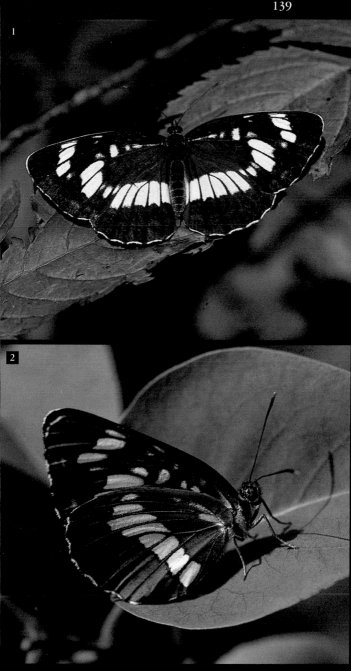

Hungarian Glider *Neptis rivularis* p.423
1. upperside; 2. underside

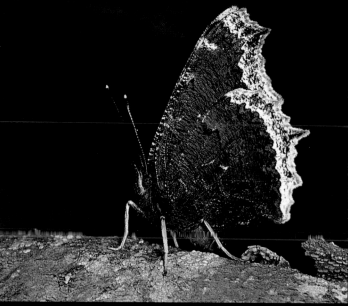

Camberwell Beauty *Nymphalis antiopa* p.424
1. upperside; 2. underside

Large Tortoiseshell *Nymphalis polychloros* p.425
1. upperside;
2. underside

Yellow-legged Tortoiseshell
Nymphalis xanthomelas p.427 upperside

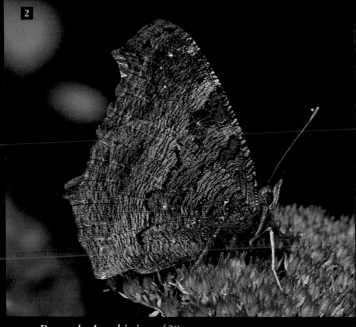

Peacock *Inachis io* p.429
1. upperside; 2. underside

Red Admiral *Vanessa atalanta* p.430
1. upperside; 2. underside

Painted Lady *Vanessa cardui* p.432

Small Tortoiseshell *Aglais urticae* p.433
1. upperside; 2. underside

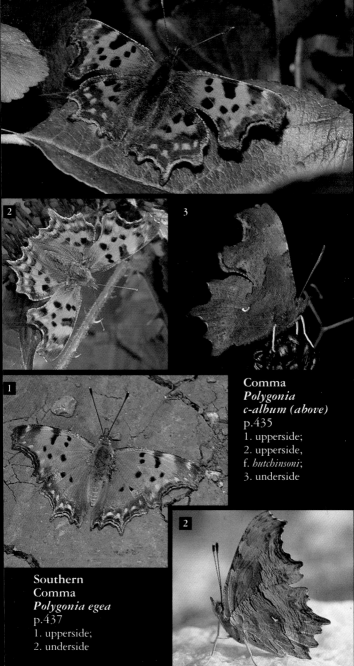

Comma
*Polygonia
c-album (above)*
p.435
1. upperside;
2. upperside,
f. *hutchinsoni*;
3. underside

**Southern
Comma**
Polygonia egea
p.437
1. upperside;
2. underside

Map Butterfly 4
*Araschnia
levana* p.438
1. upperside,
f. *levana*;
2. upperside,
f. *prorsa*;
3. underside,
f. *levana*;
4. underside,
f. *prorsa*

Cardinal *Argynnis pandora* p.439
1. male upperside; 2. female upperside; 3. underside

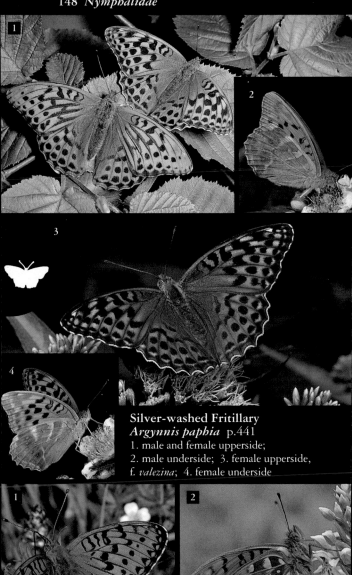

Silver-washed Fritillary
Argynnis paphia p.441
1. male and female upperside;
2. male underside; 3. female upperside,
f. *valezina*; 4. female underside

Dark Green Fritillary *Argynnis aglaja* p.443
1. upperside; 2. underside

High Brown Fritillary
Argynnis adippe
(above) p.444
1. male upperside;
2. underside

Niobe Fritillary
Argynnis niobe
p.446
1. upperside;
2. underside;
3. underside, f. *eris*

Queen of Spain Fritillary *Issoria lathonia* p.448
1. upperside; 2. upper- and underside

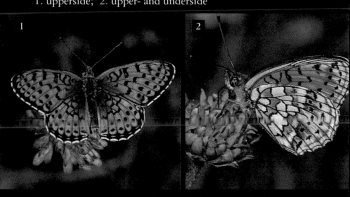

Twin-spot Fritillary *Brenthis hecate* p.449
1. upperside; 2. underside

Marbled Fritillary *Brenthis daphne* p.450
1. female upperside; 2. male underside; 3. female underside

Lesser Marbled Fritillary
Brenthis ino
p.451
1. male upperside;
2. male underside

Shepherd's Fritillary
Boloria pales p.452
1. upperside; 2. underside

Mountain Fritillary
Boloria napaea
p.453
1. male upperside;
2. underside

Cranberry Fritillary
Boloria aquilonaris
p.455
1. male upperside;
2. male underside

Balkan Fritillary
Boloria graeca
p.456
1. upperside;
2. male underside

Bog Fritillary
*Proclossiana
eunomia* p.457
1. male upperside;
2. female upperside;
3. male underside

**Pearl-bordered
Fritillary**
*Clossiana
euphrosyne*
p.458
1. upperside;
2. underside

Small Pearl-bordered Fritillary
Clossiana selene p.459
1. upperside; 2. underside; 3. underside 4. upperside, f. *hela*

Titania's Fritillary
Clossiana titania p.461
1. upperside;
2. underside

Arctic Fritillary
Clossiana chariclea
p.462
1. upperside;
2. upper- and underside

Frejya's Fritillary
Clossiana freija
p.463
1. male upperside;
2. male underside

Weaver's Fritillary
Clossiana dia
p.464
1. male upperside;
2. underside

Polar Fritillary *Clossiana polaris* p.465
1. upperside; 2. underside

Thor's Fritillary *Clossiana thore* p.466
1. male upperside;
2. male underside;
3. female upperside, *C. t. borealis*

Frigga's Fritillary *Clossiana frigga* p.467
1. upperside; 2. underside

Dusky-winged Fritillary *Clossiana improba* p.468
1. upperside; 2. underside

Glanville Fritillary *Melitaea cinxia* p.469
1. upperside; 2. underside

Freyer's Fritillary *Melitaea arduinna* p.470
1. upperside; 2. underside

161

Knapweed Fritillary *Melitaea phoebe* p.471
1. upperside; 2. upperside f. *alternans*; 3. underside

Aetherie Fritillary *Melitaea aetherie* p.472
1. male upperside; 2. underside; 3. female upperside

Spotted Fritillary *Melitaea didyma* p.473
1. male upperside; 2. male underside;
3. female upperside, *M. d. meridionalis*

Lesser Spotted Fritillary
Melitaea trivia p.475
1. female upperside;
2. underside of mating pair

False Heath Fritillary
Melitaea diamina (below)
p.476
1. male upperside;
2. female upperside;
3. underside

Heath Fritillary
Mellicta athalia
p.477
1. male upperside;
2. female upperside;
3. underside;
4. upperside,
M. a. norvegica

**Provençal
Fritillary
*Mellicta
deione*** p.479
1. male upperside;
2. female upperside;
3. upper- and
underside

Grison's Fritillary *Mellicta varia* p.480
1. upperside; 2. underside

Meadow Fritillary
Mellicta parthenoides
p.481
1. upperside;
2. underside

Nickerl's Fritillary
Mellicta aurelia
p.482 ♂
1. male upperside;
2. female upperside;
3. underside

Assmann's
Fritillary
Mellicta
britomartis
p.483
1. upperside;
2. underside

Little Fritillary *Mellicta asteria* p.484
1. female upper- and underside; 2. underside

**Scarce
Fritillary**
*Hypodryas
maturna* p.485
1. upperside;
2. underside

Asian Fritillary *Hypodryas intermedia* p.486
1. upperside; 2. underside

Cynthia's Fritillary
Hypodryas cynthia p.487
1. male upperside;
2. female upperside;
3. underside of mating pair

Lapland Fritillary
Hypodryas iduna p.489
1. upperside;
2. underside

Marsh Fritillary
Eurodryas
aurinia p.490
1. male upperside;
2. female upperside;
3. female underside;
4. pair mating;
5. upperside,
E. a. debilis;
6. underside,
E. a. debilis

Spanish
Fritillary
Eurodryas
desfontainii
p.492
1. female
upperside;
2. underside

Marbled whites pp.174–7

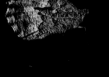

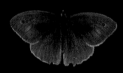

Graylings, ringlets, meadow browns, and gatekeepers pp.178–215, and walls and lattice browns pp.220–3

Heaths pp.215–19

Satyridae

These butterflies are the 'browns', most of
which are predominantly brown or orange
on both surfaces. Almost all of them have
conspicuous eye-spots or ocelli – sometimes
just at the wingtips but often all around the
outer parts of the wings. Most are small or
medium-sized butterflies: wingspans
among the European species generally
range from 25 to 60 mm (1.0–2.4 in),
although a few reach 80 mm (3.1 in). The
tiny front legs are useless for walking in
both sexes. There are several groups, but
they grade into each other with few clear-
cut differences between them.

Marbled Whites are white with extensive
black or dark brown spotting. They are
distinguished from the true whites
(Pieridae) by their eye-spots.

**Graylings, ringlets, meadow browns,
gatekeepers, walls, and lattice browns**
are brown and orange, or both, with
females tending to have larger orange
patches than males. Most are medium-sized
butterflies.

Heaths are relatively small butterflies that
are largely greyish brown on the underside.
The uppersides, rarely seen at rest, are
orange or brown with few markings apart
from the apical eye-spots.

Marbled White
Melanargia
galathea p.495
1. upperside;
2. underside;
3. upperside,
f. *magdalenae*

Esper's Marbled White
Melanargia russiae p.496
1. upperside;
2. underside

Balkan Marbled White
Melanargia larissa p.497
1. upperside;
2. underside

Western Marbled White *Melanargia occitanica* p.498
1. upperside; 2. underside

Italian Marbled White
Melanargia arge p.499
1. upperside; 2. underside

Spanish Marbled White
Melanargia ines
p.500
1. upperside;
2. underside

Woodland Grayling *Hipparchia fagi* p.501
underside

Rock Grayling *Hipparchia alcyone* p.502
underside

Eastern Rock Grayling *Hipparchia syriaca* p.504
underside

Southern Grayling *Hipparchia aristaeus* p.507
male underside

Grayling *Hipparchia semele* p.505
underside

Tree Grayling *Neohipparchia statilinus* p.508
underside

Freyer's Grayling *Neohipparchia fatua* p.509
underside

Striped Grayling *Pseudotergumia fidia* p.509
underside

The Hermit *Chazara briseis* p.510
male underside

White-banded Grayling *Pseudochazara anthelea*
p.512 underside

Grecian Grayling *Pseudochazara graeca* p.514
underside

Dil's Grayling *Pseudochazara orestes* p.515
1. upperside; 2. underside

Grey Asian Grayling *Pseudochazara geyeri* p.517
male underside

Dark Grayling *Pseudochazara mniszechii* p.517
1. upperside; 2. underside

Norse Grayling
Oeneis norna p.518
female underside

Arctic Grayling
Oeneis bore p.519
underside

Alpine Grayling *Oeneis glacialis* p.521
underside

Baltic Grayling *Oeneis jutta* p.520
1. female upperside; 2. underside

185

Black Satyr *Satyrus actaea* p.522
1. male upperside; 2. male underside

Great Sooty Satyr *Satyrus ferula* p.523
1. male upperside; 2. female underside; 3. female upperside

Dryad *Minois dryas* p.524
1. male upperside; 2. female underside

False Grayling *Arethusana arethusa* p.526

Great Banded Grayling *Kanetisa circe* p.525

Arran Brown
Erebia ligea
p.527
1. upperside;
2. underside

Large Ringlet *Erebia euryale* p.529
1. upperside; 2. male underside

Eriphyle Ringlet *Erebia eriphyle* p.530
1 upperside, 2 underside

White-speck Ringlet *Erebia claudina* p.532
1. female upperside; 2. female underside; 3. male underside

Yellow-spotted Ringlet *Erebia manto* p.531
1. upperside; 2. female underside

Mountain Ringlet *Erebia epiphron* p.533
1. upperside; 2. female underside

Yellow-banded Ringlet *Erebia flavofasciata* p.534
1. male upperside; 2. female underside

Blind Ringlet *Erebia pharte* p.535
1. upperside; 2. underside

Lesser Mountain Ringlet *Erebia melampus* p.537
1. male upperside; 2. underside

Scotch Argus *Erebia aethiops* p.539
1. male upperside; 2. male underside; 3. female underside

de Prunner's Ringlet *Erebia triaria* p.540
1. male upperside; 2. female underside

Lapland Ringlet *Erebia embla* p.540
1. upperside; 2. underside

Arctic Ringlet
Erebia disa
p.541
1. upperside;
2. underside

**Woodland
Ringlet**
*Erebia
medusa* p.542
1. female
upperside;
2. male underside

Arctic Woodland Ringlet *Erebia polaris* p.543
1. upperside; 2. underside

Almond-eyed Ringlet *Erebia alberganus* p.544
1. upperside; 2. underside

Sooty Ringlet *Erebia pluto* p.545
1. upperside, *E. p. oreas*; 2. male underside, *E. p. pluto*

Silky Ringlet *Erebia gorge* p.546
1. male upperside, f. *triopes*; 2. male underside, f. *triopes*

Mnestra's Ringlet *Erebia mnestra* p.547
1. male upperside; 2. male underside

False Mnestra Ringlet *Erebia aethiopella* p.547
1. male upperside, *E. a. rhodopensis*; 2. underside, *E. a. rhodopensis*

Gavarnie Ringlet *Erebia gorgone* p.548
1. male upperside; 2. female upperside; 3. female underside

201

Spring Ringlet *Erebia epistygne* p.549
1. upperside; 2. underside

Swiss Brassy Ringlet *Erebia tyndarus* p.550
1. male upperside; 2. female underside

Common Brassy Ringlet *Erebia cassioides* p.551
1. male upperside; 2. male underside

Spanish Brassy Ringlet *Erebia hispania* p.552
1. male upperside; 2. male upper- and underside

de Lesse's Brassy
Ringlet *Erebia
nivalis* p.553
1. female upperside;
2. female underside

Lorkovic's Brassy Ringlet *Erebia calcaria* p.554
1. female upperside; 2. male underside

Ottoman Brassy Ringlet *Erebia ottomana* p.554
1. male upperside; 2. male underside

Water Ringlet
Erebia pronoe
p.555
1. male
upperside;
2. male underside

Black Ringlet
Erebia melas
p.556
1. female
upperside;
2. male underside

Lefèbvre's Ringlet *Erebia lefebvrei* p.557
1. male upperside; 2. female upperside; 3. female underside

Larche Ringlet *Erebia scipio* p.558
1. female upperside; 2. female underside; 3. male underside

Styrian Ringlet *Erebia stirius* p.558
1. female upperside; 2. female underside; 3. male underside

Stygian Ringlet
Erebia styx
p.559
1. male upperside;
2. male underside

Marbled Ringlet *Erebia montana* p.560
1. male upperside; 2. underside

Autumn Ringlet *Erebia neoridas* p.562
1. male upperside; 2. male underside

Bright-eyed Ringlet *Erebia oeme* p.563
1. female upperside;
2. female underside

Piedmont Ringlet *Erebia meolans* p.564
1. male upperside; 2. mating pair underside (female on right)

Dewy Ringlet
Erebia
pandrose
p.565
1. upperside;
2. underside

False Dewy Ringlet *Erebia sthennyo* p.566
1. female upper- and underside; 2. female underside

Dalmatian Ringlet *Proterebia afra* p.567
1. male upperside; 2. female underside

Meadow Brown
Maniola jurtina p.568
1. male upperside;
2. female upperside;
3. male underside

Dusky Meadow Brown *Hyponephele lycaon* p.570
female underside

Oriental Meadow Brown *Hyponephele lupina* p.571
1. female upperside; 2. female underside

Gatekeeper *Pyronia tithonus* p.573
1. male upperside; 2. female upperside; 3. underside

Southern Gatekeeper *Pyronia cecilia* p.574
1. male upperside; 2. female underside

Spanish Gatekeeper *Pyronia bathseba* p.575
1. male upperside; 2. female upperside; 3. underside

Large Heath
Coenonympha
tullia p.576
male underside, *C. t. scotica*

Balkan Heath
Coenonympha rhodopensis
p.577 underside

Small Heath
Coenonympha pamphilus
p.578
underside

Corsican Heath
Coenonympha corinna
p.579 underside

Elban Heath
Coenonympha elbana
p.580 underside

Dusky Heath *Coenonympha dorus* p.580 underside

Pearly Heath *Coenonympha arcania* p.581 underside

Alpine Heath
Coenonympha gardetta
p.582 underside

Darwin's Heath
Coenonympha darwiniana
p.583 underside

Russian Heath *Coenonympha leander* p.584
1. underside; 2. underside, *C. l. orientalis*

Chestnut Heath *Coenonympha glycerion* p.585
underside

False Ringlet *Coenonympha oedippus* p.587
1. male underside; 2. female underside; 3. female upperside

Scarce Heath *Coenonympha hero* p.578
underside

Speckled Wood *Pararge aegeria* p.589
1. upperside, f. *aegeria*; 2. upperside, f. *tircis*;

Wall Brown *Lasiommata megera* p.591
1. male upperside; 2. underside

Large Wall Brown
Lasiommata maera
p.592 1. male upperside;
2. female upperside;
Scandinavian race.
3. underside; 4. female
upperside, f. *adrasta*

Northern Wall Brown *Lasiommata petropolitana*
p.594 1. female upperside; 2. female underside;
3. male upperside

Woodland Brown *Lopinga achine* p.595
1. upperside; 2. underside

Lattice Brown *Kirinia roxelana* p.596
underside

Lesser Lattice Brown *Kirinia climene* p.597
male underside

Grizzled and marbled
skippers pp.226–39

Golden skippers pp.240–3

Hesperiidae

These are all small butterflies with wingspans in the European species all under 35 mm (1.4 in). They are mainly dark brown or orange on both surfaces. The antennae are often hooked or turned strongly outwards at the tip and all six legs are fully developed. There are two main groups.

Grizzled and marbled skippers are essentially sooty brown with numerous white spots on both wing surfaces, although the underside of the hindwing is often grey or greenish.

Golden skippers are orange or rich brown on their uppersides, sometimes with paler spots. The undersides are also orange, but are often dusted with grey or green and sometimes bear silvery spots. The butterflies commonly bask with their hindwings flat and their forewings partly raised.

1

2

Grizzled Skipper *Pyrgus malvae* p.599
1 upperside; 2 underside

Large Grizzled Skipper *Pyrgus alveus* p.600
1. upperside; 2. female underside

Oberthür's Grizzled Skipper *Pyrgus armoricanus*
p.601 1. upperside; 2. mating pair

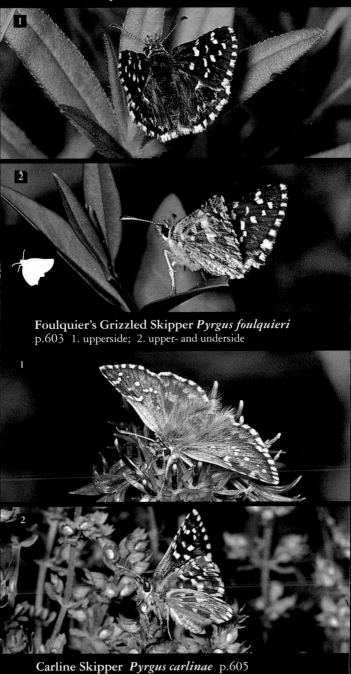

Foulquier's Grizzled Skipper *Pyrgus foulquieri*
p.603 1. upperside; 2. upper- and underside

Carline Skipper *Pyrgus carlinae* p.605
1. upperside, *P. c. carlinae*; 2. upper- and underside, *P. c. cirsii*

Olive Skipper *Pyrgus serratulae* p.604
1. male uppersides; 2. female upperside; 3. male underside

Rosy Grizzled Skipper *Pyrgus onopordi* p.606
1. upperside; 2. male underside

Sandy Grizzled Skipper *Pyrgus cinarae* p.606
1. male upperside; 2. male underside

Yellow-banded Skipper *Pyrgus sidae* p.607
1 female upperside; 2 upper- and underside

Safflower Skipper
Pyrgus carthami
p.608
1. upperside;
2. upper- and underside

Alpine Grizzled Skipper
Pyrgus andromedae
p.600
1. upperside;
2. underside

Dusky Grizzled Skipper *Pyrgus cacaliae* p.609
1. upperside; 2. underside

Northern Grizzled Skipper *Pyrgus centaureae* p.610
1. upperside; 2. underside

Red-underwing Skipper *Spialia sertorius* p.610
1. upperside; 2. underside

**Hungarian
Skipper**
Spialia orbifer
p.611
1. upperside;
2. underside

Persian Skipper *Spialia phlomidis* p.612
1. upperside; 2. upper- and underside

Tessellated Skipper *Muschampia tessellum* p.613
1. male upperside; 2. male underside

Sage Skipper *Muschampia proto* p.614
1. upperside; 2. underside

Mallow Skipper *Carcharodus alceae* p.615
1. upperside; 2. underside

Marbled Skipper *Carcharodus lavatherae* p.616
upperside

Southern Marbled Skipper *Carcharodus boeticus*
p.617 1. upperside; 2. underside

Tufted Marbled Skipper *Carcharodus flocciferus*
p.618 1. upperside; 2. underside

Oriental Marbled Skipper *Carcharodus orientalis*
p.618 1. female upperside; 2. female underside

Dingy Skipper *Erynnis tages* p.619
1. upperside; 2. upper- and underside of mating pair

Inky Skipper *Erynnis marloyi* p.620
underside

Large Chequered Skipper *Heteropterus morpheus*
p.623 1. upperside; 2. underside

Chequered Skipper *Carterocephalus palaemon* p.621
1. upperside; 2. upper- and underside

Northern Chequered Skipper *Carterocephalus silvicolus* p.622 1. male upperside; 2. female upperside

Lulworth Skipper *Thymelicus acteon* p.627
male (left) and female basking

Essex Skipper *Thymelicus lineola* p.625
1. male basking; 2. underside

Small Skipper
Thymelicus sylvestris p.624
1. male basking;
2. underside

Silver-spotted Skipper *Hesperia comma* p.628
1. male upperside; 2. female upperside; 3. underside

Large Skipper *Ochlodes venata* p.629
1. male upperside; 2. female upperside; 3. underside of mating pair

Mediterranean Skipper *Gegenes nostrodamus* p.630
underside

Pigmy Skipper *Gegenes pumilio* p.631
1. male upperside; 2. underside

PART II

FAMILY AND SPECIES DESCRIPTIONS

The number preceding each species
description in the following pages
corresponds to the page number in the
colour section on which that species can
be found.

SWALLOWTAILS, APOLLOS, AND FESTOONS (PAPILIONIDAE)

This family contains over 600 species of large and often spectacularly coloured butterflies, including the largest of all butterflies – Queen Alexandra's Birdwing from Papua New Guinea – whose female has a wingspan approaching 30 cm (12.0 in). The family has its headquarters in the tropical regions, especially in Southeast Asia. Almost a quarter of the known species live in Indonesia and the Philippines. Only 11 species occur in Europe, and of these only one – the Swallowtail – resides in the British Isles.

Members of the family vary greatly in appearance, but the inner margin of the hindwing is always noticeably concave and the abdomen is clearly visible from the side when the butterfly is perched with its wings closed. There is only one anal vein. Many species have 'tails' on the hindwings – hence the name swallowtail given to many members of the family. The tails have no obvious function in most species, although those of the Scarce Swallowtail undoubtedly help to confuse enemies (*see* p.253). The sexes are alike, although females tend to be a little larger than males. All six legs are fully developed in both sexes.

European members have wingspans ranging from about 45 mm to 100 mm (1.8–3.9 in). The flight of most swallowtails and festoons is deceptively lazy, with long periods of gliding and slow flapping, but the butterflies can show a fine turn of speed when necessary. The apollos live mainly in montane regions and prefer to stay close to the ground or the vegetation: high flying in their windy environment could result in their being swept away.

During mating, male apollo butterflies (*Parnassius* species) secrete a white fluid that is then attached to the end of the female abdomen, where it hardens to form a horny pouch called a sphragis. This acts like a chastity belt and prevents the female from mating again.

Mature caterpillar of a swallowtail with osmeterium expanded.

Caterpillar of an apollo.

Pupa of a swallowtail.

The eggs of the swallowtail family are spherical and, apart from those of the apollos, they lack any form of sculpturing, although they may have coloured patterns. The caterpillars of the true swallowtails are hairless, those of the apollos are clothed with short hairs, and those of the festoons are decorated with spiky tubercles. The first two larval instars of the true swallowtails are largely black and white and resemble bird-droppings, but then they become largely green and rely on their similarity to their foodplants to protect them from their numerous predators. The caterpillars go in for chemical defence as well: whenever one is alarmed a plump, Y-shaped scent-gland erupts from just behind its head and thrashes about as the caterpillar attempts to bring it into contact with the intruder. The sudden appearance of the gland, known as an osmeterium, is often enough to scare off small birds, but its acidic secretions play the major role in defence. They have a strong smell, which is not always unpleasant to human noses but certainly successful in warding off ichneumons and other parasites. The caterpillars of the festoon butterflies feed on poisonous birthworts (*Aristolochia* species), storing some of the poisons in their bodies and thus becoming distasteful and possibly toxic to any predator attempting to eat them. Their bright colours warn of the danger.

The pupae or chrysalises of the true swallowtails are fixed vertically to the foodplants or other supports by silken girdles around their middles. Festoons usually pupate in a similar way, although their supporting girdles are attached to their heads. They are also said to pupate on the ground, but still anchor themselves with silk fore and aft. The apollos pupate in flimsy cocoons amongst the debris on the ground.

p.42 **Swallowtail** *Papilio machaon*

Description: 30–40 mm (1.2–1.6 in). The ground colour of the wings is pale yellow on both surfaces and the basal area of the forewing is black. The dark band on the hindwing has a variable amount of blue spotting and sometimes appears almost entirely blue. The two surfaces are very similar, although the underside is usually paler and the outer edge of the broad black band on the underside of the forewing is almost straight. The summer broods tend to look paler than the spring brood because the black areas are more heavily dusted with yellow scales. The abdomen is black in the spring brood, but in later broods it is yellow with a black stripe along the back.

Similar species: Corsican Swallowtail, found only in Corsica and Sardinia, has a similar pattern but its tails are shorter and the red spot on the hindwing is smaller. The outer edge of the dark band on the underside of the forewing is very wavy.

Flight: March to September, with a single brood around midsummer at high altitude and in the northern parts of the range, and two or three broods elsewhere.

Habitat: Flowery places of all kinds, including gardens, from sea level to 2,200 m (7,225 ft), although the British race is confined to fenland (*see* below). The adults are especially fond of thistles and other purple flowers, and commonly visit garden buddleias in continental Europe. They rarely keep still when feeding, their forewings twitching continuously in readiness for a quick take-off. The larval foodplants are various umbellifers, including Fennel, Wild Carrot, and Milk-parsley.

Life-cycle: The eggs are yellow at first, becoming mottled with brown as they develop. They are laid singly on the foodplants and they hatch within a week. Until the second moult the caterpillar is black with a white 'saddle' and resembles a bird-dropping. Then it becomes bright green with black bands and red spots. If it is disturbed, its orange osmeterium shoots out (*see* p.248) and its sweet but pungent scent lingers for a surprisingly long time. Caterpillars can be found from May to October. They feed for about a month and reach lengths of about 50 mm (2.0 in) before pupating on the foodplant or some other support. Summer chrysalises tend to be yellowish green, but those produced in the autumn are more often pale brown, thus blending more effectively with the dead and dying vegetation. Winter is always passed in the chrysalis stage.

Range: Throughout Europe and North Africa and across the temperate parts of Asia to Japan, although the British race (*P. m. britannicus*) is confined to small areas of the Norfolk Broads. Also occurs in Alaska and Canada, where it is known as the Old World Swallowtail. About 35 races or subspecies are recognized.

The restriction of the British race to damp fenland seems strange in view of the fact that the continental race (*P. m. gorganus*) is so widely distributed, but it appears that the male genitalia of *P. m. britannicus* function properly only in a damp environment. British swallowtails are mainly single-brooded, with adults flying from late May to early July, but in some years a partial second brood is on the wing in August and September. Adults of the British race tend to be a little darker than their Continental relatives, some of which occasionally turn up in southeast England in the summer. Caterpillars of the British race feed almost exclusively on Milk-parsley.

---

p.43 **Corsican Swallowtail** *Papilio hospiton*

Description: 35–40 mm (1.4–1.6 in). The wings are pale yellow and heavily marked with black on both surfaces. The basal part of the forewing is always black, and all black areas are liberally sprinkled with yellow scales. The blue spots on the upperside of the hindwing are always well defined, and the outer edge of the dark band on the underside of the forewing is distinctly wavy.

Similar species: Swallowtail has longer 'tails' and a larger red spot on each hindwing. The outer edge of the dark band on the underside of the forewing is almost straight.

Flight: May to July.

Habitat: Flowery slopes, usually between 600 and 1,500 m (1,975 and 4,925 ft). The foodplants are various umbellifers, especially Giant Fennel.

Life-cycle: Eggs are laid singly and they hatch within a week. The caterpillar is much like that of the Swallowtail during the first two instars, but then it becomes yellow with black blotches on each segment. It grows to a length of about 50 mm (2.0 in) and then pupates on the foodplant. Winter is passed in the chrysalis stage. There is only one brood per year, but the adults emerge over quite a long period.

Range: Confined to Corsica and Sardinia, and extremely local in both places.

Commercial collection, habitat damage, and the destruction of the foodplants in the belief that they are poisonous to sheep have seriously reduced populations, although opinions differ as to whether the butterfly is in any real danger. It is legally protected in Corsica. The species regularly hybridizes with Swallowtail, and this further reduces the population of the true Corsican Swallowtail.

---

p.43 **Southern Swallowtail** *Papilio alexanor*

Description: 30–40 mm (1.2–1.6 in). The ground colour of the wings is a brighter yellow than that of the other swallowtails and, although conspicuously striped, the wings are less heavily marked with black. The base of the forewing is yellow and the dark band on the hindwing has a continuous blue filling. Upper and lower surfaces are almost identical. The female is usually a little larger than the male.

Similar species: Scarce Swallowtail is superficially similar, especially in flight, but it is paler and has more stripes on the forewing. It has longer 'tails' and the blue on the hindwing is broken up into crescent-shaped patches.

Flight: April to July in a single generation, with adults emerging over a long period.

Habitat: Flower-rich places, mainly in upland regions to an altitude of 1,500 m (4,925 ft). A very local butterfly, particularly fond of thistles, on which it often performs elegant pirouettes while feeding. The larval foodplants are various umbellifers, especially *Seseli montanum*.

Life-cycle: Eggs are laid singly on the foodplants and they hatch within a week. The caterpillar is like that of the Swallowtail at first, but then becomes pale green with broad black bands bearing orange spots. It reaches about 60 mm (2.2 in) in length and completes its growth within about a month. The winter is passed in the chrysalis stage.

Range: This rare and declining species occurs locally from Provence, through southern Italy to Greece and the Middle East, but is now most likely to be seen in the Alpine foothills of Provence, especially in the wilder, undisturbed corners. It is threatened with extinction elsewhere in Europe and has already disappeared from many places.

---

p.43 **Scarce Swallowtail** *Iphiclides podalirius*

Description: 30–45 mm (1.2–1.8 in). The ground colour of the wings ranges from almost white to pale yellow. The forewing has six prominent black stripes, visible on both surfaces; the inner margin of the hindwing normally has a broad black border, and blue markings on the hindwing form distinct crescents. The 'tails' are much longer than in the other European swallowtails.

Similar species: Southern Swallowtail is brighter yellow, with fewer stripes and shorter 'tails', and it has a continuous blue band on the hindwing.

Flight: March to September. In the northern parts of the range and at high altitudes there is just one brood, on the wing from April to July, but elsewhere there are two broods, flying from March to early June and from July to September. Flight is elegant, with a distinctive floating action.

Habitat: Open, flowery places, including gardens, from sea level to 2,000 m (6,550 ft); often common in orchards and light woodland. The caterpillars feed on Blackthorn and various other rosaceous trees and shrubs, including cultivated plums and cherries.

Life-cycle: Eggs are laid singly from April to August. The young caterpillar is black with a white 'saddle', but after the second moult it becomes green, with yellow stripes and red spots; it is slug-shaped, tapering towards each end. It takes up to eight weeks to mature, by which time it is about 40 mm (1.6 in) long and ready to pupate on the foodplant. The winter is passed in the chrysalis stage, but chrysalises can be found throughout the year. Overwintering chrysalises are usually brown, but summer ones are green.

Range: Throughout Europe, apart from Scandinavia and the British Isles, and on through Asia to China. Also in North Africa. Vagrants occasionally reach Scandinavia and the British Isles and the name Scarce Swallowtail refers to the butterfly's status in Britain. In many parts of the Continent it is actually much more common than the Swallowtail.

Spring-brood insects are much yellower than the summer brood. Specimens from North Africa, Iberia, and southwest France, where the males of both broods are almost white, are assigned to the subspecies *I. p. feisthamelii*. They are often larger than specimens from elsewhere and some entomologists consider them to belong to a separate species, *Iphiclides feisthamelii*.

When the butterfly perches with its wings closed, the dark patch at the rear of the hindwing gives the impression of a head, with the long 'tails' resembling antennae. On landing, the butterfly frequently turns through 180 degrees to face the direction from which it came, and the effect is totally confusing to any bird or other predator that might have seen the insect land. They peck at the 'wrong' end of the butterfly, which can then fly away unharmed apart from the loss of a bit of 'tail'.

---

p.44   ## Spanish Festoon *Zerynthia rumina*

Description: 20–30 mm (0.8–1.2 in). The ground colour of the wings ranges from cream to pale orange, with the latter occurring mainly in females. Black spots and bars vary in intensity. There is a translucent 'window' near the tip of the forewing and just before it there is an elongated red spot. There are two more red spots in the cell and another near the hind margin of the forewing. These markings appear on both upperside and underside. The underside is somewhat paler, but otherwise the two surfaces are very similar.

Similar species: Southern Festoon has no translucent 'window' and, apart from a small red spot just beyond the cell, there is no red on the upperside of the forewing. Eastern Festoon is larger and has no red on either surface of the forewing.

Flight: Between February and June in most parts of the range, but in recent years the species has been seen on the wing in September and October on the south coast of Spain (*see* below). Although brightly coloured when seen at close quarters, its mottled pattern makes it quite hard to spot and follow in its stony habitat.

Habitat: Dry, stony places from sea level to about 1,500 m (4,925 ft); most common in hilly areas, especially near the coast. The foodplants are birthworts, especially the tough *Aristolochia pistolochia*.

Life-cycle: The butterfly is at least partially double-brooded in southern Spain (*see* below), but elsewhere it produces a single brood and eggs are laid in small groups on birthworts between February and June. The caterpillar is up to 35 mm (1.4 in) long and grey or pale brown with four rows of pale, spiny outgrowths. It feeds on the birthworts until it pupates in June or July. Winter is passed in the chrysalis stage.

Range: Iberia, southern France, the extreme west of Italy, and North Africa. The ranges of the Spanish and Eastern Festoons do not overlap at all. Those of the Spanish and Southern Festoons overlap only in Provence and the extreme west of Italy.

The Spanish Festoon is a very variably coloured butterfly, the most striking variation being the form *honnoratii*, in which the red spots are much enlarged and cover a large proportion of each wing. Specimens with a red spot at the base of the hindwing, which are common in parts of France, are known as form *medesicaste*. Although the butterfly is locally common, afforestation of its rocky haunts is putting it at risk in many areas. Until recently, the species has been regarded as single-brooded in Europe, but during the last few years increasing numbers of butterflies have been seen in the Malaga region during September and October, indicating that at least in this area there is a second brood. These butterflies continue to fly well into the winter and overlap the spring brood, and in this region the species can be found on the wing from September right through to the following May. The species is also double-brooded in some parts of Morocco.

---

p.44 **Southern Festoon** *Zerynthia polyxena*

Description: 22–26 mm (0.9–1.0 in). The ground colour of the wings ranges from cream to deep yellow, often with a fair amount of white on the underside of the hindwing. The black spots and bars vary in intensity, although the bars in the front part of the forewing are usually very prominent. The underside of the forewing has two prominent red spots in the cell and another red spot beyond it, but the upperside of the forewing has no more than a small red spot close to the front margin and sometimes no red at all. The blue spots near the edge of the upperside of the hindwing are often very small or absent.

Similar species: Spanish Festoon has prominent red spots in the cell on the upperside of the forewing and also has a translucent 'window' just beyond the cell. Eastern Festoon has no red on either surface of the forewing.

Flight: April to June.

Habitat: Rough, stony places from sea level to about 1,100 m (3,600 ft): frequent in old vineyards and often in somewhat damper places than the Spanish Festoon. The caterpillars feed on birthworts, especially the succulent Round-leaved Birthwort.

Life-cycle: Single-brooded, with eggs laid in small groups on birthworts from April to June. The caterpillar is up to 35 mm (1.4 in) long, and pale brown or greyish with four rows of red tubercles tipped with black spines. It feeds between May and July, and then it pupates low down on the foodplant. The chrysalis may overwinter twice before the adult emerges, especially in the more northerly parts of the range.

Range: From southeast France (Provence) and Italy, northwards and eastwards to the Czech Republic and the Black Sea. Overlaps with the Spanish Festoon only in Provence and western Italy.

Specimens from France and Italy are darker and more heavily marked than those from elsewhere and are assigned to the subspecies *cassandra*.

Although widely distributed, the Southern Festoon is a local and declining species. The decline is believed to be the result of increasingly intensive cultivation of vineyards, which destroys the butterfly's foodplant. Many European populations are considered to be vulnerable and the species is legally protected in several countries. It is also known as the Birthwort Butterfly.

p.45 **Eastern Festoon** *Zerynthia cerisyi*

Description: 20–30 mm (0.8–1.2 in). The ground colour of the wings varies from off-white to pale yellow and there are no red spots on either surface of the forewing. The outer margin of the hindwing is strongly scalloped and usually bears a short 'tail' at the end of vein 4. Upperside and underside are alike, but females are more heavily marked than males.

Similar species: Southern Festoon resembles female but has no 'tail' and always has red spots on the underside of the forewing.

Flight: March to July.

Habitat: Rough ground from sea level to 1,500 m (4,925 ft), with a particular liking for rocky hillsides and riverbanks. The caterpillars feed on birthworts.

Life-cycle: A single-brooded species, laying its eggs in small batches on birthworts from March to June. The caterpillar – up to 40 mm (1.6 in) long – is fawn, with broad black stripes along the back and sides, and four bristly pink tubercles on each segment. It feeds until August and then pupates, usually low down on the foodplant. Winter is passed in the chrysalis stage.

Range: From the southeastern shores of the Adriatic to the Caspian Sea. A local and declining species, legally protected in Greece.

Specimens from Crete are smaller and much more yellow than those from the mainland, and they have no 'tails' on the hindwings. Although normally assigned to the subspecies *Z. c. cretica*, they are very distinct and are sometimes treated as a separate species – *Zerynthia cretica*.

p.47 **False Apollo** *Archon apollinus*

Description: 25–30 mm (1.0–1.2 in). The forewings of the male are translucent grey, with a variable amount of speckling and two prominent black spots in the cell. The hindwings have a yellowish tinge, with a black smudge at the base and a conspicuous arc of six red and blue spots near the outer margin. Upperside and underside are very similar. The female has heavier markings and a deeper-yellow tinge, especially on the hindwings.

Similar species: This butterfly cannot be confused with any other European species.

Flight: March to April.

Habitat: Rough, stony places, usually occurring in small, scattered colonies at altitudes up to 1,500 m (4,925 ft). The foodplants are birthworts.

Life-cycle: Single-brooded, with eggs found in small groups on birthworts from March to May. The caterpillar is up to 40 mm (1.6 in) long and velvety black with four red 'pimples' on each segment. It feeds until July and then pupates amongst leaf-litter on the ground. The winter is passed in the chrysalis stage.

Range: From Greece and Bulgaria to the shores of the Caspian Sea.

Although widely distributed and not uncommon in western Asia, the False Apollo is rare in Europe, where its scattered populations are considered to be vulnerable.

p.46 **Apollo** *Parnassius apollo*

Description: 35–45 mm (1.4–1.8 in). The wings are usually thinly scaled and the outer edge of the forewing is usually translucent. The ground colour is white or cream with a variable dusting of grey scales, usually heavier in the female than in the male. There are two large black spots in the cell of the forewing, and another one near the hind margin of the forewing. The upperside of the hindwing bears two conspicuous red or orange spots ringed with black, although these may be quite small. The underside of the hindwing has these same spots and some additional ones at the base. There is rarely any red on the forewing. The body is rather furry, as in all apollos, providing useful insulation in the Alpine habitat.

Similar species:	Small Apollo is a bit smaller and has one or more small red spots just beyond the cell of the forewing. The antennae are white with conspicuous black rings.
Flight:	May to September, according to altitude, usually in a single brood. Flight is sluggish and the butterfly spends a lot of time sitting on flowers or on the ground.
Habitat:	Mountain slopes and meadows from 500 to 2,000 m (1,650–6,550 ft), although it may fly much lower down in Scandinavia. The foodplants are stonecrops and houseleeks.
Life-cycle:	The dimpled white eggs have a pimply surface and are laid singly on or near the foodplants during the summer. Some hatch in the autumn, but most do not hatch until the following spring. Caterpillars leaving their eggs in the autumn soon go into hibernation amongst the stones and leaf-litter. The caterpillar feeds from March until the end of June and reaches about 50 mm (2.0 in) in length. It is velvety black with yellow or orange spots on the sides. Pupation takes place in a flimsy cocoon spun between stones and roots on the ground. The chrysalis is coated with a bluish-white powder and the adult emerges in three or four weeks. Populations inhabiting warmer areas at lower altitudes – usually those whose eggs hatch in the autumn – may feed up quickly in the spring and produce a second generation of butterflies in late summer.
Range:	Widely distributed in mountainous areas, from Scandinavia to Spain and Sicily and right across Asia to China. Absent from the British Isles.

Numerous subspecies have been described, varying mainly in the size of the red spots and in the amount of grey dusting. Scandinavian specimens are more heavily scaled and noticeably whiter than those from elsewhere. Spanish specimens often have yellow or orange spots on the hindwings.

Although locally common, the species is declining in many areas and some populations face extinction. Widespread

collection of this beautiful and easily
caught butterfly – often for trade – may
have contributed to its disappearance from
some places, and the ever-increasing
number of cars using the Alpine roads kill
a lot of the insects, because of their
fondness for basking on the roads.
However, afforestation of the mountain
slopes is generally agreed to be the major
cause of the decline. The Apollo is legally
protected in several countries, and it was
the first insect to come under the protective
umbrella of CITES (the Convention on
International Trade in Endangered Species).

---

p.47 **Small Apollo** *Parnassius phoebus*

Description: 30–40 mm (1.2–1.6 in). The ground
colour of the wings is generally pale cream
or white and there are normally one or two
black-ringed red spots just beyond the cell
of the forewing and there are two large red
spots on the hindwing. Females are often
heavily dusted with grey and more heavily
marked than the males, with a conspicuous
black spot near the hind edge of the
forewing. The underside of the hindwing
has a cluster of red spots at the base, but
otherwise the two surfaces are much alike.
The antennae are clearly ringed with black
and white.

Similar species: Apollo lacks red on the forewing and does
not have ringed antennae. It is usually a
little larger and it flies at lower altitudes.

Flight: June to September.

Habitat: Grassy mountain slopes, usually above
2,000 m (6,550 ft) and rarely far from
streams. The Small Apollo can fly at lower
temperatures than most other butterflies
and has even been known to fly in
snowstorms. The larval foodplants are
various saxifrages, especially Yellow
Saxifrage, and houseleeks.

Life-cycle: The dimpled, white eggs are laid singly or
in small clusters on the foodplants in the
summer. Some of them hatch in a few
weeks and the tiny caterpillars quickly go
into hibernation under the mats and

cushions of leaves, but most of the eggs do not hatch until the following spring. The caterpillar is velvety black with yellow or orange spots and it feeds up quickly in the spring. It reaches a length of about 48 mm (1.9 in) and pupates in a flimsy cocoon under the foodplant or surrounding stones. The chrysalis is black.

Range: A very local butterfly, living in small and widely scattered colonies in the Alps. Also occurs right across northern Asia to Siberia, and in the Rocky Mountains of North America where it is known as the Phoebus Parnassian.

The Small Apollo is a very variable species, especially with regard to the extent of the red spots and the amount of grey scaling, and numerous subspecies have been recognized. In general, the darkest races inhabit the highest altitudes. In the eastern Alps a proportion of the insects have heavy grey scaling and the red spots on the hindwing are joined by a black line. Additional red spots occur at the base of the upperside of the hindwing. Such specimens are known as f. *cardinalis*.

Living in small colonies, the butterfly is very susceptible to any kind of disturbance of its habitat and it is considered to be at risk throughout Europe.

p.47 **Clouded Apollo** *Parnassius mnemosyne*

Description: 25–32 mm (1.0–1.25 in). The wings are thinly scaled, with prominent black veins and no red spots. There are two black spots in the cell of the forewing. The grey scales around the tip of the forewing are particularly sparse and this region is almost transparent. The amount of grey varies elsewhere on the wings: it is usually greater in females and also at high altitudes. The underside is rather shiny, but otherwise similar to the upperside. Mated females carry a particularly large sphragis (*see* p.247), extending almost the whole length of the abdomen.

Similar species: Black-veined White looks very similar in flight, but has no black spots and its hindwings have strongly convex inner margins.

Flight: May to August.

Habitat: Generally in upland areas with damp meadows and open woodland, up to about 2,000 m (6,550 ft), but in Scandinavia it flies over meadows at sea level. The foodplants are various kinds of corydalis species.

Life-cycle: The domed white eggs have a pimply surface and are laid singly on the foodplant in June and July. Some eggs hatch quickly, but the majority do not hatch until the following March or April. Like those of the other apollos, the caterpillar feeds only in sunny weather, and reaches lengths of about 40 mm (1.6 in) before pupating in May or June. It is velvety black with orange spots and very much like that of the Small Apollo. The chrysalis is brown and lies in a silken cocoon spun among the leaves of the foodplant.

Range: Widely distributed in upland areas of Europe, from Scandinavia to the Pyrenees and across to the Black Sea. Also across Asia to Afghanistan. Absent from the British Isles.

Some European populations are at risk – from afforestation and the development of ski resorts, for example – and although the species is still locally common the Clouded Apollo is legally protected in several countries.

WHITES AND YELLOWS (PIERIDAE)

Most of the 1,200 or so species in this cosmopolitan family are white or yellow, although some tropical members display brilliant reds and blues. There are two anal veins and the inner margin of the hindwing is convex – never concave as in the Papilionidae – so the abdomen is usually completely concealed when the insect is at rest with its wings closed. Wingspans range from about 20–100 mm (0.8–3.9 in). All six legs are fully developed in both sexes.

Eggs of Wood White (left) and Orange-tip (right).

*Caterpillar of
Clouded Yellow.*

Small White (left)
and Bath White

Clouded Yellow

Brimstone

Pierid chrysalises.

The sexes usually differ in the amount of spotting on the wings and are sometimes markedly different in colour, as in the Brimstone and the orange-tips.

The eggs are generally skittle-shaped and usually strongly ribbed. The caterpillars are mostly green and markedly cylindrical, with a coat consisting of no more than short fine hairs. Most of the whites use members of the cabbage family as larval foodplants, while the yellows nearly all use plants of the pea family. The chrysalis tapers to a single point at the head end and is of the succinct type – held upright on its support by a silken girdle.

About 40 species live in Europe, and only six are permanently resident in the British Isles, although several others, including the Clouded Yellow, arrive in variable numbers each year and may breed during the summer. The yellows are generally strong fliers and many are great migrants. Some of the whites also migrate, but at other times they fly weakly and are content to dance and flutter over the flowers and foodplants. Their black and white colours are of a warning nature, for many of these butterflies are protected by distasteful mustard-oils obtained from their larval foodplants.

p.50 **Wood White** *Leptidea sinapis*

Description: 18–25 mm (0.7–1.0 in). This flimsy little butterfly has much narrower wings than the typical whites. The upperside is basically pure white and, although the veins may be lined with grey scales, the only obvious mark is a dark smudge near the tip of the forewing. In the first brood the smudge is solid grey in the male and reduced to streaks along the veins in the female. In later broods the patch is smaller and darker in the males and virtually absent in the females, whose wings are almost pure white. The underside is smudged with grey, most obviously in the first brood, and there is often a yellowish tip to the forewing. Irish specimens (*L. s. juvernica*) have a distinct greenish tinge on the underside. All races and all generations have a white patch underneath the antennal club, although this is not always very obvious in females.

Similar species: Eastern Wood White has no white spot on the antennal club. Fenton's Wood White, confined to Eastern Europe, has slightly more rounded apical smudges, but is otherwise very difficult to distinguish from Wood White.

Réal's Wood White (*L. reali*) has recently been separated from Wood White on the basis of genitalia differences. It occurs here and there from Spain to Sweden and Poland.

Flight: April to September, with one brood in midsummer in the north and two or three broods further south. In the British Isles the butterfly flies in May and June, and there may be a partial second brood in August in good summers – but only in the more southerly colonies. The Wood White has a very weak fluttery flight and rarely flies far above the ground. It often spends long periods hovering over or even among the stems of a single plant. Courtship in this and the other wood whites is a much more gentle affair than among the other whites: the pair sit facing each other and the male gently waves his antennae around the female's head.

Habitat: In England and Wales the species is found mainly in woodland rides and clearings, in both coppiced woodlands and young coniferous plantations. Elsewhere, including Ireland, it also occupies more open situations – roadside verges, meadows, and hillsides – as long as these are sheltered and not too far from woodland. It reaches altitudes of 2,000 m (6,550 ft). Larval foodplants include Meadow Vetchling, Tufted Vetch, bird's-foot trefoils, and various other leguminous plants.

Life-cycle: The eggs are laid singly on the foodplants, mainly on those plants protruding from the surrounding vegetation. They change from cream to bright yellow as they mature, and generally hatch within about ten days. The caterpillar rarely moves far and is very well camouflaged – bright green with a broad yellow line along each side. It feeds mainly by day and when fully grown (within three or four weeks) it is about 18 mm (0.7 in) long. It usually pupates in the surrounding vegetation. The chrysalis is pale green, and winter is spent in the pupal stage.

Range: Most of Europe and temperate Asia, but absent from Scotland and northern half of England.

After a marked decline in the early years of the 20th century, the butterfly has been increasing its range in England and Wales in recent years and has colonized several abandoned railway-lines. The increase in conifer plantations, with their wide rides, has helped the butterfly, although as the trees get larger and cast more shade the butterfly will undoubtedly disappear from these places.

The wood whites are not closely related to the crucifer-feeding whites. Apart from the noticeable differences in wing shape, with much more rounded tips in the wood whites, there are significant chemical differences in the white pigments of the two groups.

---

p.50 **Eastern Wood White** *Leptidea duponcheli*

Description: 16–21 mm (0.6–0.8 in). The first-brood upperside is white with a distinct yellow tinge and a variable amount of grey scaling on the veins. The dark smudge on the forewing is grey and well developed in both sexes. The underside of the hindwing is heavily marked with grey, but there is a prominent white patch on the outer margin. The second brood has a smaller and blacker wingtip smudge, but this is much reduced and often absent in the female. The underside lacks dark markings and generally has a strong yellow tinge. The underside of the antennal club has no white spot.

Similar species: Wood White wings are less yellow and there is a white spot under the antennal club. Fenton's Wood White also has a white spot under the antennal club, but this species is larger and prefers wooded areas. It overlaps with Eastern Wood White, if at all, only in Bulgaria and on the eastern shores of the Adriatic.

Flight: April to August in two generations.

Habitat: Upland meadows, usually below 1,000 m (3,275 ft). Larval foodplants are Meadow Vetchling and various other leguminous plants.

Life-cycle: The yellowish eggs are laid singly and the caterpillars, which are very much like those of the Wood White, can be found until September. Winter is passed in the pupal stage, which is very like that of the Wood White.

Range: Provence and neighbouring regions of southern France; the southeastern shores of the Adriatic and on through Greece and Bulgaria to Iran.

Fenton's Wood White *Leptidea morsei*

Description: 20–25 mm (0.8–1.0 in). The dark smudge at the tip of the forewing is grey and a little more rounded than in the other wood whites. First-brood females have a slightly pointed wingtip. Second-brood insects are larger and males have darker apical smudges: females have no more than a few grey streaks on the veins in this region. The underside of the antennal club has a white patch.

Similar species: Wood White is very similar, although slightly smaller on average and the apical smudge on the forewing has straighter edges. Eastern Wood White has no white on the antennal club.

Flight: April to July in two broods.

Habitat: Lightly wooded valleys, usually at low levels. The caterpillars feed on Spring Pea and the very similar Black Pea.

Life-cycle: The eggs are laid singly on the foodplant. They hatch quickly, and the caterpillars, which are very much like those of the Wood White, can be found from April to August. They pupate on the foodplants or on the neighbouring vegetation. Winter is passed in the pupal stage.

Range: From Croatia and Austria, eastwards through Hungary and Romania and across Asia to Japan. Overlaps with Eastern Wood White, if at all, only in Bulgaria and on the eastern shores of the Adriatic.

Although this species is very difficult to separate from the Wood White on external characteristics, the genitalia of the two species are quite distinct.

p.51 **Black-veined White** *Aporia crataegi*

Description: 25–40 mm (1.0–1.6 in). The upperside of the male is white with dark-brown or black veins. The underside is similar but has a variable dusting of black scales. The female is larger than the male and thinly scaled, revealing the translucent brown membrane of her wings – especially in later life. Her veins are brown.

Similar species: Clouded Apollo is superficially similar, especially in flight, but it has black spots on the forewing and the inner margin of the hindwing is dark and distinctly concave.

Flight: April to July in a single brood. Rather slow, with alternating gliding and flapping.

Habitat: Open, flower-rich habitats of all kinds, from sea level to about 2,000 m (6,550 ft). Often common on roadsides and woodland edges and in gardens and orchards. Adult butterflies feed avidly at flowers and are especially fond of purple ones, such as knapweeds, scabious, clovers, and Lucerne. They also drink a fair amount of honeydew. The larval foodplants are shrubs and trees of the rose family, especially Blackthorn and other *Prunus* species, and the caterpillars can be a real nuisance in orchards.

Life-cycle: The bright-yellow, barrel-like eggs are laid in large batches on the undersides of the leaves, usually in May and June, and they hatch after two or three weeks. The caterpillars are strongly gregarious and quickly spin a communal web under which they all shelter. After the second moult, at which time they are only about 4 mm (0.2 in) long, the caterpillars go into hibernation, safely tucked up in thick-walled tents made of grey silk. These tents, which often incorporate dead leaves as well, are firmly fixed to the twigs of the foodplant. Waking in the spring, the caterpillars bask on the outside of the web and rapidly gain weight as they feed on the opening buds. They gradually disperse as they get larger. The mature caterpillar is clothed with white and yellowish hairs and reaches a length of about 42 mm (1.7 in). The lower half of its body is grey, but the upper half is black with a fragmented orange or yellow stripe on each side. Pupation takes place between the end of March and the end of May. The chrysalis is yellow with bold black spots and is fixed succinctly to the foodplant. Adult butterflies emerge after about three weeks and may survive for eight weeks.

chrysalis

Range: Most of Europe, apart from the British Isles and the Arctic. Across Asia to Japan; also in North Africa.

The Black-veined White was widely distributed and quite common in England and Wales in the early part of the 19th century, although its numbers fluctuated wildly from year to year. It was still common in some areas in the 1850s and 1860s, but by then it had disappeared from many of its original haunts. The decline continued rapidly, and by the beginning of the 20th century only Kent could claim the butterfly in any numbers. It probably became extinct in Britain in 1922, although casual immigrants from the Continent have been seen on several more recent occasions.

Increased spraying of its orchard habitats and increased predation by birds have both been suggested as causes of the demise of the butterfly in Britain, and they would certainly have had some effect, but climatic change is the most likely cause of the extinction. Autumn rainfall was abnormally high in the early years of the

20th century, encouraging the growth of pathogenic fungi which are believed to have wiped out the hibernating caterpillars.

Black-veined Whites can often be seen drinking from muddy puddles and other damp ground, especially in upland areas. Hundreds of the butterflies may gather to drink at the sides of the roads. Almost all of them are males, but it is not the actual water that they are after: they are interested in the salts dissolved in it – especially sodium – which male butterflies require in considerable amounts for the formation of the sperm packets that they transfer to the females during mating. (*See also* p.16)

p.52 **Large White** *Pieris brassicae*

Description: 25–35 mm (1.0–1.4 in). The male upperside is almost entirely white, with black wingtips and a narrow black border at the front of the forewing. There is a small black spot on the front edge of the hindwing. The female is similar but the forewing has two large black spots in the centre and a black streak on the rear edge. The undersides of both sexes have two black spots on the forewing, while the hindwing is largely cream with a variable amount of black dusting. Spring insects have more dusting than summer ones, and the latter have much more intense black markings on the upperside. Third-brood insects are often quite small.

Similar species: Small White is smaller and has much smaller and less dense black markings. Moorland Clouded Yellow female resembles male Large White but has black borders on the upperside of both wings.

Flight: April to October in two or three broods. Flight is fast and powerful on migration, but rather weak and fluttery at other times, especially when searching for egg-laying sites.

Habitat: Flowery places of all kinds, from sea level to 2,200 m (7,225 ft). Although it is especially common in gardens and on other cultivated land, this migrant butterfly can be found in open habitats almost anywhere. The larval foodplants are mainly cultivated brassicas. Garden nasturtiums are also used, and so are various wild crucifers and Wild Mignonette.

Life-cycle: The skittle-shaped eggs are bright yellow and laid in large batches on the undersides of the foodplants from April onwards. The caterpillars are dirty green and heavily marked with black and yellow. They are gregarious for much of their lives, but they separate after the final moult. They mature in about a month, when they are about 40 mm (1.6 in) long. Pupation takes place on vertical surfaces, including garden walls and sheds, and the chrysalis, strongly pointed at the front, is greyish green, marked with yellow and black. Summer pupae give rise to new butterflies in about a fortnight, but the autumn ones overwinter and produce the spring brood.

Range: This strongly migratory butterfly occurs throughout Europe and North Africa and across temperate Asia to the Himalayas, although it is rare beyond the Arctic Circle.

The Large White and the Small White are both commonly known as cabbage whites in Britain. The caterpillars of the Large White wreck huge quantities of cabbages and other brassica crops each year, often reducing the leaves to spiky skeletons. All stages of the life-cycle are rendered distasteful to predators by the mustard-oils absorbed from the larval foodplants, and they advertise the fact with their bold colours. Feeding larvae also emit a disagreeable smell that deters most predators but, fortunately for the gardener, it does not deter the braconid wasp *Apanteles glomeratus*: this tiny parasite lays its eggs inside a caterpillar and its grubs gradually eat their way through the host, although they do not kill it until they are fully grown. Then they bore their way out and pupate in little yellow cocoons clustered around the caterpillar's shrivelled corpse – a very common sight in late summer.

Apanteles is so abundant in the British Isles, especially in the autumn, that it is doubtful whether the Large White could survive in these islands without regular immigration from the Continent each year. The Large White was introduced to Australia in the 1930s and threatened to become a serious pest, but the subsequent introduction of Apanteles quickly eliminated the butterfly.

The pupae are attacked by the tiny chalcid wasp Pteromalus puparum, hundreds of which can be seen emerging from a single chrysalis in the spring.

p.53 **Small White** Pieris rapae

Description: 15–27 mm (0.8–1.1 in). The uppersides are creamy white with greyish wingtips. The grey often extends all along the front edge of the forewing, but never spreads along the outer margin further than vein 6. There is often a dusting of grey scales over the basal areas of the wings, especially in the female. The male has a single, often ill-defined black spot near the middle of the forewing, while the female has two spots. Both sexes have a small black spot on the front edge of the hindwing. All markings are darker in the summer broods than in the spring brood. The underside of the forewing is white with a yellow tip and normally has two black spots in both sexes. The underside of the hindwing is yellow with a dusting of dark scales, the latter being most obvious in the spring brood. Late-summer and autumn specimens are often very small.

Similar species: Large White is larger and the dark wingtips extend down the outer margin at least to vein 3. Southern Small White is very similar, but dark wingtips extend at least to vein 4. Mountain Small White has a distinctly square dark patch at the wingtip.

Flight: March to October in two or more broods.

Habitat: Flowery places of all kinds, from sea level to 2,000 m (6,550 ft), but especially common in gardens and on other cultivated land. The larval foodplants are mainly cultivated brassicas, together with garden nasturtiums

and assorted wild crucifers and Wild
Mignonette.

Life-cycle: The eggs are pale yellow and are laid singly,
usually on the undersides of the leaves. They
hatch in about a week to produce velvety,
green caterpillars with a fine yellow line on
the back and a line of yellow spots on each
side. The caterpillar is extremely well
camouflaged on brassica leaves, and it often
gets right inside cabbages and broccoli
heads. About 25 mm (1.0 in) long when
mature, it normally pupates on fences and
other upright supports. The chrysalis ranges
from green to pale brown and is often heavily
speckled with black dots. The pupal stage
lasts for two to three weeks in the summer,
but autumn pupae overwinter and do not
give rise to butterflies until the spring.

Range: Throughout Europe, apart from the Arctic
coasts; and most of Asia. Introduced to
Australia and North America, where it is
called the Cabbage White. One of the
world's commonest butterflies. It is a strong
migrant, with large numbers moving
northwards through Europe in the spring
and early summer and a reverse movement
beginning during August as a result of
falling temperatures and shorter days.

The Small White can be an even worse pest
in the garden than the Large White because
it is generally more common and its
caterpillars are less easy to find and destroy.
It is attacked by the same kinds of parasites
that attack the Large White.

Together with the following four species,
the Small White is sometimes placed in the
genus *Artogeia*.

p.55 **Southern Small White** *Pieris mannii*

Description: 20–30 mm (0.8 1.2 in). The uppersides are
milky white with greyish wingtips, the grey
extending down the outer edge at least to
vein 4. The male has one or two black spots
on the forewing, but the female always has
two. The anterior spot is rectangular or
crescent-shaped (never round as in the Small

White), and in the female it is usually linked to the outer margin by two dark streaks. Both sexes have a black spot at the front of the hindwing. The underside of the forewing is white with black spots and a yellow tip, and the underside of the hindwing is yellow with a fairly heavy dusting of black scales.

Similar species: Small White has a dark wingtip patch extending back no further than vein 6. Mountain Small White has a rather square wingtip patch and no black spots on the underside of the forewing.

Flight: March to November in three or four broods.

Habitat: Rough, flower-rich places from sea level to 1,600 m (5,250 ft). Larval foodplants are candytufts and other wild crucifers.

Life-cycle: The eggs are yellow and are laid singly or in small groups on the uppersides of the leaves. The caterpillar is bluish green and velvety, with a very thin yellow line on the back. About 25 mm (1.0 in) long when mature, it pupates on plant stems and stones. Summer generations spend only two or three weeks in the pupal stage, but pupae formed in the autumn overwinter and produce adults in the spring. The chrysalis is cream with sparse black dots.

Range: The southern half of Europe, including much of France, and on to the Middle East; also in Morocco.

The butterfly is sometimes called *Artogeia*.

p.53 **Mountain Small White** *Pieris ergane*

Description: 18–25 mm (0.7–1.0 in). The upperside of the male is white with a distinctly square black mark at the tip of the forewing and a rounded spot near the centre, although this may be very faint or even absent. The female usually has a yellow tinge, especially on the hindwing, and two black spots on the forewing. The underside of the forewing is white with a yellow tip, and the underside of the hindwing is bright yellow. The undersides have no black marks, although those of the upperside may show through.

Similar species: Small White and Southern Small White

have black spots on the underside of the forewing and less square wingtip patches.

Flight: March to October in two or three broods.

Habitat: Rough, grassy slopes from sea level to about 2,000 m (6,550 ft). The larval foodplants are assorted low-growing crucifers, but especially Burnt Candytuft.

Life-cycle: The pale-yellow eggs are laid singly on the foodplant and the velvety caterpillars, about 25 mm (1.0 in) long, are bluish green with a heavy sprinkling of black dots and yellow spots around the spiracles. The chrysalis is very much like that of the Southern Small White and normally fixed to rocks or stones. Summer generations spend only a very short time in the pupal stage, but insects pupating in the autumn spend the winter as pupae.

Range: Scattered populations exist through the Mediterranean region from northern Spain to the Balkans and on to the Caspian Sea, with small outposts in Hungary.

The butterfly is sometimes called *Artogeia*.

---

p.55 **Krueper's Small White** *Pieris krueperi*

Description: 20–25 mm (0.8–1.0 in). The uppersides are white, with a black triangular mark close to the wingtip on the front edge of the forewing. (This is visible on both surfaces.) There are often heavy black triangles around the outer wing-margins, especially in females. There is a large, rounded black spot near the middle of the forewing and a triangular one at the front edge of the hindwing. The underside of the forewing is white with a yellowish tip and a large black spot near the centre. The underside of the hindwing is largely green with a white onto band in the first brood, but in later broods it is largely yellow and sometimes almost white, especially in the male.

Similar species: The triangular spot on the forewing distinguishes this from all other whites.

Flight: March to October in two to four broods.

Habitat: Rocky slopes and other uncultivated areas from sea level to about 2,000 m (6,550 ft).

The larval foodplants are primarily Golden Alyssum and Mountain Alyssum.

Life-cycle: The early stages of this butterfly resemble those of the Mountain Small White. The caterpillars feed mainly on the flowers of the food-plant and winter is passed in the pupal stage.

Range: From the Balkans and Turkey, across the Middle East to the Gulf of Oman.

The butterfly is sometimes called *Artogeia*.

---

p.54 Green-veined White *Pieris napi*

Description: 18–25 mm (0.7–1.0 in). The uppersides are creamy white with dark tips to the forewings and the veins dusted with dark scales. There are usually small dark triangles at the tips of the veins, especially on the forewings. The male usually has a single spot near the middle of each forewing and the female has two spots, the rear one normally connected to a black streak on the rear margin. As in other *Pieris* species, there is a black spot on the front edge of the hindwing. The underside of the forewing is white with a yellowish tip, while the underside of the hindwing is yellowish. The veins are lined with dark scales, especially on the hindwings where, mixed with the yellow ground colour, they appear green and give the insect its common name. In late broods the markings on the veins are much less pronounced and the insects could be mistaken for Small White.

Similar species: Late broods can resemble Small White (*see* above). Peak White has superficially similar underside, but the black spot on the forewing is at the end of the cell.

Flight: March to November. Single-brooded in the Arctic, on high mountains, and in some other regions (*see* below), but with two to four broods elsewhere.

Habitat: Flowery places of all kinds, including gardens, hedgerows, damp grassland, and woodland clearings, from sea level to 2,500 m (8,200 ft). Larval foodplants include a wide range of wild crucifers, such as Charlock, Garlic Mustard, Cuckooflower, and Watercress. Adults are fond of lavender and buddleia in gardens, although the species rarely breeds in gardens (*see* below).

Life-cycle: The eggs are greenish yellow and are laid singly on the leaves. They hatch within a week or ten days to produce velvety green caterpillars, very like those of the Small White except that they lack the yellow line along the back. The caterpillar is about 25 mm (1.0 in) long when mature, and it pupates on the foodplant or on nearby vertical surfaces. The chrysalis ranges from pale green to buff, often displaying a mixture of both colours and an assortment of brown spots. Summer pupae produce new adults in two or three weeks, but autumn pupae overwinter and produce adults in the spring.

Range: Throughout Europe, North Africa, and temperate Asia. Also in North America, where it is called the Veined White. Unlike the Large White and Small White, it does not go in for large-scale migration.

Although the adult is common in gardens and often referred to as a cabbage white, the larvae do not feed on cultivated brassicas and the species is in no way a pest. Its main breeding habitats are woodland margins, hedgerows, and riverbanks.

The butterfly is very variable, with several forms and subspecies, some of which may be distinct species. Several races, including those from the Arctic, regularly have reduced black markings on the upperside. Some races lack the yellow in the hindwing, while f. *sulphurea* is a rare Irish form in which the ground colour is bright yellow. *P. n. bryoniae*, flying at high levels in the Alps and other mountains, is sometimes regarded as a separate species – the Mountain Green-veined White (*P. bryoniae*): the female upperside is heavily dusted with yellow or grey; the male upperside is white, but the veins are blacker and more obvious than in other races. A similar race occurs in the far north, often flying over the shores of the Arctic Ocean.

In northern Britain most populations are single-brooded and largely restricted to damp moors and meadows, where the caterpillars feed entirely on Cuckooflower. Elsewhere in Britain the butterfly occupies a wider range of habitats and is normally double-brooded, although the second brood is only a partial one: less than 50 per cent of pupae from spring caterpillars produce adults in the summer, the rest going into a long diapause and not producing adults until the following spring. In good summers there may even be a partial third brood. The single-brooded populations appear to be genetically different from the rest and are certainly less mobile.

The butterfly is sometimes called *Artogeia*.

---

p.56 **Bath White** *Pontia daplidice*

Description: 20–25 mm (0.8–1.0 in). The uppersides are white and the forewing has a black tip containing a number of white spots. A prominent black spot at the end of the forewing cell is usually split by a thin white line. The upperside of the male hindwing is almost unmarked apart from a greyish smudge near the front margin, although the underside pattern shows through quite strongly. The female has more extensive dark markings, including a black spot near the hind edge of the forewing and several black spots around the edge of the hindwing. The underside of the forewing has a mottled-green tip, and the black spot at the end of the cell extends to the front margin. The underside of the hindwing is olive-green with white spots, including an isolated, rounded spot in the cell.

Similar species: Small Bath White is less heavily marked and the underside of the hindwing has a striped margin. Peak White has elongated white spots on the underside of the hindwing. Dappled White and other *Euchloe* species are usually more heavily mottled on the underside of the hindwing. In none of these other species does the black spot on the underside of the forewing reach the front margin.

Flight: February to October, with two to four broods. A fast-flying species, with a rather purposeful flight close to the ground.

Habitat: Flowery places of all kinds, from sea level to 2,000 m (6,550 ft). The adults are particularly fond of clover and Lucerne fields but, being strong migrants, they can be found almost anywhere. Larval foodplants include mignonettes and assorted wild crucifers.

Life-cycle: The bright-orange eggs are laid singly on the leaves and flowers of the foodplants, hatching in about a week to produce bluish-grey caterpillars with yellow stripes and numerous black dots. The caterpillar feeds mainly on the flowers and developing fruits, and it is fully grown in about a month, when it is about 25 mm (1.0 in) long. It pupates on the foodplant or on neighbouring rocks and other objects. The chrysalises range from pale green to pale grey or brown, with yellow lines and red or brown points. During the summer they produce adults within a couple of weeks. Pupae formed in the autumn go through the winter and do not produce butterflies until the following spring.

Range:  Resident in central and southern Europe, where it is often very common; also in North Africa, and much of temperate Asia. The species is strongly migratory and moves northwards through Europe in spring and summer, producing a summer generation as far north as southern Scandinavia, although it very rarely visits Britain. Until the 1970s it was resident in Denmark and southern Sweden but, with the possible exception of a non-migratory population on the island of Gotland, it has now disappeared from Scandinavia other than as a summer visitor. Recent biochemical research suggests that the Bath White may actually be two species – one confined largely to France and Iberia and the other one, known as the Eastern Bath White living further east.

The Bath White got its English name after being depicted on a piece of embroidery created by a young lady from Bath in the 18th century. The first recorded British specimen was captured late in the 17th century by William Vernon, and was originally known as Vernon's Half Mourner.

p.57 **Small Bath White** *Pontia chloridice*

Description: 20–25 mm (0.8–1.0 in). The uppersides are white, with a white-centred, crescent-shaped black spot at the end of the cell in the forewing. The tip and outer margin of the forewing have a fair amount of black spotting, which is heavier in the female, and usually extends on to the hindwing. The female also has a large black spot near the rear edge of the forewing. The underside of the forewing has a greenish tip; the underside of the hindwing has alternating green and white stripes in the outer region and a distinctly oval or elongate white spot in the cell. Second-brood insects are a little larger than first-brood insects.

Similar species: Bath White is larger, with heavier black markings. Peak White has a yellower underside with a band of arrowhead marks in the centre.

Flight: April to July in two broods.

Habitat: Uncultivated and rocky places with plenty of flowers, from sea level to 1,500 m (4,925 ft), but most common in the hills. The larval foodplants are various crucifers, especially species of *Sisymbrium,* and also *Cleome ornithopodioides.*

Life Cycle: The caterpillar, up to 30 mm (1.2 in) long, is white with black warts and white hair, and very like that of the Bath White. It feeds on both leaves and flowers. It pupates on rocks and stones and the black-and-white chrysalis can easily be mistaken for a bird-dropping. Winter is passed in the pupal stage.

Range: The Balkans and across temperate Asia to Siberia. Becker's White (*Pontia beckeri*) from western North America is closely related and may actually be a subspecies of Small Bath White.

p.57 **Peak White** *Pontia callidice*

Description: 20–26 mm (0.8–1.0 in). The uppersides are white with a solid black spot at the end of the forewing cell. The male has few other markings apart from a series of dark-grey triangles on the outer edge of the forewing. The female is more heavily marked, with dark wingtips enclosing oval or triangular white spots and a dark spot near the rear edge of the forewing. The underside of the forewing has a greenish tip with white spots; the underside of the hindwing is largely green with conspicuous cream or yellow arrowhead markings in the centre that will immediately identify the species. The underside pattern shows through on the upperside, which is otherwise more or less unmarked.

Similar species: Bath White lacks the arrowhead markings on the hindwing. Green-veined White has no black spot at the end of the cell. The forewings of the Peak White are more sharply pointed than in related species.

Flight: June to August, usually in a single brood, although good summers may see two broods in sheltered valleys.

Habitat: Montane grassland above 1,500 m (4,925 ft). The larval foodplants are Mignonette and various crucifers, especially treacle-mustards.

Life-cycle: The orange eggs are laid singly on the foodplants, and they hatch within about 14 days to produce bluish-grey caterpillars heavily marked with black spots and yellow blotches. Up to 32 mm (1.25 in) long when mature, the caterpillar pupates on stones and low-growing vegetation. The chrysalis is bluish grey and heavily speckled with black, and winter is passed in the pupal stage.

Range: Pyrenees and Alps; also in the mountains of Asia. The Western White (*Pontia occidentalis*) of North America may be conspecific with the Peak White.

p.58 **Dappled White** *Euchloe ausonia*

Description: 20–25 mm (0.8–1.0 in). The uppersides are white with a jet black spot at the end of the forewing cell. The wingtips are dark grey with a number of white spots. The underside of the forewing resembles the upperside but is green or yellowish at the tip, and the black spot at the end of the cell has a white centre. The underside of the hindwing is mottled green and white, and the pattern shows through on the otherwise unmarked upperside. The sexes are alike although the female is yellower under the hindwing.

Similar species: Bath White has extra black spots on the underside of the forewing in both sexes, and the black spot at the end of the cell reaches the front margin on the underside. Other *Euchloe* species are generally smaller but they are not easy to distinguish (*see* below).

Flight: March to July in two broods.

Habitat: Open, flower-rich places, including cultivated land and coastal grassland, up to 2,000 m (6,550 ft). Larval foodplants include Wild Candytuft, Woad, and many other crucifers.

Life-cycle: The yellowish-green eggs are laid singly, usually on the flowers and developing fruits of the foodplants. The caterpillar feeds mainly on the fruits. It is boldly striped with yellow and greyish blue and densely spotted with black. About 30 mm (1.2 in) long when mature, it pupates on rocks and low-growing shrubs. The chrysalises are sandy brown and they often pass through two winters before giving rise to new adults. Some pupae have been known to survive four winters before producing adult butterflies.

Range: Throughout southern Europe and on through Central Asia. The Creamy Marblewing (*Euchloe ausonides*) of North America may be conspecific with the Dappled White.

Some authors have recently split the Dappled White into two species – the Western Dappled White (*Euchloe crameri*) extending from Iberia to northwest Italy, and the Eastern Dappled White (*E. ausonia*) living further to the east. The various species of *Euchloe* are all very similar, even with regard to their genitalia, and the exact number of species is not known. It is possible that all the dappled whites are races of a single species.

p.58 **Mountain Dappled White**
Euchloe simplonia

Description: 20–25 mm (0.8–1.0 in). The uppersides are white and the forewing has a black tip containing white spots, the front one of which is noticeably rounded. There is a solid crescent-shaped spot at the end of the cell, and it commonly extends forward to reach the dark streak on the front margin. The underside of the hindwing is yellowish green with numerous white spots that are often shiny. The underside of the forewing resembles the upperside except that it has a green or yellowish tip.

Similar species: Dappled White's black forewing spot does not extend forward to the front margin. Bath White has extra black spots on the underside of the forewing.

Flight: April to August in a single brood.

Habitat: Locally common on open, flower-rich fields and hillsides generally above 1,500m (4,925 ft). Larval foodplants are candytufts and other crucifers.

Life-cycle: The yellowish-green eggs are laid singly on the flowers and developing fruits of the foodplants. The caterpillar is bluish green with yellow stripes and numerous black spots, and it feeds mainly on the developing fruits of the foodplant. It is about 28 mm (1.1 in) when mature, and it pupates in a slender brown chrysalis on rocks or low-growing vegetation. Winter is passed in the pupal stage.

Range: Mountains of northern Spain and the Western Alps. The Pearly Marblewing (*Euchloe hyantis*) of North America is closely related and may be conspecific with *E. simplonia*.

Corsican Dappled White *Euchloe insularis*

Description: 18–22 mm (0.7–0.9 in). Smaller than most similar species, this butterfly has chalky-white uppersides with little or no black dusting at the base. The black tip of the forewing encloses a few small white spots. The black spot at the end of the cell is narrow and often triangular. The underside of the forewing has a greenish tip with white spots, and the black spot at the end of the cell is very small. The underside of the hindwing has numerous small white spots on a dark-green background.

Similar species: Portuguese Dappled White is very similar, but the two species do not overlap. Female Orange-tip has more rounded wingtips.

Flight: March to April, with a partial second brood May to June.

Habitat: Rocky slopes from sea level to 1,200 m (3,925 ft), but usually between 800 and 1,000 m (2,625 and 3,275 ft). A rare and very local species. The larval foodplants are various crucifers, including Annual Candytuft.

Life-cycle: Eggs are laid singly on the flowerheads of the foodplant, and the young stages are similar to those of the Dappled White. The caterpillar feeds from April to July and winter is passed in the pupal stage.

Range: Confined to Corsica and Sardinia, where the only other similar species is the Orange-tip. Some entomologists consider the Corsican Dappled White to be merely a race of the Dappled White.

p.59 **Portuguese Dappled White** *Euchloe tagis*

Description: 15–22 mm (0.6–0.9 in). The uppersides are chalky white with a dusting of black scales at the base, and with the usual black tip to the forewing containing small white spots. The black spot at the end of the forewing cell is more or less rectangular. The underside of the forewing has a mottled black and green tip, and the underside of the hindwing is green with relatively small white spots. The hindwings are smoothly rounded at the front – not angular as in other species – and the tips of the forewings are noticeably pointed, especially in the male.

Similar species: Corsican Dappled White has much more white spotting on the underside of the hindwing. Dappled White and Mountain Dappled White are usually larger.

Flight: March to May.

Habitat: Rough grassland from sea level to about 1,000 m (3,275 ft), but usually in upland areas. A very local species. The larval food-plants are candytufts.

Life-cycle: Eggs are laid singly on the flowerheads of the foodplant. The caterpillar is bluish green with black dots and pink and white stripes, and it can be found between March and June. It is about 25 mm (1.0 in) long when mature. Winter is passed in the pupal stage, and the brownish chrysalis has a sharply pointed front end.

Range: Southern and central Iberia, southern France and northwest Italy; also in North Africa.

Butterflies from Morocco and around the southern coast of Iberia (*E. t. tagis*) have very little white spotting on the underside of the hindwing. Those from central Spain and southern France (*E. t. bellezina*) have more white spotting, but their small size – the forewing is usually under 20 mm (0.8 in) long – distinguishes them from Dappled White and Mountain Dappled White.

---

p.59   **Green-striped White** *Euchloe belemia*

Description: 16–24 mm (0.6–1.0 in). The uppersides are chalky white with a small amount of black dusting at the base. The black tips of the forewings contain the usual white spots and the black spot at the end of the cell is rather square with a faint white line through the centre. The white marks on the underside of the hindwing form distinct stripes on the green background, and the tips of the forewings are also clearly striped on the underside.

Similar species: The striped hindwings distinguish this from all other European whites.

Flight: February to June in two overlapping broods; butterflies of the second brood are often larger than those of the first brood and have less distinct stripes.

Habitat: Rough, flowery places from sea level to about 1,000 m (3,275 ft). Larval foodplants are candytufts, rockets, and other crucifers.

Life-cycle: The eggs are laid singly on the foodplants and the resulting caterpillars are bright green with pink and white stripes and numerous black dots. They are about 25 mm (1.0 in) long when mature. Winter is passed in the pupal stage.

Range: Iberia, North Africa, and across southern Asia to Pakistan. Also in the Canary Islands, where the subspecies *E. b. hesperidum* flies at up to 2,500 m (8,200 ft). In Europe, the butterfly is confined to southern Spain and Portugal.

p.61 **Orange-tip** *Anthocharis cardamines*

Description: 18–25 mm (0.7–1.0 in). The male upperside is white with a broad orange patch beyond the cell. The orange is almost as extensive on the underside of the forewing, leaving a dappled green and white tip. The female has no orange, and her wingtips are more rounded with more black at the apex. In both sexes the underside of the hindwing is irregularly mottled with green and white although, as in many of the pierids, the green is actually produced by a mingling of black and yellow scales. The mottling provides excellent camouflage when the insects are at rest.

Similar species: The male is unmistakable. The female resembles the various dappled whites, but has rounder wingtips and no white spots in the black apical patches. Female Eastern Orange-tip has yellow and green mottling on the underside.

Flight: Generally March to July in a single brood, but the occasional adult appears in late August. These could be late emergers or a genuine, if very small, second brood.

Habitat: Flower-rich places, especially woodland edges and clearings, gardens, hedgerows, and damp meadows. From sea level to about 2,000 m (6,550 ft). Larval foodplants include Cuckooflower, Garlic Mustard, and Hedge Mustard. Watercress is sometimes used, and so are garden Honesty and Sweet Rocket. A wide-ranging butterfly with an open population structure, the Orange-tip is common in many areas and can be found more or less anywhere within its range.

Life-cycle: The eggs are white at first but soon become orange; they are laid singly in the flowerheads of the foodplants. The slender caterpillar is pale orange at first but then becomes bluish green or greyish on the back, shading to dark green below, and it is incredibly difficult to spot among the developing fruits. It is cannibalistic when young, but the spacing out of the eggs ensures that it does not often get the chance to attack its siblings. Up to about 30 mm (1.2 in) long when mature, it can be found from May to August. It pupates on the foodplants and the pointed, almost boomerang-shaped chrysalis is either green or brown. Winter is passed in the pupal stage.

chrysalis

Range: Most of Europe south of the Arctic Circle, and across temperate Asia to China and Japan. Absent from much of western Scotland and from some of the Mediterranean islands.

---

p.62   **Moroccan Orange-tip** *Anthocharis belia*

Description: 18–20 mm (0.7–0.8 in). The upperside of the male is butter-yellow with a patch of black scales at the base of each wing and a broad, black-edged orange tip to each forewing. The underside, also yellow, has a smaller orange tip without the black edges and the hindwing carries an irregular greenish-black pattern, confined mainly to the basal half. The female is largely white, with a mottled orange and black tip on the upperside and a yellow tip on the underside. The underside of the hindwing is sometimes paler than that of the male but carries a similar pattern.

Similar species: The **male's** coloration is unique in south-west Europe. Eastern Orange-tip has more extensive mottling on the underside of the hindwing, and the male has a broader orange patch on the underside of the forewing: female lacks orange.

Flight: March to July in a single brood.

Habitat: Rough flowery hillsides and woodland margins from sea level to about 2,000 m (6,550 ft), although it is most common in upland areas. Males often congregate on hilltops and wait for females to arrive. Larval foodplants are Buckler Mustard and other crucifers.

Life-cycle: Eggs are laid singly on the flowerheads of the foodplants, and the caterpillars can be found feeding on the developing fruits between April and July. Up to about 32 mm 1.25 in) long when mature, the caterpillar is white with a broad yellow stripe along the back and heavily speckled with black. Pupation takes place on the foodplants and the winter is passed in the pupal stage.

Range: Mainly Iberia and southern France, with scattered populations in Italy and southern Switzerland. Also in North Africa.

Some recent classifications assign the European butterflies to the species *A. euphenoides*, with *A. belia* being restricted to the North-African race, which has less distinct markings on the underside of the hindwing.

p.63 **Eastern Orange-tip** *Anthocharis damone*

Description: 18–20 mm (0.7–0.8 in). The ground colour of the male is yellow, with a broad orange patch on both surfaces of the forewing. The female is largely white, with a broad black tip on the upperside of the forewing and a yellowish tip on the underside. The underside of the hindwing is yellow in both sexes, heavily marbled with greenish black.

Similar species: Moroccan Orange-tip has less marbling on the underside of the hindwing, and the female has an orange-tipped forewing. Female Orange-tip has more rounded forewings and the ground colour of the underside of the hindwings is white.

Flight: April to June.

Habitat: A very local butterfly of rocky hillsides, from sea level to about 1,500 m (4,925 ft). The larval foodplant is Woad.

Life-cycle: Eggs are laid singly on the flowerheads of the foodplant and the caterpillars can be found feeding on the flowers and young fruits between May and July. They are pale or yellowish green, with a yellow stripe on each side, and about 28mm (1.1 in) long when mature. Pupation takes place on the food-plant and the chrysalis is usually some shade of brown. It is very like that of the Orange-tip. Winter is passed in the pupal stage.

Range: From southern Italy and the Balkans to northern Iran.

---

p.63 **Gruner's Orange-tip** *Anthocharis gruneri*

Description: 15–18 mm (0.6–0.7 in). The ground colour of the male upperside is pale yellow, with a broad orange patch and a blackish tip on the forewing. The underside of the forewing resembles the upperside. The female's ground colour is white, with no orange patch. The upperside of her forewing carries a large black spot which extends forward to meet a dark streak on the front margin, and the dark apical patch reaches almost to the hind margin; the underside of her forewing has a yellowish tip. In both sexes, the underside of the hindwing is green with distinct white spots.

Similar species: Orange-tip is larger and whiter, with less distinct spotting on the underside of the hindwing; female has a much smaller black spot on the forewing. Moroccan Orange-tip and Eastern Orange-tip have yellow undersides to the hindwings.

Flight: March to June in a single brood.

Habitat: Rough, stony ground from sea level to about 1,600 m (5,250 ft). The main larval foodplant is Burnt Candytuft.

Life-cycle: The slender, almost cylindrical eggs are laid singly on the flowerheads of the foodplant, and the caterpillars feed on the developing fruits between April and July. They are very like those of the Orange-tip, with the greyish green back separated from the apple-green underside by a white stripe. When fully grown, they are about 25mm (1.0 in) long. Pupation takes place low down on the food-plant and the chrysalis, somewhat plumper than those of its relatives, is usually brown. Winter is passed in the pupal stage.

Range: From the south-eastern coast of the Adriatic, through Greece and Turkey and on to western Iran.

Sooty Orange-tip *Zegris eupheme*

Description: 22–25 mm (0.9–1.0 in). The uppersides of both sexes are white, with a sooty smudge containing a small orange patch at the tip of each forewing, although the orange is occasionally absent in females. There is a prominent curved black spot – larger in the female than in the male – at the end of the cell. The underside of the forewing is white with a yellowish tip. The underside of the hindwing is yellow with irregular dark markings.

Similar species: The orange patch in the black wingtip distinguishes this from all other species. Female resembles female Eastern Orange-tip and female Moroccan Orange-tip on the underside, but Sooty Orange-tip is larger and has more pointed wingtips.

Flight: April to June in a single brood. A fast-flying species.

Habitat: Rough, flowery places, including abandoned cultivations, from sea level to about 1,500 m (4,925 ft). The larval foodplants are Hoary Mustard, Woad, and various other brassicas.

Life-cycle: The strongly-ribbed eggs are greenish white at first, but become cherry-red after a while. They are laid singly on the food-plant and the caterpillars feed on the flowers and developing fruits. The mature caterpillar is dirty white with heavy black spots forming a dark band on each segment. 35–40 mm (1.4–1.6 in) long when mature, it pupates in a flimsy cocoon low down on the food-plant. The chrysalis is greyish brown and the bulbous abdomen is heavily spotted with black. Winter is passed in the pupal stage.

Range: Eastern Spain and North Africa, and across southern Asia to Iran.

Desert Orange-tip *Colotis evagore*

Description: 15–18 mm (0.6–0.7 in). The uppersides of
both sexes are white with an orange tip to
the forewing and black dots around the
outer margins of both wings. There is a
conspicuous black smudge on the rear edge
of the forewing and a variable amount of
black dusting on the hindwing. The body
varies from grey to black. The undersides
are largely white, with a pink or orange
tinge on the hindwing and an orange
smudge near the tip of the forewing.

Similar species: No other European butterfly has a similar
colour pattern. The other orange-tips all
have mottled hindwings.

Flight: April to October, in several broods.

Habitat: Hot, rocky places, mainly around the coast
but rising to about 500m (1,650 ft). The
larval foodplants are capers.

Life-cycle: The spindle-shaped egg is largely green.
The caterpillar is chestnut brown, with a
white stripe on each side and violet-ringed
spiracles. The whole body is covered with
white spots, each of which sprouts a little
white hair. The mature caterpillar is about
28 mm (1.1 in) long and it pupates on or
near the food-plant. The chrysalis is bright
green with brown streaks and spots. Winter
is passed in the pupal stage.

Range: Southern Spain, much of Africa, and
Arabia, where it usually flies in the desert.

The species is not closely related to the
other orange-tips of Europe.

---

p.60 **Greenish Black-tip** *Elphinstonia charlonia*

Description: 14–18 mm (0.6–0.7 in). The uppersides are
sulphur-yellow in both sexes, with a black tip
to the forewing that may contain a number of
indistinct pale spots. A conspicuous black
spot, larger in the female than in the male,
sits at the end of the cell and extends forward
towards the front edge of the wing. The
underside of the forewing is yellow with a
greyish-green tip, and the underside of the
hindwing is entirely greyish green.

Similar species: No other yellow butterfly has the large black spot on the forewing.

Flight: March to June in two broods.

Habitat: Rocky slopes from sea level to about 500 m (1,650 ft). The larval foodplants are Eruca and wild stocks.

Life-cycle: The eggs are usually laid on the flowerheads of the foodplants and the caterpillars feed on the developing fruits. The caterpillar is bluish green with black dots, and about 25 mm (1.0 in) long when mature. The chrysalis is brownish and has a very prominent head-spike. Winter is spent in the pupal stage.

Range: The butterfly is widely distributed from the Canary Islands, through North Africa, to India, but in Europe it is found only in Spain and in northern Greece and neighbouring regions. Butterflies from eastern Europe (*E. c. penia*), often larger than Spanish ones, have a yellow collar instead of a pink one. They have recently been treated as a separate species – the Eastern Greenish Black-tip.

---

p.66 **Clouded Yellow** *Colias croceus*

Description: 20–30 mm (0.8–1.2 in). The upperside is deep orange-yellow, with sooty-black margins and a large black spot at the end of the cell in the forewing. The black margins are crossed by faint yellow veins in the male, and in the female they contain a variable number of yellow spots. The margins are wider in females than in males. The upperside of the female hindwing has an extensive dusting of black scales. The underside is golden yellow in both sexes, with a greenish tinge on the hindwing and around the outer edge of the forewing. Prominent black spots, which are larger in females than in males, cross the outer part of the forewing.

Similar species: Several other *Colias* species are superficially similar. Danube Clouded Yellow, Greek Clouded Yellow, and Balkan Clouded Yellow are all deeper orange on the upperside, especially in the males. Danube

Clouded Yellow lacks yellow veins in black margins of the male, and underside has only very small black spots. Lesser Clouded Yellow is usually smaller and the undersides are greener, especially in the female. Northern Clouded Yellow is smaller and darker, and does not overlap range of Clouded Yellow.

Flight: April to October, in several broods. A very fast-flying species which, like the other clouded yellows, hardly ever opens its wings when perched.

Habitat: Open, flowery places from sea level to about 2,200 m (7,225 ft). Adults are especially fond of Lucerne and clover fields, but this migratory butterfly can turn up almost anywhere. Larval foodplants include Lucerne, Bird's-foot Trefoil, clovers, and many other leguminous species.

Life-cycle: The eggs are laid singly, usually on the uppersides of the leaves. They are pale yellow at first but become deep pink before they hatch about a week later. The caterpillar is bluish green with a velvety texture and is about 33 mm (1.3 in) long when mature. Each side carries a prominent white stripe with black and orange spots. Larval life for the summer generations lasts for about a month, after which the caterpillar pupates on the foodplant. Caterpillars hatching in the autumn normally go into hibernation, although they may remain active in the warmest areas.

Range:  A permanent resident in the Mediterranean region, where it produces several broods each year. It is a great migrant and moves northwards every spring to reach nearly all parts of Europe except the far north, although the numbers of butterflies reaching the British Isles and other northern regions vary enormously from year to year. One or more broods can be produced in the north during the summer, but the species cannot survive frost or prolonged damp weather and the insects all die in the autumn. It is unlikely that the Clouded Yellow can survive the winter anywhere north of the Alps. The species also occurs in the Canaries, North Africa, and eastwards to Iran.

About 10 per cent of all Clouded Yellow females are creamy white instead of the normal golden yellow and are known as f. *helice*. The genetic factors responsible for controlling this form and maintaining it at about 10 per cent of the female population are so far unknown (*see* p.29). The Pale Clouded Yellow is often confused with f. *helice*, but has far less black, especially on the upperside of the hindwing.

---

p.65 **Greek Clouded Yellow**
Colias aurorina

Description: 25–30 mm (1.0–1.2 in). The upperside is deep orange, with a purple sheen when viewed at certain angles. The sooty-black borders are crossed by narrow yellow veins in the male and contain yellow spots in the female. The male underside is uniformly yellowish green with a few small dark spots towards the margins, but the female underside is greyish green with an orange patch in the middle of the forewing. Very pale females, similar to f. *helice* of the Clouded Yellow, occasionally occur.

Similar species: Danube Clouded Yellow male has no yellow veins in the black margins, and the underside is a rich yellow in both sexes. Balkan Clouded Yellow forewing is largely orange on the underside, with a greenish border and relatively large black spots. Clouded Yellow uppersides are much less orange.

Flight: May to July in a single brood.

Habitat: Dry grassland, usually above 1,000 m (3,275 ft). The larval foodplants are milk-vetches.

Life-cycle: Eggs are laid singly on the foodplants and the resulting larvae go into hibernation when partly grown, finishing their growth and pupating in the spring.

Range: Confined to a few mountain slopes in Greece and not overlapping the ranges of the Balkan and Danube clouded yellows that it most resembles.

p.67 **Balkan Clouded Yellow** *Colias caucasica*

Description: 25–30 mm (1.0–1.2 in). The upperside is deep orange, often with a heavy suffusion of black scales on the hindwing, especially in the female. The black borders are rather broad, with yellow spots in the female. In the male they are crossed by only very faint yellow veins, mainly near the tip. The upperside of the male has a very conspicuous pale-yellow sex-brand close to the body at the front of the hindwing. Other species have sex-brands, but they are much less obvious. The underside of the forewing is largely orange with a yellowish-green border. The underside of the hindwing is yellowish green with much dark scaling.

Similar species: Danube Clouded Yellow underside is brighter yellow, and the male upperside has no yellow veins in the dark borders. Greek Clouded Yellow male has a uniformly yellowish-green underside and strong-yellow veins in the borders on the upperside. Clouded Yellow uppersides are much less orange.

Flight: June to August.

Habitat: Open grassland and light woodland, usually above 1,600 m (5,250 ft). The main larval foodplant is Hairy Broom.

Life-cycle: The early stages of this species are similar to those of Danube Clouded Yellow but little is known of the life history.

Range: A very local butterfly confined to the Balkan mountains from Croatia to Bulgaria and northern Greece. It does not overlap the range of the very similar Greek Clouded Yellow. The range may overlap that of Danube Clouded Yellow in Bulgaria, but the latter is a lowland butterfly and the two species are rarely, if ever, found together.

p.65 **Danube Clouded Yellow** *Colias myrmidone*

Description: 22–25 mm (0.9–1.0 in). The upperside is bright orange, though not quite as dark as that of the Greek and Balkan clouded yellows, and the male has no yellow veins in the black borders. The female has the usual yellow spots in the border. The underside is largely orange with a yellow or greenish border to the outer edge of the forewing.

Similar species: Greek and Balkan clouded yellows have darker uppersides and the males have yellow veins in the black margins. The underside of male Greek Clouded Yellow is more uniformly green. Clouded Yellow and Lesser Clouded Yellow have larger black spots on the underside.

Flight: May to September in two broods.

Habitat: Heaths and dry grasslands up to about 500m (1,650 ft). The larval foodplants are various brooms.

Life-cycle: The eggs, like those of the other clouded yellows, are yellowish green at first but become pink or orange shortly before hatching. The caterpillars are green with a conspicuous white stripe on each side and are about 35 mm (1.4 in) long when fully grown. Caterpillars hatching in August go into hibernation when still very small and complete their growth in April.

Range: From southern Germany, along the Danube Basin to the Black Sea, and on through western Asia.

The Danube Clouded Yellow has a very local distribution and, although still common in some areas, is considered to be at risk throughout its European range. Being a lowland species, it rarely flies with the Balkan Clouded Yellow, although their ranges may overlap in Bulgaria.

Lesser Clouded Yellow *Colias chrysotheme*

Description: 20–25 mm (0.8–1.0 in). The forewings are rather pointed in both sexes. The male upperside is bright orange-yellow, and the spot at the end of the forewing cell is small and often red. The black borders are crossed by strong-yellow veins. The underside is pale yellow. The female has a similar ground colour but is heavily dusted with black on both surfaces, especially on the hindwing. She has the usual yellow spots, and a broad greyish-green border on the front margin of both surfaces of her forewing.

Similar species: Clouded Yellow male has deeper-yellow undersides and less obvious yellow veins in forewing borders. Clouded Yellow and Danube Clouded Yellow females are very similar but lack the greyish-green border on the forewing.

Flight: May to October in two or more broods.

Habitat: Open, grassy places up to about 1,000 m (3,275 ft). The larval foodplants include Hairy Tare and milk vetches.

Life-cycle: The young stages resemble those of the other clouded yellows, with the caterpillars hatching in August, going into hibernation when quite small, and waking to complete their growth in the spring.

Range: From Austria to the northern shores of the Black Sea and on through much of central Asia.

The butterfly is characteristic of steppe vegetation and, although common and widely distributed in Asia, it is rare and local throughout its European range.

---

p.67 **Northern Clouded Yellow** *Colias hecla*

Description: 20–25 mm (0.8–1.0 in). The male upperside is orange with a rosy sheen when seen from certain angles. The dark borders have a liberal sprinkling of yellow scales and are usually crossed by faint yellow veins. The female's ground colour is similar but she is altogether duskier, with a heavy dusting of dark scales that sometimes obscure the yellow spots in the dark borders. The undersides of both sexes are greyish green, with an orange patch in the centre of the forewing.

Similar species: Apart from the occasional Clouded Yellow that strays into northern Norway, this is the only butterfly of this colour living in the far north. The Clouded Yellow has much brighter undersides.

Flight: June to August in a single brood.

Habitat: Rough grassland and tundra, from sea level to about 1,000 m (3,275 ft), but usually in upland areas above the birch scrub. The usual

larval foodplant is Alpine Milk-vetch, but
Bilberry and related shrubs may be eaten.

Life-cycle: The eggs resemble those of the other clouded
yellows and are laid singly or in small groups
either on the foodplants or on neighbouring
vegetation. They hatch in a week or two but
the caterpillars quickly go into hibernation
and do not reappear until May. In the
warmer coastal areas they may complete
their growth and pupate in late summer, but
many hibernate a second time and pupate in
the spring. Winter can thus be spent in
either the larval or pupal stage. The
caterpillar is green with a white stripe and a
row of black dots on each side; it is about
25 mm (1.0 in) long when fully grown.

Range: Throughout the Arctic region, including
Northern Scandinavia and Greenland. In
North America it is known as the
Greenland Sulphur.

p.64 **Mountain Clouded Yellow**
Colias phicomone

Description: 20–25 mm (0.8–1.0 in). The upperside of
the male is pale greenish yellow, heavily
dusted with black or dark grey. The dark
bands on the outer margin are indistinct
and contain pale-yellow spots. There is a
prominent yellow spot in the centre of the
hindwing. The underside of the forewing is
greenish or greyish white with a yellow tip.
The underside of the hindwing has a yellow
border with a distinctly wavy inner margin,
the rest of the wing being heavily dusted
with grey. The female is similarly marked,
but the ground colour of the upperside is
almost white. Both sexes have conspicuous
red fringes on both surfaces.

Similar species: Pale Arctic Clouded Yellow is very similar,
especially the female, but the ranges of the
two species do not overlap. Pale Clouded
Yellow and Berger's Clouded Yellow
females have dense black wingtips.

Flight: June to August, with a second brood in
September in some areas.

Habitat: Grassy mountain slopes, mostly above about
1,800 m (5,900 ft) and often on rather wet

ground. The larval foodplants are vetches and other members of the pea family.

Life-cycle: In most areas there is just one brood. The eggs hatch within about ten days and the caterpillars go into hibernation after the second moult – usually firmly attached to their foodplants with silk. Growth is completed in the spring and the fully grown caterpillar is about 35 mm (1.4 in) long. It is deep green, often with a bluish tinge, and has a narrow white stripe on each side. In some of its more southerly habitats the butterfly is double-brooded: caterpillars feed up quickly in July and August and second-brood adults are on the wing in September.

Range: Widely distributed and often common in the Alps, Pyrenees, and Cantabrian Mountains.

---

p.64 **Pale Arctic Clouded Yellow** *Colias nastes*

Description: 22–25 mm (0.9–1.0 in). The ground colour of the male upperside ranges from lemon-yellow to greenish white, with dusky-grey margins and prominent pink fringes. The female is similar, but with more obvious spotting in the marginal bands. The underside is predominantly white in both sexes, but the hindwing is heavily dusted with yellow and grey scales. Specimens from high altitudes are smaller and paler than those from the valleys.

Similar species: Mountain Clouded Yellow female has a large yellow spot in the centre of the hindwing, but the ranges of the two species do not overlap. Moorland Clouded Yellow is larger and has solid black margins. Small White and other *Pieris* species are 'cleaner' and have no pink fringes.

Flight: May to July, being one of the earliest butterflies to fly in the Arctic spring.

Habitat: Rough moorland and grassland, up to about 1000 m (3,275 ft): often common in marshy clearings in the birch forests. The main larval foodplants at the lower altitudes are bilberries and related shrubs, but higher up the caterpillars feed mainly on Alpine Milk-vetch.

Life-cycle: The eggs, more barrel-like than those of other *Colias* species, are laid singly on the foodplants. The caterpillar is green, with yellow and red stripes on each side. Although some caterpillars hibernate when only partly grown, most of them feed up quickly and pupate in August. Winter is therefore normally passed in the pupal stage, and many pupae actually pass through two winters.

Range: Northern Scandinavia, Greenland, and Arctic North America – where it is called the Labrador Sulphur. The butterfly probably occurs throughout the Arctic region.

p.65 **Moorland Clouded Yellow** *Colias palaeno*

Description: 25–30 mm (1.0–1.2 in). The ground colour of the upperside of the male ranges from almost white to lemon-yellow, with solid black margins and red fringes. There is a small black spot or ring in the centre of the forewing. The female is white with similar markings and a dusting of grey scales on the hindwing. There are no pale spots in the black margins. The undersides are largely greenish yellow, but the female forewing is white with a yellow tip. Both sexes have a clear white spot in the centre of the otherwise rather plain hindwing.

Similar species: The pale colour and solid black margins on the upperside distinguish this from all other clouded yellows. Large White resembles the female, but has black spots on the forewing and less extensive black margins.

Flight: June to July in a single brood; occasionally extending into August – especially in Scandinavia, where it is one of the commonest butterflies.

Habitat: Bogs, moorland, and Arctic heaths, usually in areas sheltered by trees or scrub, from sea level (in the north) to well over 2,000 m (6,550 ft) in the Alps. The larval foodplants are Bilberry and Bog Bilberry.

Life-cycle: Eggs are laid singly on the foodplants, and normally hatch quickly to produce velvety green caterpillars with a yellow stripe on each side. The partly grown caterpillar hibernates and finishes its growth in late spring. When mature it is about 35 mm (1.4 in) long. Both caterpillar and chrysalis are extremely well camouflaged on the foodplants. In the far north some of the eggs do not hatch until the spring, and the resulting caterpillars feed up very quickly.

Range: Central and northern Europe and across the cooler parts of Asia to Japan. Also in North America, where it is called the Palaeno Sulphur.

The Moorland Clouded Yellow has several geographical races or subspecies. Males are very pale in the far north, but those living in the Alps are smaller and quite yellow, without any obvious spot on the forewing. Elsewhere the butterflies are of an intermediate colour. Unlike the other clouded yellows, this species readily opens its wings to bask in the sunshine, especially in the northern parts of its range.

---

p.68 **Pale Clouded Yellow** *Colias hyale*

Description: 20–30 mm (0.8–1.2 in). The upperside of the male is pale yellow with triangular black wingtips and black borders that taper off towards the rear of the hindwing. There is a small amount of dark scaling at the base of the forewing and rather more on the hindwing. The female upperside is almost white, with dark markings like the male. The dark borders contain pale-yellow spots in both sexes. The male underside is bright yellow, with a row of black spots on the forewing. The underside of the female hindwing is bright yellow, but her forewing is largely cream or white.

Similar species: The pale upperside and bright-yellow underside distinguish this species from almost all other clouded yellows. Clouded Yellow f. *helice* resembles female but has broader black borders and more black scaling on the hindwing. Eastern Pale Clouded Yellow female resembles Pale Clouded Yellow male but has broader black borders on upperside and heavier black spots on the underside. Berger's Clouded Yellow cannot be reliably separated on external features (*see* below), although the larvae are very different.

Flight: May to October in one, two, or three broods.

Habitat: Flowery places of all kinds, from sea level to 2,000 m (6,550 ft). Adults are particularly fond of clovers and Lucerne. The larval foodplants include Lucerne, vetches, and other leguminous species.

Life-cycle: Eggs are laid singly on the leaves and stems of the foodplants. They hatch within a week or so to produce bright-green caterpillars with a pale-yellow stripe on each side. The stripes are dotted with red and orange. Summer caterpillars pupate after about a month, when they are some 32 mm (1.25 in) long, but caterpillars from eggs laid in late summer go into hibernation and complete their growth in the spring. The chrysalis is green with a yellow stripe on each side and not at all easy to spot among the foodplants.

Range: Resident in most of central Europe, where it is regularly double-brooded, but it is a strong migrant and many butterflies fly northwards in spring to reach southern Britain and southern Scandinavia, where a summer brood may be produced. Also present in southern France and parts of Spain, but absent from Greece and all other Mediterranean regions. The species also extends eastwards to central Asia.

---

p.68 **Berger's Clouded Yellow**
Colias alfacariensis

Description: 20–27 mm (0.8–1.1 in). The upperside of the male is bright yellow and that of the female is white, with relatively little black scaling at the base of the wings. Both sexes have black wingtips containing pale spots. The black borders are very narrow in the hindwings and virtually absent from the rear half. The undersides are essentially lemon yellow, although the female forewing is largely white.

Similar species: Male Pale Clouded Yellow is usually less
bright on the upperside and has slightly
more pointed forewings. The orange spot
on the hindwing is usually brighter in
Berger's Clouded Yellow; and the black
scaling at the base of the forewing rarely
invades the cell in Berger's Clouded Yellow.
But no single external feature will reliably
separate the two species. Female Eastern
Pale Clouded Yellow has much broader
black borders on the upperside and heavier
black spots on the underside.

Flight: May to October in two or three broods.

Habitat: Rough, flowery places, preferring dry
uncultivated hillsides to the Lucerne fields
and meadows frequented by the Pale
Clouded Yellow. The foodplants are
Horseshoe Vetch and Crown Vetch.

Life-cycle: Eggs are laid singly on the foodplants,
hatching quickly to produce turquoise-green
caterpillars. When mature, the caterpillar is
about 32 mm (1.25 in) long, with four
yellow stripes and four rows of conspicuous
black spots – and thus very different from
the caterpillar of the Pale Clouded Yellow.
Young caterpillars generally feed low down
on the foodplants and move to the upper
leaves as they get older. Those of the final
generation go into hibernation and complete
their growth in the spring; but hibernation
appears to be less intense than in the Pale
Clouded Yellow, and the caterpillars
occasionally wake and feed in the winter. In
some areas the third generation is only a
partial one, with some of the summer
caterpillars feeding up quickly to produce
the autumn adults while others go into
hibernation. The chrysalis is bright green,
and in warm weather the adult emerges in as
little as a week.

Range: Resident in southern and central Europe
and much less of a migrant than the Pale
Clouded Yellow. The species has
occasionally reached southern Denmark,
but in Britain it has not been recorded
north of the Thames.

Berger's Clouded Yellow is named after the
Belgian entomologist L. A. Berger, who

first distinguished it from the Pale Clouded Yellow on the basis of its larvae and genitalia in 1945. Even now, because of their similarity, the precise ranges of the two species are not known.

p.69 **Eastern Pale Clouded Yellow** *Colias erate*

Description: 20–27 mm (0.8–1.1 in). The male upperside is bright yellow (not orange) with broad black borders, especially on the forewing. The female is similar, but with yellow spots in the black borders. In both sexes there is a prominent orange spot in the centre of the hindwing. The undersides of both sexes are bright yellow, with large black spots on the forewing. Red fringes are usually clearly visible on both surfaces and in both sexes.

Similar species: Males of Berger's Clouded Yellow and Pale Clouded Yellow resemble female Eastern Pale Clouded Yellow, but have narrower black borders on the upperside and smaller black spots on the underside. Male Lesser Clouded Yellow has a similar, although more orange, upperside and a greener underside.

Flight: March to October in three or more broods. Numbers are probably augmented in summer by immigration from the east.

Habitat: Mainly lowland grassland, but occurs up to 1,500 m (4,925 ft) in some areas. The main foodplant is Lucerne.

Life-cycle: Little is known of the early stages of this butterfly in Europe.

Range: Eastern Europe, from southern Poland to northern Greece. Also throughout temperate Asia and in the Horn of Africa.

p.69 **Brimstone** *Gonepteryx rhamni*

Description: 25–40 mm (1.0–1.6 in). The upperside of the male is brilliant yellow with just a small red spot on each wing. The underside is paler, with a brown spot on each wing, and when the butterfly is resting with its wings closed it looks remarkably like a leaf. The female is greenish-white on both surfaces and even more leaf-like at rest. In flight she is often mistaken for the Large White. The wingtips of both sexes are distinctively pointed, and the front margin of the forewing is very slightly concave near the middle. The uppersides are never displayed at rest.

Similar species: Cleopatra female is very similar to Brimstone female, but is slightly more yellow and has a narrow orange streak on the underside of the forewing. Powdered Brimstone male has the hindwing paler than the forewing; female is almost identical to female Brimstone but the hindwing is often more strongly toothed.

Flight: June to September and again in the spring after hibernation. A strong-flying and wide-ranging butterfly.

Habitat: Woodland margins, fens, and flowery places of all kinds, including gardens, from sea level to over 2,000 m (6,550 ft). Adults are especially fond of purple flowers and regularly visit garden buddleias. The larval foodplants are various *Rhamnus* species, especially Buckthorn, and Alder Buckthorn.

Life-cycle: Mating takes place only in the spring. The pale-green or yellow, skittle-shaped eggs are laid singly on the undersides of the leaves or on the twigs and buds of the foodplant just as the buds are beginning to open in spring. In southern Europe they may be laid as early as the beginning of April, but further north laying may not take place until June. The caterpillar is bluish green with a narrow pale stripe along each side. It is beautifully camouflaged on the foliage, although young caterpillars are quite easy to find because they attack the upper surfaces of the leaves and chew out conspicuous small holes. The caterpillar matures in about a month, when it is about 33 mm (1.3 in) long, and it usually pupates in low-growing vegetation. The adults start to emerge about two weeks later, usually in July in Britain. They fly until early September and then settle down to hibernate in evergreen trees and shrubs – especially hollies and ivies – where their shape and colour give them excellent protection. They are among the first butterflies to wake in the spring, but they can survive well into June or July and often fly with their offspring. With a total life-span of about a year they are among the longest-lived of all adult butterflies.

Range: Throughout Europe except Scotland and the far north. Also in North Africa and across Asia to Japan. Overlaps with Cleopatra and Powdered Brimstone only in southern Europe.

It is often suggested that the word butterfly was derived from 'butter-coloured fly' a name that might have been applied to the Brimstone at some time, but the writer believes that the word butterfly is more likely to have been derived from the same root as the word beauty. 'Beauty fly' is a name that could have been applied to almost any butterfly and not just a yellow one, and butterfly is a simple corruption.

---

p.69 **Cleopatra** *Gonepteryx cleopatra*

Description: 25–35 mm (1.0–1.4 in). The deep-orange flush covering much of the upperside of the male's forewing is unlike that of any other European butterfly. His underside is pale green with a yellow flush on the forewing. The female upperside is very pale yellow, with slightly darker margins. Her underside is similar, although often with a blue-green tinge, but she lacks the yellow margins and has a faint orange (not yellow) streak running through the front half of the forewing.

Similar species: Brimstone and Powdered Brimstone females resemble Cleopatra female but are slightly greener and lack the orange stripe on the underside of forewing, although Brimstone female may have a faint yellow stripe.

Flight: May to August, and again in the spring after hibernation. Possibly a partial second brood in August and September in southern Spain.

Habitat: Open woodland and scrub, mainly between 500 and 1,500 m (1,650 and 4,925 ft). The larval foodplants are various buckthorns.

Life-cycle: Mating takes place in the autumn, before hibernation, but the pale-yellow eggs are

not laid until the following spring. They are laid singly on the undersides of the foodplant leaves and they hatch in seven to ten days. The bluish-green caterpillar is very like that of the Brimstone, but it has a more conspicuous yellow stripe on each side. It reaches 35 mm (1.4 in) in length and normally pupates in May. The new adults start to fly in June, while many of their overwintered parents are still on the wing. The butterflies disappear into a long hibernation in August.

Range. Resident in Iberia and the Mediterranean region, but individuals of this strong-flying butterfly often turn up much further north.

---

p.69 **Powdered Brimstone** *Gonepteryx farinosa*

Description: 25–35 mm (1.0–1.4 in). The upperside of the male forewing is bright yellow, but paler around the outer margin. The scales are slightly upturned, giving the wing a slightly rough or dull appearance. The hindwing is very much paler. The undersides of both wings are pale yellow. The female is greenish white on both surfaces.

Similar species: Brimstone male has both wings bright yellow. Brimstone female is very similar, but the front edge of the forewing is slightly concave in the middle. Female Cleopatra has an orange streak through the underside of the forewing. The hindwing of the Powdered Brimstone is usually more strongly toothed than in the other species.

Flight: June to July, and again in spring after hibernation.

Habitat: Rough, uncultivated areas from sea level to about 1,500 m (4,925 ft), mainly in dry upland regions. The larval foodplants are various buckthorns and also Christ's-thorn.

Life-cycle: A single-brooded species, laying its eggs in May and June and passing the winter in the adult state. It may also go into a torpor during the summer drought. The caterpillar and chrysalis resemble those of the Brimstone.

Range: From the south-eastern shores of the Adriatic, across Greece and Bulgaria to Iran.

HAIRSTREAKS, COPPERS, AND BLUES (LYCAENIDAE)

This worldwide family contains well over 6,000 species – about one third of all known butterflies. Their wingspans range from about 15 to 75 mm (0.6–3.0 in), although the largest European species span no more than about 40 mm (1.6 in). The hindwings often bear slender 'tails' at the rear. These are never very long in the European species, but in some tropical lycaenids they are as long as or longer than the body and they resemble antennae. There is often a black spot on the underside of the wing-margin as well, creating the impression of a false head and undoubtedly diverting the attention of predators away from the real head and towards the expendable wing-margins. The butterflies enhance the illusion even further by gently moving their hindwings up and down when they land and simulating the movement of the antennae. This movement can be seen in most members of the family and is not restricted to those with prominent 'tails'.

Many male blues and coppers exhibit gleaming metallic colours. Sexual dimorphism is the rule and is particularly marked among the blues, where the females are often brown and quite unlike their shiny blue mates. Gynandromorphs (see p.31) are thus most frequently reported in this group, although they are not necessarily more common here than in any other family. Female coppers are often quite colourful, but they lack the intense brilliance of some of the males. The hairstreaks, which are named for the slender stripes on the underside, show fewer differences between the sexes.

Flight is generally rather jerky, although often quite fast, and, apart from some of the hairstreaks, most species keep quite close to the ground. The antennae are usually clearly ringed with white. All six legs are used for walking, but the front legs differ in the two sexes: those of the male have just

Small Copper

White-letter
Hairstreak

Black Hairstreak

Lycaenid eggs.

Black Hairstreak

Common Blue

*Lycaenid
caterpillars.*

Black Hairstreak

Large Copper

Chrysalises.

one long tarsal segment with a single claw,
while those of the female have five tarsal
segments and two claws.

Lycaenid eggs are mostly slightly
flattened hemispheres resembling
miniature buns or doughnuts, although
some are much flatter and look like tiny
pearl buttons. Most of them are exquisitely
sculptured with hexagonal patterns, and
they often appear quite spiny when seen
under a strong lens. The larvae are rather
flat, and a flange on each side usually
conceals the short legs. When not feeding,
the head is withdrawn into the thorax.
Many of the larvae taper at each end and,
although most of them are quite downy or
hairy, they are often described as slug-like
or woodlouse-shaped.

Hairstreak caterpillars all feed on trees
and shrubs, copper larvae use docks and
sorrels, and most of the blues use
leguminous plants – feeding on flowers and
fruits as well as the leaves. The caterpillars
of many of the blues are regularly associated
with ants, which are attracted by sweet
secretions from various abdominal glands,
and they commonly caress the caterpillars
to initiate the flow. The caterpillars also
emit pheromones that calm the ants'
aggressive tendencies. Many different ant
species are involved in such associations,
but none of the ants is dependent on the
caterpillars and they can all live perfectly
well without them. Most of the caterpillars
can also survive without the attentions of
the ants, although various investigations
have shown that caterpillars living with
ants are less likely to be attacked by
predators and parasites. There are, however,
a few species that cannot survive without
the aid of ants. These include the Large
Blue and its relatives, whose caterpillars
spend a large part of their lives inside the
ants' nests and often feed on the ants' grubs
(*see* pp.347–52).

Lycaenid pupae are dumpy and smoothly
rounded without any points. They often lie
freely on or just under the ground,
although some are bound to leaf-litter or

the lower parts of their foodplant by a few strands of silk. Some are buried and guarded by ants. Many can emit faint squeaking sounds when handled.

About 90 members of the family occur in Europe, but only fifteen, including the artificially maintained Large Copper, are resident in the British Isles and only seven are found in Ireland. Three further species reach Britain on rare occasions as migrants from the Continent.

---

p.72 **Brown Hairstreak** *Thecla betulae*

Description: 16–20 mm (0.6–0.8 in). The ground colour of the upperside is dull brown, with a broad orange crescent on the female forewing and a faint yellowish smudge on the male forewing. The male also has a black spot at the end of the cell. Both sexes have conspicuous orange 'tails' on the hindwing. The underside is quite unmistakable – bright orange with narrow white streaks and a red margin in both sexes. The female is a little brighter than the male, and the colour is also said to vary with the type and quality of the larval food.

Similar species: None, although several other hairstreaks, especially Ilex Hairstreak, have similar uppersides.

Flight: July to October, usually in a single brood although there is evidence of a second brood in some southern areas. The butterflies fly mainly in the treetops, where they feed on honeydew and on sap oozing from wounded trunks and branches, but females can also be seen at lower levels, flitting around with rapid changes of direction as they seek out blackthorn bushes for egg-laying. They normally perch with their wings closed, but sometimes bask with wings open in weak sunshine.

Habitat: Open woodland and forest edges, hedgerows, and scrubby hillsides, from sea level to about 500 m (1,650 ft). The principal larval foodplant is Blackthorn, but other *Prunus* species are eaten and the caterpillars are said to be pests of cultivated plums and cherries in some places. Birch is used in some parts of Europe, especially in the north. The adults occasionally drink from bramble blossom and other flowers.

Life-cycle: The domed eggs are like tiny pearly-white buttons, with an exquisitely sculptured surface. They are laid singly or in pairs on the twigs, usually at the bases of buds, and they do not hatch until the spring. The slug-shaped caterpillar is pale green with yellow stripes and a dark head, and is easily mistaken for a withered leaf. It usually feeds at night and rests underneath the leaves by day. It is up to 23 mm (0.9 in) long when mature and turns purplish grey shortly before pupating – usually amongst the leaf-litter on the ground but occasionally on the foodplant. The chrysalis is smooth and brown.

Range: Most of Europe except the far north, and on through temperate Asia to Korea. Absent from Scotland and most of Iberia.

---

p.72 **Purple Hairstreak** *Quercusia quercus*

Description: 12–15 mm (0.5–0.6 in). The ground colour of the upperside is sooty black, with a deep-purple or violet iridescence visible from certain angles. This sheen covers almost the whole of the male's upperside, but in the female it is confined to the basal region of the forewing. The underside is silvery grey in both sexes, with a dark-edged white streak on each wing and some small orange patches near the slender black 'tails'.

Similar species: Spanish Purple Hairstreak has orange submarginal bands on the underside and virtually no 'tails'.

Flight: June to September, usually keeping high in the trees where they feed on honeydew, but freshly emerged insects can often be seen sunning themselves near the ground and occasionally sipping nectar.

Habitat: Usually mature woodland, but the butterfly can be found almost anywhere with large oaks, from sea level to over 2,000 m (6,550 ft). The larval foodplants are normally oaks, including evergreen species, but ash is sometimes used.

Life-cycle: The eggs are like tiny silvery-grey buttons covered with a network of minute spines, and they are laid singly on the twigs – usually at the base of a bud. They hatch in the spring, and the young caterpillars spend the first instar feeding inside the buds. Later instars feed openly on the leaves at night, but hide by day in flimsy silken nests at the bases of the leaves. The mature caterpillar is greyish brown and slug-shaped, although the segments are clearly visible and it is rather furry. It is up to about 20 mm (0.8 in) long and it pupates in bark-crevices or leaf-litter, surrounded by a few strands of silk. The chrysalis is very smooth and reddish brown with darker spots. It is attractive to ants and can sometimes be found in their nests.

Range: All Europe except the far north, and on through temperate Asia to Korea.

---

p.73 **Spanish Purple Hairstreak**
Laeosopis roboris

Description: 12–15 mm (0.5–0.6 in). The uppersides are sooty black, with a violet iridescence visible from certain angles. This iridescence is bluer, duller and less extensive than that of the Purple Hairstreak. It is confined to the basal wing areas and often missing from the female hindwing. An arc of whitish or pale purple submarginal spots is often present on the upperside of the hindwing, especially in the female. The underside is brownish grey, with an orange submarginal band bordered internally by black and white triangles and externally by a silvery line. This band is usually well developed on both wings in the female, but often much reduced on the male forewing. There are no obvious 'tails'.

Similar species: Purple Hairstreak has no orange bands on the underside, and usually has a white streak on each wing.

Flight: May to July, usually keeping to the tops of ash trees, although both sexes may descend to feed on various flowers, including umbellifers and the nectar-rich domes of Dwarf Elder.

Habitat: Light woodland and other areas with ash trees, from sea level to about 1,500 m (4,925 ft). The larval foodplant is Ash and the caterpillars are sometimes so common that the trees are damaged. Privet is also eaten.

Life-cycle: The eggs are ornately sculptured. They do not hatch until the spring and the very flat caterpillars are pale green with diagonal brown or yellow stripes. They are about 20 mm (0.8 in) long when mature and they pupate amongst the leaf-litter.

Range: Iberia and southern France.

p.73 **Sloe Hairstreak** *Satyrium acaciae*

Description: 15 mm (0.6 in). The uppersides, rarely seen at rest, are dull brown in both sexes, with no markings apart from a small orange spot near the short 'tail' on the hindwing. The undersides are pale brown with a thin, dark-edged white line crossing both wings although it is often broken and indistinct on the forewing. There are dark-edged orange marginal lunules on the hindwing, at least on the rear half, with a faint white line beyond them. The female abdomen has a black tuft at the tip.

Similar species: Ilex Hairstreak has darker undersides and longer 'tails'. False Ilex Hairstreak also has longer 'tails', and its marginal lunules have very little black on them.

Flight: June to July, often gathering in large numbers to feed at the flowers of Bramble, Privet, and Dwarf Elder.

Habitat: Rough ground with blackthorn bushes and scrub, from sea level to about 1,800 m (5,900 ft) but especially common in hilly regions. The larval foodplant is Blackthorn, although oaks are said to be used on occasion.

Life-cycle: The dome-shaped eggs are laid singly on the twigs. They are pale grey at first, and each is partly covered with scales from the tuft on the female's abdomen. They hatch in the spring, by which time they have become greyish brown. The young caterpillar is green and brown and looks

very similar to the buds bursting around it, but it gradually becomes yellowish green with paler stripes. The mature caterpillar is about 20 mm (0.8 in) long and it pupates either in a withered leaf on the foodplant or, more often, amongst the leaf-litter on the ground. The chrysalis is brown and rather furry.

Range: Southern and central Europe, and on into Asia. Absent from the British Isles and neighbouring parts of the Continent.

---

p.74 **Ilex Hairstreak** *Satyrium ilicis*

Description: 15–20 mm (0.6–0.8 in). The uppersides, rarely seen at rest, are dark brown in both sexes, with a small orange spot near the 'tail' on the hindwing. The female, usually a little larger than the male, often has an orange patch on the forewing, but this varies in extent and is often very faint or completely absent. The underside is a little paler, with a dark-edged and rather wavy white line on each wing. This line is often broken into dots and is usually more strongly developed on the hindwing. The hindwing also has a row of reddish marginal lunules, usually bordered with black on both sides and with a faint white line beyond them.

Similar species: False Ilex Hairstreak is a little paler, and red lunules on the hindwing are usually brighter and better developed. Sloe Hairstreak has very short 'tails'.

Flight: June to August, often swarming around dwarf oaks in huge numbers. The butterfly feeds avidly at the flowers of bramble, Dwarf Elder, and Privet, and also at Wild Thyme.

Habitat: Light woodland and oak scrub, from sea level to about 1,500 m (4,925 ft). The larval foodplants are oaks, especially the Downy Oak and the evergreen species.

Life-cycle: The shiny white eggs are hemispherical and decorated with shallow dimples rather like a golf ball. They are laid singly on the twigs, where they pass the winter. On hatching in the spring, the caterpillar feeds

on the buds at first and then turns its attention to the opening leaves. The mature caterpillar is up to 22 mm (0.9 in) long and is bright greenish yellow with a coating of fine red hair. The head and feet are dark brown or black. Shortly before pupating amongst the vegetation or dead leaves at the base of the foodplant, the caterpillar becomes pink. The chrysalis is brownish grey and densely speckled with black.

Range: Southern and central Europe, as far as southern Sweden, and on to southwest Asia. Absent from the British Isles.

---

p.74 **False Ilex Hairstreak** *Satyrium esculi*

Description: 15–20 mm (0.6–0.8 in). The uppersides, rarely seen at rest, are dull brown in both sexes, although in the more southerly parts of the range the female may have a faint orange smudge on the forewing. There is a small orange or red spot near the 'tail' on the hindwing. The undersides are light greyish brown, with a white streak across each wing and a submarginal band of bright red or orange spots on the hindwing. These spots are clearly separated and often have no more than a faint black edging.

Similar species: Ilex Hairstreak is darker underneath, normally with more obvious black edges to the red spots. Sloe Hairstreak has very short 'tails' and the red spots are confined to the rear half of the hindwing.

Flight: June to August, often feeding at bramble blossom.

Habitat: Stony, scrub-covered hillsides, from sea level to about 1,500 m (4,925 ft). The larval foodplants are oaks, especially the low-growing species, and possibly *Prunus* species.

Life-cycle: The eggs are very like those of Ilex Hairstreak and are laid singly on the twigs. They probably do not hatch until the spring, but little is known of the early stages of this butterfly.

Range: Iberia and southern France: also in western Italy, where it is rare.

p.74 **Blue-spot Hairstreak** *Satyrium spini*

Description: 14–18 mm (0.6–0.7 in). The uppersides, hardly ever seen at rest, are dark brown, with an inconspicuous oval sex-brand near the front edge of the forewing in the male. There may be some small orange spots near the 'tail' on the hindwing and there may be a slight orange flush in the middle of the forewing, especially in the female. The underside is greyish brown in both sexes, with a bold white streak across each wing and a prominent square blue spot near the 'tail' on the hindwing. There is also a row of orange or red submarginal spots on the hindwing, but these vary a good deal in development.

Similar species: Several hairstreaks have similar uppersides, but no other species has the large blue spot underneath.

Flight: June to August, feeding avidly at the flowers of Wild Thyme and other low-growing plants.

Habitat: Dry, scrubby fields and hillsides from sea level to about 1,800 m (5,900 ft). The larval foodplants are several buckthorn species and Christ's-thorn.

Life-cycle: The densely sculptured, hemispherical white eggs are laid in ones or twos on the twigs, where they remain until the spring. The caterpillar is yellowish green, with yellow stripes along the back, and about 15 mm (0.6 in) long when mature. Just before pupating, it turns bluish or violet. The chrysalis is usually attached to a leaf or twig of the foodplant and is mid-brown with darker speckles. Both larval and pupal stages are commonly attended by ants.

Range: Southern and central Europe, and on through southern Asia as far as Iran. Absent from the British Isles. The species appears to be declining in most parts of its range.

Throughout Iberia and the Pyrenees, the females often have an orange flush over much of the upperside. This form is called *vandalusica*.

p.74   **White-letter Hairstreak** *Satyrium w-album*

Description: 15–18 mm (0.6–0.7 in). The uppersides, never seen at rest, are dark brown and, apart from the indistinct, grey sex-brand on the male's forewing, the only markings are one or two faint orange spots at the rear corner of each hindwing. The undersides are dull brown with a white streak on each wing, the streak on the hindwing usually forming a distinct W. There are four or five confluent orange lunules, outlined in black, beyond the W. In addition to the prominent white-tipped black 'tail' at the end of vein 2, there is a small projection at the end of vein 3.

Similar species: No other hairstreak has such a dark upperside or the incipient second tail.

Flight: June to August, usually staying high in the trees and feeding on honeydew, although individual butterflies often come down to feed at bramble blossom and other flowers, including scabious and knapweed.

Habitat: Light woodland, woodland margins, and hedgerows with elms and Bramble, from sea level to about 1,500 m (4,925 ft). The larval foodplants are elms, especially Wych Elm, and occasionally limes. Small colonies have sometimes established themselves on limes and elms in city streets.

Life-cycle: The flanged, discus-shaped or button-like eggs are usually laid singly on the twigs. They are green at first, but soon turn dark brown. They hatch in the spring and the caterpillars feed on the flowers for a while before moving to the young leaves. The caterpillar is bright yellowish green and rather hairy, with a darker-green stripe along the back. It blends very well with the leaves and is about 15 mm (0.6 in) long when mature. It becomes purplish brown just before pupating on the underside of a leaf or on a twig. The chrysalis is brown and hairy.

Range: Most of Europe except the far north and much of Iberia, and on through temperate Asia to Japan. Absent from Scotland and Ireland. The species has become rare in many regions in recent decades, mainly because of the destruction of elms by Dutch elm disease, but it is increasing again in some places.

p.75 **Black Hairstreak** *Satyrium pruni*

Description: 15–20mm (0.6–0.8 in). The uppersides of the male are sooty brown, with an inconspicuous, grey sex-brand near the front of the forewing and some small orange patches near the 'tail' on the hindwing. The female, often a little paler than the male, has an orange band nearly all round the hindwing and usually has an orange flush towards the outer edge of the forewing. The uppersides are never seen at rest. The undersides are mid-brown with a strong golden sheen and a prominent black-edged white streak on each wing. The hindwing has a bright-orange submarginal band, edged with eye-catching black spots on the inside. A similar band may be seen on the forewing, but it is usually rather faint, especially in males.

Similar species: White-letter Hairstreak is darker, and the orange band on the underside is narrower and with less obvious black spotting.

Flight: June to July. The butterfly does not fly a great deal and spends much of its time feeding on honeydew in the treetops, but it sometimes drinks from privet flowers.

Habitat: Woodland clearings, scrub, and mature hedgerows, from sea level to about 1,200 m (3,925 ft). The larval foodplant is Blackthorn, although other *Prunus* species are sometimes used.

Life-cycle: The flat, brown, button-shaped eggs are finely sculptured and are laid singly on the twigs. They hatch early in the spring. The caterpillar is chestnut-brown at first, while feeding on the buds of the foodplant, but it eventually becomes bright green with a few purple or rust-coloured spots on the back. The mature caterpillar is about 15mm (0.6 in) long and it pupates on a twig or, less often, on the upperside of a leaf. The chrysalis is black and white and bears a strong resemblance to a bird-dropping, although this does not seem to prevent a high level of predation by birds.

Range: Much of Europe, as far as southern Finland, and across Asia to Japan. Absent from most of the Mediterranean area, Iberia, and the

Atlantic seaboard. In the British Isles it occurs only in a small area of the English Midlands.

---

p.75   **Green Hairstreak** *Callophrys rubi*

Description: 10–15 mm (0.4–0.6 in). The upperside, hardly ever seen at rest, is chocolate-brown, and the only marking is a small, oval, grey sex-brand near the front edge of the male's forewing. The underside is bright green In fresh specimens, with a light-brown patch at the rear of the forewing. There is sometimes a row of small white dots on both wings, but most specimens have just a few white dots on the hindwing and some have no dots at all. Complete rows of dots seem to be most common in northern and upland areas. The green scales fall easily, and older specimens may look quite brown on the underside. The outer edge of the hindwing is slightly scalloped.

Similar species: None in the British Isles. Chapman's Green Hairstreak of southwest Europe usually has a continuous white line rather than a row of dots on the underside, and its eyes are edged with brick-red instead of white.

Flight: March to July, usually in a single brood, although there may be a partial second brood in some southern areas. The butterflies rarely visit flowers and feed mainly on honeydew and sap oozing from tree-trunks. The males are strongly territorial and often take up positions on exposed shrubs and other plants. When warming up, the butterflies keep their wings closed and keel over so that they lie almost flat on the leaves, and then they are very hard to spot. Flight is rapid and jerky and very difficult to follow.

Habitat: Rough grassland, scrub, woodland edges and clearings, moorland, and heathland, from sea level to over 2,100m (6,900 ft). Larval foodplants include rock-rose, Gorse, Broom, Bird's-foot Trefoil, Heather, Bramble, Raspberry, Cranberry, and many other plants.

Life-cycle: The delicately sculptured, pale-green, hemispherical eggs are laid singly in the flower-buds or on the young leaves. They

hatch within about ten days and the resulting caterpillars often feed on smaller larvae of their own kind. The fully-grown caterpillar is slug-shaped and rather furry, and up to 18 mm (0.7 in) long. It is bright green with two rows of diagonal yellow stripes on the back. It pupates in the leaf-litter under the foodplant, where the downy, brown chrysalis may be attached to a dead leaf by a few strands of silk. The chrysalis is attractive to ants, which probably lick secretions from its surface and often cover it with soil. Winter is passed in the pupal stage.

Range: Throughout Europe and on through temperate Asia to northern China. Also in North Africa.

p.75 **Chapman's Green Hairstreak**
Callophrys avis

Description: 13–16 mm (0.5–0.6 in). The upperside is chocolate-brown, often with a reddish tinge, and the only marking is the small oval, greyish sex-brand on the male's forewing. The underside is bright green with a greyish patch at the rear of the forewing, and there is usually a white line on the underside of each wing. This line is continuous apart from tiny breaks at the veins, but may be poorly developed on the forewing. The edge of the hindwing is not obviously scalloped.

Similar species: Green Hairstreak has a row of dots on the underside rather than a continuous line, and the upperside tends to be a little duller. Close examination reveals that the eyes are edged with white in the Green Hairstreak and reddish brown in Chapman's Green Hairstreak.

Flight: April to June. Flight is jerky and very difficult to follow.

Habitat: Maquis and other scrubby areas, rarely far from the coast. The larval foodplant is the Strawberry Tree.

Life-cycle: The eggs, very like those of Green Hairstreak, are laid singly and the caterpillar is usually attended by ants. It is green with yellow lines and about 20 mm (0.8 in) long when mature. It pupates on the ground at the base of the foodplant and the dumpy, brown chrysalis is attended by ants just like that of Green Hairstreak. Winter is passed in the pupal stage.

Range: Iberia and southern France, rarely far from the Mediterranean coast. Also in the mountains of North Africa, where it reaches heights of about 1,500 m (4,925 ft).

p.75 **Provence Hairstreak** *Tomares ballus*

Description: 15 mm (0.6 in). The male upperside is dull greyish brown, with faint orange spots at the rear of the hindwing. The female has a similar ground colour but has large orange patches on all wings. The upperside is hardly ever seen at rest. In both sexes, the underside of the forewing is orange with black spots and the underside of the hindwing is green with a brown or grey border and scattered spots of the same colour.

Similar species: None, although it may be mistaken for Small Copper in flight.

Flight: January to May.

Habitat: Rough, stony areas, generally below about 500 m (1,650 ft). The main larval foodplants are *Astragalus lusitanicus* and various kinds of medicks, but the caterpillars also eat Bladder Vetch and several other low-growing leguminous plants.

Life-cycle: The eggs are laid singly or in small groups on young leaves or flowerheads, and the caterpillars feed mainly on the flowers and developing seedpods in the spring. They are usually attended by ants. Growth is usually completed by May, when the caterpillar is about 13 mm (0.5 in) long, and the insects then pupate in the soil – probably in ants' nests. The chrysalis is smooth and brown with yellowish wingcases. Up to 11 months is spent in the pupal stage. There is no possibility of a second brood because there is no food for the larvae during the hot summer months.

Range: Local in southern Iberia and around the Mediterranean coasts of France. Also in North Africa.

p.76 **Violet Copper** *Lycaena helle*

Description: 14 mm (0.6 in). The male upperside has a bright-purple sheen on all wings. Black spots show through it on the forewing, and a good deal of the underlying orange may show through from certain angles. The hindwing has an orange submarginal band, although this is often much reduced in northern specimens. The female forewing commonly appears purple with a broad orange border, but sometimes has no purple at all. The hindwing is brown with an orange submarginal band, although this may be missing from the front half of the wing. Both wings may have an arc of bluish post-discal spots or lunules. In both sexes, the underside of the forewing is orange with heavy black spots and the hindwing is brown with black spots and a bright-orange submarginal band. Both wings are crossed by an irregular line of white lunules.

Similar species: None.

Flight: May to October in one or two broods, usually keeping close to the ground and often basking on stones or on low-growing vegetation.

Habitat: Damp meadows and moorland, from sea level to about 1,800 m (5,900 ft). The larval foodplants include sorrels, bistorts, and knotgrasses.

Life-cycle: The eggs are white and hemispherical, with large dimples. They are laid singly. The caterpillar is pale green with a darker line along the back and, although somewhat furry, it has a very slug-like appearance. About 15 mm (0.6 in) long when mature, it pupates low down on the stems of the foodplants or in the surrounding leaf-litter. The chrysalis, which overwinters, is yellowish brown with black spots.

Range: Northern Europe, including the Arctic coast, and then in scattered colonies in a fairly narrow band from the Baltic to the Pyrenees. Also across Asia to Siberia and northern China. The species is always local and is declining in most parts of its range as a result of land drainage.

p.77 **Small Copper** *Lycaena phlaeas*

Description:
10–17 mm (0.4–0.7 in). The upperside of the forewing is a gleaming coppery red or orange with a sooty-brown outer margin. The cell contains two conspicuous black spots and there is an irregular row of seven spots beyond these. The spots tend to be rather square, although they are sometimes reduced to tiny dots. The upperside of the hindwing is brown with an orange submarginal band, and there is sometimes a row of shiny blue spots just inside this band. The underside of the forewing resembles the upperside, although the orange is less intense. The underside of the hindwing is pale brown or grey with small black spots and a faint red or orange marginal line. The rear corner of the wing is drawn out into a triangular point, and there is often a second point or 'tail' just in front of it. The male forewings are slightly more pointed than those of the female, but otherwise the sexes are alike.

Similar species:
Female Sooty Copper is similar above, but much greyer underneath.

Flight:
February to November in two, three, or four broods. The butterfly has a fast, darting flight and usually keeps close to the ground. The males are strongly territorial, each one adopting a patch of vegetation in the morning and often defending it all day.

Habitat:
Heaths, wasteland, and grassland of all kinds, including roadsides, from sea level to about 2,500m (8,200 ft). It also visits neighbouring gardens. The usual larval foodplants are sorrels and docks, but knotgrasses are also used in some places.

Life-cycle:
The doughnut-shaped, greenish-white eggs are heavily dimpled and resemble tiny, squashed golf balls. They are laid singly and usually hatch within a week. The caterpillar is green, often marked with longitudinal pink or crimson stripes; and, in common with many other copper caterpillars, the early instars feed by stripping tissue from the lower surfaces of the leaves and creating translucent 'windows'. Caterpillars of the final generation become brownish green and pass

the winter in a sluggish condition low down on the foodplant, waking to feed sporadically on mild days. Growth is completed early in spring when the caterpillars are about 15 mm (0.6 in) long. They pupate on the foodplants or in the surrounding leaf-litter. The chrysalis is light brown with darker spots.

Range: All Europe, northern and eastern Africa, and across temperate Asia to Japan. Also in North America, where it is called the American Copper. Although populations have decreased in many areas in the face of agriculture, the Small Copper remains one of the commonest grassland butterflies in Europe.

---

p.78 **Large Copper** *Lycaena dispar*

Description: 15–22 mm (0.6–0.9 in). The male upperside is a brilliant coppery red or orange, with black borders and a slender black bar at the end of the cell in both wings. The border of the hindwing is clearly toothed on the inner edge. The female forewing is largely orange, although less shiny than that of the male, with large sooty spots and a broad sooty border. The hindwing is essentially orange, but is often so heavily dusted with sooty-brown scales that only the submarginal band and a few veins remain orange. In both sexes the underside of the forewing is orange with large black spots and a broad grey border. The hindwing is grey with black spots and a broad orange submarginal band.

Similar species: No other copper has such a grey underside to the hindwing or such a marked grey border under the forewing.

Flight: May to September in one or two broods, although the Dutch race (*L. d. batavus*) is always single-brooded.

Habitat: Damp grassland and wasteland, including ditches and riverbanks, from sea level to about 1,000 m (3,275 ft). The larval foodplants are docks and bistorts. The Dutch race is confined to very wet, lowland marshes and its caterpillars feed almost entirely on Water Dock.

Life-cycle: The pearly-grey eggs look like tiny dimpled buttons and they are laid singly or in twos or threes on the leaves of the foodplant. The bright-green, slug-like caterpillars feed on the undersides of the leaves; they are extremely hard to find in their early stages because each one lies in a narrow groove which it has excavated in the lower layers of the leaf. Older caterpillars chew large holes in the leaves. Autumn caterpillars go into hibernation amongst the leaf-litter at the base of the foodplant and in this state they can survive total immersion in water for several months. Growth is completed in the spring. Mature caterpillars are rather downy and about 20 mm (0.8 in) long. They pupate low down on the stems. The chrysalis is pinkish brown with darker spots.

Range: Scattered over much of central and southeastern Europe and across Asia to northern China. There is also a small population in southern Finland. The species is very local and is threatened over much of its range by land-drainage.

The British race of the Large Copper (*L. d. dispar*) was once widely distributed in the English fenland, but it died out in 1851 – mainly as a result of the drainage of the fens, although continued collecting of the dwindling populations may have hastened the end. The very similar Dutch race (*L. d. batavus*) is bright, silvery or bluish grey on the underside of the hindwings. It was introduced to Woodwalton Fen, near Huntingdon, in 1927 and has been artificially maintained there ever since; otherwise it is confined to the Netherlands. The more widely distributed *L. d. rutilus* is a little greyer on the underside, and also a little smaller.

p.79 **Scarce Copper** *Lycaena virgaureae*

Description: 12–20 mm (0.5–0.8 in). The male upperside is a gleaming coppery red or orange with sooty-brown margins. An arc of dark spots runs close to the border of the hindwing and is often joined to it, giving the border a toothed or notched appearance. Spanish specimens generally have a few black spots near the front of the forewing. The female upperside is orange, but much less shiny than that of the male, and carries several large sooty spots on both wings. The hindwing may be heavily dusted with brown scales, leaving just an orange border. The underside of the forewing is orange in both sexes, with conspicuous black spots and often with a yellowish outer margin. The underside of the hindwing is orange, often with a greenish or yellowish tinge, and carries an interrupted arc of white spots in addition to the scattered black ones. There is also a faint, wavy, red submarginal band.

Similar species: Grecian Copper lacks white under the hindwing.

Flight: June to September, visiting a wide range of flowers but especially attracted to composites. The butterfly is particularly fond of Golden Rod, from which it gets its scientific name.

Habitat: Rough, flowery grassland, especially near water, from sea level to over 2,000m (6,550 ft). The larval foodplants are docks and sorrels.

Life-cycle: The greyish-green or white eggs are hemispherical and deeply sculptured into hexagonal dimples. They are laid singly or in pairs. Some of the eggs hatch in late summer and the resulting caterpillars go into hibernation, but most eggs do not hatch until the spring. The caterpillar is green, slug-shaped and rather furry; and, like most other copper caterpillars, it spends the early part of its life stripping tissue from the lower surfaces of the leaves. The upper surface is left intact in the form of translucent 'windows', which are a reliable indication of the caterpillar's presence. The mature caterpillar is about 20 mm (0.8 in) long and it pupates on the foodplant or in the leaf-litter. The chrysalis is pale bluish green and heavily spattered with black, especially on the wingcases.

Range: Most of Europe except the far north, and on through Asia to Mongolia. Absent from the British Isles and neighbouring parts of the Continent.

p.79 **Grecian Copper** *Lycaena ottomana*

Description: 15 mm (0.6 in). The male upperside is gleaming coppery red with wide and slightly crenulate black borders. There are three very small black dots near the tip of the forewing, and the hindwing bears a short 'tail' at the rear corner. The female upperside is golden orange and is sometimes heavily dusted with brown on the hindwing; black spots form regular bands across both of the wings. The 'tail' on the female hindwing is longer than that of the male. The underside of the forewing is orange with black spots in both sexes. The underside of the hindwing is paler, and can often be quite yellow in the female. It has small black spots and a wide grey border containing red submarginal lunules.

Similar species: Scarce Copper has white on the underside of the hindwing and no 'tails'.

Flight: March to August in two broods: strongly attracted to daisies and other composites.

Habitat: Rough, stony grassland, including roadsides and wasteland, from sea level to about 2,000 m (6,550 ft). The larval foodplant is Sheep's Sorrel, but other *Rumex* species may be eaten as well.

Life-cycle: The caterpillar is yellowish green with shiny hairs. Caterpillars of the second generation go into hibernation early to avoid the summer drought. They wake early in the spring, often in January, and feed up quickly to produce the first brood of butterflies in March. Pupation takes place low on the foodplant or amongst the leaf litter and the chrysalis is greyish yellow with black freckles.

Range: Southern Balkans and southwest Asia.

The genus of the previous two species used to be *Heodes*.

p.80 Sooty Copper *Lycaena tityrus*

Description: 15 mm (0.6 in). The male upperside is sooty brown, with white fringes and variably developed orange submarginal lunules. Scattered black spots usually show through the brown, especially on the forewing, although they are more obvious from some angles than from others. The hindwing is sharply angled at the rear and, in some southern areas, second-brood insects have conspicuous tails. The female's forewing is orange with black or sooty-brown spots, which may be linked to form a cross-line in the outer part of the wing. Her hindwing, more rounded than that of the male, is brown with a band of orange submarginal lunules containing black spots, which are usually detached from the wing-margin. The undersides of both sexes are yellowish grey with black spots although the forewing may be flushed with orange, especially in the female. Both wings normally have a conspicuous orange submarginal band.

Similar species: Brown Argus and some female blues superficially resemble the male, but lack the black spots. Small Copper is much browner under the hindwing. Female Lesser Fiery Copper is browner under the hindwing.

Flight: April to October in two overlapping broods, with a possible third brood in the south. The males are strongly territorial and may defend a sunny spot on the ground for hours on end.

Habitat: Flower-rich grassland, scrub, and wasteland from sea level to about 2,500 m (8,200 ft). The larval foodplants are docks and sorrels.

Life-cycle: The hemispherical eggs are pearly or greenish white and deeply sculptured with a honeycomb pattern. They are laid singly or in twos or threes on the leaves. The dull-green caterpillars are slug-like in appearance and are usually closely attended by ants. Those of the final brood hibernate in the leaf-litter and complete their growth early in the spring. The mature caterpillar is about 20 mm (0.8 in) long, and it pupates in the leaf-litter. The chrysalis varies enormously in colour, from pale yellow to brown or pinkish grey, but always has black spots.

Range: Southern and central Europe and on through temperate Asia to Mongolia. Absent from the British Isles and most of Iberia.

At high altitudes in the Alps, both sexes may be sooty brown on the upperside with conspicuous white fringes and little or no trace of orange on either surface.

The species used to be called *Heodes tityrus*.

---

p.81 **Purple-shot Copper** *Lycaena alciphron*

Description: 15–20 mm (0.6–0.8 in). There are two main races or subspecies of this butterfly in Europe: *L. a. alciphron* and *L. a. gordius*. The *alciphron* male has a coppery upperside but this is heavily suffused with purple or violet, especially on the forewing. The front part of the hindwing is often clear orange. The *alciphron* female is dark brown with an orange outer border on the hindwing. Dark spots can be seen on the forewing in both sexes; those of the post-discal area form a very irregular row. The *gordius* male has a reduced purple sheen on its gleaming coppery wings and the dark spots show up clearly. The *gordius* female is also copper-coloured, with sooty-brown margins and heavy spotting. The two races are alike on the underside, the forewing being orange with a greater or lesser amount of grey and the hindwing grey or yellowish grey with an orange submarginal band. Both wings bear black spots, those near the outer edge of the forewing often being distinctly triangular.

Similar species: Female Purple-edged Copper has post-discal spots of the forewing in a regular row.

Flight: May to September, commonly drinking from the flowers of Wild Thyme, Bramble, and Privet.

Habitat: Rough, flower-rich grassland and scrub, especially on hot, dry hillsides. From sea level to about 2,000 m (6,550 ft). The larval foodplants are sorrels and docks.

Life-cycle: The pearly-white hemispherical eggs have a honeycomb pattern and are usually laid singly on the foodplant. The downy, slug-shaped, green caterpillar hibernates when partly grown and completes its growth in the spring. It is commonly attended by ants. The mature caterpillar is about 20 mm (0.8 in) long and it pupates among the dead leaves and stones on the ground. The chrysalis, sometimes surrounded by a few strands of silk, is greenish grey with black spots.

Range: Southern and central Europe, North Africa, and across temperate Asia to Mongolia. Absent from the British Isles and neighbouring parts of the Continent. *L. a. alciphron* is widely distributed in central and eastern Europe, while *L. a. gordius* occupies the southwest, from Iberia and central France to the Alps and peninsular Italy.

This species used to be called *Heodes alciphron*.

p.82 **Lesser Fiery Copper** *Lycaena thersamon*

Description: 15 mm (0.6 in). The upperside of the male forewing is a shiny golden orange with faint grey spots and a narrow black outer border. The hindwing is largely reddish brown, with a golden or coppery submarginal band and a border of black spots beyond it. The female is similarly coloured but has browner hindwings and black spots on both wings. In both sexes, the underside of the forewing is orange with heavy black spots and a narrow grey border, and the underside of the hindwing is greyish brown with black spots and a conspicuous orange or red submarginal band. The spots on the undersides are more clearly ringed with white than in most other coppers. Second-brood insects may have a short 'tail' at the rear of the hindwing. This is just a tiny, easily over-looked point in the male, but quite distinct in the female.

Similar species: Female Sooty Copper is much greyer under the hindwing.

Flight: April to October in two or three broods: a regular visitor to the flowers of Wild Thyme and Dwarf Elder.

Habitat: Rough, flowery grassland and wasteland, from sea level to about 1,500 m (4,925 ft). The larval foodplant is knotgrass, although sorrels are often quoted.

Life-cycle: The eggs are laid singly on the foodplants and the larvae feed on leaves and flowers. They are often tended by ants. Pupation takes place on the leaves of the foodplant.

Range: Italy, eastern Europe, and the Balkans, and then on through southern Asia to Iran.

The species used to be called *Thersamonia thersamon*.

---

p.82 **Fiery Copper** *Lycaena thetis*

Description: 15 mm (0.6 in). The male upperside is a gleaming flame-red, with black outer borders that are noticeably expanded at the tip of the forewing. There are small black spots around the edges of the hindwing. The female is less brightly coloured, with two bands of small dark spots in the outer part of each wing. There is a heavy dusting of brown on the hindwing, which is sometimes virtually brown with an orange sub-marginal band. In both sexes the underside of the forewing is pale orange or yellow with grey borders and heavy black spots, including a particularly large one at the rear corner. The underside of the hindwing is yellowish grey with faint spots and a faint orange submarginal band. Both sexes usually sport a slender 'tail' on each hindwing.

Similar species: Grecian Copper and Scarce Copper have much brighter undersides.

Flight: July to August, regularly drinking from the flowers of Wild Thyme and thistles.

Habitat: Mountain slopes, usually above 1,500 m (4,925 ft). The larval foodplant is Prickly

Thrift, making the species the only European copper not feeding on members of the dock family.

Life-cycle: The larvae are very difficult to spot among the tussocks of the foodplant. They hibernate when very small, but little else appears to be known of the life-cycle of this species.

Range: Southern Balkans and on through southern Asia to Iran.

The species used to be called *Thersamonia thetis*.

p.83 **Purple-edged Copper** *Lycaena hippothoe*

Description: 12–20 mm (0.5–0.8 in). There are several races or subspecies in Europe. In *L. h. hippothoe*, the male upperside is a gleaming flame-red with dark brown or black borders, and a distinct purple sheen on the front edge of the forewing and on the rear half of the hindwing. *L. h. eurydame* lacks the purple sheen and has a broad brown inner border to the hindwing, but otherwise the two races are very similar. The female *L. h. hippothoe* has an orange forewing with a wide brown border and a smoothly curved row of brown post-discal spots. The hindwing is deep brown with an orange submarginal band. The female *L. h. eurydame* is almost entirely brown above, but may have a faint orange flush on the forewing and a few faint orange spots at the rear of the hindwing. In all forms, the underside of the hindwing is grey with the usual small black spots, and there may be a faint or incomplete orange submarginal band on the hindwing. The underside of the female forewing is largely orange in *L. h. hippothoe*, but that of *eurydame* is grey with no more than a faint orange flush.

Similar species: Purple-shot Copper female has larger spots and a stronger submarginal band on the underside.

Flight: May to September.

Habitat: Damp grassland from sea level to about 2,500 m (8,200 ft) in the Alps. The larval foodplants are Common Sorrel and Bistort.

Life-cycle: The pearly-white or greenish eggs are
hemispherical with deep hexagonal
depressions; they are laid singly. The
caterpillar is bright green and rather furry.
It goes into hibernation after the first
moult, and growth is completed in the
spring. The mature caterpillar is about
20 mm (0.8 in) long. It pupates low down
on the foodplant or in the leaf-litter, and
the chrysalis is cream with heavy black
spots.

Range: Most of Europe, except the British Isles and
southern Iberia, and on through Asia to
northern China. *L. h. hippothoe* is
distributed over much of north and central
Europe and northern Spain. *L. h. eurydame*
occurs in the Alps and most other upland
areas of southern Europe.

In the far north the butterfly is represented
by *L. h. stiberi*, which is paler and much
more golden and also much smaller than
the typical race. The underside of the male
forewing is largely orange. *L. h. candens* is a
very large race from parts of the Balkans,
sometimes treated as a separate species –
the Balkan Copper.
    The species used to be known as
Palaeochrysophanus hippothoe.

p.84 **Long-tailed Blue** *Lampides boeticus*

Description: 15–20 mm (0.6–0.8 in). This butterfly
gets its name because of its slender 'tail'
on the rear of the hindwing. This tail is
longer than that of any other European
blue butterfly. The male upperside is
violet-blue with narrow black borders,
while the female upperside is largely
sooty brown, with a variable amount of
blue or violet in the basal and central areas
of the forewing. Both sexes have two
small black spots near the 'tail' and the
female usually has pale lunules around the
edge of the hindwing. The underside is
greyish brown with thin, wavy, white lines
in both sexes, and there is a broad white
post-discal stripe on the hindwing. There

are also two colourful eye-spots near the 'tail'.

Similar species: Lang's Short-tailed Blue is smaller and lacks the broad white band underneath.

Flight: April to October in two or three broods, flying with a fast and rather jerky motion and rarely opening its wings for long at rest.

Habitat: This strongly migratory butterfly can be found in any flowery habitat, including gardens, but is most common in rough, uncultivated areas, from sea level to about 2,000 m (6,550 ft). The caterpillars feed mainly on legumes, including Bladder-senna, Gorse, Broad-leaved Everlasting Pea, lupins, and cultivated peas and broad beans. The caterpillars feed inside the seedpods. They are also said to attack Caper Spurge.

Life-cycle: The delicately sculptured, white eggs are laid singly on the flowers of the foodplant. The caterpillar eats various parts of the flower at first but gradually makes its way into the young seed pods, where it feeds on the developing seeds and on the pod-lining. Dark green at first, the caterpillar becomes pinkish brown as it matures, and begins to leave the seedpod. The fully grown caterpillar is about 15 mm (0.6 in) long and it pupates under stones or dead leaves. The chrysalis, which is attached by a few flimsy strands of silk, is pink or cream with brown blotches. Winter is passed in the pupal stage.

Range: The Long-tailed Blue is found throughout the warmer parts of the Old World. It is resident in southern Europe and North Africa and migrates northwards to central Europe in the spring, but it is only a sporadic visitor to Britain and rarely seen north of the Thames. The butterfly has not been recorded in Ireland.

The Long-tailed Blue is very common in tropical and subtropical regions, where it is continuously brooded and often a serious pest of leguminous crops.

p.85 **Lang's Short-tailed Blue**
Leptotes pirithous

Description:	12 mm (0.5 in). The male upperside is violet-blue with narrow black borders and two faint black spots near the 'tail' on the hindwing. The female upperside is dull brown, with a bluish flush near the centre of the forewing and two strong black spots near the 'tail'. The underside is light brown with wavy white lines in both sexes, and there are two eye-spots near the 'tail' on the hindwing.
Similar species:	Long-tailed Blue is larger and has a broad white post-discal stripe under the hindwing.
Flight:	March to December, with up to four broods, but it can be seen on the wing throughout the year in the far south. It rarely opens its wings at rest.
Habitat:	This is a migratory species and can be found in almost any habitat, but it is most common on rough, flowery grassland and wasteland, especially near the sea. It is generally a lowland species, but has been seen at 3,000 m (9,850 ft) on migration. The main larval foodplants are various leguminous species, such as Broom, Gorse, and Lucerne, but Heather and many other plants are also eaten.
Life-cycle:	The very ornate eggs are laid singly on the foodplant and the caterpillars feed mainly on the flowers. They are pale green or white at first but usually turn dark green or chestnut-brown with black lines on the back. On some flowers they may stay white throughout their lives. They are said to be tended by ants. Final-brood caterpillars go into a short hibernation if the weather is unusually cold and complete their growth early in the spring. The mature caterpillar is about 12 mm (0.5 in) long and it pupates low down on the foodplant or in the leaf-litter in a flimsy cocoon of leaf fragments held together with strands of silk. The chrysalis is shiny brown.
Range:	Probably resident all around the Mediterranean, and in much of southwest Asia. Although the species is a strong

migrant and moves northwards in the spring, it is rarely seen north of the Alps, and only one undoubted specimen has been caught in Britain – in 1938.

p.84 Geranium Bronze *Cacyreus marshalli*

Description: 20 mm (0.8 in). The uppersides are dark chocolate-brown in both sexes, and the outer margins are conspicuously chequered with white. There are a few faint, blue-ringed eye-spots at the rear of the hindwing, which also carries a prominent 'tail'. The undersides are brownish grey, with white streaks and rings, and chequered fringes. A dark band crosses each wing, although it may be broken on the hindwing. There is a small blue-ringed eye-spot at the base of the 'tail'.

Similar species: No similarly marked species has chequered fringes on the underside.

Flight: May to October, flying weakly and never far above the ground.

Habitat: Mainly in gardens in Europe. The larval foodplants are mainly cultivated pelargoniums (geraniums), but the caterpillars will eat wild *Geranium* species.

Life-cycle: The eggs are laid in the flowers. The caterpillars, which are pale green with red markings and white hairs, feed mainly on the developing seeds. The chrysalis is also green with reddish markings.

Range: This is a South African butterfly that has recently become established in southern Europe, having undoubtedly been brought in with pelargoniums for the horticultural trade. First discovered on Mallorca in 1989, it has now spread to the other Balearic Islands and to mainland Spain, and it has recently been found in Italy and Britain.

The Geranium Bronze has become a serious pest of pelargoniums in several places. Although it is still found mainly in areas where pelargoniums are cultivated, there seems no reason why the butterfly should not establish itself in the wild in the warmer parts of Europe.

p.86 Common Tiger Blue *Tarucus theophrastus*

Description: 10–12 mm (0.4–0.5 in). The male upperside is violet-blue with narrow black borders and a large black mark at the end of the forewing cell. The female is dusky brown with a few indistinct white patches and a light dusting of blue scales at the base. Both sexes have a slender 'tail' on the hindwing. The undersides are white with black streaks and spots in both sexes. There are two complete rows of black spots in the outer part of each wing, and the outer row on the hindwing contains tiny silvery-blue dots.

Similar species: Little Tiger Blue has a continuous post-discal line instead of spots on the underside, and the male has more black spots on the upperside.

Flight: April to September in three or more broods, keeping close to the ground and rarely flying more than a few metres at a time. It rarely opens its wings at rest.

Habitat: Dry, stony places with Jujube and Christ's-thorn scrub. The butterfly is found mainly in low-lying coastal areas in Europe. The larval foodplants are Jujube and Christ's-thorn.

Life-cycle: The eggs are laid singly on the foodplant and the caterpillars feed by chewing narrow channels in the lower leaf-surfaces. Translucent 'windows' in the upper surface show where they have been at work. Winter is passed in the pupal stage.

Range: Probably confined to southern Spain in Europe, although the species may occur in southern Italy. Widely distributed in Africa and western Asia.

p.87 Little Tiger Blue *Tarucus balkanicus*

Description: 10 mm (0.4 in). The male upperside is purplish blue with dark borders (somewhat wider than those of the Common Tiger Blue) and several black spots on the forewing. The female is dull brown, with the underside pattern showing through, and sometimes with a dusting of blue scales

at the base. She may also have some black spots on the outer margin of the hindwing. Both sexes have a slender 'tail' on the hindwing. The undersides are white with black streaks and spots in both sexes. There is a complete submarginal row of black spots on each wing, but the post-discal spots are united to form a continuous line. The submarginal spots of the hindwing enclose tiny silvery-blue dots.

Similar species: Common Tiger Blue has a row of post-discal spots on the underside instead of a continuous line, and the male has only one black mark on the upperside of the forewing. The ranges of the two species do not overlap.

Flight: April to September in two or three broods, usually keeping close to the ground and making only the shortest of darting flights. Much of its time is spent on the ground with its wings firmly closed, often on very warm surfaces.

Habitat: Dry, stony places with Christ's-thorn bushes – the larval foodplant. The butterfly is most common near the coast, but rises to altitudes of about 600 m (1,975 ft).

Life-cycle: The eggs are laid on the stems of the foodplant, and the caterpillars feed by chewing narrow galleries in the lower surfaces of the leaves. Winter is passed in the pupal stage.

Range: Scattered through the Balkans and North Africa and on across Asia to Iran, although absent from southern Greece.

---

p.87 **African Grass Blue** *Zizeeria knysna*

Description: 10–12 mm (0.4–0.5 in). The male upperside is a deep violet-blue with wide, sooty-black borders. The female is sooty brown, generally with a violet flush towards the rear of each wing. The undersides are greyish brown with small black dots, including faint marginal markings, in both sexes.

Similar species: Lorquin's Blue is similar above but pale blue on the underside.

Flight: April to September in two broods.

Habitat: Damp grassland, usually near the coast.
The larval foodplants include Lucerne,
various medicks, and possibly mallows and
Oxalis species.

Life-cycle: Little is known of the early stages of this
butterfly.

Range: Scattered all round Iberia, mainly in eastern
coastal areas, and also in Sicily and all
round the coast of North Africa.

p.88 **Short-tailed Blue** *Everes argiades*

Description: 10–15 mm (0.4–0.6 in). This butterfly is
named for its very fine, short 'tail' that is
easily overlooked. The upperside of the
male is purplish blue with narrow dark
borders, and often a number of
submarginal black spots on the hindwing.
The female is sooty brown with a light
dusting of purple scales near the base,
although this is often absent in the second
brood, and one or more small orange spots
near the rear of the hindwing. Both sexes
have conspicuous white fringes. The
undersides of both sexes are pale greyish
blue, often with a silvery sheen, and
decorated with small black spots. There are
two prominent black spots near the 'tail',
often ringed with orange although this
may be very faint.

Similar species: Eastern Short-tailed Blue and Provençal
Short-tailed Blue have no bright-orange
spots underneath. Female Short-tailed Blue
is often confused with Small Blue in flight,
but the latter has neither 'tails' nor orange
spots and is generally browner underneath.

Flight: April to September in two or three broods,
fluttering delicately over the vegetation and
rarely moving very far. It spends much of
its time perched on grass-stems with its
wings partly raised.

Habitat: Grassy fields and hillsides, roadsides, and
wasteland, especially in damp areas, from
sea level to about 1,000 m (3,275 ft). The
larval foodplants are clovers, trefoils, and

other low-growing legumes, although Gorse is also eaten.

Life-cycle: The pearly-white, finely sculptured, hemispherical eggs are laid singly in the flowerheads of the foodplants, and the caterpillars feed mainly on the petals. The slug-like caterpillar is pale green with a dark line along the back. It is about 10 mm (0.4 in) long when mature, and pupates on the stems or leaves of the foodplant. The chrysalis is green or pale brown with black spots, and rather hairy. Mature caterpillars of the final brood take on a brownish tinge in the autumn and hibernate in the leaf-litter. They pupate in the spring without further feeding.

Range: Resident in southern and central Europe, and across temperate Asia to Japan, but absent from most of Iberia. The species migrates northwards in spring and reaches southern Finland, but it is a very rare visitor to southern Britain. The butterfly was once known as the Bloxworth Blue, from the Dorset locality where the first British specimens were taken.

p.88 **Eastern Short-tailed Blue** *Everes decoloratus*

Description: 12 mm (0.5 in). Both sexes have a very short 'tail' on the hindwing, but it is not easy to see. The male upperside is blue with black borders and white fringes, and a small black line at the end of the forewing cell. The female upperside is sooty brown with white fringes, and no more than the slightest trace of blue scales at the base. The undersides are silvery blue or grey in both sexes, with scattered black spots but no orange on the underside.

Similar species: Short-tailed Blue has orange spots under the hindwing. Male Provençal Short-tailed Blue has no dark line on the forewing, but the females are difficult to distinguish. Other superficially similar blues have no 'tails'.

Flight: April to September in two or three broods.

Habitat: Flowery fields and hillsides, from sea level to about 900 m (2,950 ft). The larval foodplants are Black Medick and related legumes, including Lucerne.

Life-cycle: The larvae feed on the flowers of the foodplant and hibernate when fully grown, but little seems to be known of the early stages of this butterfly.

Range: Confined to southeast Europe, from Austria to northern Greece.

p.89 **Provençal Short-tailed Blue** *Everes alcetas*

Description: 12–16 mm (0.5–0.6 in). Both sexes of this butterfly have a short 'tail' on the hindwing. The upperside of the male is bright violet-blue with narrow black borders. The female is sooty black and unmarked. The undersides of both sexes are pale grey or silver with small black spots, and Balkan specimens occasionally show traces of orange near the 'tail'.

Similar species: Short-tailed Blue has orange spots under the hindwing. Male Eastern Short-tailed Blue has wider borders and a black mark on the upperside of the forewing, but the females are very difficult to separate. Other superficially similar blues have no 'tails'.

Flight: April to September in one, two, or three broods. Flight is rather weak and the butterflies spend much of their time basking on the vegetation with their wings partly raised.

Habitat: Open, flower-rich grassland, including roadsides, from sea level to about 1,500m (4,925 ft): usually near water in the south. The larval foodplants are low-growing legumes, especially Goat's-rue, Crown Vetch, and Lucerne.

Life-cycle: The densely sculptured, pearly-white eggs are laid singly or in twos and threes, and they hatch in about a week. The caterpillar is bright green with darker longitudinal stripes, and it feeds mainly on the flowers of the foodplants. It is rather downy, and is about 10 mm (0.4 in) long when mature. Final-brood caterpillars go into hibernation when fully grown, and they pupate in the spring without further feeding. Pupation takes place low down on the foodplant or in the surrounding leaf-litter. The chrysalis is white or cream with black spots and long white hairs.

Range: Southern Europe, from the Pyrenees to Bulgaria and Greece, and also extending half-way up the west coast of France.

---

p.90 **Little, or Small, Blue** *Cupido minimus*

Description: 8–12 mm (0.3–0.5 in). This is Britain's smallest butterfly. The uppersides are sooty brown with white fringes in both sexes, and unmarked except for a dusting of silvery-blue scales, mainly near the base, in the male. The undersides of both sexes are pale greyish brown, with a blue flush near the base and a number of small, white-ringed black dots. The post-discal dots of the forewing lie in an almost straight line running parallel to the outer margin.

Similar species: Female Lorquin's Blue is blacker on the upperside, but the ranges hardly overlap. Female *Everes* species have short 'tails' and are silvery blue underneath. Osiris Blue is larger.

Flight: April to September in one or two broods; they keep close to the ground or the vegetation and spend a lot of time basking with their wings wide open or partly raised.

Habitat: Rough grassland, including roadsides, from sea level to about 2,000 m (6,550 ft), but never in very exposed places. The butterfly occurs mainly on chalk and limestone. The main larval foodplant is Kidney Vetch, but medicks are eaten in some areas.

Life-cycle: The pearly-blue eggs are doughnut-shaped with reticulate white sculpturing; they are laid singly, deep in the flowerheads of the foodplant. The caterpillar is woodlouse-shaped and pale brown or pinkish grey with a darker line along the back. It feeds on the developing seeds and is rarely seen. The mature caterpillar is about 10 mm (0.4 in) long, and it pupates low down on the foodplant. The chrysalis, which is often attended by ants, is cream or pale grey, with brown spots and conspicuous silvery hairs. Caterpillars of the final brood hibernate in soil-crevices when fully grown and pupate in the spring.

Range: Most of Europe, and on across temperate Asia to Mongolia, but absent from most of Iberia.

Carswell's Little Blue (*Cupido carswelli*), restricted to southeast Spain, is almost identical to Small Blue, but male may have a small basal purple patch on the upperside. It is often regarded as a subspecies of Small Blue.

---

p.90 **Osiris Blue** *Cupido osiris*

Description: 12–15 mm (0.5–0.6 in). The male upperside is a bright violet-blue, unmarked except for its narrow black margins and white fringes. The female upperside is dark sooty brown, sometimes with a slight blue flush at the base of the forewing. The undersides are pale bluish grey with small, white-ringed black dots, those of the forewing more or less in a straight line. There is usually a brighter flush of blue at the base of the hindwing.

Similar species: *Everes* species have small 'tails'. Mazarine Blue underside is browner and has larger spots. Small Blue female is smaller.

Flight: April to September in one or two broods, basking for long periods with its wings wide open or partly raised.

Habitat: Flower-rich grassland, usually above 500 m (1,650 ft) and reaching altitudes of about 2,000 m (6,550 ft) in the Alps. The larval foodplants are various legumes, especially sainfoins.

Life-cycle: The pearly-white or pale-green eggs are doughnut-shaped and heavily sculptured. They are laid on the flowers of the foodplant and the caterpillars feed on both the flowers and the developing seeds. The mature caterpillar is up to 15 mm (0.6 in) long, bright green with rust-coloured stripes, and very well camouflaged in the sainfoin flowerheads. It pupates between two leaves. The chrysalis is cream and hairy, with dark spots and streaks. Final-brood

caterpillars hibernate when fully grown and pupate in the spring.

Range: Southern Europe, as far north as Switzerland, and eastwards to central Asia. A very local butterfly.

p.91 **Lorquin's Blue** *Cupido lorquinii*

Description: 10–15 mm (0.4–0.6 in). The male upperside is violet-blue with broad sooty-black margins and white fringes. The female upperside is sooty brown with just a few blue scales near the base. The underside is pale bluish grey in both sexes, with a row of small white-ringed black spots on each wing but no marginal markings.

Similar species: African Grass Blue underside is browner and has faint marginal markings. Female Small Blue is very similar, but ranges overlap only in central Portugal.

Flight: April to June.

Habitat: Rough grassy places, from sea level to about 1,500m (4,925 ft). The larval foodplant is Kidney Vetch.

Life-cycle: The eggs are laid in the flowers of the foodplant and the caterpillars feed on the flowers and developing seeds. Winter is passed in the pupal stage.

Range: Confined to southern Iberia and North Africa. The European population is considered vulnerable.

p.89 **Holly Blue** *Celastrina argiolus*

Description: 12–18 mm (0.5–0.7 in). The male upperside is bright violet-blue with narrow black margins and lightly chequered white fringes. The female upperside is usually more of a sky-blue, with much wider black borders, especially in the second brood. The underside is very pale blue, with black spots that are not ringed with white. The spots on the forewing are confined to the post-discal region and they are distinctly elongate. Specimens from the far north often have very small spots.

Similar species: Provençal Short-tailed Blue and Eastern
Short-tailed Blue have 'tails', and the
underside spots are rounded and ringed
with white.

Flight: April to September in two broods, often
high in hollies and other trees where it likes
to bask with its wings partly raised. Apart
from the Long-tailed Blue, it is the only
European blue likely to be seen high in the
trees. It feeds mainly on honeydew and
oozing sap, although it can also be seen at
Brambles and other flowers. In Scandinavia,
males often gather to drink from elk-
droppings.

Habitat: Open woods and woodland margins, parks,
gardens, and hedgerows, from sea level to
about 1,500m (4,925 ft). It is not
uncommon in towns. Holly is the main
foodplant for the caterpillars of the first
brood, although Dogwood, Spindle, Gorse,
Bell Heather, Bramble, Raspberry, Hop,
and many other shrubs and herbaceous
plants may be used. Ivy is the usual
foodplant for second-brood caterpillars.

Life-cycle: The disc-shaped eggs are greenish white,
elaborately sculptured, and laid singly on
the flower-buds of the foodplants. The
caterpillars feed on the flowers and
developing fruits. They are bright green
and slug-shaped, with a bumpy dorsal
surface. Many have pink or purple stripes,
and become redder towards maturity, when
they are about 12 mm (0.5 in) long. Both
caterpillars and pupae may be attended by
ants. Caterpillars of the spring brood often
pupate on the leaves, but autumn larvae
usually pupate on the larger ivy stems or in
neighbouring crevices. The chrysalis looks
rather like a contracted brown slug. The
pupae of the autumn caterpillars do not
produce adults until the following spring.

Range: Almost all of Europe, although absent from
Scotland and much of northern
Scandinavia; across Asia to Japan and also
in North Africa.

The Holly Blue was once considered to be
conspecific with the Spring Azure of North
America, but recent work has shown that the

two butterflies are distinct species, and the Spring Azure is now called *Celastrina ladon*.

p.92 **Green-underside Blue** *Glaucopsyche alexis*

Description: 12–18 mm (0.5–0.7 in). The male upperside is bright blue, tinged with violet, but unmarked apart from the sooty-brown borders and white fringes. The female upperside is sooty brown with no more than a faint blue flush at the base. The undersides of both sexes are pale grey, with a variable greenish-blue flush at the base of the hindwing. The forewing has large, round or oval, white-ringed black spots in the post-discal area of the forewing, but the spots are much smaller on the hindwing and sometimes missing, especially in the north.

Similar species: Mazarine Blue underside is browner, with much smaller spots on the forewing.

Flight: April to July, possibly with a partial second brood in August in some areas.

Habitat: Warm, well-drained grassland with Lucerne and other leguminous flowers, from sea level to about 2,000 m (6,550 ft) although the butterfly is most common in upland areas. The larval foodplants include brooms, vetches, Lucerne, and many other leguminous shrubs and herbs.

Life-cycle: The eggs are pale green, disc-shaped and heavily sculptured with white. They are laid singly on the upper leaves and flower-buds and the caterpillars eat both leaves and flowers. They are usually green or pink, with a brown line and yellow blotches along the back, but the colour is very variable. The mature caterpillar is up to 20 mm (0.8 in) long. It pupates in the leaf-litter, and winter is normally passed in the pupal stage, although the caterpillar may hibernate in some of the more northerly parts of its range. The chrysalis is yellow and brown and very smooth.

Range: Most of Europe except the British Isles and the far north, and on through Asia to China.

p.93 **Black-eyed Blue**
Glaucopsyche melanops

Description: 10–15 mm (0.4–0.6 in). The male
upperside is a clear violet-blue with narrow,
sooty-brown borders. The female upperside
is basically blue with wide brown margins,
but it is heavily dusted with brown scales
and the blue is often visible only at the base
of each wing. The undersides are grey in
both sexes, with some pale marginal
markings and a blue smudge near the base
of the hindwing. The forewing carries an
arc of very large, white-ringed black spots.
The hindwing of the female also bears
conspicuous black spots, but those of the
male hindwing are much smaller.

Similar species: Green-underside Blue is much paler under
the hindwing. Mazarine blue is browner
underneath, with smaller spots.

Flight: March to May.

Habitat: Heaths and open woodland, from sea level
to about 900 m (2,950 ft). The larval
foodplants are Dorycnium and various other
low-growing leguminous herbs and shrubs.

Life-cycle: The eggs are laid in the flowerheads of the
foodplant, where the caterpillars feed on the
flowers and the developing seeds. They are
regularly attended by black ants. The
caterpillar normally hibernates when fully
grown and pupates early in the spring, but
some individuals may pupate in the
autumn and pass the winter as pupae.

Range: Iberia, southern France, and northwest Italy.

---

p.93 **Odd-spot Blue** *Turanana endymion*

Description: 10 mm (0.4 in). The male upperside is deep
violet-blue with broad sooty-black borders
and a black bar at the end of the forewing
cell. The female upperside is dark brown,
usually with a trace of blue at the base of
each wing. The undersides of both sexes are
grey with white-ringed black spots on both
wings. The post-discal spots on the
forewing are very large, that in S3 being
displaced towards the margin and giving
the butterfly its common name.

Similar species: None.
Flight: May to July.
Habitat: Dry mountain slopes between 1,500 and 2,300 m (4,925 and 7,550 ft). The larval foodplant is Prickly Thrift.
Life-cycle: The eggs are very small and are laid in the flowerheads of the foodplant. The caterpillars feed mainly on the flowers. Winter is passed in the pupal stage.
Range: Southern Greece and through southwest Asia to the Caspian.

p.94 **Alcon Blue** *Maculinea alcon*

Description: 12–20 mm (0.5–0.8 in). There are two quite distinct races or subspecies – *M. a. alcon* and *M. a. rebeli*. The male upperside of *alcon* is pale violet-blue with narrow black borders, but *rebeli* is a deeper and brighter blue. The females of both races are basically violet-blue, but they have broad, sooty-black borders and are sometimes so heavily dusted with sooty scales that the blue is hardly visible. There is an arc of black post-discal spots on the forewing of *rebeli*, but this is often missing from *alcon*. The undersides are greyish brown in both races, with rather faint marginal markings and a somewhat wavy line of white-ringed, jet-black post-discal spots on each wing. The hindwing may have a blue smudge at the base.
Similar species: Scarce Large Blue has similar underside, but male has post-discal spots on the upperside, and female upperside has more blue. Iolas Blue has post-discal spots under the forewing almost in a straight line.
Flight: June to August.
Habitat: The two races have very different habitat requirements. *M. a. alcon* is a butterfly of damp meadows, from sea level to about 900 m (2,950 ft), where the young larvae feed on Marsh Gentian and Cross Gentian. *M. a. rebeli* inhabits both damp and dry grassland and usually flies between about 1,200 and 2,200 m (3,925 and 7,225 ft). Its main larval foodplants are Cross Gentian and Chiltern Gentian.

Life-cycle: The disc-shaped white eggs are identical in
the two races and are laid singly on the
flowers and upper leaves of the foodplant,
although the plants often carry the eggs of
several females. The pink, maggot-like
caterpillars feed on the leaves and flowers
during the first three instars and, unlike
those of other *Maculinea* species, they are not
cannibalistic. After the third moult the
caterpillars stop feeding and develop no
further unless they are adopted by red ants:
Myrmica rubra and *M. ruginodis* are the usual
hosts. Inside the ants' nest, the caterpillars
start to exude a sugary liquid from small
glands all over the body, and the ants lick
them regularly. In return, the caterpillars lap
up fluids regurgitated by the ants and they
also receive some of the ants' prey – in fact,
they are treated almost exactly the same as
the ants' own grubs. They may also eat some
of the ants' grubs, but not on the scale of the
other *Maculinea* species and this may explain
why as many as twenty *alcon* caterpillars have
been found in a single ants' nest. The
caterpillars spend the winter in the ants'
nests, and pupate there in the spring. Mature
caterpillars are flesh-coloured and up to
15 mm (0.6 in) long. The chrysalis is also
flesh-coloured, and very smooth.

Range: South and central Europe, including
southern Sweden (*M. a. alcon*), but absent
from the British Isles and most of Iberia.

The Alcon Blue is a rare species, in danger
of extinction in Europe through overgrazing
of its upland habitats and drainage of the
lowland meadows. Although the two races
are connected by many intermediate forms,
some entomologists consider them to be
separate species, with *M. a. rebeli* known as
the Mountain Alcon Blue.

---

p.94 **Large Blue** *Maculinea arion*

Description: 15–20 mm (0.6–0.8 in). The male
upperside is bright sky-blue, with a broad
black border and an arc of wedge-shaped,
black post-discal spots on the forewing.

The post-discal spots are small or absent on the hindwing and the outer border may consist only of small black spots. Both wings have white fringes. The female is similar, but she has larger post-discal spots and the hindwing generally has a complete black border. In montane regions, both sexes may be heavily dusted with dark scales, with the blue showing only in the basal parts of the wings. The undersides are greyish brown with large black spots, those in the post-discal area of the forewing being distinctly elongate or oval. The wings are often quite shiny and there is a faint clear-blue flush at the base of the hindwing.

Similar species: Alcon Blue female has a more violet upperside. Scarce Large Blue has a duller upperside, with smaller spots, and no blue flush on the underside.

Flight: June to August, usually keeping fairly close to the ground. The butterflies may bask with their wings open early in the day or in overcast conditions, but otherwise the wings usually stay closed at rest.

Habitat: Rough grassland, usually on well-drained sunny slopes, with Wild Thyme and red ants – the two essential requirements of the caterpillars, although Marjoram is used as a foodplant in some areas. It is also a favourite nectar source for the adults. Scandinavian populations often occur in forest clearings. *Myrmica sabuleti* is the principal host ant, and is the only one used in Britain, but other *Myrmica* species may be used on the Continent. The butterfly can be found from sea level to about 2,000 m (6,550 ft).

Life-cycle: The eggs are bluish white and almost spherical, with fine, white, lace-like sculpturing. They are laid singly, deep in the unopened flowerheads of the foodplant, although several females may lay in a suitable flowerhead. First-instar larvae are strongly cannibalistic, and it is rare for more than one larva to survive on each flowerhead. The caterpillars feed on the flowers and developing seeds until the third moult, and their pink colour provides excellent camouflage. After the third moult, the caterpillars fall to the ground and wait to be discovered by the ants. As soon as an ant starts to nuzzle a caterpillar, the latter exudes a drop of sweet liquid, which is eagerly lapped up by the ant. The ant becomes very excited and continues to 'milk' the caterpillar for a while, and eventually carries it back to its nest. Any caterpillar not found within a day or two will die. The caterpillar is still very small at this stage, although it is in its third instar, but once in the ants' nest it gorges itself on the ant grubs and quickly puts on weight. It gives out no more 'nectar' and, despite its attacks on their grubs, it is virtually ignored by the ants. Ant-calming pheromones emitted by the caterpillar are probably responsible for this, although the caterpillars are attacked if the worker ants bring too many into the nest. It is rare to find more than four or five individuals in one nest, and most nests contain no more than one caterpillar. The caterpillar stays in the nest throughout the winter and pupates there in the spring, when it is about 15 mm (0.6 in) long. The chrysalis is smooth and flesh-coloured.

Range: Most of Europe except the far north, and on to central Asia. The butterfly is rare everywhere and threatened with extinction through overgrazing or undergrazing of its habitat – both of which render the environment unsuitable for the ants.

The Large Blue was widespread in southern England in the past, but its range contracted as many grassland areas were ploughed up. Rabbit grazing kept a few small areas in a suitable condition, and the butterfly remained locally common until the 1950s, but the arrival of myxomatosis and the consequent crash of the rabbit population spelt disaster for the Large Blue. Scrub developed on the hillsides and the ants died out – and so did the butterfly. It was declared extinct in Britain in 1979, but it has since been reintroduced from Sweden and seems to be doing well in carefully monitored sites.

p.95 Scarce Large Blue *Maculinea telejus*

Description: 15–20 mm (0.6–0.8 in). The male upperside is a rather dull blue with broad, sooty-brown borders and white fringes. There is usually a row of small, elongated post-discal spots on both wings, although these spots are sometimes very small or absent. The female is similar but has broader borders and a sooty-brown front edge to the forewing, and she rarely lacks post-discal spots. The undersides of both sexes are greyish brown with conspicuous black post-discal spots, and no blue flush on the hindwing. The marginal spots are very faint, especially on the forewing.

Similar species: Large Blue is more of a sky-blue above and has a blue flush on the underside. Alcon Blue is more of a violet-blue, with no spots on the male upperside and broader dark borders in the female. Dusky Large Blue has a much browner underside.

Flight: June to August. The butterfly may bask with its wings open in overcast weather, but the uppersides are otherwise rarely seen.

Habitat: Damp grassland and moorland, from sea level to about 1,800 m (5,900 ft). The young larvae feed on Great Burnet, but older ones live in ants' nests.

Life-cycle: The eggs are pearly white or pale green and much smoother than those of other *Maculinea* species. They are laid singly in the flowerheads of the foodplant. The young caterpillar is pink or purple, and it feeds in the flowerheads until after the third moult, when it falls to the ground and awaits its ant hosts. *Myrmica scabrinodis* is the usual host species, and the caterpillars are taken into their nests in much the same way as those of the Large Blue. Feeding mainly on the ant grubs, the caterpillar grows rapidly, but does not pupate until the spring, when it is about 15 mm (0.6 in) long.

Range: Central Europe, mainly in the east, and across temperate Asia to Japan. Absent from the British Isles and most areas west of the Alps, although it occurs here and there near the Atlantic coast of France. A very local species, in danger of extinction throughout its European range because of the drainage of its wetland habitat.

---

p.95 **Dusky Large Blue** *Maculinea nausithous*

Description: 15–20 mm (0.6–0.8 in). The male upperside is a deep violet-blue with broad dark-brown borders to all margins except the rear edge of the forewing. There are small, elongate post-discal spots on both wings, although they are sometimes indistinct. The female is dark brown with at most a faint blue flush near the base. Both sexes have brown fringes, but the uppersides are very rarely seen at rest. The undersides are chocolate-brown, with conspicuous, white-ringed black post-discal spots in a strongly curved arc on each wing. There are no marginal markings.

Similar species: Scarce Large Blue has much paler undersides. Iolas Blue has paler undersides with the post-discal spots of the forewing in a straighter line.

Flight: June to August.

Habitat: Lakesides and other marshy areas, up to about 1,500 m (4,925 ft). The caterpillars feed on Great Burnet during the first three instars but are then taken into ants' nests.

Life-cycle: The eggs are slightly flattened, white spheres with a faint honeycomb pattern, and they are normally laid singly on the flowerheads of the foodplant. The young caterpillar is deep pink or maroon and well camouflaged on the flowers. After the third moult, when it is still very small, the caterpillar drops to the ground and awaits the arrival of a suitable ant. *Myrmica rubra* and *M. scabrinodis* are the normal host ants and the caterpillar is taken into the nests in just the same way as the Large Blue caterpillar. It feeds on the ant grubs and pupates in the nest in the spring. The chrysalis is pinkish brown and very smooth.

Range: Across central Europe, in widely scattered colonies, from eastern France to the Caucasus and the Urals. Also recorded in northern Spain. The species is endangered throughout its range by drainage of its wetland habitat.

p.99 **Iolas Blue** *Iolana iolas*

Description: 17–22 mm (0.7–0.9 in). The male upperside is a pale and rather shiny violet-blue, unmarked apart from the narrow sooty-brown borders. The female upperside is a deeper blue, with wide sooty borders that are often so extensive that the upper surface looks completely brown apart from a small patch of blue near the base. The undersides are silvery grey in both sexes, with prominent white-ringed, black, post-discal spots on each wing. Those on the forewing are particularly large and form an almost straight line parallel to the outer margin. There are faint grey marginal spots on each wing and a slight blue flush at the base of the hindwing.

Similar species: Alcon Blue has post-discal spots under the forewing in a strong curve.

Flight: May to September in one or two broods, although the second brood is usually only a partial emergence.

Habitat: Rough grassy and rocky slopes and light woodland, from sea level to about 1,800 m (5,900 ft). The larval foodplant is Bladder-senna and the caterpillars feed inside the seedpods.

Life-cycle: The eggs, like tiny white dishes with a conspicuous honeycomb pattern, are quite unmistakable. They are usually laid singly in the flowers or pods of the foodplant and the caterpillars feed on the developing seeds. The caterpillar is up to 20 mm (0.8 in) long and is pale green, often tinged with brown, for much of its life. It becomes reddish brown when mature, and leaves the foodplant to pupate amongst the stones and leaves on the ground. The chrysalis is cream with brown freckles. Winter is passed in the pupal stage.

Range: Southern and central Europe, mainly to the east of the Rhône although it maintains a precarious existence in Spain. Also in North Africa and across southern Asia to Iran. A rare species throughout its European range.

p.96   **Baton Blue** *Pseudophilotes baton*

Description: 10–12 mm (0.4–0.5 in). The male
upperside is pale blue with a dark bar at the
end of the cell in each wing. There may be a
faint row of marginal black spots on the
hindwing. The female is largely brown,
with a variable amount of purplish blue on
the basal half of each wing and usually some
indication of black marginal spots on the
hindwing. Both sexes have chequered
fringes on both surfaces, but these are
especially noticeable on the forewing. The
undersides of both sexes are pale grey, often
with a brownish tinge, and heavily spotted
with black. The underside of the hindwing
has a conspicuous arc of orange submarginal
spots, bordered by black spots on both sides.

Similar species: Bavius Blue of southeast Europe has orange
lunules at the rear of the hindwing, and the
orange spots on the underside form a
continuous band. Chequered Blue is larger,
with much heavier markings on the
underside.

Flight: April to October in one or two broods, but
the insect does not fly a great deal and
spends much of the daytime resting on the
ground or on low-growing vegetation with
its wings closed or half open. It regularly
takes nectar from Wild Thyme, but rarely
visits other flowers.

Habitat: Dry, sunny grassland and stony slopes, from
sea level to about 2,000 m (6,550 ft). The
main larval foodplant is Wild Thyme, but
other labiates are also used, especially by
second-brood caterpillars.

Life-cycle: The eggs are pale green and are laid singly in
the flowerheads of the foodplant. The
caterpillar feeds mainly on the flowers and is
regularly tended by ants. It is green with
longitudinal maroon stripes, and matches the
thyme flowers extremely well. It is about
10 mm (0.4 in) long when mature and it
pupates among the leaves at the base of the
foodplant. The chrysalis is pale green or cream
with maroon lines and is without any trace of
a girdle. The winter is usually passed in the
larval stage, although some single-brooded
populations may overwinter as pupae.

Range: Most of Europe, as far north as southern Finland although absent from the rest of Scandinavia, and on through Asia to the Himalayas. Absent from the British Isles and from southern Iberia.

Western and eastern populations, distinguishable only by a small difference in the male genitalia, have long been regarded as races or subspecies, but have recently been treated as distinct species – *P. baton* in the west (as far as Italy and western Poland) and *P. vicrama* in the east.

p.96 **False Baton Blue** *Pseudophilotes abencerragus*

Description: 10 mm (0.4 in). The male upperside is basically a dark violet-blue with wide, sooty-brown borders, but the brown scales often encroach over the whole surface and restrict the blue colour to a small area at the base of each wing. There is a black spot at the end of the cell in each wing. The female upperside is sooty brown or grey with a variable amount of blue at the base. The undersides are greyish brown with white-ringed black spots in both sexes, the spots on the forewing being particularly large. There may be a faint orange band between the submarginal and marginal black spots on the hindwing. Both sexes have strongly chequered white fringes on both surfaces.

Similar species: Panoptes Blue male is slightly paler; female is almost identical, although the black spots under the forewing may be a little smaller in Panoptes Blue.

Flight: April to May, keeping close to the ground and commonly taking nectar from thyme flowers.

Habitat: Rough hillsides, usually between 700 and 1,200 m (2,300 and 3,925 ft). The major larval foodplant is the labiate *Cleonia lusitanica*, but Wild Thyme may also be used.

Life-cycle: The eggs are laid singly low down on young plants, although the caterpillars feed on the flowers. Little else seems to be known of the early stages of this butterfly.

Range: Iberia and North Africa.

p.97 **Panoptes Blue** *Pseudophilotes panoptes*

Description: 10 mm (0.4 in). The male upperside is bright violet-blue with strong, although not particularly broad, black borders. There is a prominent black bar at the end of the cell in each wing. The female upperside is dark brown with a variable amount of blue at the base. Both sexes have conspicuously chequered white fringes. The undersides are greyish brown with white-ringed black spots, although the marginal and submarginal spots may be quite faint.

Similar species: False Baton Blue male has darker uppersides: females are almost identical although False Baton Blue may have larger spots under the forewing.

Flight: April to July in two broods. Flights are short and never far from the ground and the butterfly commonly basks on low vegetation with its wings wide open.

Habitat: Rough hillsides, usually between 800 and 2,000 m (2,625 and 6,550 ft). The larval foodplants are thymes.

Life-cycle: The eggs are laid singly on the foodplant. Nothing else seems to be known of the early stages of the butterfly, but the life-cycle is likely to be very similar to that of Baton Blue.

Range: Confined to Spain and Portugal, where it may be just a race of Baton Blue.

Sardinian Blue *Pseudophilotes barbagiae*

Description: 10 mm (0.4 in). The male upperside is greyish brown with a small patch of blue scales at the base. The female upperside is dark brown all over. Both sexes have strongly chequered margins. The undersides are greyish brown with black spots just like those of Panoptes Blue.

Similar species: Distinguished with certainty from Panoptes Blue and False Baton Blue only by examination of the male genitalia.

Flight: May to June.

Habitat: Rocky hillsides between 800 and 1,500m (2,625 and 4,925 ft). The larval foodplants are thymes.

Life-cycle: Nothing seems to be known of the early stages of this butterfly.

Range: Confined to a small area of Sardinia.

---

p.97 **Bavius Blue** *Pseudophilotes bavius*

Description: 10–15 mm (0.4–0.6 in). The male upperside is a bright violet-blue, with orange submarginal lunules towards the rear of the hindwing. Both wings have dark borders merging gradually with the blue ground colour. The female is sooty brown or black, with blue dusting at the base and orange lunules like those of the male. Both sexes have strongly chequered fringes. The undersides are pale grey with black spots, and there is a conspicuous orange submarginal band on the hindwing.

Similar species: Baton Blue has no orange on the upperside and the orange band under the hindwing consists of separate spots.

Flight: May to June.

Habitat: Rough grassland, usually between 500 and 1,200 m (1,650 and 3,925 ft). The larvae feed on Silver Sage and possibly other *Salvia* species (claries).

Life-cycle: The caterpillars feed mainly on the flowers of the foodplants and are either green or pink. Winter is passed in the pupal stage.

Range: The Balkans and Romania and eastwards to the Caucasus. Also in North Africa. The butterfly is considered to be endangered in Europe, where it is right on the edge of its range.

---

p.98 **Chequered Blue** *Scolitantides orion*

Description: 14 mm (0.6 in). The uppersides of both sexes generally appear sooty brown or black, with the underlying blue showing through mainly on the forewing. Both wings carry a line of greyish-blue submarginal lunules, although these are often partly obscured by dark scales in the female, and a large dark spot is usually visible at the end of the cell in the forewing. The fringes are strongly chequered on both surfaces. The undersides are dirty white with large black spots that are often rather square on the forewing. There is a bright-orange submarginal band on the hindwing. Scandinavian males are largely blue on the upperside, with wide black borders sometimes broken into separate spots. The females may be yellowish underneath.

Similar species: Baton Blue is smaller and less heavily marked below.

Flight: April to August in one or two broods, keeping fairly close to the ground and feeding regularly at the flowers of stonecrops. It is one of the earliest blues to fly in the Alps.

Habitat: Dry, stony hillsides and coastal cliffs, from sea level to about 1,000 m (3,275 ft). The larval foodplants are various stonecrop species.

Life-cycle: The little eggs look like flat, white buttons covered with elaborate sculpturing. They are laid singly or in small groups on the leaves or flowerheads of the foodplant. The caterpillar is yellowish green and very slug-like, with short hairs and variable brown or purplish stripes. It possesses a nectar-gland and is attended by ants. The mature caterpillar is up to 15 mm (0.6 in) long and it pupates under stones or moss. The chrysalis is yellowish or reddish brown with darker mottling. Winter is passed in the pupal stage.

Range: Patchily distributed from the Mediterranean to southern Scandinavia, and on through central Asia to Japan. Absent from the British Isles and much of central Europe. A rare and local butterfly throughout its European range.

p.99 **Grass Jewel** *Chilades trochylus*

Description: 8 mm (0.3 in). The uppersides are brown in both sexes, with orange lunules and black spots around the rear of the hindwing. The undersides are pale greyish brown with white-ringed black spots. There is a short row of orange lunules near the rear of the hindwing, and beyond these are some black spots ringed with gleaming bluish-green scales – the jewels referred to in the name.

This is one of the world's smallest butterflies.

Similar species: None.

Flight: March to October in three or more broods. The butterfly keeps close to the ground and spends much of its time settled with wings closed.

Habitat: Dry, stony ground, including roadsides, from sea level to about 1,000 m (3,275 ft). The larval foodplant is Andrachne, but caterpillars may also eat heliotropes.

Life-cycle: Winter is passed in the pupal stage, but little else seems to be known of the early stages of this butterfly.

Range: Confined to Greece in Europe, but widely distributed in Africa and in the warmer parts of Asia.

---

p.100 **Zephyr Blue** *Plebejus pylaon*

Description: 14–17 mm (0.6–0.7 in). The male upperside ranges from a bright-violet to a royal blue, with narrow black borders and conspicuous white fringes. There are a number of small black spots around the edge of the hindwing and these are sometimes edged with red on the inside. The female upperside is rich brown, usually with bright-orange submarginal lunules on the hindwing and occasionally with some on the forewing. Specimens from the Alps (*P. p. trappi*) may lack the orange. The undersides are pale greyish brown, with conspicuous black spots and a bright-orange submarginal band on each wing. The band may be broken into separate lunules. A whitish area, especially noticeable in Alpine specimens, lies between the band and the post-discal black spots. There may be a slight blue flush near the base of the hindwing, especially in the male.

Similar species: Silver-studded Blue, Idas Blue, and Reverdin's Blue all have silvery spots under the hindwing.

Flight: May to August, usually keeping low over the vegetation and spending much of its time basking with wings open.

Habitat: Rough, flowery grassland, from sea level to about 2,000 m (6,550 ft) but most commonly found in upland areas. The larval foodplants are milk-vetches.

Life-cycle: The eggs are pale green and almost spherical, with a finely sculptured surface. They are laid singly or in small groups. In some of the hotter and drier areas the eggs may not hatch until the following spring, but elsewhere they hatch within a week or two. The slug-like caterpillar is yellowish green with short hairs, and with a hint of pink on the sides. In most areas it goes into hibernation when half-grown and completes its growth in the spring, reaching up to about 12 mm (0.5 in) long when mature. It is regularly attended by ants and it often pupates in a small chamber in the ants' nest. The chrysalis is pale green and cream.

Range: In scattered colonies across southern and eastern Europe, including the Alps, and on through Asia to Iran. European colonies are considered to be vulnerable. *P. p. trappi*, confined to the Alps of Switzerland and northern Italy, is a deeper blue than the other subspecies.

p.101 **Silver-studded Blue** *Plebejus argus*

Description: 10–18 mm (0.4–0.7 in). The male upperside is a deep blue, often with a strong violet tinge. There are strong black borders, at least 1 mm wide, on the forewing, but the hindwing may have a row of black spots instead of a continuous border. Both wings have conspicuous white fringes. The female is chocolate-brown, usually with orange submarginal lunules on the hindwing and sometimes on the forewing as well, although they are often very faint. There is sometimes a faint dusting of blue scales near the base. The underside of the male is some shade of grey, while that of the female is smoky brown. Both sexes have black spots. There is usually a conspicuous orange submarginal band on both wings, and on its inside there is a clear white area, especially obvious in the female. The marginal black spots of the hindwing contain shiny, blue or greenish centres – the silver studs that give the butterfly its name.

Similar species: Zephyr Blue has no silver studs. Idas Blue and Reverdin's Blue are difficult to distinguish in the field but males generally have narrower black borders and females have slightly darker fringes. The male Silver-studded Blue has a strong spine at the tip of the front tibia, but this is visible only at close quarters with a good lens.

Flight: May to September in one or two broods, keeping low over the vegetation and rarely flying far at a time. The butterflies spend a lot of time resting with their wings closed, although they bask readily in the sunshine.

Habitat: Heaths and grasslands, including coastal dunes and montane grassland to about 2,500 m (8,200 ft). The larval foodplants include Heather, Rock-rose, and a wide range of leguminous plants such as Kidney Vetch, Bird's-foot Trefoil, and Gorse. British populations are now found only on lowland heaths and in a few coastal areas. The butterfly is most common in areas where heathland is regenerating after clearance or fire and there is plenty of young heather growth for the larvae, although some more mature plants may be necessary to provide shelter for the adults.

Life-cycle: The greenish-white eggs are disc-shaped and beautifully sculptured. They are laid singly on or near the foodplant – commonly in areas occupied by ants, which may provide a certain amount of protection from predators and parasites. In double-brooded populations, the first-brood females usually lay on the foodplant, but females of the second brood often lay on leaf-litter under the plants, as do the females of single-brooded populations. Eggs of the second brood and of all single-brooded populations remain dormant through the winter and hatch in the spring. The caterpillar is pale green to pinkish brown, with a white-edged dark stripe along the back. It feeds on the flowers and young shoots of the foodplants and is regularly attended by ants of the genus *Lasius*. The mature caterpillar is 12–13 mm (0.5 in) long and, in sandy areas, it usually pupates in a silk-lined chamber in the ground; elsewhere it may lie freely on the surface, although it is quickly buried by ants. The chrysalis is green, with a brown tinge to the wingcases. Ants often occur in the pupal chambers and may even build new nests around the pupae.

Range: Throughout Europe except the far north, and across temperate Asia to Japan. Absent from Scotland and Ireland.

Widespread deterioration and destruction of its heathland habitat has greatly reduced the population of the Silver-studded Blue in Britain, although it is still quite common in some favourable localities. Most grassland populations died out when myxomatosis destroyed the rabbits and the grasslands became overgrown with scrub.

---

p.102 **Idas Blue** *Plebejus idas*

Description: 10–15 mm (0.4–0.6 in). The male upperside is generally bright blue with narrow black borders and relatively long white fringes, although in Corsica and parts of southeast Europe the ground colour is a deep violet-blue and the black borders are quite wide. The rear border of the hindwing may be broken into separate black spots, although these are not as large as in the Silver-studded Blue. The female is largely chocolate-brown, with orange submarginal lunules on the hindwing and often on the forewing as well. There is often a blue flush at the base of the wings, and females from the far north can be almost as blue as the males. The undersides of both sexes are pale brownish grey with black spots, and there is often a blue flush at the base of the hindwing. There is an orange submarginal band on both wings, although this is often rather faint on the forewing, and the black marginal spots of the hindwing contain shining blue or blue-green centres. At least some of the black lunules on the inner edge of the orange band on the hindwing are distinctly triangular.

Similar species: Silver-studded Blue generally has broader black borders and the male has a spine on the front tibia, but the two species cannot be accurately distinguished in the field. Reverdin's Blue is not easily separated, but the black lunules on the inner edge of the orange band under the hindwing are less pointed and male upperside is usually a little darker.

Flight: May to September in one or two broods, regularly feeding at lavender flowers in southern Europe. The butterfly keeps close to the ground and, in common with many other blues, the males frequently gather in large numbers to drink from muddy puddles and seepages.

Habitat: Rough, stony grassland from sea level to about 2,500 m (8,200 ft). The larval foodplants are mainly leguminous plants, including Bird's-foot Trefoil, Broom, and various clovers, but in the French Alps *P. i. calliopis* feeds on Sea Buckthorn. Heather may also be used in the north.

Life-cycle: The disc-shaped eggs are greenish white and elegantly sculptured. In double-brooded populations the first-brood females usually lay on the flowers of the foodplants, but otherwise the eggs are distributed over the leaves of the foodplants and also those of the surrounding vegetation. Second-brood eggs and those of the single-brooded populations do not normally hatch until the spring, although it is possible that some of them hatch in late summer and that the larvae are taken into ants' nests for the winter. The caterpillar is usually green, with a white stripe on each side and a white-edged brown stripe along the back, but some individuals are dark brown with a pale stripe on the back. It is constantly attended by ants, especially those of the genus *Formica*. The mature caterpillar is up to 15 mm (0.6 in) long. It pupates on the ground, but the pupa, which is brownish green, is quickly buried by ants or taken into their nests.

Range: Throughout Europe, except the British Isles, and all across temperate Asia. Many subspecies have been described, differing slightly in size and colour pattern.

p.103 **Reverdin's Blue** *Plebejus argyrognomon*

Description: 12–18 mm (0.5–0.7 in). The male upperside is a clear violet-blue, with narrow black borders and white fringes. The rear edge of the hindwing may have some small black spots just inside the black border. The female upperside is chocolate-brown, with orange submarginal lunules, although these may be missing from the forewing. The hindwing has black marginal spots associated with the lunules and both wings may have an extensive blue flush. Scandinavian females are particularly blue. The male underside is pale grey or almost white, with an orange submarginal band. This band is best developed on the hindwing, and is bordered on the inside by an arc of curved black lunules. The marginal spots on the hindwing contain shiny blue centres. The female underside has the same pattern as the male, but the ground colour is pale greyish brown and the orange band is well developed on both wings.

Similar species: Although Reverdin's Blue is visually almost identical to Idas Blue, the male genitalia of the two species are quite different. The black lunules lining the orange band under the hindwing are noticeably heavier in Idas Blue. Silver-studded Blue has broader black borders and female is browner underneath. Amanda's Blue female is much paler underneath.

Flight: May to September. There are two broods in most places, but there is probably one only brood in Scandinavia.

Habitat: Rough grassland from sea level to about 1,500 m (4,925 ft). The main larval foodplant is Crown Vetch, but various other legumes are also eaten. Wild Liquorice is the normal foodplant in Scandinavia.

Life-cycle: The ornately patterned eggs are white and resemble tiny buttons. They are laid singly or in small groups, and those laid by the final brood do not usually hatch until the following spring. The slightly hairy, slug-like caterpillar and is pale green with a yellowish stripe on each side, and it is constantly attended by ants of various species. It is about 20 mm (0.8 in) long when mature and it pupates on a leaf or in a flowerhead. The chrysalis is bright green.

Range: Mainly southern and central Europe, but absent from Iberia, the British Isles, and all western coastal areas. Scattered populations occur in southern Scandinavia, where the species is considered to be in some danger although it is quite common in some localities. The butterfly ranges over much of temperate Asia, and also occurs in North America, where it is known as the Northern Blue.

p.103 **Cranberry Blue** *Vacciniina optilete*

Description: 10–15 mm (0.4–0.6 in). The male upperside is a deep violet-blue, unmarked apart from the narrow, jet-black borders. The female is sooty brown with a variable amount of violet dusting at the base. Both sexes have white fringes. The undersides of both sexes are brownish grey, with conspicuous white-ringed, black post-discal spots on both wings. The other spots on the forewing are relatively faint and often no more than grey dashes, especially in far northern specimens. The hindwing has two rows of black lunules near the margin and a prominent red submarginal spot in S2. This is bordered on the outside by shiny blue scales, and there may be a smaller red spot on each side of it.

Similar species: None.

Flight: June to August, skipping low over the ground and vegetation but spending a lot of time at rest, often with its wings wide open.

Habitat: Moors, bogs, and mountain slopes, from sea level to about 2,500 m (8,200 ft): rarely far from the forest edge and, in the north, may be locally common in forest clearings. The larval foodplants include Cranberry, Bell Heather, Bog Rosemary, and bilberries.

Life-cycle: The greenish-white eggs are hemispherical and densely sculptured. They are laid singly or in small groups on the foodplant, and the caterpillar feeds on the flowers and young leaves. It goes into a long hibernation when half-grown, and completes its growth in spring and early summer. The caterpillar is bright green, with a darker stripe along the back and a pink or purple stripe on each side. Up to 12 mm (0.5 in) long when mature, it pupates on the stems of the foodplant or among the mosses at the base. The chrysalis is smooth and rather variable in colour, although it is often green or purplish brown.

Range: Central and northern Europe, from the Alps to the North Cape, and on through northern Asia to Japan. Absent from the British Isles and all areas west of the Alps. A small population may survive in the Balkans. Also in North America, where it is called the Yukon Blue.

The Cranberry Blue is a very local species, declining rapidly as its wetland habitats are being drained, especially in lowland areas, and it faces extinction in several areas.

Cretan Argus *Kretania psylorita*

Description: 13 mm (0.5 in). The uppersides of both sexes are chocolate-brown, with small orange or yellow submarginal lunules. There are a few black marginal spots on the hindwing. The markings tend to be best developed in the female. The undersides are grey, with small black dots and faint orange or yellow submarginal lunules.

Flight: June, keeping low over the ground.

Habitat: Mountain slopes up to 2,000 m (6,550 ft). The larval foodplant is a milk-vetch.

Life-cycle: Nothing is known of the early stages of this butterfly.

Range: Restricted to the mountains of Crete where, although sometimes locally abundant, the population is vulnerable and legally protected.

p.107 **Geranium Argus** *Eumedonia eumedon*

Description: 14–18 mm (0.6–0.7 in). The uppersides of both sexes are dark brown with an occasional trace of blue at the base. The female usually has faint orange lunules near the rear of the hindwing. The undersides are greyish brown with white-ringed black spots. Apart from the anterior one, the post-discal spots of the forewing lie almost in a straight line. The hindwing often has a dusting of blue at the base, and there is normally a short white streak running along vein 5 from the cell to the post-discal spots, although this is often missing in eastern Europe. There may be an arc of triangular, orange submarginal lunules, but this is not always well developed, and in many males it is imperceptible.

Similar species: Brown Argus has much brighter lunules and, as in other *Aricia* species, the post-discal spots under the forewing do not form a straight line.

Flight: May to August, making short, darting flights low over the vegetation.

Habitat: Rough grassland and moorland, from sea level to about 2,500 m (8,200 ft) but most common in damp upland areas; rarely far from woodland or scrub. The larval foodplants are various crane's-bills, especially Wood Crane's-bill.

Life-cycle: The eggs are pale green and hemispherical, with a delicate reticular pattern, and they are laid singly on the flowers or upper leaves of the foodplant. The slug-like caterpillar hibernates and completes its growth in the spring. It is green with pale flecks and stripes, and clothed with short yellowish hairs. It is regularly tended by ants. The mature caterpillar is about 12 mm (0.5 in) long and it pupates low down on the vegetation or amongst the

leaf-litter, sometimes in a flimsy cocoon.
The chrysalis is dull green, often tinged
with yellow or brown.

Range: Most of Europe from the Alps eastwards,
with outlying populations in central France
and Spain. The species appears to be
spreading westwards in Scandinavia, but is
generally considered to be rare in Europe.
The species is also widely distributed in the
cooler parts of Asia.

In some recent literature this butterfly is
called *Aricia eumedon*.

---

p.104 **Brown Argus** *Aricia agestis*

Description: 10–15 mm (0.4–0.6 in). The uppersides of
both sexes are rich chocolate-brown, usually
with a full set of orange or red lunules
around the margins of both wings although
the lunules may be quite small on the male
forewing. There is an inconspicuous black
spot or bar at the end of the forewing cell.
There is never any trace of blue on the
wings, although there may be a few bluish
hairs on the body. The undersides are
greyish brown, with a full set of orange
submarginal lunules and numerous white-
ringed black spots, but there is no spot in
the forewing cell. The two anterior spots on
the hindwing sit one above the other in the
form of a colon. Vein 4 usually carries a
white streak, which may broaden into a
triangular patch towards the margin.

Similar species: Mountain Argus is often darker, with fewer
and smaller orange lunules on the
upperside. Female Blue Argus and several
female blues are superficially similar, but
the spots under the hindwing do not form
an obvious colon. Spanish Argus has fainter
orange lunules on the underside.

Flight: April to September in two or three broods,
commonly basking with wings open but
closing their wings as soon as the sun
disappears.

Habitat: Open grassland, including grass heaths and
coastal dunes, from sea level to about
1,000 m (3,275 ft); mainly on sunny slopes

with short turf and some shelter from the wind. The main larval foodplants are rock-roses on alkaline soils and stork's-bills and crane's-bills on acid soils.

Life-cycle: The eggs are pale green with white sculpturing, and they are laid singly on the undersides of the leaves. The young caterpillars burrow in the lower layers of the leaves, but older ones feed more openly. Those of the final brood go into hibernation while still quite small, usually in the third instar, and complete their growth in the spring. The mature caterpillar, about 12 mm (0.5 in) long, is pale green, with a maroon stripe on each side, and rather hairy. It is regularly attended by ants. It pupates in the leaf-litter, but the pale-green or yellowish chrysalis is quickly buried by ants.

Range: Southern and central Europe and much of temperate Asia. The species just creeps into southern Sweden but is absent from Ireland and Scotland.

p.104 **Mountain Argus** *Aricia artaxerxes*

Description: 12 mm (0.5 in). The uppersides of both sexes are dark, sooty brown and sometimes almost black when fresh, but older specimens tend to have more of a chocolate colour. There are usually orange or yellowish submarginal lunules on both wings, but these are fairly small and they fade away towards the wingtip. They are sometimes absent altogether, especially in butterflies of the far north and on some of the higher mountains. The Scottish race (*A. a. artaxerxes*) is a little paler and has a conspicuous white spot on the forewing. The undersides range from pale brown to grey, with pale-orange submarginal lunules on both wings and the usual scattering of white-ringed, black spots, although the latter may be much reduced. The two anterior spots on the hindwing form a colon. Scottish specimens commonly have pure-white spots, and there is usually a conspicuous white wedge in spaces 3 and 4.

Similar species: Brown Argus is generally a brighter brown, with larger orange lunules but never with a white spot on the forewing. Female Blue Argus is very similar, but spots at the front of the hindwing do not form a colon. Spanish Argus has hardly any orange lunules on the upperside.

Flight: June to August, flying low over the vegetation and commonly basking with its wings wide open in weak sunshine.

Habitat: Flower-rich grassland, mainly on limestone; most common in upland areas and reaching 2,500 m (8,200 ft) in the Alps and Pyrenees, but flying at sea level in the far north. The principal larval foodplant is Common Rock-rose, but stork's-bills and crane's-bills are used in some areas.

Life-cycle: The eggs are pale green or cream with white sculpturing and very like those of the Brown Argus. They are laid singly, usually on the uppersides of the leaves, and they hatch within about a week. The caterpillar is pale green with a darker green line on the back and a pink line on each side. It hibernates in the leaf-litter after the third or fourth moult, and completes its growth in the spring. The mature caterpillar is up to 14 mm (0.6 in) long and it pupates in the turf or leaf-litter. The chrysalis is yellowish green with pink lines on the abdomen. Both caterpillar and chrysalis are attractive to ants and the chrysalis is often buried by them.

Range: Widely distributed from Greece and Spain to the Arctic, but confined to mountains in the southern parts of its range. It is absent from Ireland and its British range extends from Derbyshire to northern Scotland. Also occurs in North Africa and across temperate Asia to Mongolia.

The Mountain Argus, also known as the Northern Brown Argus, has several races or subspecies. The Scottish race (*A. a. artaxerxes*) always has a white spot on the forewing. This spot is usually absent in the English race (*A. a. salmacis*), but it is present in some specimens from Durham, where the two races grade into one another.

A. a. salmacis may be confused with the Brown Argus, although the two butterflies do not overlap in Britain. Continental butterflies usually have greyer undersides than British ones, and the spots are clearly black with white rings.

p.105 **Spanish Argus** *Aricia morronensis*

Description: 12–15 mm (0.5–0.6 in). The uppersides of both sexes are dark brown, with lightly chequered fringes. There is a prominent black spot, occasionally ringed with white, at the end of the forewing cell, and the hindwing may have a couple of small orange lunules at the rear. The undersides are light brown and the white-ringed, black spots are sometimes unusually large on the forewing. The front two spots on the hindwing normally line up to form a colon. Both wings carry pale-orange submarginal lunules.

Similar species: Brown Argus, Mountain Argus, and female Blue Argus have more orange lunules on the upperside.

Flight: May to August in one or two broods.

Habitat: Rough hillsides from 900 to 3,000 m (2,950–9,850 ft). The larval foodplants are various stork's-bills.

Life-cycle: Winter is passed in the caterpillar stage.

Range: Confined to Spain, where it flies in small, isolated colonies.

p.105 **Blue Argus** *Ultraaricia anteros*

Description: 15 mm (0.6 in). The male upperside is a shining pale blue with black borders, the inner edges of which are rather indistinct. There is a short black bar at the end of the cell in the forewing, and the hindwing carries an arc of black marginal spots bordered internally by small orange submarginal lunules. The female is rich brown, usually with rich-orange lunules on the hindwing and often on the forewing as well. The black marginal spots are prominent on the hindwing, and there is a strong black spot at the end of the cell in the forewing. The undersides range from grey to light brown, with the usual white-ringed black spots and an arc of bright-orange submarginal lunules on each wing. There is no black spot in the forewing cell.

Similar species: Female is like Brown Argus and other *Aricia* species, but lacks the colon-like mark under the hindwing. Eros Blue and other *Polyommatus* species have a black spot in the cell under the forewing.

Flight: May to September in one, two, or three broods.

Habitat: Flower-rich mountain slopes, usually between 1,000 and 2,000 m (3,275 and 6,550 ft). The larval foodplants are various crane's-bills.

Life-cycle: Nothing is known of the life-cycle of this butterfly.

Range: From the Adriatic coast, across the Balkans and Turkey to Iran.

---

p.106 **Silvery Argus** *Pseudaricia nicias*

Description: 12 mm (0.5 in) The male upperside is a pale, silvery blue with variable sooty-brown borders. These are wide in specimens from the mountains of southern Europe (*P. n. nicias*), but much narrower in *P. n. scandica* from Scandinavia. Both wings usually carry a small, but clearly visible black bar at the end of the cell, although this may be absent on the hindwing. The female upperside is entirely sooty brown. Both sexes have greyish fringes. The undersides of both sexes are pale greyish brown with small black spots, and a conspicuous white streak across the hindwing. There may be some faint orange submarginal lunules.

Similar species: Damon Blue is larger, and male has no spots at the end of the cell.

Flight: July to August.

Habitat: Montane slopes, between 900 and 2,000 m (2,950 and 6,550 ft) in the south but at much lower levels in the north; usually in sheltered spots, including woodland clearings. The larval foodplants are Wood Crane's-bill and Meadow Crane's-bill.

Life-cycle: The slightly flattened round eggs are pearly
white with a densely sculptured surface,
and they are laid singly or in small groups
on the stems of the foodplant. The eggs are
said to overwinter in Scandinavia, but in
the south they hatch soon after they are laid
and the caterpillars go into hibernation
when they are half-grown. The fully grown
caterpillar is about 12 mm (0.5 in) long; it
is pale green with a darker green line on the
back, and narrow brown and white stripes
on the side. It is clothed with short white
hair. It pupates on the ground, sometimes
surrounded by a few strands of silk. The
chrysalis is yellowish green.

Range: Alps, Pyrenees, and lightly wooded
mountain slopes in Sweden and Finland,
where it seems to be spreading into derelict
farmland. A local and generally rare
butterfly, although it is said to be more
widely distributed in Russia.

The butterfly is also called *Aricia nicias*.

p.107 **Alpine Argus** *Albulina orbitulus*

Description: 12–15 mm (0.5–0.6 in). The male
upperside ranges from a deep, shining sky-
blue to a greyish or steely blue, and is
unmarked apart from the narrow black
borders. The female is brown, often with a
slight blue dusting at the base. Both sexes
have clear white fringes, with brownish-
grey, rather hairy undersides that are often
tinged with green. There is usually an arc
of small, black post-discal spots under the
forewing, although these are sometimes
absent. The spots under the hindwing are
pure white with no black centres and are
very conspicuous.

Similar species: Female Arctic Blue is superficially similar
but the underside of the forewing usually
has dark-grey submarginal spots.

Flight: June to August, commonly basking on
the ground with wings open. The males
often gather to drink at cow-pats, in
common with the males of many other
montane blues.

Habitat: Montane grassland, between 1,000 and
2,500 m (3,275 and 8,200 ft) in the Alps
but down to about 800 m (2,625 ft) in
Scandinavia. The butterfly favours stream
banks and other damp spots. The major
larval foodplants are milk-vetches,
especially Alpine Milk-vetch, although a
few other leguminous plants may be eaten.

Life-cycle: The eggs are white and hemispherical with
a fine reticulate pattern and they are laid
singly on the leaves. The caterpillar is leaf-
green with fine brown hair and a faint
brown line along the back; and it is very
difficult to spot on the leaves. It hibernates
while still quite small and completes its
growth in the spring. The mature
caterpillar is about 12 mm (0.5 in) long
and it pupates at the base of the foodplant.
The chrysalis ranges from bright green to
yellowish brown.

Range: The Alpine Argus is widely distributed in
northern and central Asia, but in Europe it
is confined to the Alps and to a small area
of central Norway and Sweden.

---

p.108   **Glandon Blue** *Agriades glandon*

Description: 12–15 mm (0.5–0.6 in). The male upperside
is a pale, shining blue, with wide brown
borders whose inner margins merge
imperceptibly with the blue and sometimes
extend beyond the middle of the wing,
especially in specimens from southern Spain.
There may be a black spot at the end of the
cell in the forewing, and small dark spots
may be visible in the border of the
hindwing. The female is sooty brown, with
traces of marginal spots on the hindwing.
The undersides are generally greyish brown,
although sometimes dark brown in the
female. The forewing has a conspicuous
black spot in the cell and another at the end
of the cell, and there is an arc of black post-
discal spots. The submarginal spots beyond
them are grey. The underside of the
hindwing has a prominent white spot in the
centre, and there are usually one or two pale-
orange submarginal lunules near the rear.

Similar species: Gavarnie Blue male is greyer above, and both sexes have black submarginal spots under the forewing. Arctic Blue is smaller, with very few black spots underneath.

Flight: July to August, flying quickly but keeping close to the ground and frequently settling to bask in the sunshine.

Habitat: Montane slopes, often with very sparse vegetation, from about 1,500 m (4,925 ft) right up to the snow-line. The larval foodplants are snowbells, rock-jasmines, and other members of the primrose family.

Life-cycle: The eggs are yellowish white and hemispherical, and they are laid singly on the upper leaves of the foodplant. The slug-shaped caterpillar is bright green with a dark line on the back, the line being edged with white and crossed by a pink bar in each segment. There is also a pink stripe on each side of the body. The caterpillar hibernates deep in the leaf-rosettes and completes its growth in the spring. The mature caterpillar is about 10 mm (0.4 in) long and it pupates under stones or amongst the moss and leaf-litter. The chrysalis is green with red spots at first, but becomes brown with darker stripes.

Range: Alps, eastern Pyrenees, and Sierra Nevada.

---

p.109 **Arctic Blue** *Agriades aquilo*

Description: 10 mm (0.4 in). The male upperside is basically silvery grey with a pale-blue flush and variable brown borders that merge gradually into the general wing colour. There may be a few buff-ringed, darker spots around the outer margin of the hindwing. The female is shiny brown, usually with pale submarginal lunules around the hindwing and sometimes with a band of grey post-discal spots on the forewing. The undersides of both sexes are greyish brown with paler borders. There are usually a few white-ringed black spots on the forewing but the hindwing spots are plain white and the post-discal ones form wedges that extend to the outer border.

Similar species: Glandon Blue and Gavarnie Blue have much heavier spotting under the forewing.

Flight: June to August, darting rapidly from place to place but always keeping close to the ground and frequently settling to bask in the shelter of stones.

Habitat: Rocky areas with sparse vegetation, where the resting butterflies are very well camouflaged, from sea level to about 1,000 m (3,275 ft), but only where there is shelter from the wind. The usual larval foodplants are Purple Saxifrage and Yellow Mountain Saxifrage.

Life-cycle: The eggs are bluish or greenish white and are laid singly or in small groups. The caterpillar is green with reddish spots and a pale-edged dark stripe on the back, and with a reddish line on each side. It hibernates and then completes its growth in the spring. The mature caterpillar is about 10 mm (0.4 in) long and it pupates on the ground. The chrysalis is pale brown with darker stripes.

Range: Arctic Scandinavia, mainly on the coastal lowlands.

The Arctic Blue is sometimes regarded as a subspecies of the Glandon Blue. The High Mountain Blue (*Agriades franklinii*) of North America is closely related and may be conspecific.

---

p.109   **Gavarnie Blue** *Agriades pyrenaicus*

Description: 14 mm (0.6 in). The male upperside is silvery grey with narrow, sooty-brown borders. There is a small dark spot at the end of the cell in the forewing, and there may be some faint white submarginal lunules on the hindwing. The female is dull brown with a conspicuous black spot on the forewing, and there may be white submarginal markings on both wings. Both sexes have white fringes. The undersides are grey or brown and the forewing has black submarginal spots and an irregular line of post-discal spots. The underside of the hindwing has large white blotches but hardly any black.

Similar species: Glandon Blue has a bluer male, and the underside has grey submarginal spots and a more regular post-discal line.

Flight: June to August, usually keeping close to the ground.

Habitat: Montane grassland and scree, between 1,500 and 2,400 m (4,925 and 7,875 ft). The larval foodplants are rock jasmines and possibly snowbells.

Life-cycle: The hemispherical, pale-green eggs are laid singly on the foodplant and the caterpillar hibernates when partly grown, but little else is known of the life-cycle of this butterfly.

Range: In scattered, isolated colonies in the Pyrenees, the Cantabrian Mountains of northern Spain, and the Balkans, and on through Turkey to the Caucasus.

Butterflies from the Cantabrian Mountains (*A.p. asturiensis*) usually have well-marked white submarginal lunules on the hindwing in both sexes. In the Balkans, where the species is in danger of extinction, the male upperside is heavily dusted with brown.

p.110 **Mazarine Blue** *Cyaniris semiargus*

Description: 12–18 mm (0.5–0.7 in). The male upperside is deep violet-blue and unmarked apart from the narrow black borders. The female upperside is chocolate-brown, sometimes with a faint violet flush at the base. Both sexes have prominent white fringes. The undersides are pale brown in both sexes, with small, white-ringed black spots and a slight blue flush near the base. There are no marginal markings.

Similar species: Greek Mazarine Blue male has similar uppersides but has red markings below. Osiris Blue has much greyer undersides.

Flight: May to October in one, two, or three broods, but probably single-brooded in most areas. Usually flies quite slowly and keeps close to the ground. Males sometimes gather in large numbers to drink from muddy puddles and seepages, and both sexes bask on the ground or on short turf with their wings wide open.

Habitat: Flower-rich grassland, from sea level to about 2,200 m (7,225 ft). The major larval foodplant is Red Clover, but other leguminous plants are probably used as well.

Life-cycle: The hemispherical eggs are bluish or greenish white and heavily sculptured. They are laid singly on or near the flowers of the foodplant. The caterpillar tunnels into the flowerheads and feeds on the developing seeds at first, but older larvae feed on the leaves. It is slug-like, up to 14 mm (0.6 in) long when mature, and pale green with a darker line on the back. Final-brood caterpillars go into hibernation in dead flowerheads when half-grown and complete their growth in the spring. Pupation takes place on the foodplant, to which the speckled brown chrysalis is attached by strands of silk.

Range: Throughout Europe except the British Isles and the Arctic, and across temperate Asia to Mongolia. Once resident in the British Isles, it became extinct towards the end of the 19th century and now occurs only as a very occasional summer visitor.

---

p.110 **Greek Mazarine Blue** *Cyaniris helena*

Description: 14 mm (0.6 in). The male upperside is a rich violet-blue, with narrow black borders. The female upperside is chocolate-brown, with orange submarginal lunules on the hindwing and in the rear half of the forewing. Both sexes have white fringes. The undersides are pale brown or greyish brown in both sexes, with large orange lunules in the rear half of the hindwing and small white-ringed, black post-discal spots on both wings.

Similar species: Mazarine Blue and several others have similar uppersides, but none has the red pattern under the hindwing.

Flight: April to July.

Habitat: Montane grassland, usually between 1,200 and 1,500 m (3,925 and 4,925 ft). The larval foodplants are clovers, especially *Trifolium physodes*.

Life-cycle: The early stages of this butterfly are very like those of Mazarine Blue in both appearance and behaviour, although hibernation and pupation are more likely to take place on the ground.

Range: Southern Greece and the eastern Mediterranean.

The Greek Mazarine Blue is variously regarded as a subspecies of the Mazarine Blue or as a true species. In some recent literature it has been renamed *Cyaniris antiochena*.

p.111 **Damon Blue** *Agrodiaetus damon*

Description: 14–18 mm (0.6–0.7 in). The male upperside is generally a pale shiny blue, although the intensity varies a good deal from place to place. There are wide greyish-brown borders, and the dark scales extend along the veins towards the middle of the wings. The female is dull brown, sometimes with a few blue scales at the base. Both sexes have white fringes. The undersides are greyish brown in both sexes, but usually browner in the female, and the black spots are much larger on the forewing than on the hindwing. The latter has a prominent white streak running through the centre.

Similar species: Furry Blue underside has a much less obvious white streak and the male upperside has a patch of brownish scent-scales near the base of the forewing. The anomalous blues have brownish fringes.

Flight: July to September, often gathering to drink from dung and muddy puddles.

Habitat: Upland scrub and grassland, usually on calcareous soils, from 400 to about 3,000 m (1,300–9,850 ft). The larval foodplants are sainfoins.

Life-cycle: The hemispherical eggs are greenish white and clothed with short spines. They are laid singly or in two and threes on the flowers and fruiting heads of the foodplant. Winter

is passed either in the egg stage or as a small caterpillar. The caterpillar feeds on the flowers and leaves and is regularly attended by ants. The mature caterpillar is green with a darker line along the back and it is about 15 mm (0.6 in) long. It pupates in the leaf-litter and the chrysalis is dull yellow or olive green.

Range: Scattered through southern and central Europe, as far north as Estonia, and on through temperate Asia to China. Absent from the British Isles and neighbouring areas of the Continent. The butterfly is very local and endangered in several parts of its European range.

---

p.111 **Chelmos Blue** *Agrodiaetus iphigenia*

Description: 15 mm (0.6 in). The male upperside is shiny sky-blue with black borders. The outer regions of some of the veins may carry dark scales and there is a brownish smudge of scent scales near the middle of the forewing. The female is brown and unmarked. Both sexes have white fringes. The undersides are brownish grey in both sexes, with a scattering of deep-blue scales near the base and a narrow white streak through the centre of the hindwing. The post-discal spots are well marked on both wings, but noticeably larger on the forewing.

Similar species: Male Damon Blue has paler uppersides, but the females are very hard to distinguish – look for the slightly darker brown underside of the Damon Blue. The anomalous blues have brown fringes.

Flight: June to July.

Habitat: Rough montane grassland between 500 and 1,500 m (1,650 and 4,925 ft). The larval foodplants are sainfoins.

Life-cycle: The larvae feed in the seed pods of the foodplant and hibernate while still quite small.

Range: Southern Greece, where it is known only from Mount Chelmos, and eastwards through Asia to the Caspian.

p.112 **Furry Blue** *Agrodiaetus dolus*

Description: 15–20 mm (0.6–0.8 in). The male upperside ranges from silvery white to a very pale silvery blue, with indistinct brown borders of variable width. The outer parts of the veins are usually heavily marked with brown, and there is a large patch of brown scent-scales at the base of the forewing. This area is rather fluffy and gives the butterfly its common name. The female is plain brown, with dark veins in the outer region and sometimes with dark spots around the edge of the hindwing. Both sexes have white fringes. The male underside is pale grey and that of the female is pale brown. The black post-discal spots are larger on the forewing than on the hindwing. There is often a faint white streak through the centre of the hindwing in both sexes.

Similar species: Chalk-hill Blue is similar in flight, but the underside is very different. Damon Blue has a stronger white streak under the hindwing, and the male lacks the furry patch on the upperside of the forewing. The anomalous blues have brown fringes.

Flight: June to August.

Habitat: Rough grassland, from lowlands to about 1,800 m (5,900 ft). The larval foodplants are sainfoins and Lucerne.

Life-cycle: The eggs are laid singly on the foodplants and the caterpillar is regularly tended by ants. It hibernates when it is still quite small, and it pupates in the leaf-litter.

Range: Confined to northern Spain, southern France, and Italy. The species is local and generally rare.

The Italian race (*A. d. virgilius*), with its silvery-white male, is sometimes regarded as a separate species. Forster's Furry Blue (*A. ainsae*), found only in northern Spain, is visually identical and, although it may be a little smaller, it is distinguished from the Furry Blue only by its lower chromosome number.

Anomalous Blues

The following seven species, confined mainly to the Mediterranean area, have brown uppersides in both sexes and are very difficult to separate. The only sure way to distinguish some of the species may be to examine the chromosomes. Each species seems to have a different chromosome number, but the taxonomy of the group is by no means settled. Several of the species have been discovered only during the last few years, and more may well await discovery.

Although the anomalous blues are listed here in the genus *Agrodiaetus*, some entomologists have proposed putting them and all other *Agrodiaetus* species into the genus *Polyommatus*, together with the genera *Plebicula* and *Lysandra*.

p.113   **Anomalous Blue** *Agrodiaetus admetus*

Description: 15–20 mm (0.6–0.8 in). The uppersides of both sexes are plain brown with brown fringes, although the male can be distinguished by the patch of hairy scent-scales at the base of the forewing. The female sometimes has faint orange lunules near the rear corner of the hindwing. The undersides are yellowish brown with conspicuous white-ringed, black post-discal spots and pale-brown marginal and submarginal lunules. These lunules are most obvious in the female.

Similar species: Most other anomalous blues lack obvious marginal markings on the underside, but accurate determination can be made only by examining the chromosomes. Ripart's Anomalous Blue has a white streak under the hindwing.

Flight: June to August.

Habitat: Dry, stony slopes from sea level to about 1,000 m (3,275 ft). The larval foodplants are sainfoins.

Life-cycle: Winter is passed in the larval stage.

Range: Eastern Europe, from the Czech Republic to Greece, and on through Turkey. A local species, occurring in widely scattered colonies.

p.114 Ripart's Anomalous Blue
Agrodiaetus ripartii

Description: 14–18 mm (0.6–0.8 in). The uppersides of both sexes are plain brown with brown fringes, although the male has a large patch of hairy scent-scales at the base of the forewing. The female may have a few faint orange spots near the rear corner of the hindwing. The undersides are yellowish brown, with a white streak through the centre of the hindwing. There are white-ringed, black post-discal spots on both wings, but marginal spots are very faint or absent.

Similar species: Higgins' Anomalous Blue is slightly darker above. Apart from Andalusian Anomalous Blue, the other anomalous blues lack the white stripe under the hindwing. Damon Blue and Furry Blue females have white fringes.

Flight: June to August, often feeding at lavender flowers.

Habitat: Dry, sunny slopes from sea level to 1,000 m (3,275 ft) or more. The larval foodplants are sainfoins, especially Rock Sainfoin.

Life-cycle: The eggs are greenish white and hemispherical. The caterpillar is pale green and rather hairy, with numerous greyish spots. It hibernates when half-grown and completes its growth in the spring. It pupates in leaf-litter, and the chrysalis is yellowish brown.

Range: Southern Europe, in scattered areas from northern Spain to Greece, and eastwards into Turkey.

The Greek race (*A. r. pelopi*), which reaches altitudes of about 1,500 m (4,925 ft), has sometimes been regarded as a distinct species and named the Chestnut Anomalous Blue, but recent studies suggest that it may actually be conspecific with the Grecian Anomalous Blue.

Oberthür's Anomalous Blue
Agrodiaetus fabressei

Description: 18 mm (0.7 in). The uppersides of both sexes are plain brown with brown fringes, although the male has an extensive patch of hairy scent-scales at the base of the forewing. The undersides are pale brown with conspicuous white-ringed, black post-discal spots, but the marginal spots, if present at all, are very faint.

Similar species: Anomalous Blue has more obvious marginal spots on the underside. Grecian Anomalous Blue is a little darker on the upperside.

Flight: June to August.

Habitat: Sunny hillsides and mountain slopes, usually between 900 and 1,500 m (2,950 and 4,925 ft), although the slightly darker and larger Catalonian race (*A. f. agenjoi*) flies at low altitudes. The larval foodplants are sainfoins, especially Rock Sainfoin.

Life-cycle: Winter is passed as a small caterpillar. The mature caterpillar is about 25 mm (1.0 in) long and is lime green with darker diagonal stripes and a purple and white stripe on each side.

Range: Confined to Spain, in small and scattered colonies.

The subspecies *A. f. agenjoi*, which is confined to northeast Spain, has sometimes been treated as a separate species and called Agenjo's Anomalous Blue.

p.114 Grecian Anomalous Blue
Agrodiaetus aroaniensis

Description: 15–18 mm (0.6–0.7 in). The uppersides of both sexes are dark brown with brown fringes, and the male has a large patch of hairy scent-scales at the base of the forewing. The undersides are yellowish or reddish brown with conspicuous white-ringed, black post-discal spots, but there is rarely any hint of marginal markings. Some specimens have a faint white streak across the hindwing.

Similar species: Higgins' Anomalous Blue has a white streak on the underside of the hindwing. The other anomalous blues, apart from the Piedmont Anomalous Blue and the Catalonian race of Oberthür's Anomalous Blue, are noticeably paler on the upperside.

Flight: June to August.

Habitat: Grassland, usually between 700 and 1,800 m (2,300 and 5,900 ft) although it sometimes occurs at lower altitudes. The larval foodplants are sainfoins, especially Small Sainfoin.

Life-cycle: Winter is probably passed as a small larva, as in related species.

Range: Confined to Greece.

Andalusian Anomalous Blue
Agrodiaetus violetae

Description: 15 mm (0.6 in). The uppersides of both sexes are plain brown with brown fringes. The male has a large patch of hairy scent-scales at the base of the forewing. The undersides are pale brown with the usual prominent post-discal spots and there is usually a white streak across the hindwing, although this is sometimes quite faint.

Similar species: Ripart's Anomalous Blue is visually identical, but the two species do not overlap and no other anomalous blues are known from southern Spain.

Flight: July to August.

Habitat: Montane slopes up to about 1,600 m (5,250 ft). The larval foodplants are sainfoins.

Life-cycle: Winter is probably passed as a small caterpillar.

Range: Confined to southern Spain, where it occurs in just a few scattered colonies.

It is possible that this butterfly is merely a race of Ripart's Anomalous Blue.

Higgins' Anomalous Blue
Agrodiaetus nephohiptamenos

Description: 15 mm (0.6 in). The uppersides of both sexes are plain brown, with a slightly golden sheen and relatively pale fringes. The male has a large patch of hairy scent-scales at the base of the forewing. The undersides are pale yellowish grey, with a prominent white streak across the hindwing. The white-ringed, black post-discal spots are noticeably larger on the forewing than on the hindwing.

Similar species: Ripart's Anomalous Blue has a slightly paler upperside and lacks the golden sheen. Most other anomalous blues lack the white streak under the hindwing. Female Damon Blue has white fringes.

Flight: July to August.

Habitat: Grassy slopes between 1,600 and 2,000 m (5,250 and 6,550 ft). The larval foodplant is Mountain Sainfoin.

Life-cycle: As in the related species, winter is probably passed in the caterpillar stage.

Range: Greece and southern Italy.

The Italian race (*A. n. galloi*), which is a little smaller than the nominate race in Greece, is probably a distinct species – Gallo's Anomalous Blue. It is more common than the Greek race, which is very local and possibly in danger of extinction.

---

p.115 **Piedmont Anomalous Blue**
Agrodiaetus humedasae

Description: 17–20 mm (0.7–0.8 in). The male upperside is dark brown, with dark fringes and a large patch of hairy scent-scales at the base of the forewing. The female is a little smaller, with paler fringes and one, two or three faint orange lunules at the rear of the hindwing. Both sexes have a black mark at the end of the cell in the forewing. The undersides are pale brown and the post-discal spots of the forewing are generally much larger than those of the hindwing. There are darker smudges around the edges of both wings, although these are not always obvious in the male.

Similar species: Only Ripart's Anomalous Blue occurs in the same area, and this has a white streak under the hindwing.

Flight: July to August.

Habitat: Montane meadows on warm slopes at about 900 m (2,950 ft). The larval foodplants are sainfoins.

Life-cycle: The eggs are laid singly on the foodplant, usually on the flowers, and the young caterpillars hibernate in the surrounding turf or leaf-litter. Mature caterpillars are green and about 15 mm (0.6 in) long.

Range: Restricted to a few valleys on the Swiss–Italian border.

This butterfly was originally regarded as a subspecies of Oberthür's Anomalous Blue.

---

p.115 **Escher's Blue** *Agrodiaetus escheri*

Description: 15–20 mm (0.6–0.8 in). The male upperside is bright blue, often with a violet sheen, and has black borders and white fringes, the latter being lightly chequered on the hindwing. There is a silvery patch at the front of the forewing. The female is chocolate-brown, sometimes with a slight blue dusting at the base, and with dirty-white fringes without any chequering. There is usually a full set of orange submarginal lunules on each wing, although these may be reduced on the forewing. The undersides are grey in the male and brown in the female, with a slight blue dusting at the base of the hindwing and usually a white wedge in the outer part of the wing. The white-edged, black spots are quite heavy and orange submarginal lunules are usually present on both wings. There is no black spot in the cell of the forewing.

Similar species: Adonis Blue has fully chequered fringes in both sexes, and a black spot in the cell under the forewing. Common Blue has a black spot in the cell under the forewing and no chequered fringes. Amanda's Blue has no

chequered fringes and has smaller, more oval
post-discal spots under the forewing.

Flight: May to August, frequently feeding at the
flowers of Wild Thyme.

Habitat: Rough, flowery grassland from sea level to
about 2,000 m (6,550 ft), although most
common in upland areas. The main larval
foodplants are milk-vetches, but sainfoins
and possibly Wild Thyme may be used in
some areas.

Life-cycle: The eggs are pale green and elegantly
sculptured like tiny cup-cakes. They are
laid singly on the foodplant. The caterpillar
is green with longitudinal yellow stripes
and it feeds on the flowers and leaves. It
goes into hibernation when still quite small
and completes its growth in the spring,
usually with ants in attendance. The
mature caterpillar is up to 18 mm (0.7 in)
long and it pupates among the stones and
leaf-litter at the base of the foodplant. The
chrysalis is bronzy green and rather shiny.

Range: Southern Europe and North Africa.

A. e. dalmaticus from the Balkans has wider
black borders on the male than the typical
race and also has a very pale underside.

---

p.116 **Amanda's Blue** *Agrodiaetus amanda*

Description: 15–20 mm (0.6–0.8 in). The male
upperside is a bright sky-blue, sometimes
with a silvery appearance, and with dark-
grey borders of variable width. The dark
scales extend inwards along the outer parts
of the veins, and the hindwing may bear
black or grey spots around the outer edge.
The female is chocolate-brown, often
dusted with blue at the base and usually
with orange submarginal lunules on the
hindwing. Both sexes have white fringes.
The underside is pale grey in the male and
somewhat browner in the female, with
relatively small, white-ringed, black spots
that are markedly oval on the forewing.
There is a basal blue flush on the hindwing.
Both sexes have orange submarginal lunules
on the hindwing, and the female may have

some on the forewing as well. The forewing has rather faint marginal markings and there is no black spot in the cell.

Similar species: Escher's Blue has heavier spotting on the underside and the female has more extensive orange lunules. Turquoise Blue has white borders on the underside.

Flight: May to August, flying quite strongly but keeping fairly close to the ground. The males commonly drink from animal dung and damp ground.

Habitat: Flower-rich grassland, both wet and dry, from sea level to about 2,000 m (6,550 ft); most common in upland regions, including Alpine hay-meadows, although the species is declining in many parts of its range. The main larval foodplant is Tufted Vetch, but other vetches are frequently used.

Life-cycle: The eggs are greenish white and hemispherical with a densely sculptured and rather spiky surface. They are laid singly on the foodplant. The caterpillar goes into hibernation in the leaf-litter while still quite small, and growth is completed in the spring, often with ants in close attendance. The mature caterpillar is grass-green with yellow or white stripes, and clothed with white hair. It is about 24 mm (1.0 in) long. It pupates among leaves on or near the ground and the chrysalis is green or brown.

Range: Most of Europe, but absent from the far north, the British Isles, and most of France. Also in North Africa and Southwest Asia.

---

p.116 **Chapman's Blue** *Agrodiaetus thersites*

Description: 15 mm (0.6 in). The male upperside is light blue, tinged with violet and with narrow black borders. The female is dark brown, extensively dusted with blue in the first brood. There are orange submarginal lunules on the hindwing and sometimes on the forewing as well. The hindwing also has black and blue marginal spots. Both sexes have white fringes. The underside is pale brownish grey in both sexes, with orange submarginal lunules on both wings and the usual white-ringed black spots. There is no spot in the cell of the forewing. There is a blue flush at the base of the hindwing in the first brood, although it is reduced or absent in second-brood insects, and there is usually a white flash in the outer part of the wing.

Similar species: Common Blue has a very similar upperside but has a black spot in the forewing cell on the underside. Escher's Blue is slightly larger and the male is less violet.

Flight: April to September in two or possibly three broods.

Habitat: Flower-rich fields and hillsides, including hay-meadows, from sea level to about 2,000 m (6,550 ft). The larval foodplants are sainfoins.

Life-cycle: The greenish-white eggs are disc-shaped with a strongly sculptured surface, and they are laid singly on the foodplant. The rather hairy caterpillar is grass-green with paler stripes. Final-brood caterpillars go into hibernation and complete their growth in the spring. The mature caterpillar is about 15 mm (0.6 in) long and it pupates in the leaf-litter. The chrysalis is light green and smudged with brown at each end.

Range: Southern and central Europe, and eastwards to central Asia; also in North Africa. Absent from the British Isles.

p.117 **Pontic Blue** *Neolysandra coelestina*

Description: 12 mm (0.5 in). The male upperside is deep blue with wide black margins. The female is plain brown with traces of yellow lunules at the rear of the hindwing. Both sexes have white fringes. The undersides are grey with few spots other than the post-discal arcs, and there is a shiny blue flush on the hindwing. The female may have a few yellowish submarginal lunules on the hindwing.

Similar species: Green-underside Blue has larger spots under the forewing. Mazarine Blue has narrower black borders and is generally browner underneath.

Flight: June to July.

Habitat: Mountain slopes up to about 1,500 m (4,925 ft). The larval foodplants are vetches – mainly Tufted Vetch.

Life-cycle: The caterpillar hibernates while still quite small and completes its growth in the spring. It is green with a dark brown dorsal stripe and it pupates in the soil or leaf litter when mature. The chrysalis is light brown.

Range: Southern Greece and eastwards to the Caucasus.

---

p.118 **Turquoise Blue** *Plebicula dorylas*

Description: 15–18 mm (0.6–0.7 in). The male upperside is a shiny sky-blue with a slight turquoise sheen when seen from certain angles and a violet tinge when viewed from another direction. There are narrow black borders, from which black scales extend inwards along the extremities of the veins. The female, which is noticeably smaller than the male, is brown, often with a blue dusting at the base. There are usually orange submarginal lunules on the hindwing, and sometimes on the forewing as well. Both sexes have white fringes. The male underside is brownish grey with broad white borders, faint orange submarginal lunules, and very pale marginal markings. The black spots are noticeably larger on the forewing than on the hindwing. The female underside is similar but the ground colour is pale brown.

Similar species: Nevada Blue is smaller. Female Mother-of-Pearl Blue usually has better developed orange lunules on the upperside and less obvious white borders on the underside.

Flight: May to September in one or two broods, flying strongly in the sunshine and feeding avidly at Wild Thyme.

Habitat: Flowery fields and scrubby hillsides, often with sparse vegetation but always with a sunny, sheltered aspect, on well-drained soils. Most colonies are found above about 600 m (1,975 ft), and usually between 900 and 2,000 m (2,950 and 6,550 ft). The larval foodplants are Kidney Vetch and possibly other leguminous species.

Life-cycle: The eggs are bluish white and button-shaped, with conspicuous hexagonal sculpturing. They are laid singly on the

foodplant. The caterpillar is pale green and downy, with white flecks and stripes, and it is usually attended by ants. Final-brood caterpillars go into hibernation and complete their growth in the spring. The mature caterpillar is about 15 mm (0.6 in) long and it pupates on the ground, in the leaf-litter or amongst young shoots. The chrysalis is greenish yellow.

Range: Southern and central Europe, including southern Sweden, and eastwards into western Asia. Absent from the British Isles.

p.119 **Nevada Blue** *Plebicula golgus*

Description: 15 mm (0.6 in). The male upperside is deep blue with a violet tinge and prominent black borders, especially on the forewing. The female upperside is brown, usually with orange lunules on the hindwing. Both sexes have white fringes. The undersides are greyish or golden brown with white borders and orange submarginal lunules, although the latter are often very faint in the male. The black spots are larger on the forewing than on the hindwing, but there is no spot in the cell of the forewing.

Similar species: Turquoise Blue is larger, especially the male, and has more obvious white borders on the underside, but the two species do not overlap. Common Blue has a black spot in the cell under the forewing.

Flight: July.

Habitat: Rocky montane slopes, from 2,000 to 3,000 m (6,550–9,850 ft), where the snows remain for nine months and the ground is often very wet. The larval foodplant is believed to be an upland race of Kidney Vetch.

Life-cycle: Eggs are laid singly on the foodplant, and the caterpillars are regularly tended by ants. They hibernate in the third instar and complete their growth in the following summer before pupating in the ground at the base of the foodplant.

Range: Confined to the Sierra Nevada of southern Spain.

p.119 **Mother-of-pearl Blue** *Plebicula nivescens*

Description: 15–18 mm (0.6–0.7 in). The male upperside is a shining silvery grey or pearly colour, often becoming pale blue towards the dark-grey borders. The latter are broken into separate spots on the hindwing. The female is brown, usually with orange submarginal lunules on both wings. Both sexes have plain-white or off-white fringes. The undersides are pale yellowish grey, with faint orange lunules and indistinct grey marginal markings. The black spots on the forewing are much larger than those on the hindwing, especially in the female, and there is no spot in the cell of the forewing.

Similar species: Spanish Chalk-hill Blue and Provençal Chalk-hill Blue both have chequered fringes and a black spot in the cell on the underside of the forewing. Female Turquoise Blue has more obvious white borders on the underside.

Flight: June to August.

Habitat: Mountain slopes, generally between 1,000 and 2,000 m (3,275 and 6,550 ft). The larval foodplant is Kidney Vetch.

Life-cycle: Winter is passed as a small caterpillar.

Range: Confined to the eastern half of Spain.

p.120 **Meleager's Blue** *Meleageria daphnis*

Description: 18–20 mm (0.7–0.8 in). The upperside is shiny blue with sooty-black borders in both sexes, but the borders are noticeably wider in the female, and she also has a sooty front margin to the forewing and a conspicuous black spot at the end of the cell. Both sexes have plain-white fringes, and the rear of the hindwing is lightly scalloped – more so in the female than in the male. The undersides are grey or light brown, with black post-discal spots and grey marginal markings but no orange lunules.

Similar species: The scalloped hindwings should distinguish this butterfly from all other blues.

Flight: May to August.

Habitat: Warm, dry grasslands and roadsides from
            sea level to about 1,500 m (4,925 ft), but
            most common in upland areas. The usual
            larval foodplants are Crown Vetch and
            Wild Liquorice, but Wild Thyme may be
            used in some places.

Life-cycle: The greenish-white eggs are button-shaped
            and heavily sculptured. They are laid
            singly. Some eggs produce caterpillars
            within a week or two, but others do not
            hatch until the following spring;
            caterpillars produced in the summer go
            into a long hibernation when still quite
            small and complete their growth in the
            spring. The slug-like, but rather hairy
            caterpillar is leaf-green with darker stripes
            separated by yellow patches on the back. It
            is about 18 mm (0.7 in) long when mature
            and it pupates in the leaf-litter.

Range: A rather local butterfly in northern Spain
            and southern France, but more widely
            distributed in Italy and in eastern Europe
            from Greece to the Czech Republic and
            southern Poland. Also across southern Asia
            to Iran.

            In some areas many of the females have
            sooty-brown uppersides with just a light
            dusting of blue scales at the base. This form
            is known as f. *steeveni*.

---

p.121 **Chalk-hill Blue** *Lysandra coridon*

Description: 15–20 mm (0.6–0.8 in). The male
             upperside is silvery blue, with a wide sooty-
             brown border on the forewing. The
             hindwing border is broken up into separate
             oval spots. The female is brown, with faint
             orange submarginal lunules on the
             hindwing. Beyond these lunules are black
             spots, ringed on their outer edges by white
             scales. There is often a dusting of blue
             scales at the base, and in some areas this is
             quite extensive. Both sexes have chequered
             white fringes, although this is not always
             obvious on the male hindwing. The male
             underside is pale grey with abundant black
             spots, including a spot in the cell of the

forewing, and faint orange submarginal lunules on the hindwing. There is often a triangular white mark near the centre of the hindwing and usually a white flash near the outer edge. The female underside is similar except that the ground colour is pale brown.

Similar species: Mother-of-Pearl Blue does not have chequered fringes. Spanish Chalk-hill Blue is paler in both sexes, and female has orange lunules on the upperside of the forewing. Provençal Chalk-hill Blue male is paler, but females are virtually identical. Female Adonis Blue has blue scales beyond the lunules on the upperside of the hindwing.

Flight: June to September, usually keeping close to the ground and flying only in the sunshine. It feeds at a wide range of flowers and commonly basks with wings wide open.

Habitat: Open grassland on lime-rich soils, from sea level to about 2,000 m (6,550 ft). The larval foodplant is Horseshoe Vetch, although Bird's-foot Trefoil and some other low-growing leguminous plants are sometimes used as temporary food sources.

Life-cycle: The eggs are greenish white and button-shaped, with a coarsely sculptured surface. They are laid singly on or near the foodplant, and in most parts of Europe they do not hatch until the following spring. In the far south they hatch in the autumn and the caterpillars go into hibernation in the first or second instar. The caterpillar is regularly attended by and protected by ants after the first moult. It feeds mainly at night and the ants may even bury the caterpillar during the daytime to give it additional protection. The mature caterpillar is slug-like and downy, and about 15 mm (0.6 in) long. It is leaf-green with longitudinal yellow stripes. It pupates on the ground, and the smooth, olive-green or brownish-yellow chrysalis is usually carried away and buried by the attendant ants.

Range: Southern and central Europe, including southern Britain, and eastwards to the Urals.

The Chalk-hill Blue is a very variable butterfly and has several hundred named varieties and aberrations. The differences between them often concern the relative amounts of blue and brown on the wings. The female f. *syngrapha*, for example, is largely blue. It is possible that some of the geographical races – such as the Spanish *L. c. caelestissima*, which has bright-blue males – will turn out to be separate species.

p.122 **Provençal Chalk-hill Blue**
Lysandra hispana

Description: 15–18 mm (0.6–0.7 in). The male upperside is pale bluish grey, often becoming even paler towards the smoky-grey borders. The latter are broad and continuous on the forewing but broken into separate spots on the hindwing. The female is brown, with orange submarginal lunules on both wings. Both sexes have lightly chequered fringes. The undersides are pale grey in the male and pale brown in the female, with markings just like those of the Chalk-hill Blue.

Similar species: The typical Chalk-hill Blue male is a little bluer, but otherwise the two species are very difficult to separate; the females are visually identical. Spanish Chalk-hill Blue male is a more yellowish grey and has larger marginal spots on the upperside.

Flight: April to September in two broods, usually flying before and after the Chalk-hill Blue in the same area.

Habitat: Rough, flower-rich grassland from sea level to about 1,000 m (3,275 ft). The major larval foodplant is Crown Vetch, but other low-growing leguminous plants may also be used.

Life-cycle: Winter is probably passed in the larval stage.

Range: Northern Spain, southern France, and northwest Italy.

p.122 **Macedonian Chalk-hill Blue**
Lysandra philippi

Description: 15–19 mm (0.6–0.75 in). The male upperside is shiny blue with a continuous sooty-grey border on the forewing, and a border of dark-grey spots on the hindwing. Dark scales extend inwards along the outer parts of the veins. The female has a smoky-brown or greyish ground colour, but the wings are sometimes heavily suffused with blue and the hindwing may be almost entirely blue with a border of grey spots. Both sexes have chequered fringes. The ground colour of the undersides ranges from pale brown to almost white, with the usual black spotting although the spots on the hindwing are very much smaller than those on the forewing. There are orange submarginal lunules on the hindwing of the male and on both wings in the female.

Similar species: Both sexes are visually indistinguishable from some Spanish races of the Chalk-hill Blue.

Flight: July.

Habitat: Mountain slopes from about 600 to 2,000 m (1,975–6,550 ft), where the males bask on the sun-drenched scree. The larval foodplant is Horseshoe Vetch.

Life-cycle: Winter is passed in the larval stage.

Range: Known only from northeast Greece, where it was discovered in the 1970s, and must be considered a rare and vulnerable species.

Despite its similarity to Spanish races of the Chalk-hill Blue, chromosome studies indicate that the Macedonian Chalk-hill Blue is not conspecific with them.

p.122 **Spanish Chalk-hill Blue** *Lysandra albicans*

Description: 18–21 mm (0.7–0.8 in). The male upperside is mostly yellowish grey or cream, but specimens from the hot south may be almost white. Some specimens have a blue tinge all over, but others have no more than a blue dusting at the base and some have no blue at all. The wide, smoky-grey borders contain darker spots, which are much more obvious on the hindwing than on the forewing. The female is dull brown with spotted borders and often with faint orange submarginal lunules on both wings. Both sexes have lightly chequered fringes. The underside of the male forewing is white with relatively small black spots, including one in the cell. The underside of the hindwing is pale yellowish brown with faint orange submarginal lunules. The female underside is greyish brown with the usual pattern of black spots, but those of the forewing are noticeably larger than in the male and clearly ringed with white.

Similar species: Provençal Chalk-hill Blue male lacks the yellowish tinge and has less obvious spotting on the forewing. Mother-of-Pearl Blue lacks chequered fringes. Chalk-hill Blue is always much bluer where the two species overlap.

Flight: June to August.

Habitat: Rough, grassy slopes, usually between 900 and 1,500 m (2,950 and 4,925 ft). The larval foodplants are Horseshoe Vetch and probably other low-growing leguminous plants.

Life-cycle: Winter is probably passed in the larval stage.

Range: Eastern Spain and neighbouring parts of North Africa.

---

p.123 **Adonis Blue** *Lysandra bellargus*

Description: 14–18 mm (0.6–0.7 in). The male upperside is a brilliant sky-blue, unmarked apart from the thin black marginal line. The female is rich chocolate-brown, often dusted with blue near the base. There are orange-red submarginal lunules on the hindwing, with black spots and blue scales beyond them. Both sexes have strongly chequered white fringes. The undersides are greyish brown in both sexes, with a hint of blue near the base of the hindwing. There are orange submarginal lunules on both wings and there is a conspicuous white wedge in the outer part of the hindwing. The black spots are well developed and include a small but conspicuous one in the middle of the forewing cell.

Similar species: The intense sky-blue of the wings together with the chequered fringes distinguishes the male from all other blues. The female can be distinguished from the Chalk-hill Blue female by the marginal spots on the hindwing: there are blue scales beyond them in the Adonis Blue, but white ones in the Chalk-hill Blue.

Flight: May to September, usually in two broods. It often basks on flowers with wings wide open, and males frequently drink from moist ground.

Habitat: Warm, well-drained slopes on calcareous soils, from sea level to about 2,000 m (6,550 ft). The butterfly requires short turf and plenty of bare ground. The main larval foodplant is Horseshoe Vetch, but Crown Vetch and other low-growing leguminous plants are used on the Continent.

Life-cycle: The white eggs are button-shaped, with spiky sculpturing, and they are laid singly on the young leaves – usually on those shoots growing close to the ground. The caterpillar is pale green in the first instar but then becomes deep green with two rows of yellow streaks on the back and a yellow line on each side. Unlike the very similar larva of the Chalk-hill Blue, the caterpillar feeds by day and is rarely without attendant ants, which even put the caterpillar to bed at night by burying it in a shallow chamber. Second-brood caterpillars hibernate in any of their first three instars, attached to a silken pad spun on one of the lower leaves of the foodplant. The mature caterpillar is about 15 mm (0.6 in) long. It pupates on the ground, but the greenish chrysalis is quickly buried by ants, close to or even inside their nests, and the ants continue to lavish attention on it throughout the pupal stage.

Range: Southern and central Europe, and on across southern Asia to Iran. British populations

are confined to southern England and rarely found north of a line joining the Thames and Severn estuaries.

Occasional females (f. *ceronus*) have an extensive blue suffusion on the upperside, sometimes covering the whole surface except for a small brown marginal strip. The Adonis Blue was known as the Clifden Blue until the end of the 19th century.

p.124 **Common Blue** *Polyommatus icarus*

Description: 12–18 mm (0.5–0.7 in). The male upperside is bright blue with a strong-violet tinge, especially in the second brood, and unmarked apart from the thin black marginal line on each wing. The fringes are plain white. The female upperside is basically brown with a variable dusting of violet or blue although some specimens, especially in the north, are effectively blue with brown borders. Orange submarginal lunules are usually present on both wings, and the hindwing also has marginal black spots between the veins. The fringes range from white to brown, but are never chequered. The male underside is brownish grey or fawn with a blue or turquoise dusting at the base and well developed white-ringed black spots, including one in the middle of the cell of the forewing. Orange submarginal lunules are usually present on both wings, although they are much larger and brighter on the hindwing than on the forewing. A white wedge extends along vein 4 from the post-discal spots to the orange lunules. The ground colour of the female underside is mid-brown, with all markings heavier than in the male.

Similar species: The plain fringes and the black spot in the cell under the forewing will distinguish the Common Blue from most similar blues. Eros Blue and False Eros Blue males generally lack the violet sheen and have broader black borders; females have poorly developed orange lunules on the upperside.

Flight: April to October, usually in two or three broods but with just one brood in northern areas, including Scotland and northern parts of Ireland. The insects stay close to the ground and, like many other blues, they bask in weak sunshine with their wings wide open and separated. Males are strongly attracted to wet ground and to animal dung and urine.

Habitat: Almost any rough, grassy habitat, including roadsides and woodland clearings, from sea level to about 2,500 m (8,200 ft). The larval foodplants include Bird's-foot Trefoil, Restharrow, and a wide range of other low-growing leguminous plants.

Life-cycle: The eggs are greenish white and bun-shaped, with reticulate surface sculpturing. They are usually laid singly on the young shoots of the foodplant, and the caterpillars feed on both leaves and flowers. The caterpillar is leaf-green and rather downy, with a darker stripe along the back and a white stripe on each side. Final-brood caterpillars hibernate in the third instar, after attaching themselves to the lower parts of the foodplant or to the surrounding leaf-litter. Although many females select plants growing on or near ant-hills for egg-laying, the caterpillar is not attractive to the ants until the final instar, when it is eagerly sought out and 'milked', although the degree of attraction for the ants seems to depend on the quality of the plants on which the caterpillars are feeding. The mature caterpillar is about 13 mm (0.5 in) long. It normally pupates on the ground, often under cover of a few strands of silk, but the chrysalis, which is green with brown smudges, is quickly buried by ants.

Range: Throughout Europe, temperate Asia, and North Africa. One of Europe's commonest butterflies.

Single-brooded populations, occurring mainly in the north, tend to be larger and bluer than others and often have reduced spotting on the underside.

p.125 **Eros Blue** *Polyommatus eros*

Description: 12–15 mm (0.5–0.6 in). The male upperside is pale, shining sky-blue, with conspicuous black borders from which dark scales extend inwards along the outer parts of the veins. The hindwing also has black marginal spots between the veins. The female upperside is dark brown, often lightly dusted with pale-blue scales at the base. Orange submarginal lunules may be present on both wings, although they are often very faint, and the hindwing has an arc of black marginal spots. Both sexes have plain white fringes. The undersides are brownish grey in both sexes, with blue dusting at the base. Orange submarginal lunules occur on the hindwing and sometimes on the forewing as well. The black spots are just like those of the Common Blue, always with one in the cell of the forewing.

Similar species: Common Blue male has much narrower black margins and female has stronger-orange lunules on both surfaces. False Eros Blue is usually a little larger, except in southern Greece, and has larger orange lunules on the underside.

Flight: June to September, often feeding at Wild Thyme and basking with wings wide open on other low-growing vegetation. The males often congregate to drink from damp ground.

Habitat: Montane slopes, mostly between 1,500 and 2,500 m (4,925 and 8,200 ft). The larval foodplants include milk-vetches, especially the Yellow Milk-vetch and Silky Milk-vetch.

Life-cycle: The eggs are pale green and bun-shaped, and they are laid on the upper surfaces of the leaves. The caterpillar goes into hibernation while still quite small and completes its growth in the spring. The caterpillar is grass-green, with pale longitudinal stripes, and quite downy. It is about 12 mm (0.5 in) long when mature and may be attended by ants in its later stages. It pupates at the base of the foodplant, and the chrysalis is olive-green.

Range: A local and generally quite rare butterfly, found in scattered colonies in the Alps and other mountains of southern Europe and eastwards into central Asia.

P. e. menelaos from southern Greece is slightly larger and paler than the typical race and is sometimes regarded as a distinct species – the Taygetos Blue.

---

p.125 **False Eros Blue** *Polyommatus eroides*

Description: 15–18 mm (0.6–0.7 in). The male upperside is shiny sky-blue with prominent black borders from which dark scales extend inwards along the outer parts of the veins. The hindwing has black marginal spots between the veins. The female upperside is dull greyish brown with little or no blue dusting and with variably developed orange submarginal lunules. Both sexes have plain-white fringes and greyish-brown undersides, usually with orange lunules on both wings. There is a black spot in the cell of the forewing and all black spots tend to be larger than in the Eros Blue.

Similar species: Eros Blue is generally a little smaller, except in southern Greece, and has smaller black spots on the underside. Common Blue male has a violet sheen, and female is rarely without any blue dusting at the base.

Flight: June to July.

Habitat: Montane slopes, mainly between 1,200 and 1,800 m (3,925 and 5,900 ft). The larvae probably feed on shrubby leguminous plants.

Life-cycle: Winter is passed in the larval stage.

Range: Scattered across eastern Europe, from Poland to Greece, and then eastwards into Turkey. A local and generally rare species, endangered throughout its European range.

METALMARKS BUTTERFLIES
(RIODINIDAE)

Caterpillar.

This family owes its common name to the brilliant metallic splashes adorning the wings of many of its 1,200 or so species. Most of them live in tropical America and only one occurs in Europe. The front legs are fully developed in the female, but those of the male are short and clawless and are not used for walking. The family is sometimes treated as a subfamily – the Riodininae – of the Lycaenidae. It is also known as the Nemeobiidae.

Chrysalis.

---

p.128 **Duke of Burgundy** *Hamearis lucina*

Description: 13–18 mm (0.5–0.7 in). The upperside is dark brown, with orange spots forming three fairly distinct transverse rows on the forewing. The spotting on the hindwing may be limited to the submarginal band, which has a dark centre to each orange spot. All spots tend to be larger in the female, which also has slightly more rounded wingtips. Second-brood insects have smaller orange spots. The underside is largely orange, with two distinct bands of white spots crossing the hindwing. Insects from southern areas are often noticeably larger than those from the north of the range. Because of its similarity to a small fritillary, the butterfly is often called the Duke of Burgundy Fritillary.

Similar species: Chequered Skipper is similar when at rest with wings open, but its spots are much yellower and those around the edges contain no dark spots. It also lacks the white bands on the underside and its antennae are hooked at the tip. The two butterflies have a similar dancing flight. Some of the smaller fritillaries also resemble the Duke of Burgundy, but these have largely orange uppersides and less obvious white bands on the underside.

Flight: April to September, with two broods in most areas although there is just one brood in the more northerly parts of its range.

British populations are normally single-brooded, although there is sometimes a partial second brood in August. Flight is swift and darting, very like that of many skippers, and the butterfly rarely flies far above the ground. It does not visit flowers with any great regularity and may get much of its food from the honeydew dropped by aphids. The butterfly commonly basks on the ground and on low-growing vegetation.

Habitat: Open woodland and scrubby hillsides from sea level to about 1,500 m (4,925 ft). The caterpillars feed on Cowslip, Primrose, and Oxlip.

Life-cycle: The round, pearly eggs are laid singly or in small groups on the undersides of the leaves in May and June, and – where there is a second generation – in July and August. The brown hairs of the developing caterpillars gradually show through the shells as the eggs develop. The caterpillar is slug-shaped, pale brown at first but becoming darker and hairier as it matures. It feeds at night and hides in the leaf-litter during the daytime, although young caterpillars may cling to the undersides of their foodplants all day. Up to 15 mm (0.6 in) when mature, it pupates in clumps of grass or in the surrounding leaf-litter. The hairy chrysalis is cream with black spots and is attached by a silken girdle. Winter is always passed in the pupal stage.

Range: Most of Europe, but absent from southern Iberia and most of Scandinavia. In the British Isles it is confined mainly to the southern counties of England, although there are colonies in the Lake District and in Yorkshire.

The butterfly lives in small colonies and rarely moves more than a few hundred metres during its life. Although originally a butterfly of coppiced woodlands, most Duke of Burgundy colonies in England now exist on scrub-covered hillsides. The decline of coppicing destroyed most of its original habitats, but the decline of sheep grazing on many hillsides allowed scrub to develop and this provided a new and very acceptable habitat for the butterfly. The advent of myxomatosis and the consequent fall in the rabbit population in the 1950s opened up even more habitat for the butterfly. But much of the scrub that developed has now become too dense to support it – or has been ploughed up and converted to arable land – and, although the butterfly still flourishes in some areas, it is declining rapidly in most places and is now one of Britain's more vulnerable species. It is still common in many parts of Europe, mainly in open woodland.

SNOUT BUTTERFLIES (LIBYTHEIDAE)

Caterpillar of Nettle-tree Butterfly.

This small family has only about ten known species, but it is represented on all continents apart from Antarctica and also on many remote oceanic islands – thanks to the migratory habits of several of the species. There is rarely more than one species in any given area. The maxillary palps, which are sometimes half the length of the abdomen, point forwards and account for the family's common name. The strongly toothed forewing is another family characteristic. The front legs of the females are fully developed, but those of the males are short and useless for walking, so the family is often treated as a subfamily – the Libytheinae – of the Nymphalidae (*see* p.412). The caterpillars feed mainly on plants of the elm family. There is just one European species.

p.128   **Nettle-tree Butterfly** *Libythea celtis*

Description: 15–25 mm (0.6–1.0 in). The ground colour of the upperside is chocolate-brown, with large orange spots. There is a small white spot on the front edge of the forewing, and the outer edge of the wing is drawn out to form a prominent tooth or beak. The outer margin of the hindwing is lightly scalloped. The underside of the forewing resembles the upperside, although it is a little paler, but the underside of the hindwing is dull brown with just a thin white streak through the middle. The projecting palps are nearly four times as long as the head. The sexes are alike.

Similar species: Comma is superficially similar when at rest with wings closed, but it has more 'ragged' margins, especially on the hindwing, and the hindwing has a conspicuous white comma-shaped mark.

Flight: June to September, and again from March to May after hibernation.

Habitat: Light woodland and wooded river valleys, and not uncommon in villages and small towns where the larval foodplant – the Nettle Tree – is grown for shade and ornament. Occurs from sea level to about 1,500 m (4,925 ft), although individuals are occasionally seen flying at much higher altitudes in late summer.

Life-cycle: The oval, ribbed eggs are laid in small groups on the foodplants as soon as the leaves open in March and April. The slender caterpillar is smooth and either green or brown with a pale stripe along each side. It can be found on the Nettle Trees from April until July. When fully grown at a length of about 35 mm (1.4 in) it pupates on the underside of a leaf. The bluish-green chrysalis is rather angular, with a white V on the back. Adults emerge about 12 days after pupation and are on the wing from June until they go into hibernation in August or September. They are fond of the flowers of Christ's-thorn bushes, and also frequent visitors to bramble flowers and fruits. They hibernate in dense undergrowth, looking just like dead leaves, and emerge again in the spring.

Range: Iberia and the Mediterranean region, extending northeastwards to Hungary and Slovakia and on through Asia to Japan. Also in North Africa. The butterfly is rare in the more northerly parts of its European range.

Although the butterfly is generally stated to be single-brooded, some authors state that there are two broods, with the caterpillars feeding up very rapidly in spring to produce a short-lived adult generation in June. Double-brooded populations may be restricted to certain areas.

MILKWEED BUTTERFLIES (DANAIDAE)

Most of the 150 or so species in this group hail from tropical Asia. None is native to Europe, although the widely distributed Monarch and the Plain Tiger are occasional visitors and could possibly settle down as permanent residents. Wingspans range from about 50 to 180 mm (2.0–7.1 in), and many species have striking colours in association with their being distasteful to predators (*see* below). The front legs are much reduced and useless for walking. During courtship, the males evert tufts of fine hairs, called hair-pencils, from their abdomens and use them to scatter scent particles picked up from small pouches on the hindwings. The hair-pencils are waved in front of the females and the scent encourages them to mate.

Egg of Monarch.

Milkweed eggs are conical and strongly ribbed. The caterpillars are usually boldly coloured and, except during the first instar, they are decorated with a number of long, fleshy filaments. They feed on a variety of poisonous plants, belonging mainly to the milkweed and dogbane families, and the ingested poisons give the caterpillars the toxic qualities of which their bold colours give warning. The pupae, which are suspended from the foodplants, are short and smoothly rounded and often decorated with gold or silver spots.

Caterpillar of Monarch.

The poisons stored in the caterpillars' bodies are passed on to the adults, where they are concentrated in the blood and in the wing-scales. Birds attempting to eat the butterflies quickly learn their lesson and

Chrysalis of Monarch.

rarely molest them again. In common with many other insects displaying warning colours, the milkweeds have rather tough bodies and they are not seriously harmed when young birds peck at them. The Monarch is famed for its powerful migration flights, but at other times its flight is rather relaxed and unhurried, like that of most other milkweeds. Many of the species actually have considerably less muscle than other butterflies of a similar size. The butterflies are usually easy to approach when settled, as if they know that their poisons will provide adequate protection. In many parts of the world the poisonous milkweed butterflies are mimicked by an assortment of non-poisonous species. The mimics, which belong to several different families, benefit from their similarity to the poisonous models because birds that have learned their lesson with the milkweeds also leave the mimics alone. Natural selection, favouring the best mimics in each generation, has led to some truly amazing similarities between models and mimics, but there are no clear-cut examples of this kind of mimicry among the European butterflies.

The milkweeds are often treated as a subfamily – the Danainae – of the Nymphalidae because of their reduced front legs (*see* p.412), but the possession of hair-pencils distinguishes them from all the other nymphalids.

---

p.129 **Monarch** *Danaus plexippus*

Description: 35–50 mm (1.4–2.0 in). The ground colour of the upperside is a rich chestnut-brown or orange, with broad, white-spotted black margins. All veins are lined with black. The male has a small black sex-brand on vein 2, near the middle of the hindwing. The underside of the forewing resembles the upperside, but the underside of the hindwing is paler and the veins are very heavily lined with black. The sexes are similar but the female has darker veins and lacks the sex-brand.

Similar species: Plain Tiger has similar colours, but with less prominent veins and with conspicuous white patches near the tip of the forewing. It is usually a little smaller.

Flight: This casual visitor is most often seen in Europe in late summer, but it has been seen in almost every month of the year.

Habitat: Almost anywhere, but most likely to be found in open places with plenty of flowers. The foodplants are various milkweeds (*Asclepias* species).

Life-cycle: The eggs are pale green or yellow, strongly ribbed, and shaped like tiny truncated lemons. They are laid singly on the foodplants. The caterpillar, up to 50 mm (2.0 in) long, is basically white with yellow and black bands and a pair of black filaments at each end. The chrysalis is plump and pale green and studded with golden spots.

Range: The Monarch is essentially an American species, but it is a great traveller and during the last 150 years or so it has expanded its range enormously. It is now one of the world's most widely distributed butterflies, occupying Indonesia and Australasia as well as most of the Pacific islands. It has also crossed the Atlantic Ocean and established itself in the Azores and the Canary Islands. Most specimens seen in Europe turn up in the south and west and probably come from the Canaries, but some may well fly all the way from North America. In recent years the species has established small breeding colonies in southern Spain.

Several species of milkweed plants, notably *Asclepias curassavica*, are grown as ornamentals in southern Europe, and it is these cultivated plants that the Monarch caterpillars have been able to use in Spain. As the plants are quite successful escapes to waste ground, it seems quite possible that the Monarch will be able to establish itself more securely in Europe.

In North America the Monarch undertakes a spectacular autumn migration, with millions of butterflies converging on small areas of Mexico, Florida, and California to spend the winter dozing in groves of conifer and eucalyptus trees. Some of these butterflies cover more than 3,200 km (2,000 miles) from summer haunts in southern Canada. The return trip in the spring is a more relaxed affair, with the butterflies leaving at intervals and travelling in small groups. They breed on the way and it is their offspring that complete the journey to the summer breeding grounds.

The Monarch is also known as the Wanderer and the Milkweed.

---

p.129 **Plain Tiger** *Danaus chrysippus*

Description: 35–45 mm (1.4–1.8 in). A bright-orange or brick-red butterfly with narrow black veins. The upperside of the forewing has an extensive black tip with prominent white spots. The hindwings have narrow black borders, and the male has a conspicuous black sex-brand on vein 2 just below the cell. The underside is similar but the tip of the forewing is paler and the black border of the hindwing contains large white spots.

Similar species: Monarch has similar colours but lacks the conspicuous white spots on the forewing. It is normally a little larger.

Flight: Throughout the summer months.

Habitat: Any open area with flowers can attract this infrequent summer visitor. The foodplants are various kinds of milkweed.

Life-cycle: The pale-green eggs resemble those of the Monarch and are laid singly during the summer. The caterpillar, up to 70 mm (2.75 in) long, is largely pale blue with black and yellow banding and it has three pairs of long black filaments. The chrysalis is pale green or pink and resembles that of the Monarch. In the African tropics the species has one of the quickest of all butterfly life-cycles and produces up to 12 generations in a year, but in cooler regions it has only one or two broods each year.

Range: Another very widely distributed species, probably originating in Africa – where it is one of the commonest butterflies – but now occurring right across southern Asia to Japan and Australia. It also occurs in Fiji and the Canary Islands, and specimens occasionally turn up in southern Europe.

Most European specimens have been seen singly in Italy and Greece – undoubtedly having arrived as vagrants from Africa, especially from the Nile Valley – but larger numbers began to appear in Europe during the 1980s. Breeding was recorded in Spain and, although the species may not be able to survive the winter in Europe, the spread of introduced milkweed plants may well allow the butterfly to establish itself as a breeding summer visitor just like the Painted Lady.

The Plain Tiger is also known as the African Monarch and the Lesser Wanderer.

EMPERORS, ADMIRALS, AND FRITILLARIES (NYMPHALIDAE)

This very large family occurs all over the world, although it is centred on the northern hemisphere. There are about 3,000 species, but some modern schemes of classification incorporate several other families here, including the Satyridae and Danaidae, and thus increase the total to about 6,000 species – nearly a third of all the world's butterflies. Even in its restricted sense, the family contains several distinct groups of butterflies, but they all have greatly reduced front legs that are useless for walking. These legs, which are more severely reduced in males than in females, often carry tufts of hair-like scales, and these insects are commonly known as brush-footed butterflies. Wingspans range from about 25 mm (1.0 in) to a little over 100 mm (4.0 in), although the largest European species are no more than about 85 mm (3.4 in) across. The antennae are fairly rigid and strongly clubbed.

Red Admiral showing reduced nature of legs and their brush-like appearance.

White Admiral egg.

Camberwell Beauty eggs.

Purple Emperor

Dark Green Fritillary

Caterpillars.

Silver-washed Fritillary

Glanville Fritillary

Chrysalids.

There are about 70 European species, 15 of which regularly breed in the British Isles, and they include some of our most colourful butterflies. Most of them are fast-flying insects, and several species, including the White Admiral, are great gliders as well. Many, such as the Painted Lady and the Red Admiral, are great migrants. The fritillaries can be distinguished from the rest of the family by their generally orange uppersides with black spots and their pretty undersides – often with silvery markings. The other nymphalids fall into several groups or subfamilies, the most familiar of which is the Nymphalinae: sometimes known as vanessids, these include the colourful tortoiseshells, the Peacock, and the Red Admiral.

The sexes are generally similar and often indistinguishable without careful examination of the front legs, although some male fritillaries have streaks of dark scent-scales on their forewings.

The eggs are quite variable, but usually barrel-shaped with prominent ribs. Many are exquisitely sculptured and decorated with glass-like spines. The larvae commonly bear elaborately branched or bristly spines or tubercles. They use a wide range of foodplants, including stinging nettles – which are used by no other butterfly family. The pupae are suspended and have two prominent horn-like projections on the head. Many have other spiky outgrowths as well and are commonly decorated with golden spots, and it was for these pupae that the word chrysalis, meaning golden, was originally coined.

p.132 **Two-tailed Pasha** *Charaxes jasius*

Description: 36–45 mm (1.4–1.7 in). The ground colour of the upperside is dark chocolate-brown with yellow or orange borders and a variable amount of orange spotting or smudging on the forewing. A broad white stripe divides the underside into a brown basal region with white-edged black spots and a variable outer region which is largely orange or yellow with blue spots on the hindwing. The rear edge of the hindwing is drawn out into two prominent 'tails'.

Similar species: Camberwell Beauty looks similar in flight, but has no real 'tails'; Two-tailed Pasha is the only European butterfly with two tails on the hindwing.

Flight: May to October in two broods. A fast-flying and strongly territorial butterfly, fond of feeding at ripe fruit and often patrolling orchards; quite common at Fig trees in the autumn.

Habitat: Scrubby places and orchards from sea level to 1,000 m (3,275 ft). The larval foodplant is the Strawberry Tree.

Life-cycle: The globular yellow eggs are laid singly on the foodplant, and the young caterpillars are pale brown with four small horns on the head and two more at the rear. The mature

caterpillar

caterpillar is up to 60 mm (2.4 in) long, deep green, and heavily speckled with yellow. There are two conspicuous blue and yellow eye-spots in the middle of the back, and a yellow line runs along each side of the body to end in two short prongs at the rear. The head, which is paler green than the

chrysalis

body, has a yellow border and four red-tipped, backward-pointing horns. The whole insect is beautifully camouflaged among the leaves of the foodplant. First-brood caterpillars mature in about six

weeks and pupate in July, but autumn caterpillars go into hibernation and complete their growth in April. The chrysalis is smooth and green and suspended from the foodplant.

Range: Portugal and the Mediterranean region, rarely far from the coast. Widely distributed in Africa.

p.133 Purple Emperor *Apatura iris*

Description: 30–40 mm (1.2–1.6 in). The ground colour of the upperside is brownish black, with white spots on the forewing and a white stripe across the centre of the hindwing. There is a black spot close to the margin in space 2 of the forewing, and an orange-ringed black spot near the rear of the hindwing. The male displays a brilliant iridescent blue or purple when viewed at certain angles. The female is larger than the male, paler brown with larger white markings, and no iridescence. The undersides are largely brown and white in both sexes, with silvery-grey markings on the inner and outer edges of the hindwing.

Similar species: Lesser Purple Emperor has a conspicuous orange ring round the black spot in space 2 of the forewing and is more orange underneath. Freyer's Purple Emperor is paler and has orange bands and spots on the upperside.

Flight: July and August. A fast-flying species, generally staying in the treetops and feeding on honeydew, although males sometimes come down to drink from muddy ground, dung, and carrion.

Habitat: Mature oakwoods, with tall trees – the 'master oaks' – on which the males establish their territories while waiting for the females to appear; from sea level to about 1,000 m (3,275 ft). The larval foodplants are various sallows, especially Goat Willow and Grey Willow.

Life-cycle: The ribbed, dome-shaped eggs are bright green with a purple band at the base. They are laid singly on the upper surfaces of the leaves and hatch in about ten days. The caterpillar is yellowish green until the second moult and is extremely well camouflaged as it sits on the midrib close to the tip of the leaf. After the second moult, the caterpillar becomes purplish brown and goes into hibernation, usually pressed tightly against the bark in the fork of a small twig. It wakes when the buds open in the spring and gradually turns green again. Growth is completed in June, when the caterpillar is bright green with yellow stripes on the sides and two slender horns on the head. Pupation takes place under a leaf. The chrysalis is silvery green and very hard to spot.

egg

Range: Most of Europe – except Norway and Sweden and the Mediterranean region –

and on through Asia to Japan. Restricted in
the British Isles to a few localities in
southern England.

p.134   **Lesser Purple Emperor** *Apatura ilia*

Description: 30–38 mm (1.2–1.5 in). The ground colour
of the upperside is dull brown, with white
spots on the forewing and a white stripe
across the centre of the hindwing. There is
an orange-ringed black spot in space 2 of
the forewing and a similar spot near the
rear of the hindwing. The male displays a
bright-purple iridescence when viewed
from certain angles. The female, which has
larger white markings, has no such
iridescence. The undersides of both sexes
are greyish brown with orange mottling
and black and white spots.

Similar species: Purple Emperor lacks the orange ring
round the black spot on the forewing and
has much less orange on the tips of the
antennae. Freyer's Purple Emperor is much
paler and has orange spots and bands on the
upperside.

Flight: May to September in one or two broods,
usually seen flying around the treetops. It
feeds mainly on honeydew, although males
often come down to feed at muddy pools
and at dung and carrion.

Habitat: Light woodland, with tall trees that the
males can use as territories, from sea level
to about 1,000 m (3,275 ft). The larval
foodplants are poplars, especially Aspen,
and willows.

Life-cycle: The ribbed, dome-shaped eggs are green
with a purple zone near the top, and they
are laid singly on the upper surfaces of the
leaves. The mature caterpillar is about
50 mm (2.0 in) long and tapers strongly
towards the tail end. It is very like that of
the Purple Emperor – leaf green with
yellow dots and a pair of yellow horns on
the head, although the horns of Lesser
Purple Emperor have a dark stripe on the
underside. In southern areas, where there
are two broods, the summer caterpillars
grow up and pupate in July and August,

but autumn larvae, like those of the single-brooded populations elsewhere, become brown in the third instar and hibernate on the bare twigs just like those of the Purple Emperor. The silvery-green chrysalis hangs from a leaf or a twig.

Range: Southern and central Europe and on through Asia to China. Absent from the British Isles, the Netherlands, Greece, and most of Iberia.

Most populations contain a proportion of butterflies in which the uppersides have pale-yellow markings instead of white, although the white spots remain near the tip of the forewing. The wings also have orange submarginal bands. This striking variety is known as f. *clytie*, and in some populations it is more common than the normal form. It is very similar to Freyer's Purple Emperor, from which it can be distinguished by the arc of black post-discal spots on the hindwing.

---

p.135 **Freyer's Purple Emperor** *Apatura metis*

Description: 30–35 mm (1.2–1.4 in). The ground colour of the uppersides is orange-brown, with orange submarginal bands and a wavy, yellowish discal band on each wing. The band is broken into separate spots on the forewing. Males exhibit a slight purple iridescence when viewed from certain angles. There is a distinct black-centred orange eye-spot in space 2 of the forewing. There are no obvious eye-spots on the hindwing. The undersides are orange-brown and grey with an irregular pale discal band.

Similar species: Lesser Purple Emperor f. *clytie* is very similar but has an arc of dark post-discal spots on the hindwing.

Flight: May to August in one or two broods. The adults feed avidly on bramble nectar.

Habitat: Open woodland, with some tall trees, especially in river valleys and on other damp slopes, from sea level to about 1,000 m (3,275 ft). The main larval foodplant is White Willow, but other willows and poplars are also eaten.

Life-cycle: The early stages of this butterfly are very like those of Lesser Purple Emperor, although the eggs are laid in batches and the newly hatched caterpillars immediately bind the leaves with silk to form feeding chambers. The caterpillar is greenish yellow at first, but becomes reddish brown before settling down to hibernate on an exposed twig. It becomes green again in the spring, with a conspicuous white streak on each side.

Range: Austria and Hungary and southeastwards to the Black Sea and northern Greece, but rare and local. Also across Asia to Korea and Japan.

This butterfly was once considered to be a subspecies of Lesser Purple Emperor. Almost all European specimens are of the orange-brown form described above, but dark individuals similar to the normal form of the Lesser Purple Emperor are occasionally found.

---

p.136 **Poplar Admiral** *Limenitis populi*

Description: 35–40 mm (1.4–1.6 in). The ground colour of the uppersides is sombre greyish brown, with white spots on the forewing and a broad white band in the centre of the hindwing. The white markings are smaller in the male than in the female and, apart from the three small apical spots, they are sometimes missing from the male forewing. The hindwing has a bluish-grey margin, inside which there is a row of black spots and orange lunules. The forewing has similar markings but they are smaller and much less distinct. The underside is largely orange with a bluish-grey margin and white markings similar to those on the upperside.

Similar species: White Admiral and Southern White Admiral are smaller and darker, with no orange on the upperside and no grey borders on the underside. Female Purple Emperor lacks orange bands.

Flight: June and July, paying little attention to flowers and feeding mainly on honeydew.

Habitat: Light woodland, especially in river valleys and other damp places, from sea level to about 1,600 m (5,250 ft). The larval foodplants are poplars, especially Aspen.

Life-cycle: The pale-green eggs are elaborately decorated with dimples and glassy spines. They are laid singly on Aspen, and occasionally on other poplars. The caterpillar resembles a bird-dropping at first, being brown and warty with a white belt, and soon prepares a tubular hibernation chamber. This is made from a partly eaten leaf, bound tightly to a twig with silk, and it is extremely difficult to spot. Growth is completed in the spring, when the fully grown caterpillar reaches about 50 mm (2.0 in) in length. It is green

Chrysalis.

with a straw-coloured band on each side and purplish blotches on its back, and two spiky horns just behind the head. Pupation takes place on a leaf that has been moulded into a protective cradle with silk. The shiny chrysalis is basically black and white, with a yellow bulge in the middle that looks as if the body fluids are oozing out. Birds, presumably having learnt that many black and yellow insects taste unpleasant, rarely molest this chrysalis.

Range: Northern, central, and southeast Europe, but absent from the British Isles and, apart from Brittany, the whole of western France.

---

p.136 **White Admiral** *Limenitis camilla*

Description: 25–30 mm (1.0–1.2 in). The ground colour of the uppersides is velvety black in fresh specimens, but soon becomes brownish black. Both wings carry a broad white band, although this is broken in the centre of the forewing, and an indistinct row of black submarginal spots. The underside is largely orange or brick-coloured, with the same white pattern as the upperside. There are two rows of black dots beyond the white band, and the inner or lower margin of the hindwing is silvery grey. There are a number of varieties and aberrations in which the white spots are almost or completely obliterated.

Similar species: Southern White Admiral has a clear white spot in the forewing cell and its underside is much redder, with only one row of black submarginal dots and a larger silvery area at the base. Hungarian Glider has more rounded wings and no silvery patch on the underside of the hindwing. Poplar Admiral is much larger, with orange submarginal lunules.

Flight: June to August, often gliding gracefully for long distances. Basks in dappled sunlight, where it is very difficult to detect. It regularly feeds at Bramble blossom and also sips honeydew.

Habitat: Woodland with plenty of glades or rides, from sea level to about 1,500 m (4,925 ft). The larval foodplants are honeysuckles.

Life-cycle: The eggs are globular and greyish green, with a delicate honeycomb pattern and a coating of fine glassy spines. They are laid singly on the leaves and they hatch in about a week. The caterpillar is spiky brown in the early stages and, like its relatives, feeds by stripping the outer parts of the leaves and leaving the midribs sticking out like spines. After the second moult the caterpillar prepares for hibernation by binding the stalk of a partly eaten leaf to a twig with silk, and then folding the blade over to form a little cradle. The cradle remains on the foodplant throughout the winter, with the little caterpillar safely tucked up inside it. Activity resumes when the new leaves open in the spring, and after its next moult the caterpillar becomes bright green, with branched red spines on its back. It is up to 30 mm (1.2 in) long when mature and it pupates head-down on the foodplant. The chrysalis is green and purplish brown, with two ear-like points on the head and a number of silvery spots, and it is very well camouflaged amongst the foliage. The pupal stage may last no more than a week.

Range: Southern and central Europe, but absent from much of Iberia and southeast Europe.

In the British Isles, the White Admiral is confined to the southern half of England

caterpillar

chrysalis

and Wales, but it has been spreading in recent decades. There was also a noticeable expansion in Denmark and southern Sweden in the 1940s and 1950s, but the butterfly has now declined there and has recently disappeared from Sweden – possibly through the destruction of honeysuckle in the plantations. The insect certainly seems happy in the slightly shaded rides of conifer plantations in Britain, where the females can find the spindly growths of honeysuckle that they seem to favour for egg-laying.

p.137 **Southern White Admiral** *Limenitis reducta*

Description:

Chrysalis.

20–30 mm (0.8–1.2 in). In fresh specimens, the ground colour of the uppersides is velvety black, sometimes with a bluish tinge, but it soon becomes brownish black. The forewing is variably marked with white but, except in certain rare aberrations in which almost all the white is obliterated, there is always a prominent spot in the cell. The hindwing has a central white stripe. The undersides are largely chestnut-brown with the same white markings as the upperside, but the basal third of the hindwing is silvery grey. There is a single row of black submarginal spots, most noticeable on the hindwing.

Similar species: White Admiral has no white spot in the forewing cell, and the underside is more orange with two rows of black submarginal spots. Hungarian Glider has no silvery basal patch on the underside of the hindwing. Poplar Admiral is much larger, with orange submarginal lunules.

Flight: May to September in one, two, or possibly three broods: slow and graceful, with much gliding. The butterfly feeds at Bramble and other flowers and is often common in the lavender fields of Provence. It also feeds on honeydew.

Habitat: Light woodland and scrubby areas, from sea level to about 1,500 m (4,925 ft). The larval foodplants are honeysuckles.

Life-cycle: The eggs, very much like those of the White Admiral, are laid singly on the upper surfaces of the leaves. The caterpillar – brown at first and then bright green – is also similar to that of the White Admiral, but with purplish legs and even longer, branched reddish spines on its back. It is about 25 mm (1.0 in) long when mature. Early broods feed up quickly and pupate on the foodplant. Late-summer caterpillars, just like those of the White Admiral, go into hibernation in a folded leaf while still quite small and complete their growth in the spring. The chrysalis is pale brown and rather lumpy, and very hard to distinguish from a shrivelled leaf.

Range: Southern and central Europe, as far north as Slovakia and Brittany, but absent from southern Iberia.

p.138   **Common Glider** *Neptis sappho*

Description: 23 mm (0.9 in). The uppersides are velvety black, with a broad, broken white streak running through the centre of the forewing. There is a band of elongated white spots beyond the streak, and a band of small white spots near the outer margin. The upperside of the hindwing bears two conspicuous white bands. The undersides are rust-coloured, with white markings similar to those on the uppersides. The hindwings are markedly rounded.

Similar species: Hungarian Glider, White Admiral, and Southern White Admiral all lack the white streak on the forewing and have just one white band on the hindwing.

Flight: May to September in two broods, the butterfly gliding elegantly from perch to perch, where it commonly basks with wings wide open.

Habitat: Lowland woods and scrubby hillsides to about 500 m (1,650 ft). The foodplant is Spring Pea, but the caterpillar has also been reported to eat the leaves of False Acacia.

Life-cycle: The dimpled, pearly eggs are laid singly on the foodplant and hatch in about two weeks. The caterpillar feeds in curled-up

leaves at first, but then more openly on the leaves. When mature, it is pale brown with darker patches and about 45 mm (1.75 in) long. Second-brood caterpillars go into hibernation in curled-up leaves when nearly fully grown. The chrysalis, which hangs from the foodplant, is pale green with brown flecks and is easily mistaken for a folded leaf.

Range: Eastern Europe, from Slovakia to northern Greece, and then across Asia to Japan. Rare in the westernmost parts of its range, where it is in danger of extinction.

---

p.139 **Hungarian Glider** *Neptis rivularis*

Description: 25 mm (1.0 in). The uppersides are velvety black with a white band across each wing, although this is broken and irregular in the forewing. There are a few small white spots in the cell of the forewing. The undersides are rusty brown with white markings similar to those on the uppersides. The hindwings are markedly rounded.

Similar species: Common Glider has two white bands on the hindwing and more white on the forewing. White Admiral and Southern White Admiral have less rounded hindwings, with conspicuous silvery patches on the undersides.

Flight: June to August in a single brood. Glides elegantly from perch to perch – as its name suggests – with only an occasional flap of the wings. It often basks on the vegetation with its wings wide open.

Habitat: Light woodland and forest margins to an altitude of about 1,200 m (3,925 ft). The larval foodplants are Goat's-beard Spiraea, Meadowsweet, and various species of *Spiraea*.

Life-cycle: The pearly, dimpled eggs are laid singly on the foodplant and they hatch in about two weeks. The young caterpillar lives in a pouch made from partly eaten leaves, but later feeds openly on the leaves. During the third instar, the caterpillar makes a hibernaculum by folding one or more leaves and securing them to the foodplant, and it

spends the winter there. Growth is completed in the spring. The mature caterpillar is about 50 mm (2.0 in) long and sports an attractive mixture of light and dark brown with spiky outgrowths at each end. The chrysalis is pale green with brown flecks and can easily pass for a folded leaf.

Range: Eastern Europe, from Switzerland and Northern Italy to Northern Greece, and on through Asia to Japan. Like the Common Glider, it is becoming rare in the western parts of its range.

---

p.140 **Camberwell Beauty** *Nymphalis antiopa*

Description: 33 mm (1.3 in). The uppersides are largely purplish brown or chocolate-coloured, and each wing has a pale-yellow or cream border with a line of blue spots just inside it. There are two white flecks near the tip of the forewing. The undersides are sooty brown with dirty-white borders.

Similar species: None, although Two-tailed Pasha can appear similar in flight.

Flight: June to September and again in spring after hibernation. Flight is fast and powerful and the insects can often be seen high in the trees as well as basking with their wings wide open on the ground. They feed mainly on fallen fruit and on sap oozing from wounded tree-trunks, but regularly visit sallow catkins in the spring. They tend to be strongly territorial.

Habitat: Open woods and scrub, from sea level to 2,500 m (8,200 ft): most common in hilly areas but, being a strongly migratory insect, it can turn up almost anywhere. The foodplants are mainly sallows, poplars, and birches, but elm is also used.

Life-cycle: The strongly ribbed orange eggs are laid in large clusters on the twigs of the foodplants in spring or early summer, and the resulting caterpillars live and feed in communal webs until they are fully grown. They move to a new site and spin a new web after each moult. The adult caterpillar is about 50 mm (2.0 in) long, and black with brick-red patches on the back and numerous branched black spines. The chrysalis, which can be found throughout the summer months, is light brown with black and orange speckles. It is suspended from the foodplant or from some other nearby support. The adult butterfly goes into hibernation from August onwards, usually in a hollow tree, log-pile, or a hollow in a stone wall. Unlike the related tortoiseshells, it rarely uses buildings. The hibernated butterfly may survive well into the summer and thus have a total life-span of well over a year. It often overlaps with its adult offspring, but the two generations are easily distinguished because the older butterflies are rather tattered and their pale borders are usually white – if there is anything left of them at all. But loss of the outer-wing regions does not seem to impair their flight.

Range: Throughout Europe, but absent from most of Iberia and occurring in the British Isles only as a casual visitor. Also occurs right across the cooler parts of Asia, and in North America where it is called the Mourning Cloak butterfly.

The Camberwell Beauty was so named because the first specimen recorded in Britain was found at Camberwell, in London. It was once known as the Grand Surprise.

The species is declining in many areas and has completely disappeared as a breeding species in some parts of the low countries and neighbouring parts of Germany. Numbers vary a great deal, possibly because the caterpillars are heavily attacked by ichneumons and related parasites.

p.141 **Large Tortoiseshell** *Nymphalis polychloros*

Description: 30 mm (1.2 in). The ground colour of the upperside is dull orange or brick-coloured, with black spots and dark borders. The latter have well-defined inner margins, especially on the hindwing. The border of the hindwing contains a row of blue spots, but there are very rarely any blue spots on the forewing. The underside is mottled brown, darker towards the base and with a faint greyish-blue band around the edge of each wing. The legs and palps are clothed with dark brown or black hair.

Similar species: Yellow-legged Tortoiseshell has broader dark margins on the upperside and yellowish brown hairs on its legs and palps. Small Tortoiseshell has brighter uppersides, with blue spots on the forewing and much more black on the hindwing. False Comma has broad black wingtips with white spots.

Flight: June to September, and again in spring after hibernation. In most areas there is just a single brood, but in some places to the south of the Alps there may be two broods. Flight is fast and strong, but the butterflies spend a lot of time basking in the sunshine, often in a head-down position on walls and tree-trunks. They visit sallow catkins in the spring, but otherwise show little interest in flowers and get most of their nourishment from honeydew or from sap oozing from wounded tree-trunks.

Habitat: Light woodland and forest edges, tall hedges, parks, and orchards, from sea level to about 2,000 m (6,550 ft). The main foodplants of the caterpillars are elms, but sallows, poplars, and several other deciduous trees, including cultivated fruit trees, may be used.

Life-cycle: The yellow, ribbed eggs are laid in the spring, deposited in large batches on twigs high in the trees. The resulting caterpillars remain together until they are fully grown, spending most of their lives in communal silk tents draped over the branches. The fully grown caterpillar is black, with brownish spines, narrow orange stripes, and numerous tiny white dots. It is about 45 mm (1.0 in) long. The chrysalis is suspended freely from the foodplant or other convenient support, often at a much lower level than the larval feeding site. It is pale brown with golden spots, and its spiky nature gives it a strong similarity to a withered leaf. The adult goes into hibernation from August onwards, hiding in a hollow tree, log-pile, attic, or outbuilding, and re-emerges from March onwards.

Range: Throughout Europe except Ireland and the northern half of Scandinavia, but now only a rare visitor to Britain.

Scandinavian specimens tend to be paler than those from further south, although they are of a more normal colour in years with really warm summers. The species has declined in many areas since the 1950s and is now decidedly rare in western Europe. The loss of so many elm trees through Dutch elm disease may be partly responsible.

---

p.141 **Yellow-legged Tortoiseshell**
Nymphalis xanthomelas

Description: 32 mm (1.25 in). The ground colour of the upperside is orange, with dark margins and black spots. The margin of the hindwing contains a row of blue, crescent-shaped spots, and its inner border merges gradually into the general wing colour. The underside is brown, with a dark basal area and a blue marginal band – best developed on the hindwing. The legs and palps bear a lot of yellowish brown hairs.

Similar species: Large Tortoiseshell has black legs and more sharply defined dark margins. False Comma has conspicuous white spots on both wings.

Flight: June to September, and again in spring after hibernation. Flight is strong, but the butterfly spends a lot of time basking on the ground or on tree-trunks.

Habitat: Lowland woodland, usually near water: generally from sea level to about 600 m (1,975 ft), but sometimes much higher. The main foodplants are willows, although some other deciduous trees may be used.

Life-cycle: The eggs, very like those of the Large Tortoiseshell, are laid in batches on twigs in spring. The caterpillars are gregarious for much of their lives, inhabiting large

silken tents that are sometimes very conspicuous on the willow trees. The mature caterpillar is black and yellow with branching black spines, and about 45 mm (1.8 in) long. The chrysalis, which is suspended from the foodplant, is very much like that of the Large Tortoiseshell. The adult goes into a long hibernation from August onwards, and reappears in March or April.

Range: Eastern Europe. Individuals sometimes migrate to the west, but the species is rarely seen west of a line linking the Baltic and the Adriatic.

False Comma *Nymphalis vau-album*

Description: 32 mm (1.25 in). The ground colour of the upperside is orange, heavily marked with black. The forewing has a broad, dark outer border and a large black apical patch containing a conspicuous white spot. The black spots in the outer part of the forewing are often rectangular and may run together. There is a large white spot on the front edge of the hindwing, and the black submarginal band is clearly edged with yellow. The underside is mottled brown, with a darker basal area and an indistinct blue band near the outer edge. Both wings are strongly toothed.

Similar species: Large Tortoiseshell and Yellow-legged Tortoiseshell lack the white spots and both have blue marginal bands on the upperside of the hindwing. Comma and Southern Comma have similar undersides, but are much smaller and have no white on the upperside.

Flight: July to September and again in spring after hibernation.

Habitat: Lowland woodland and surrounding scrub and grassland; never far from trees. The larval foodplants are mainly elms and willows, although several other deciduous trees may be used.

Life-cycle: The eggs are laid in the spring, clustered around twigs like those of the Large Tortoiseshell. The caterpillars are gregarious for much of their lives, living and feeding under extensive silken tents. They are about 45 mm (1.8 in) long when mature and pupate, suspended from the foodplants, in midsummer. The adult goes into hibernation from late August onwards and re-emerges in March.

Range: Eastern Europe – mainly Hungary and Romania – and on through Asia to Japan. Also in North America, where it is known as the Compton Tortoiseshell. The butterfly is a strong migrant and occasionally reaches the Baltic coasts of Sweden and Finland, but it is rarely seen in Europe west of a line joining the Baltic to the Adriatic.

p.142 **Peacock** *Inachis io*

Description: 28 mm (1.1 in). The ground colour of the upperside is a rich chestnut-brown or maroon, with sooty-brown margins and a conspicuous eye-spot on each wing. The eye-spots, which make the butterfly quite unmistakable, are blue and black with grey rings on the hindwings, but those of the forewings are largely red with blue and yellow surrounds. The undersides, which are sooty brown with little obvious pattern, provide excellent camouflage during hibernation.

Similar species: None.

Flight: June to October and again in spring after hibernation. The butterfly commonly basks and feeds at flowers with its wings open, but it also feeds with its wings closed; if it is disturbed it will flash its eye-spots to scare potential enemies.

Habitat: A wide-ranging butterfly with no fixed home area, it can be found almost wherever there are suitable nectar-rich flowers. It is common in town parks and gardens, where it is especially fond of buddleia flowers, as well as on rough grassland and wasteland. It is often abundant in woodland rides. The larval foodplant is Stinging Nettle.

Life-cycle: The ribbed, green eggs are generally laid in April and May. They are laid in clumps on the undersides of nettle leaves and are often piled several deep – probably a way of reducing the effects of egg-parasites. The caterpillars are black with branching black spines and numerous tiny white spots, and they live together in flimsy webs until after the final moult. The mature caterpillar is about 40 mm (1.6 in) long, and it often pupates in trees and shrubs well away from its foodplant. The chrysalis is yellowish green with reddish points. The adult butterfly emerges within about a fortnight and flies until the autumn, when it seeks out a hollow tree, attic or outbuilding for hibernation. Total adult life may exceed one year, with the hibernated individuals often hanging on until their offspring are on the wing. In some of the warmer parts of Europe there may be two broods, one flying in July and August and the second appearing in late September and going into hibernation almost straightaway.

Range: Throughout Europe, apart from the northern half of Scandinavia. It is a strong migrant and has occasionally been found in Iceland.

p.143 **Red Admiral** *Vanessa atalanta*

Description: 30 mm (1.2 in). The uppersides of this handsome butterfly are velvety black, with a red stripe through the centre of the forewing and a red margin to the hindwing. There are also several white spots near the tip of the forewing. The undersides are mottled greyish brown, marked with red, white, and blue on the forewing.

Similar species: There are no similar resident species, but Indian Red Admiral may occasionally arrive from the Canaries. It can be distinguished by the broader and very irregular red band on the forewing.

Flight: May to October and again in early spring in the south, after a short hibernation. In most places there is just one brood, but two broods possibly occur in some parts of southern Europe. The adults often bask with their wings wide open, but frequently feed with their wings closed. They often drink sap oozing from wounded trees and are also fond of over-ripe and fermenting fruit, often indulging to such an extent that they become a little 'drunk'.

Habitat: This wide-ranging migratory butterfly can be found almost anywhere with flowers and ripe fruit. It is often common in gardens and orchards. The larval foodplant is Stinging Nettle, but Hop and a few other related plants are occasionally used.

Life-cycle: The eggs are green with prominent glassy ribs, and they are laid singly, or occasionally in pairs, on the upsides of the leaves. The young caterpillar soon makes itself a little tent by folding the leaves and fixing them together with silk, and it lives and feeds there until it has outgrown the space or eaten all the food. It then makes a larger tent, and the process is repeated several times during the caterpillar's life. The tents are not hard to find around the edges of nettle beds during the summer, with the rather spiky caterpillars curled up inside them. The mature caterpillar is about 35 mm (1.4 in) long and ranges from yellowish brown to almost black, densely speckled with white. There is a prominent row of yellow spots, often linked into a continuous band, on each side. The chrysalis is greyish brown with golden points and is usually concealed in the last larval tent. The pupal stage lasts for two or three weeks.

egg

Range: Throughout Europe, including Iceland, and also in North Africa, western Asia, and North America.

Although the Red Admiral occurs throughout Europe in the summer, relatively few individuals seem to survive the winter north of the Alps. Adults emerging in late summer tend to fly south, but most of them perish with the first frosts and repopulation of the northern half of Europe depends on migrants moving up from their Mediterranean breeding grounds each spring. There is evidence of successful over-wintering in some sheltered areas of northern and central Europe, however, and global warming could make this a normal occurrence in the future.

---

p.143 **Painted Lady** *Vanessa cardui*

Description: 28 mm (1.1 in). The ground colour of the upperside is orange-buff, often with a strong rosy tinge, and overlaid with a pattern of black spots and patches. The forewing tip has an extensive black patch containing white spots. The hindwing has an arc of prominent black spots just inside the outer margin. The underside of the forewing resembles the upperside, but the underside of the hindwing is mottled grey and brown with a row of bluish eye-spots near the outer margin.

Similar species: American Painted Lady, a very scarce vagrant to southwest Europe from the Canary Islands, is superficially similar but has just two large eye-spots on the underside of the hindwing.

Flight: Mainly April to October, in one or two broods, but the butterfly can be seen in any month in the south. It often basks on the ground or the vegetation with its wings wide open, and readily launches into a powerful gliding flight when approached. It feeds from a wide range of flowers and also enjoys a drink from ripe fruit.

Habitat: A far-ranging migrant, this butterfly can be found almost wherever there are flowers, including gardens, roadsides, and even montane grassland. The larval foodplants are mainly thistles, but mallows are often used, especially in the south: Stinging Nettle, Viper's Bugloss, and knapweeds are occasionally used as well. During the 1996 'Painted Lady year', when huge numbers bred in the British Isles, the caterpillars were reported to have caused severe damage to fields of borage.

Life-cycle: The eggs are green with conspicuous glassy ribs, and they are laid singly on the uppersides of the leaves. The young

caterpillar feeds on the underside of the leaf, concealed under a thin sheet of silk, but it can usually be tracked down by looking for the clear 'windows' that it leaves in the upper surface. Older caterpillars feed in tents of silk and leaves. The fully grown caterpillar is about 30 mm (1.2 in) long and is black with pale dots and branched black or yellowish spines. A broken yellow line runs along each side. The chrysalis is greyish, tinged with pink and overlaid here and there with gold. It is usually formed inside a tent of leaves. The pupal stage lasts for about two weeks.

Range: This is one of the world's most widely distributed butterflies, being found almost all over the world, apart from South America. In North America it is often called the Thistle Butterfly.

Although found all over Europe, including Iceland, in the summer, the Painted Lady cannot survive the European winter in any stage except possibly in the far south of Spain. Adults emerging in late summer usually fly southwards and some may reach North Africa, but the majority perish with the first frosts. The insects breed throughout the year in North Africa, where clouds of them can be seen flying wherever there is vegetation. Huge swarms can sometimes be seen flying northwards through southern Europe in the spring.

p.144 **Small Tortoiseshell** *Aglais urticae*

Description: 23 mm (0.9 in) The ground colour of the upperside is a rich orange or brick-red, with a blue-studded black border to all wings. The front edge of the forewing has three conspicuous black patches with yellowish patches between them, and there are usually three more black spots further back. The basal half of the hindwing is sooty brown. The undersides are mottled brown, rather sooty towards the base and with a submarginal band of blue spots. The overall effect is very much like the bark of a tree and it provides excellent camouflage for the resting or hibernating butterfly.

Similar species: Large Tortoiseshell, extremely rare in Britain, is larger, with much less black on the hindwing.

Flight: May to October in one, two, or three broods, and again in early spring after hibernation. The adults normally bask and feed with their wings wide open and are very fond of buddleias and the garden 'ice-plant' in the autumn. Flight consists of long glides separated by bouts of flapping.

Habitat: This is a very mobile species and is found wherever there are flowers, including town parks and gardens, wasteland, and montane pastures up to 2,750 m (9,000 ft). It is one of our commonest garden butterflies. The major larval foodplant is Stinging Nettle, but Annual Nettle is also used and Roman Nettle is possibly used quite a bit in the south. Caterpillars have also been seen feeding on Hop.

Life-cycle: The pale-green, ribbed eggs are laid in large clusters on the undersides of young leaves after hibernation. The caterpillars live communally in silken tents until after the final moult. When fully grown, the caterpillar is about 22 mm (0.9 in) long, and generally brown or black, densely speckled with white or yellow. There are two yellowish bands on each side and the branching black spines may have yellow bases. The chrysalis is grey or brown with a golden sheen and hangs from the foodplant or from some neighbouring support. The adult butterfly emerges within two or three weeks. A second and even a third brood may appear during the summer in the southern half of Europe, with adults from the final brood going into hibernation after feeding up on the autumn flowers. They hide in hollow trees and all kinds of building, where their sombre undersides make them difficult to spot. They are among the first butterflies to reappear in the spring – often as early as February if the weather is warm.

Range: Throughout Europe and temperate Asia. *A. milberti* of North America is very similar and may be conspecific.

The subspecies *A. u. ichnusa* from Corsica and Sardinia appears brighter, having slightly less black on the hindwing and no black spots in the rear half of the forewing.

p.145 **Comma** *Polygonia c-album*

Description: 23 mm (0.9 in). The uppersides are some shade of orange with sooty-brown markings, and with paler spots close to the deeply indented or jagged margins. The undersides are mottled brown and resemble dead leaves, and the hindwing carries the white comma-shaped mark that gives the butterfly its common name.

Similar species: There is no other British butterfly with which the jagged-winged Comma can be confused, although some of the fritillaries are similar in flight. Southern Comma of southeast Europe has fewer and smaller dark spots on the upperside and a faint white V or Y on the underside. Nettle-tree Butterfly is superficially similar at rest, but hindwing is less jagged and has no comma-mark.

Flight: June to September in two broods, and again in spring after hibernation. Flight consists mainly of long, elegant glides, and the butterfly enjoys basking on the vegetation with its wings wide open. It is very fond of Bramble blossom, and garden buddleia and 'ice-plant', and second-brood insects also enjoy blackberries and pears.

Habitat: This wide-ranging species can turn up anywhere from sea-level to about 2,000 m (6,550 ft), but its main habitats are woodland glades and clearings, hedgerows, gardens, and orchards. The larval foodplants include Hop, Stinging Nettle, elms, sallows, and currants.

Life-cycle: This butterfly exhibits a rather complex life-cycle, with two distinct forms. The hibernating insects are all of the dark-orange form and they mate and lay their eggs in the spring. The eggs are green and glassy, with prominent ribs, and they are laid singly or in twos and threes on the edges of the leaves. They hatch in two or three weeks and the caterpillars then follow one of two paths of development. One group feeds up quickly and produces new adults in midsummer, but these new butterflies are much paler than the spring ones and are known as f. *hutchinsoni*. The second group of larvae develop more slowly and produce new adults of the normal dark form in late summer. Meanwhile, the *hutchinsoni* adults mate and produce a second generation of rapidly maturing larvae, which develop into dark commas identical to their slower-developing relatives. Both groups of late-summer butterflies go into hibernation in hollow trees and outhouses and in dense hedgerows and shrubs, where their leaf-like appearance affords them plenty of protection from predators. It is not known what causes the spring larvae to separate into fast and slow lanes. The caterpillar is largely brown with branched spines, and when mature it has a large white patch on the rear end, giving it a striking resemblance to bird-droppings and effective immunity from predation. The mature caterpillar is about 35 mm (1.4 in) long, and it turns into a dark-brown chrysalis that is very hard to distinguish from a dead leaf.

Range:  Throughout Europe apart from Scotland, Ireland and the far north. Also in North Africa and right across temperate Asia to Japan. The Comma of North America is a very similar species, *Polygonia comma*.

The Comma has had a very chequered history in Britain during the last 100 years or so. It was widely distributed during the 18th and 19th centuries, but then the population crashed and, until the 1930s, the butterfly survived only in a small area around the River Severn. It then began to spread again and is now quite common throughout Wales and the southern half of England. The decline may have been caused by a period of cold, wet winters and the decline in hop-growing. The subsequent spread of the species may have been brought about by its ability to use nettles and elms as foodplants, as well as an improvement in the climate.

---

p.145 **Southern Comma** *Polygonia egea*

Description: 23 mm (0.9 in). The ground colour of the upperside is bright orange, with a few sooty-brown or black patches. The underside has a mottled-brown pattern reminiscent of a fine wood grain, with an indistinct blue submarginal band and a faint white V or Y in the centre of the hindwing. Both wings are edged with brown and yellow and have deeply indented outer margins.

Similar species: Comma has rather heavier dark markings on the upperside, especially in the overwintering generation, and has a distinctly comma-like white mark on the underside of the hindwing. Apart from the Nettle-tree Butterfly, which has a very different upperside, no other species has such jagged wing-margins.

Flight: May to October in two or three broods, and again in early spring after hibernation. First-brood insects are a little paler than later ones, especially on the underside. The butterfly likes to bask on walls and tree-trunks, often in a head-down position, and also on the ground.

Habitat: Orchards, gardens, roadsides, and waste ground, usually in dry areas up to about 1,000 m (3,275 ft). The normal larval foodplant is Pellitory-of-the-Wall, but Stinging Nettle and elms may also be used.

Life-cycle: The eggs, which are very much like those of the Comma, are laid singly or in small groups on the foodplant. The caterpillar is largely black and yellow on the top and brown below, with conspicuous branched spines. It is about 35 mm (1.4 in) long when mature, and it pupates on or near the foodplant. The chrysalis is brownish yellow and rather spiny.

Range: The Mediterranean region, from southern France to Greece and on to Iran.

---

p.146 **Map Butterfly** *Araschnia levana*

Description: 18 mm (0.7 in). This butterfly exists in two very different seasonal forms, which can easily be taken for two different species. The spring brood, known as f. *levana*, has predominantly orange uppersides, heavily spotted with black and with conspicuous white spots near the tip of the forewing, and there is a row of small blue spots around the outer margin of the hindwing. The butterfly is often mistaken for a small fritillary. The summer brood, known as f. *prorsa*, is more like a small White Admiral. It has dark-brown uppersides, with a cream band running through the centre of each wing, and there is a thin reddish or orange submarginal band on the hindwing and sometimes on the forewing as well. The undersides of both forms exhibit a complex pattern of white veins and lines on a purplish-brown background, and it is this pattern that gives the insect both its English name of Map Butterfly and its scientific name *Araschnia*, which is derived from the Greek word for a spider's web.

Similar species: The underside pattern is unique and the butterfly cannot be confused with any other species when seen at close quarters.

Flight: April to October, usually in two broods but often with a partial third brood in some areas. Insects of both spring and summer broods enjoy basking with their wings wide open, often on bare ground. They fly with a dainty, floating motion and rarely stay airborne for long before returning to a favourite perch.

Habitat: Light woodland and rough ground, including roadsides, up to about 1,000 m (3,275 ft). The larval foodplant is Stinging Nettle, and this restricts the species to disturbed habitats.

Life-cycle: The ribbed, pale-green eggs are laid in chains on the undersides of the nettle leaves. There are usually between 6 and 15 eggs in a chain, although there may be as many as 20, and the chains resemble small nettle catkins. The female has to bend her body a good deal to add eggs to the end of the chain and may end up with her abdomen perpendicular to the rest of her body. The caterpillar is black, with branched black or brownish spines on its body and two prominent 'horns' on the head. It feeds in loose colonies until fully grown – at a length of about 20 mm (0.8 in) – and then pupates on the foodplant. The chrysalis is greyish brown, often with a purplish tinge, and marked with pale-golden or brassy spots. Summer pupae produce *prorsa* adults in two or three weeks, but pupae formed in the autumn – often as late as the end of October – go through the winter and produce *levana* adults in the spring. Experimental work has shown that it is the varying day-length experienced by the larvae that determines their adult form.

Range: Central Europe, from the Baltic to the Alps and western France, and on across Asia to Japan. Also in northern Iberia and northern Greece, but absent from the Mediterranean region.

The butterfly is not native in the British Isles, but it was introduced to the Forest of Dean early in the 20th century and colonies survived there for some years until they were deliberately destroyed. The species is at present increasing its range in western Europe and has reached Finland and southern Sweden in recent years, and there seems no reason why it should not become established in the British Isles in the future.

p.147 **Cardinal** *Argynnis pandora*

Description: 40 mm (1.6 in). The upperside is orange, heavily suffused with green and boldly marked with black, including two complete rows of spots in the outer part of each wing. The male is slightly less green than the female, from which he is readily distinguished by the presence of two narrow black streaks, containing scent-scales, along the veins in the rear half of his forewing. In both sexes, the underside of the forewing is largely salmon pink, heavily marked with black spots and with a pale green tip. The underside of the hindwing is pale green, often with a bluish tinge, and striped with silver in the outer half, although the stripes are sometimes very faint and usually most apparent in the female.

Similar species: Silver-washed Fritillary has a similar pattern, but usually lacks the green suffusion and the green tips under the forewings.

Flight: May to July. Flight is often fast and powerful, although when moving from flower to flower the butterfly more often travels in a series of elegant glides. It is very fond of thistles and can also be seen in large numbers at freshly opened lime blossom (*Tilia*) and at the flowers of the Oleaster tree, which is often planted around the shores of the Mediterranean.

Habitat: Flowery meadows, woodland margins, and waste ground, up to an altitude of about 1,500 m (4,925 ft). The larval foodplants are Wild Pansy and other *Viola* species.

Life-cycle: The yellowish-green eggs are conical and strongly ribbed, and they are laid singly on or near the foodplant. They hatch within two or three weeks, but the caterpillars go into hibernation among the leaf-litter when still quite small and do not complete their growth until the following April or May. The fully grown caterpillar is about 35 mm (1.4 in) long and largely brown, with branched spines and a broad black band along the middle of the back. The chrysalis, suspended low down on the foodplant or neighbouring vegetation, is greyish brown with metallic spots.

Range: Mainly southern Europe, but extending up the Atlantic coast to Brittany and also reaching The Czech Republic. Also in western Asia and North Africa.

441

p.148 **Silver-washed Fritillary** *Argynnis paphia*

Description: 35 mm (1.4 in). Some Scandinavian specimens may be much smaller. The upperside is normally bright orange, heavily spotted with black. The male is somewhat brighter than the female and carries four black streaks of scent-scales near the middle of the forewing. The underside of the forewing is normally orange in both sexes, lightly marked with black, while the underside of the hindwing is greenish with silver stripes and a purplish tinge towards the outside. Some females are lightly dusted with green scales on the upperside, but a small proportion of them have a quite different appearance: these females have a pale-fawn ground colour and are very heavily coated with green, giving them an olive-green appearance overall. Known as f. *valezina*, they are most common in the more densely wooded areas, including England's New Forest, where up to 15 per cent of females may be of this form.

Similar species: Cardinal resembles female but the underside of the forewing is salmon-pink with a broad green tip. No other fritillary has silver stripes on the underside.

Flight: May to August. Flight is fast, with long glides interspersed with periods of flapping. The adults often bask with their wings wide open and are very partial to Bramble blossom. They also flock to any buddleia blossom within range.

Habitat: Woodland rides and clearings, especially in coppiced woodlands, and the surrounding scrub and grassland, reaching altitudes of about 1,500 m (4,925 ft). The larval foodplants are various violets.

Life-cycle: The ribbed, conical eggs are laid singly in bark-crevices and amongst the mosses on tree-trunks, usually about a metre (3 ft) above the ground. They are pale cream at first, but become slate-coloured before hatching – usually about two weeks after they are laid. The young caterpillars eat their eggshells and then immediately go into hibernation in a crevice or among the moss. They wake in spring and crawl down the trunks to begin feeding on the violet leaves. Some caterpillars may actually stay in their eggshells until the spring. The fully grown caterpillar is about 38 mm (1.5 in) long and velvety brown with two bright yellow stripes along the back. It has numerous branched brown spines, but the two anterior ones are black and point forward over the head like a pair of horns. The chrysalis is brown and spiky with large silvery spots that look like dew, and it is very hard to spot amongst the vegetation. It is often suspended from sprawling Bramble stems.

Range: Most of Europe and across temperate Asia to Japan. Absent from Scotland and northern England and from northern Scandinavia, and apparently declining in several other areas although it is still doing well in some places. Also in North Africa.

Pallas's Fritillary *Argynnis laodice*

Description: 28 mm (1.1 in). The uppersides are bright orange, heavily marked with rounded or oval black spots, although those near the centre of the forewing may be rather square. The male has two slender black streaks of scent-scales near the rear of each forewing, while the female has a very small white spot near the tip. The underside of the forewing is orange, with heavy black spots near the centre and very faint greyish spots around the edge. The underside of the hindwing has a greenish-yellow basal half and a purplish-brown outer half, the two areas being separated by a ragged white line. Specimens from the western edge of the range tend to be smaller and less heavily marked than those from further east.

Similar species: Marbled Fritillary is smaller and lacks the white line on the underside of the hindwing. High Brown Fritillary and Dark Green Fritillary have similar uppersides, but their undersides are very different.

Flight: July to August. A fast-flying species with frequent long glides.

Habitat: Damp, open woodland and surrounding fields and scrub, mainly in the lowlands. The principal larval foodplant is Marsh Violet, but other violets are sometimes used.

Life-cycle: The eggs, which are laid singly or in small groups, are conical and pale yellow with brown mottling and they hatch within two or three weeks of laying. The caterpillars hibernate in the first instar and complete their growth in the spring.

Range: Eastern Europe, from the eastern shores of the Baltic to Hungary, and on across temperate Asia to China. A rare vagrant in Sweden. The species is rapidly declining and endangered in the western parts of its range.

p.148 **Dark Green Fritillary** *Argynnis aglaja*

Description: 25–30 mm (1.0–1.2 in). The male uppersides are rich orange with dark-brown or black spots. The markings are variable, but there is always an arc of five post-discal spots on the hindwing, and the central spot is usually noticeably smaller than the others. The female ground colour is paler than that of the male and there is a conspicuous row of pale spots around the margin of each wing. There is often a heavy brown suffusion at the base of each wing. The underside of the forewing is pale orange in both sexes, with black spots and a faint submarginal row of silvery spots or dashes. The underside of the hindwing is largely green with large silver spots. Both wings are rather less angular than in the other large fritillaries, with straight or slightly convex outer edges.

Similar species: High Brown Fritillary and Niobe Fritillary are similar on the upperside, but both have an arc of rust-coloured eye-spots on the underside of the hindwing. Marbled Fritillary has neither green nor silver on the underside.

Flight: June to August. The butterfly usually flies fast and low, with a powerful flapping flight, and rarely settles for long even when

feeding. It is particularly attracted to
thistles and knapweeds, and also to the
flowers of Red Clover.

Habitat: Open country of all kinds, including
heathland and the northern tundra, but
most common on rough grassland. Many
colonies occur on coastal cliffs and dunes,
but the butterfly can also be found on
mountains to a height of about 2,500 m
(8,200 ft). It is sometimes found in
woodland rides and clearings, and is a
regular inhabitant of light woodland in the
northern parts of its range. The larval
foodplants are various species of violet.

Life-cycle: The pale-green, conical, ribbed eggs are
laid singly on or near the foodplant, and
they hatch after about two weeks. The
young caterpillars eat their eggshells, but
then go straight into hibernation in the
turf or leaf-litter. They feed during the
spring. The fully grown caterpillar is about
38 mm (1.5 in) long, and velvety black
with a row of red spots on each side. It is
clothed with branched black spines. The
chrysalis, which is enclosed in a tent of
leaves and silk low down in the vegetation,
is brown and black with a deep notch
between the thorax and abdomen.

Range: Throughout Europe, from the
Mediterranean to the shores of the Arctic
Ocean, although uncommon north of the
Arctic Circle. Also in North Africa and
across temperate Asia to Japan.
Surprisingly for such a powerful flier, it is
absent from Corsica and Sardinia.
Scandinavian specimens are relatively
small and often heavily dusted with dark
scales in both sexes, as are some high-
altitude specimens. It is the commonest
and most widespread of the fritillaries in
the British Isles.

p.149 **High Brown Fritillary** *Argynnis adippe*

Description: 25–30 mm (1.0–1.2 in). The male
upperside is bright orange, with a variable
pattern of dark-brown or black spots; there
are two indistinct dark streaks, containing

scent-scales, near the rear edge of the forewing. There is an arc of rounded, post-discal spots on the hindwing but the central one is either very small or absent. The female ground colour is paler, but her spots are heavier and she is often heavily dusted with greenish scales, especially on the hindwing. In both sexes the underside of the forewing is orange with heavy black spotting, with or without silvery spots at the yellowish tip. The underside of the hindwing is yellowish brown, often heavily tinged with green, and usually with large silver spots. There is always an arc of rust-coloured post-discal spots containing silvery pupils.

Similar species: Dark Green Fritillary lacks the eye-spots on the underside of the hindwing. Niobe Fritillary has more prominent veins on the underside of the hindwing, and the pale spot at the base of the cell has a central black dot.

Flight: June to August, flying rapidly in sunshine and often staying quite high in the trees, although readily coming down to feed at Bramble blossom and thistles.

Habitat: Woodland rides and clearings, scrub, and rough grassland, from sea level to about 2,000 m (6,550 ft). The larval foodplants are various violets.

Life-cycle: The conical, lightly ribbed eggs are laid singly on or near the foodplant. They are yellowish green at first, but turn orange after a few days. They do not hatch until the following spring. The caterpillar is dark brown, with black patches on the back and often with a white line along the middle. It has branching, rust-coloured spines on each segment and is about 40 mm (1.6 in) long when fully grown. The chrysalis is dark brown with shiny points and is usually concealed in a tent of leaves low down amongst the vegetation. In warm weather the adult may emerge in under three weeks.

Range: Most of Europe, but absent from the far north and from Scotland and Ireland. Also in North Africa and across temperate Asia to Japan.

The High Brown Fritillary is one of Britain's rarest butterflies, now confined to a few western areas, although some colonies seem to be surviving quite well, especially those in the Lake District that inhabit fairly open scrub and bracken-covered hillsides. Changes in woodland management, especially the reduction of coppicing, have been largely responsible for the decline of this butterfly in Britain, for the caterpillars need plenty of open areas in which they can soak up the sunshine.

The High Brown Fritillary exists in several distinct forms and geographical races, which differ mainly in the pattern of the underside of the hindwing. In Greece and neighbouring parts of southeast Europe it is represented by f. *cleodoxa*, which has virtually no silver on the underside: f. *chlorodippe* from Iberia has large silver spots on a bright-green background.

---

p.149 **Niobe Fritillary** *Argynnis niobe*

Description: 23–30 mm (0.9–1.2 in). The ground colour of the upperside is orange, heavily marked with dark-brown or black spots, although these vary a good deal in size. The post-discal arc on the hindwing usually contains three spots of normal size and two very small ones, although the small ones may be absent. The underside of the forewing is largely orange, with a yellowish tip and the usual dark spots. The underside of the hindwing is yellowish, with or without silver spots and often heavily dusted with green at the base; the veins are lined with black, and the pale spot at the base of the cell generally contains a tiny black dot.

Similar species: High Brown Fritillary lacks the black veins and the small black dot in the cell spot on the underside of the hindwing.

Flight: June to August, feeding at thistles, knapweeds, and many other flowers. It flies rapidly, but each flight is usually quite short.

Habitat: Flower-rich grassland from sea level to about 2,500 m (8,200 ft). The larval foodplants are violets and occasionally plantains.

Life-cycle: The ribbed, conical eggs are pale yellow at first, but they soon become rust-coloured. They are laid singly on or near the foodplant and do not usually hatch until the following spring. In some southern areas they may hatch in two or three weeks, but then the caterpillars go into a long hibernation and do not start feeding in earnest until the spring. The fully grown caterpillar is very like that of the High Brown Fritillary – dark brown with paler spines and with angular black patches and a pale stripe on the back. It is about 40 mm (1.6 in) long and it pupates in a flimsy silken tent low down on the vegetation. The chrysalis is smooth and brown, with silvery points.

Range: Most of Europe apart from the British Isles and northern Scandinavia. Also in North Africa and on through temperate Asia to the Caspian Sea and Iran.

The Niobe Fritillary exists in two main forms: f. *niobe* has numerous silver spots on the underside of the hindwing, while f. *eris* has no silver and its hindwing is essentially chequered with yellow. In most areas, *eris* is far more common than *niobe*, although the latter is the commoner of the two forms in central France. Only *eris* is known in Iberia south of the Pyrenees.

Corsican Fritillary *Argynnis elisa*

Description: 25 mm (1.0 in). The uppersides are rich orange with relatively small black spots, although there are two or three quite large oval ones near the tip of the forewing. There is a slightly paler discal band in the hindwing. The underside of the forewing is orange, with two large black spots near the centre and a greenish tip with a few silver spots. The underside of the hindwing is yellowish green, liberally decorated with small silver spots and with a post-discal arc of small, rust-coloured eye-spots.

Similar species:	High Brown Fritillary and Niobe Fritillary are larger, with fewer and larger silver spots below, but neither occurs in Corsica or Sardinia.
Flight:	June to July.
Habitat:	Maquis and open woodland, usually in upland areas from 900 to 1,500 m (2,950–4,925 ft). The larval foodplants are violets.
Life-cycle:	The eggs are laid singly on the foodplant and they hatch within two or three weeks. Winter is probably passed in the egg stage, although some individuals may hibernate as small caterpillars.
Range:	Confined to Corsica and Sardinia.

The Corsican Fritillary is very similar to the Niobe Fritillary in many ways and may be no more than a subspecies of that butterfly.

p.150 **Queen of Spain Fritillary** *Issoria lathonia*

Description:	14–22 mm (0.6–0.9 in). The uppersides are bright orange, often with a metallic-green sheen when fresh, and they have a fairly full pattern of black spots, including two complete rows of spots near the outer margin of each wing. The outer margin of the forewing is distinctly concave, and this distinguishes the butterfly from most of the other fritillaries, but the best diagnostic features are found on the underside of the hindwing, where the silver spots are extremely large and shiny. The underside of the forewing is pale orange with black spots and a few silver spots near the tip.
Similar species:	None.
Flight:	February to October in two or more broods. The butterfly is a great migrant and covers large distances on the Continent, but for much of the time it is content to float lazily from flower to flower.
Habitat:	Flower-rich places of all kinds, including gardens, from sea level to about 2,500 m (8,200 ft). The larval foodplants are various species of *Viola*, mainly of the pansy type.
Life-cycle:	The pale, conical eggs are laid singly on the foodplants and usually hatch within about a week. The caterpillar is essentially

chrysalis

black, speckled with white, and with two narrow white lines running along the back. There are brown patches on the sides, and the branched spines are rust-coloured. The caterpillar is about 35 mm (1.4 in) long when fully grown and it pupates low down on or near the foodplant. The chrysalis is dark brown with a white 'saddle' and other white splashes that give it more than a passing resemblance to a bird-dropping. Winter can be passed in the larval, pupal, or adult stage, and possibly in the egg stage as well.

Range: Most of Europe apart from the far north and the British Isles, where it occurs only as an occasional vagrant. Also in North Africa and across Asia to China. The butterfly's failure to establish itself in the British Isles is strange in view of the fact that it flourishes so well elsewhere in Europe, including the southern parts of Scandinavia.

---

p.150 **Twin-spot Fritillary** *Brenthis hecate*

Description: 20 mm (0.8 in). The uppersides have the typical fritillary coloration of dark brown or black spots on an orange background, with two complete rows of uniform small spots running parallel to the margin in the outer part of each wing – in the post-discal and submarginal areas. Some females are heavily dusted with brown scales. The underside of the forewing resembles the upperside, but has a yellowish tip. The underside of the hindwing is orange and yellow and, like the upperside, it has two complete rows of black spots.

Similar species: Marbled Fritillary and several others have two rows of spots on the upperside of each wing, but these spots are not uniform and none of the species has two rows on the underside as well.

Flight: May and June

Habitat: Rough, grassy slopes, usually between 600 and 1,500 m (1,975 and 4,925 ft). The major larval foodplant is Meadowsweet, but *Dorycnium* species and various other legumes may also be eaten.

Life-cycle:

The ribbed, conical eggs are laid singly or in small groups. The caterpillars go into a long hibernation when still quite small, and growth is completed in the spring. The mature caterpillar is about 35 mm (1.4 in) long. It is dark brown with broken white lines and pale spines. The head is orange and the face is yellowish. Pupation takes place on or near the foodplant and the chrysalis is pale brown with prominent silvery spikes.

Range: Iberia and the Mediterranean region, extending northwards in eastern Europe to Hungary and Slovakia and on to central Asia. A local species in western Europe, but more generally distributed in the east.

p.151 **Marbled Fritillary** *Brenthis daphne*

Description: 20–26 mm (0.8–1.0 in). The upperside is orange with dark spots. The spots of the post-discal row are very uneven in size, especially on the forewing. Both wings carry a more or less complete arc of submarginal spots, which are often rather angular. The underside of the forewing resembles the upperside, except that it has a yellowish tip. The underside of the hindwing is very distinctive, with a largely yellow basal half and a strong purple cast on the outer half. There is a faint arc of post-discal spots in the purple area. The front edge of the forewing is strongly curved, giving the outstretched butterfly a much more rounded appearance than most other fritillaries.

Similar species: Lesser Marbled Fritillary is smaller and usually has an unbroken dark margin on the hindwing.

Flight: May to August, often floating from flower to flower with hardly a flap of the wings. It is very fond of Bramble blossom.

Habitat: Open woodland and scrubby habitats, with plenty of flowers and plenty of exposure to sunshine, from sea level to about 1,500 m (4,925 ft). The normal larval foodplants are Bramble and Raspberry, but violets are occasionally used as well.

Life-cycle: The ribbed, conical eggs are laid singly or in small groups on or near the foodplants. They are pale yellow at first, but soon become rust-coloured. In southern Europe the eggs hatch within about ten days and the caterpillars go into hibernation while still quite small. In central areas of Europe, however, the eggs do not hatch until the following spring. The caterpillar is black with white markings, including two conspicuous white lines on the back and numerous bristly, reddish-brown spines. It is about 35 mm (1.4 in) long when mature and it pupates on the foodplant. The chrysalis is silvery grey with prominent shiny spines.

Range: Southern and central Europe and on through temperate Asia to Japan. Absent from the British Isles and neighbouring parts of the Continent.

p.151 **Lesser Marbled Fritillary** *Brenthis ino*

Description: 20 mm (0.8 in). The uppersides are orange with dark spots, which tend to be more uniform in size than in the Marbled Fritillary. The margins are usually entirely black or dark brown, especially on the hindwing, and there is a female form that is heavily dusted with brown scales. The underside of the forewing resembles the upperside except that it has a yellowish tip and no dark margin. The underside of the hindwing is largely yellow in the basal half, with an orange or brick-coloured band near the base surrounding a conspicuous yellow spot in space 4. Beyond the middle, the wing is purplish brown, with paler patches and an indistinct row of eye-spots.

Similar species: Marbled Fritillary generally has more purple on the underside of the hindwing and lacks the distinct yellow spot at the base. The dark margins on the upperside tend to be broken into separate spots.

Flight: June to August, keeping fairly close to the ground with a rather weak and fluttery motion. It is especially fond of the nectar of Marsh Thistle, knapweeds, Ragged Robin, and Bramble.

Habitat: Damp, flower-rich grassland, including hay-meadows, from sea level to about 2,000 m (6,550 ft). Also on bogs and in damp forest clearings. The larval foodplants include numerous rosaceous species, such as Meadowsweet, Great Burnet, Cloudberry, and Raspberry.

Life-cycle: The conical, strongly ribbed eggs are laid singly or in pairs on the foodplant. They turn from pale yellow to orange just before hatching. In northern parts of the range the eggs do not hatch until the following spring, but elsewhere they hatch about two weeks after they are laid and the caterpillars go into hibernation when about half-grown. The mature caterpillar is about 35 mm (1.4 in) long. It is essentially brown, with numerous yellowish-grey streaks and two conspicuous white or yellow lines on the back. The spines or tubercles are pale orange with black bristles. Pupation takes place on the foodplant, and the chrysalis is purplish brown with prominent silvery points.

Range: Most of Europe, apart from the British Isles and the extreme south, and on through temperate Asia to Japan. The species is declining in many areas as a result of land-drainage, for this species is very much tied to damp situations.

Scandinavian specimens are somewhat smaller than those from elsewhere and the underside of the hindwing may be almost entirely pale yellow.

---

p.152 **Shepherd's Fritillary** *Boloria pales*

Description: 16–19 mm (0.6–0.75 in). The upperside is orange with black markings, including two more or less complete rows of spots – the post-discals and submarginals – in the outer part of each wing. The discal spots are often rather square and linked together and there is usually an extensive dark smudge in the basal half of the hindwing. The underside of the forewing is orange with indistinct black markings and with yellow spots around the tip. The underside of the hindwing is brightly marked with red and yellow, although the pattern is variable. There is usually a rust-red band near the base and another, usually broken, in the discal area. There is a large yellow patch close to the margin at the tip of space 3. There is usually a band of white spots around the margin.

Similar species: Mountain Fritillary is a little larger and may be a little paler, but very difficult to distinguish in the field. Cranberry Fritillary is much redder under the hindwing.

Flight: June to September, usually keeping close to the ground.

Habitat: Montane pastures, including intensively grazed areas, usually between 1,500 and 3,000 m (4,925 and 9850 ft), although sometimes as low as 1,200 m (3,925 ft). The larval foodplants are *Viola* species, especially Long-spurred Pansy, and occasionally plantains.

Life-cycle: The conical, slightly ribbed, yellowish eggs are laid singly or in small groups, and they hatch in two or three weeks. The caterpillar goes into hibernation when partly grown, and when fully grown in late spring it is about 32 cm (1.25 in) long. It is pale brown with darker blotches and a broad cream stripe along the back, and the pale spines are clothed with dark bristles. Pupation takes place low down on the foodplant and the chrysalis is greyish brown with small silvery points.

Range: The mountains of southern and central Europe, and on through Asia to the Himalayas.

Specimens from the highest levels are often quite small.

---

p.152 **Mountain Fritillary** *Boloria napaea*

Description: 16–22 mm (0.6–0.9 in). The uppersides are orange, often with a strong yellowish tinge and with an extensive dark patch in the basal half of the hindwing. The black spots include more or less complete post-discal and submarginal series on each wing, while the discal spots are rather linear and often linked into a continuous zig-zag line. The underside of the forewing is orange with a yellow tip and faint black spots, while the underside of the hindwing is largely orange and yellow with white marginal spots. There is a particularly large yellow patch near the tip of space 3. Females are generally larger, and on both surfaces they are paler or 'dustier' than males: the markings are heavier and the underside of the hindwing often has a greenish tinge at the base.

Similar species: Shepherd's Fritillary is usually smaller. Cranberry Fritillary is largely red and white under the hindwing.

Flight: June to August. A rather restless species, generally flying close to the ground.

Habitat: Stony mountainsides, usually from close to the tree-line to about 3,000 m (9,850 ft), in the Alps, but down to sea level in northern Scandinavia: usually in damp places. The larval foodplants are violets and Alpine Bistort.

Life-cycle: The conical eggs are pale yellow and lightly ribbed, and they are laid singly on the foodplant. They hatch within two or three weeks and the resulting caterpillars go into a long hibernation when still quite small. They wake and continue feeding in the spring. In the less extreme habitats they complete their growth within a few weeks, but in the far north and at high levels in the Alps they hibernate for a second time before reaching maturity. The fully grown caterpillar is about 35 mm long. It is dark brown with cream flecks and black spots, and conspicuous, pale, bristly spines. The purplish or greyish-brown chrysalis is attached to the foodplant or to a stone.

Range: The Alps and the extreme eastern end of the Pyrenees, and Scandinavia – where it extends to the North Cape and the shores of the Arctic Ocean. Also in much of Arctic Asia, and the northern parts of North America, where it is called the Napaea Fritillary.

Scandinavian specimens are generally smaller than those from the Alps and have smaller markings.

p.153 **Cranberry Fritillary** *Boloria aquilonaris*

Description: 17–22 mm (0.7–0.9 in). The ground colour of the upperside is usually bright orange, although often somewhat paler in the north, with a strong pattern of black streaks and spots. The discal spots on the forewing are often V-shaped and frequently linked to form a conspicuous zig-zag line. There is a large dark area at the base of the hindwing. The underside of the forewing is orange with yellow spots at the tip and fairly heavy black spotting. The underside of the hindwing is largely rust-red with white spots, including a conspicuous white patch right at the base and a rather square spot in the middle of the front margin. The marginal spots are silvery white.

Similar species: Mountain Fritillary and Shepherd's Fritillary are similar above, but much yellower on the underside of the hindwing and with much less black under the forewing.

Flight: June to August. Rather quick and very agile, flying only in the sunshine and usually keeping very close to the ground. Marsh Cinquefoil is one of its favourite flowers.

Habitat: Bogs and wet heaths, including the open birch forests of the far north. Although found at sea level in the north, it reaches heights of about 2,000 m (6,550 ft) in the Alps. The larval foodplant is normally Cranberry, although Marsh Violet and Common Bistort are said to be used in some areas.

Life-cycle: The conical, greenish-yellow eggs are laid singly on the stems and leaves of the foodplant, and they hatch within two or three weeks. The caterpillar feeds for a while before going into hibernation, often inside the stems of the foodplant. In the less extreme parts of its range, the caterpillar matures during the following spring, but in the higher and more northerly regions it takes two years to mature. The fully grown caterpillar is about 32 mm (1.25 in) long and is dark brown with pale spots and two thin white lines on the back. The spines are pale, but densely clothed with dark bristles. Pupation takes place low on the foodplant and the chrysalis is greyish with short points.

Range: North and central Europe, extending right to the North Cape and then eastwards to Siberia. Scattered and rare to the west of the Rhine, and absent from the British Isles.

Specimens from the far north are generally smaller than those from further south, with the largest ones inhabiting lowland bogs in the southern part of the range. The insect occurs in small, localized colonies, and as a result of land-drainage it is endangered in most parts of its range.

p.153   **Balkan Fritillary** *Boloria graeca*

Description: 16–20 mm (0.6–0.8 in). The uppersides are bright orange with black spots and chequered fringes. There are two complete arcs of spots towards the margin of each wing, the outer or sub-marginal spots being distinctly triangular. The hindwing has a black patch at the base but this is relatively narrow and does not take in the outer part of the cell. The underside of the forewing is pale orange with a yellow tip and a spot pattern similar to that of the upperside. The underside of the hindwing is basically straw-coloured with rusty-brown and green marbling, and there is a prominent silvery spot at the end of the cell. There is an arc of well-defined brown ringed eye-spots in the post-discal region. Females tend to be greener below than males, and specimens from the western parts of the range also have more green and fewer rusty patches.

Similar species: Mountain and Shepherd's fritillaries have more extensive black areas on the upperside of the hindwing and much less spotting under the forewing. Cranberry Fritillary is superficially similar but does not occur in the same areas.

Flight: July to August.

Habitat: Montane meadows, usually above 1,500 m (4,925 ft). The larval foodplants are violets.

Life-cycle: Winter is passed as a small caterpillar.

Range: The Balkans and a small area of the Alpes-Maritimes on the French/Italian border. Greek specimens tend to be larger than those from elsewhere.

---

p.154 **Bog Fritillary** *Proclossiana eunomia*

Description: 16–23 mm (0.6–0.9 in). The uppersides are bright orange and the rounded post-discal spots of the forewing lie in an almost straight line, but the most obvious feature is the dark zig-zag line around the edge of each wing. This zig-zag is repeated on the undersides, which are essentially pale orange with yellow borders. The underside of the hindwing has a bright-yellow band near the middle and an arc of dark rings with pale centres in the outer half. In the Scandinavian race (*P. e. ossiana*) the yellow areas are replaced by white or silvery patches. Scandinavian insects are also smaller than those from elsewhere and often heavily dusted with brown on the upperside. Females from other areas may also have an attractive dusky suffusion.

Similar species: Pearl-bordered and Small Pearl-bordered fritillaries lack the fully developed eye-spots on the underside of the hindwing.

Flight: June to July.

Habitat: Bogs and other wet, grassy places, including the northern tundra, from sea level in the north, to about 1,500 m (4,925 ft) in the mountains further south. The main larval foodplant is Common Bistort, but Cranberry and other *Vaccinium* species are also eaten.

Life-cycle: The pale eggs have numerous keels and are laid singly or in small groups. They hatch within two or three weeks and the caterpillars generally take two years to mature. The fully grown caterpillar is about 22 mm (0.9 in) long; it is purplish brown with many white spots and a pale-yellow stripe along the back. The spines are brown with black bristles. The chrysalis is grey with silvery spots, and it hangs from a rock or a low-growing plant.

Range: From the Alps to the shores of the Arctic Ocean and eastwards across northern Asia to Siberia. Scattered populations exist on some of the mountains of Bulgaria and northern Spain. Also in North America.

The butterfly is endangered throughout its European range as a result of land-drainage and afforestation.

---

p.154 **Pearl-bordered Fritillary**
Clossiana euphrosyne

Description: 18–23 mm (0.7–0.9 in). The ground colour of the upperside varies a good deal, possibly as a result of temperature differences during development, but it is generally a rich orange with black streaks and spots, including a well-marked post-discal arc of spots on each wing. The hindwing has a dark basal patch of variable extent. The underside of the forewing is pale orange with heavy black spotting and a yellowish tip. The underside of the hindwing is orange and yellow with seven silver spots – the 'pearls' – on the outer edge. The inner edges of the pearls are outlined with deep orange or brown. An arc of often indistinct dark eye-spots lies just inside the silvery margin. There is a large silver spot right in the middle of the wing and a smaller one close to the base of the wing.

Similar species: Small Pearl-bordered Fritillary is almost identical above but never has an isolated silver spot in the middle of the underside of the hindwing.

Flight: April to August in one or two broods, usually keeping quite close to the ground with a dainty dancing movement. The butterflies are especially attracted to the flowers of Bugle in the spring. The second brood occurs only rarely in the British Isles.

Habitat: Woodland rides and clearings, especially in coppiced woodlands, from sea level to about 2,000 m (6,550 ft); also on heathland and damp, scrubby grassland, mainly in coastal areas in the British Isles. The larval foodplants are violets, mainly Common Dog-violet and Marsh Violet.

Life-cycle: The conical, strongly ribbed eggs are pale yellow or pearly white. They are laid singly on or near the foodplant and they hatch in two to three weeks. In double-brooded populations the summer caterpillars mature very quickly, but other larvae go into hibernation when still quite small and complete their growth in the spring. The fully grown caterpillar is up to 25 mm (1.0 in) long; it is black with a row of white spots on each side and bristly black or yellow spines. Pupation takes place low down in dense cover. The greyish-brown chrysalis has silvery spots near the front and its irregular shape makes it look very like a dead leaf.

Range: Almost all of Europe, and on across temperate Asia to the Pacific. The butterfly has disappeared from most of eastern England since the Second World War and is declining in other areas, but it is still locally common in some western districts. The Irish population is confined to the Burren National Park.

---

p.155 **Small Pearl-bordered Fritillary**
Clossiana selene

Description: 17–22 mm (0.7–0.9 in). The orange uppersides, with their scattered black markings, are almost identical to those of the Pearl-bordered Fritillary. The underside of the forewing is also more or less the same in both species, but the butterflies can be distinguished very easily by looking at the underside of the hindwing. The seven marginal 'pearls' are edged with black on their inner margins, and there is no isolated silver spot in the middle of the wing: the central band usually has three silver spots or else the whole band is silver. There are commonly two or three more silvery spots at the base of the wing, but all silver areas on the underside of the hindwing may be replaced by yellow. There is a large black spot in the otherwise orange cell, and this spot can also be seen on the upperside in some specimens. Many northern specimens (f. *hela*) have an extensive black patch on the upperside of the hindwing.

Similar species: Pearl-bordered Fritillary has orange inner borders to the marginal 'pearls', and a solitary silver spot in the middle of the underside of the hindwing.

Flight: April to August in one or two broods, usually keeping close to the ground and strongly attracted to Bugle flowers. A second brood is uncommon in the British Isles but does appear in some years.

Habitat: Woodland rides and clearings, especially in damp areas, and also on moors, heaths, and damp grassland, from sea level to about 2,000 m (6,550 ft). The larval foodplants are mainly violets, especially Common Dog-violet and Marsh Violet, but Bilberry, Strawberry and Raspberry are also mentioned in the literature as occasional foodplants.

Life-cycle: The pale-yellow, strongly ribbed eggs are usually laid singly on or near the foodplant, although they are sometimes scattered freely in flight. The eggs hatch after about ten days, and the caterpillars feed for a few weeks before going into hibernation when they are about half-grown. Growth is completed in the spring, when the caterpillar reaches length of about 22 mm (0.9 in). It is dark brown with numerous conical yellow spines or tubercles, each bearing black bristles. The front pair of spines are long and horn-like. Pupation takes place low down in the vegetation and the chrysalis is dark brown with silvery points. In double-brooded populations, the summer caterpillars feed up quickly and produce a second generation of adults in August.

Range: Almost everywhere in Europe, from the North Cape to central Spain, but absent from southern Iberia and the Mediterranean area and also from Ireland. The butterfly has disappeared from much of eastern England in recent decades. It also occurs throughout temperate Asia and in North America, where it is known as the Silver-bordered Fritillary.

The species has been dubbed the '7.30 butterfly' because of the shape of the dark marks in the cell of the forewing, although these are not always recognizable as 7 and 30.

p.156 **Titania's Fritillary** *Clossiana titania*

Description: 20–25 mm (0.8–1.0 in). The orange uppersides, paler in females than in males, are heavily marked with dark spots and often have a fair dusting of dark scales. The margins are frequently solid brown or black with chequered fringes and the submarginal spots are distinctly triangular. The underside of the forewing is pale orange with large black spots, yellow smudges around the outer margin, and often some prominent, brown, finger-like marks near the wingtip. The underside of the hindwing is generally rust-coloured, with a broad cream or yellow band, often dusted with brown, across the centre and two or three pale spots at the base. The black submarginal marks are strongly triangular and often extend inwards to meet the post-discal spots. Most specimens from the Alps have a strong purple tinge to the underside of the hindwing.

Similar species: Several fritillaries have similar uppersides, but the underside, with its triangular submarginal marks, is quite distinctive.

Flight: June to August.

Habitat: Light woodland and flower-rich forest clearings in upland areas, from about

500 m (1,650 ft) to the tree-line. Bistort is the main larval foodplant, but violets may also be eaten.

Life-cycle: The eggs are ribbed and conical and have a pearly or silvery appearance. The mature caterpillar, about 25 mm (1.0 in) long, is jet-black with conspicuous yellowish spines carrying black bristles. The two anterior spines are darker and project forward over the head like horns. Pupation takes place on the vegetation and the rather lumpy chrysalis is silvery grey with darker spotting. Winter is passed either in the egg stage or as a first-instar caterpillar.

Range: Alps and Balkan mountains, and from the eastern shores of the Baltic across Asia to Siberia. Also in North America.

---

p.156 **Arctic Fritillary** *Clossiana chariclea*

Description: 17 mm (0.7 in). The ground colour of the upperside is tawny yellow or orange with an extensive area of dark brown on the hindwing and a variable amount of dusting at the base of the forewing. The spots are dark brown and quite heavy, those of the discal band being linked into a continuous, wavy band. The underside of the forewing resembles the upperside, although it is paler and has pale spots around the edge. The underside of the hindwing is mainly rust-brown, with a broad silvery-white discal band and silvery margin.

Similar species: Polar Fritillary has T-shaped silvery marginal spots on the hindwing. Frejya's Fritillary lacks the broad white discal band.

Flight: June to August, usually flying quite fast and keeping very close to the ground.

Habitat: Exposed tundra slopes, from sea level to about 1,400 m (4,600 ft). The larval foodplant is unknown, although Cassiope has been suggested as a likely candidate. Violets may also be used.

Life-cycle: The eggs are pale yellow and thimble-shaped. Nothing is known of the life-cycle in nature, but it seems likely that the caterpillars take two years to mature.

Range:  Arctic Europe, where it is quite common in some areas but absent from others. Also in Greenland and Arctic North America. The Arctic Fritillary has been seen further north than any other butterfly – at a latitude of over 81°N.

The species probably occurs throughout the Arctic, but there are few records from Asia so far.

p.157 **Frejya's Fritillary** *Clossiana freija*

Description:  14–22 mm (0.5–0.9 in). The ground colour of the upperside is orange, with an extensive brown smudge at the base of the hindwing. The spots are dark brown and quite heavy, and those of the discal band are joined to form a thick zig-zag band. The post-discal spots in spaces 2 and 3 are noticeably larger than the rest and often markedly triangular. The underside of the forewing is pale orange with somewhat blurred dark spots and with white or cream smudges near the tip. The underside of the hindwing is largely rust-coloured, with a conspicuous black zig-zag line in the discal area and a narrow, broken white band beyond it. The marginal lunules are silvery white, sometimes arrow-shaped, and, in mountain specimens, often very narrow.

Similar species: Arctic and Polar fritillaries lack the black zig-zag under the hindwing.

Flight: May to July. Flight is low over the vegetation and rather jerky. The butterfly commonly feeds at Moss Campion.

Habitat: Moorland, peat-bogs, and tundra; usually at low levels, but rising to about 1,000 m (3,275 ft) in some areas. Apparently absent from coastal areas. The larval foodplants include Cloudberry, Bog Bilberry, and Bearberry.

Life-cycle: The conical eggs are yellow and ribbed, and they hatch within three or four weeks of being laid. The caterpillars hibernate, and emerge to complete their growth a soon as the snow melts in spring. The mature caterpillar is black, with bristly orange spines, and about 20 mm (0.8 in) long.

Range: Northern Europe, and across northern Asia to Japan. Also in North America, where it is called Freya's Fritillary.

---

p.157 **Weaver's Fritillary** *Clossiana dia*

Description: 15–17 mm (0.6–0.7 in). One of the smallest of the European fritillaries, this species is most easily identified by the very sharp angle – almost a right-angle – of the front edge of the hindwing. The ground colour of the upperside is orange and the dark markings are relatively large. Those in the basal part of the forewing are strongly angular, while the hindwing bears a complete arc of large, oval post-discal spots. The underside of the forewing is largely orange with black spots, but the tip is yellowish with rust-coloured markings. The underside of the hindwing is largely brown, with a strong violet tinge and a discal band containing three or four large silvery spots. There are also six silvery marginal spots and, just inside these there is an arc of dark post-discal spots, often containing silvery centres.

Similar species: No similar fritillary has such a sharply angled hindwing, and there is no other species within its range with a similar pattern under the hindwing.

Flight: March to October. There are two or three broods in most areas, but only one brood in the mountains. The butterfly usually keeps close to the ground and flies in a rather 'fidgety' fashion.

Habitat: Light woodland, scrub, and rough grassland, from sea level to about 1,500 m (4,925 ft). Violets are the main larval foodplants, but Bramble and various other low growing plants may also be used.

Life-cycle: The ribbed, conical eggs are laid singly on the foodplants or, in the autumn, on neighbouring grasses and other plants. They are yellow at first, becoming purple before hatching about two weeks after they are laid. The mature caterpillar is about

22 mm (0.9 in) long; it is slate grey with white flecks and pale spines. Caterpillars of the final generation go into hibernation and reappear to complete their growth early in spring – as early as mid-February in some areas. Pupation takes place low down in the vegetation and the chrysalis is brownish grey.

Range: Southern and central Europe and on across temperate Asia to China. Absent from the British Isles and most of Iberia.

The species is also known as the Violet Fritillary.

---

p.158 **Polar Fritillary** *Clossiana polaris*

Description: 19 mm (0.75 in). The ground colour of the upperside is tawny yellow, with a large brown patch at the base of the hindwing. The discal spots of the forewing are linked into an irregular band, and the outer spots may be quite faint. The underside of the forewing is a paler version of the upperside, but the underside of the hindwing is purplish brown with a lot of small white spots. The latter may link up to form a continuous band in the discal area, and there is another band of spots, often triangular, in the post-discal area. The silvery-white marginal spots are more or less T-shaped.

Similar species: Frejya's Fritillary has much less white on the underside. Arctic Fritillary lacks the white post-discal spots under the hindwing and marginal spots are not T-shaped.

Flight: June to August, keeping close to the ground and flying fast and erratically.

Habitat: Dry tundra slopes, from sea level to about 1,000 m (3,275 ft). The larval foodplant is possibly Mountain Avens, but the butterflies will lay on Cassiope in captivity and this may also be used in the wild.

Life-cycle: The pale-yellow eggs are conical or thimble-shaped, but little else is known of the early stages of this butterfly. The caterpillars probably take two years to mature.

Range: Throughout the Arctic, but uncommon and
          very local in Europe where it forms small,
          isolated communities in the far north.
          Specimens from Greenland are often very
          pale. Also in North America where it is
          known as the Polaris Fritillary.

p.158   **Thor's Fritillary** *Clossiana thore*

Description: 17–25 mm (0.7–1.0 in). The ground colour
                of the upperside is orange in the Alpine
                subspecies *C. t. thore*, but it is always
                heavily dusted with dark brown and
                sometimes almost obliterated: the pattern
                of dark spots is then indistinct. The
                hindwing has a broad brown border. The
                underside of the forewing is orange and
                yellow with heavy black spots. The
                underside of the hindwing is largely
                reddish brown and has a conspicuous
                yellow discal band with a number of white
                spots just beyond it. The marginal spots are
                lead-coloured and often form a continuous
                band. Scandinavian specimens (*C. t. borealis*)
                are usually smaller than the Alpine race and
                much paler on both surfaces, with paler
                spots and less brown suffusion: the pale
                band under the hindwing is buff rather
                than yellow and much less obvious.

Similar species: The yellow band under the hindwing and
                    the lack of bright, silvery marginal spots
                    distinguish this butterfly from most other
                    fritillaries.

Flight: June to July, flying quite slowly and
           staying close to the ground.

Habitat: Woodland clearings and margins, usually
            near water, between about 800 m (2,625 ft)
            and the tree-line in the Alps, but
            sometimes close to sea level in Scandinavia.
            The larval foodplants are violets, especially
            the Yellow Wood-violet.

Life-cycle: The eggs are thimble-shaped, ribbed, and
               greenish yellow. They hatch within two or
               three weeks and the caterpillars usually
               hibernate twice before maturing, although
               in some southern localities a small
               proportion may produce adults after just
               one year. The mature caterpillar is about

25 mm (1.0 in) long; it is jet-black with dark-brown bristly spines, but many specimens bear three conspicuous pale spots on each side. Pupation takes place amongst the vegetation and the chrysalis is grey with black spots.

Range: Alps and Northern Europe, including the far north, and on through northern Asia to Japan.

p.159 **Frigga's Fritillary** *Clossiana frigga*

Description: 20–25 mm (0.8–1.0 in). The ground colour of the upperside is yellowish orange or pale brown, with an extensive dark-brown suffusion at the base – especially on the hindwing. The dark spots are fairly large, those of the basal half of the forewing being rather angular and linked up to form zig-zag cross-lines. The underside of the forewing is largely orange with black spots and a yellowish tip. The underside of the hindwing is chestnut-brown in the basal half, with a yellowish discal band and two or three large pale patches near the front. The outer half of the wing is purplish brown, with no white marginal spots.

Similar species: Scandinavian specimens of Thor's Fritillary are paler beneath and lack the large white marks. Most other Arctic fritillaries have white or silvery marginal spots.

Flight: June to July.

Habitat: Bogs, moors, and damp clearings in Arctic birch and willow scrub, usually at low levels. The larval foodplant is Cloudberry.

Life-cycle: The cone-shaped, salmon-coloured eggs are laid singly on the foodplant. Before hibernation, the caterpillar is dark green and hairy, with branched black spines, but after hibernation it is brown with rows of indistinct pale spots. The mature caterpillar is about 25 mm (1.0 in) long. It pupates amongst the vegetation and the brown chrysalis is very hard to find.

Range: Northern Europe, beyond about 60°N, and on through northern Asia. In Europe it is most common above the Arctic Circle, but it is a local butterfly and never found in large numbers. It also occurs in North America.

p.159 **Dusky-winged Fritillary** *Clossiana improba*

Description: 16 mm (0.6 in). This well-named fritillary has yellowish-brown uppersides, but appears dirty brown because the wings are heavily dusted with brown or grey scales that often almost obliterate the dark spots. The underside of the forewing resembles the upperside, but the underside of the hindwing is purplish brown in the basal half and greyish brown in the outer half. The front edge is white and the discal area has two prominent white patches. In some specimens there is a pale band right across the discal area. Fresh specimens have rather hairy wings, especially in the outer region, but the hairs gradually fall off in flight.

Similar species: None.

Flight: July to August, flying close to the ground, and sometimes simply crawling over the vegetation. It feeds at saxifrages and Moss Campion. It basks with its wings wide open in the sunshine, but it drops down to hide in the vegetation as soon as the sun disappears.

Habitat: Tundra slopes with sparse vegetation, usually at low levels but reaching 1,000 m (3,275 ft) in some places. Although the caterpillars have not been seen feeding in Europe, they probably feed on dwarf willows as they do in North America. Alpine Bistort is another possibility.

Life-cycle: The eggs are thimble-shaped and deep yellow, and the early larval instars are dark brown and very hairy, but little else is known of the early stages of this butterfly. In some localities the adults are seen only in alternate years and it seems likely that the caterpillars take two years to mature.

Range: Throughout the Arctic, although records are sparse from Asia. European populations are very local, but the insect is quite common in some areas. In North America, where it extends southwards through the Rockies to Wyoming, it is called the Dingy Arctic Fritillary.

---

p.160 **Glanville Fritillary** *Melitaea cinxia*

Description: 14–23 mm (0.5–0.9 in). The uppersides range from deep orange to sandy brown with a dark-brown reticulate pattern formed by the veins and cross-lines. The hindwing may be heavily dusted with brown, but there is always an arc of orange spots near the outer margin and most of these spots carry a conspicuous black dot in their centres. The underside of the forewing is orange with indistinct dark spots and a cream tip. The underside of the hindwing is banded with cream and orange, with the two orange bands outlined in black. The outer of these bands contains dark spots. The cream bands also contain black spots; those near the outer margin are often triangular.

Similar species: Heath Fritillary has a similar upperside, but no black spots near the outer edge of the hindwing. Spotted Fritillary has a similar underside, but the upperside is distinctly spotted. Freyer's Fritillary has a similar underside, but with heavier spotting under the forewing.

Flight: April to September in one or two broods, usually gliding low over the vegetation.

Habitat: Rough, flower-rich grassland from sea level to about 2,500 m (8,200 ft). It is most common on steep slopes and on roadsides where disturbance allows plantains to flourish. The principal larval foodplant is Ribwort Plantain, but the caterpillars will accept other plantains and occasionally take violets, speedwells, hawkweeds, and knapweeds.

egg

Life-cycle: The yellow, thimble-shaped eggs have numerous shallow ridges in the upper half, and they are laid in large batches on the undersides of the leaves. They hatch in two to three weeks. The caterpillars are black and bristly, with numerous white dots, and

caterpillar

they spend most of their lives living gregariously in silken webs. These colonies are very conspicuous when basking or feeding in the sunshine. The caterpillars separate as they reach maturity. Autumn caterpillars spin dense hibernation nests amongst the vegetation and complete their growth in the spring. The mature caterpillar is about 25 mm (1.0 in) long. It has a chestnut-coloured head and can be mistaken for an old plantain head when resting. Pupation takes place in dense vegetation and the chrysalis is greyish purple with orange spots.

Range: Southern and central Europe, as far north as southern Sweden, and on through temperate Asia to Mongolia and China. Also in North Africa. The British population is now confined to the southern coast of the Isle of Wight, although the species was widely distributed in southeast England until early in the 18th century.

Although it is one of Britain's rarest butterflies, it thrives quite happily on the Isle of Wight and does not seem to be in any danger. The butterfly was named after a Mrs Eleanor Glanville, who collected the first authentic British specimens at the end of the 17th century. It is said that some of her relations contested her will on the grounds that no person of sound mind would go in pursuit of butterflies!

---

p.160 **Freyer's Fritillary** *Melitaea arduinna*

Description: 20–25 mm (0.8–1.0 in). The male upperside is orange, with continuous brown borders and dark spots, including very heavy discal spots on both wings. The post-discal area of the hindwing encloses an arc of dark-brown spots. The female has a paler ground colour but the dark markings are bigger and the wings are heavily dusted with brown. The underside of the forewing is largely orange with heavy black spots and a pale yellow tip. The underside of the hindwing is banded cream and orange. The orange bands are bordered with black and the outer one contains black spots. The dark marginal spots under the hindwing form a continuous line.

Similar species: Glanville Fritillary has a similar pattern on both surfaces, but has much lighter spotting under the forewing. Spotted Fritillary has a more obviously spotted upperside and no black spots in the orange band on the underside.

Flight: May to July.

Habitat: Flowery slopes in mountainous areas, usually above about 1,000 m (3,275 ft). The larval foodplants are knapweeds.

Life-cycle: The caterpillars are black above and yellowish grey below, with greyish-brown spines. They feed and hibernate communally in a silken web.

Range: Scattered colonies exist in the Balkans, from where the species extends eastwards to Iran and central Asia.

---

p.161 **Knapweed Fritillary** *Melitaea phoebe*

Description: 17–25 mm (0.7–1.0 in). This is an extremely variable butterfly, whose uppersides usually exhibit a conspicuous mixture of light and dark orange overlaid with dark-brown streaks and cross-lines. In some parts of the Alps much of the orange is replaced by yellow, giving a very bold pattern, but the hindwing always has a well-defined orange band in the outer part. The pale submarginal lunule in space 3 of the forewing is much bigger than the rest. The underside of the forewing is orange with black spots, but grades to yellow at the tip and the outer margin. The underside of the hindwing varies from almost white to butter-yellow, with several wavy black lines and an irregular orange band near the base. Towards the edge of the wing there is an orange or yellow band, edged with black and containing reddish spots.

Similar species: Freyer's Fritillary has dark spots in the orange band on the underside of the hindwing. Aetherie Fritillary has no

obvious orange band on the upperside of
the hindwing.

Flight: April to October in one to three broods,
specimens of the third brood being rather
small. Flight consists of long, graceful
glides interspersed with short bursts of
rapid wingbeating. The adults often
congregate to drink from wet ground,
especially at high altitude.

Habitat: Flower-rich grassland, from sea level to
about 2,000 m (6,550 ft). The larval
foodplants are knapweeds, but thistles and
plantains may be used on occasion.

Life-cycle: The eggs are yellowish green and are laid in
large clumps on the underside of the lower
leaves of the foodplant. They hatch within a
couple of weeks or so, and the caterpillars
live gregariously in silken nests until they
are almost mature. The fully grown
caterpillar is up to 30 mm (1.4 in) long; it
is sooty black with orange-yellow spines,
and liberally spotted with white. Autumn
caterpillars hibernate communally in silken
nests and complete their growth in the
spring. Pupation takes place amongst the
vegetation and the chrysalis is greyish
brown with yellow and white spots.

Range: Southern and central Europe, but absent
from the British Isles, Belgium, and
Holland. Also in North Africa and across
temperate Asia to China.

---

p.161 **Aetherie Fritillary** *Melitaea aetherie*

Description: 20–24 mm (0.8–1.0 in). The uppersides are
bright orange with a variable black or dark-
brown pattern. The discal spots are usually
quite large and there is usually a
conspicuous zig-zag submarginal line on
both wings. The female is often heavily
dusted with greyish scales. The underside
of the forewing is orange with a yellow tip,
and the black spots are often quite small.
The underside of the hindwing has two
deep-orange bands on a cream or yellow
background. The inner band is very
irregular and the outer one contains a series
of large red spots.

Similar species: Knapweed Fritillary is darker with an orange band near the outer edge of the upperside of the hindwing. Spotted Fritillary's underside is similar but has black spots around the edge.

Flight: April to July.

Habitat: Flower-rich grassland and open woodland, generally at low levels in its European haunts but occasionally up to 1,000 m (3,275 ft). The larval foodplants are knapweeds.

Life-cycle: The eggs are laid in large groups and the caterpillars live communally. They pass through a resting stage in the summer, when drought renders their foodplants inedible, and have a second spell of dormancy in the winter, although they usually become active again by the end of January. The mature larva is very dark and hairy, with a pale stripe on each side. It is about 28 mm (1.1 in) long and it pupates on the foodplant or on nearby stones. The chrysalis is very much like those of its relatives.

Range: This is essentially a North African butterfly, flying at high altitude in the Atlas Mountains. Its European range is restricted to Sicily and the far south of Spain and Portugal, where it is threatened by coastal development.

---

p.162 **Spotted Fritillary** *Melitaea didyma*

Description: 15–24 mm (0.6–0.9 in). Marked seasonal and regional variations added to strong sexual dimorphism make this one of Europe's most variable butterflies – and to make matters worse the various forms and races grade into each other with a bewildering array of intermediates. The upperside of the male is bright orange or brick-red, and in the nominate race *M. d. didyma* – found in the northern parts of the range – it has large but well-separated black spots. *M.d. meridionalis* from some of the more southerly parts of the range has an even brighter ground colour and the spotting is much reduced in the post-discal area of the forewing: there may also be an extensive black border on the inner margin of the hindwing. The female ground colour is paler than that of the male in all races and the black spots are larger, but the insects are usually heavily dusted with grey scales, especially in *M. d. meridionalis*, and the true ground colour often shows only at the front of the hindwing. The undersides show much less variation. The forewing is orange, lightly spotted with black and with a yellow or cream outer margin. The hindwing is cream or yellow with two orange bands bordered with black spots. The inner band is very irregular, but always continuous. There are numerous other black spots, those near the outer margin being clearly rounded or oval.

Similar species: Lesser Spotted Fritillary is very similar on both surfaces, but the black marginal spots under its hindwing are more angular and often distinctly triangular.

Flight: April to September in one, two, or three broods, usually gliding or fluttering low over the vegetation and visiting a wide range of flowers.

Habitat: Flower-rich grassland, including roadside verges and montane meadows, from sea level to about 2,000 m (6,550 ft). The larval foodplants are mainly plantains, but the caterpillars also eat toadflaxes, mulleins, speedwells, and foxgloves.

Life-cycle: The pale-green, thimble-shaped eggs are laid in clumps on the foodplant and they hatch within about two weeks. The caterpillars feed gregariously in silken tents in their early stages, but they separate before they are fully grown. The mature caterpillar is up to 28 mm (1.1 in) long; it is essentially white with a brown head and a dense black pattern on the back. The bristly spines are orange on the back and white on the sides. Pupation takes place on the vegetation and the chrysalis is white with black and yellow spots. The final brood of the year goes into hibernation when the caterpillars are still quite small.

They commonly spin dead leaves or flowerheads together to make a hibernaculum.

Range: Southern and central Europe, but absent from the British Isles. Also in North Africa and across temperate Asia to western China.

p.163 **Lesser Spotted Fritillary** *Melitaea trivia*

Description: 13–22 mm (0.5–0.9 in). The upperside is typically orange with black or dark-brown spots, but there is a good deal of variation in both ground colour and spot pattern. Some specimens are heavily dusted with brown scales. In most areas, the orange marginal lunules are completely enclosed in a brown band, but in Iberia and a few other southern localities the inner brown border is fragmented and the insect has a much spottier appearance (*M. t. ignasti*). The underside of the forewing resembles the upperside except that it has a yellow tip, but the underside of the hindwing is cream or pale yellow with two black-edged orange bands and various black spots. The marginal spots are clearly triangular.

Similar species: Spotted Fritillary male is very similar, but the ground colour is usually redder and the marginal spots under the hindwing are rounded.

Flight: May to August in two broods. Second-brood insects are usually somewhat smaller than those of the first brood.

Habitat: Rough, flower-rich grassland from sea level to about 1,500 m (4,925 ft); most common in upland areas. The larval foodplants are mulleins, especially Great Mullein.

Life-cycle: The eggs are laid in batches under the leaves and the caterpillars stay together in silken tents for much of their lives. The mature caterpillar is white with a heavy black pattern on the back and very bristly pale spines. The head is chestnut-brown. Winter is passed in the caterpillar stage, hibernating communally in their webs.

Range: Northern Iberia, Italy, and southeast Europe, and on through southern Asia.

p.163 **False Heath Fritillary** *Melitaea diamina*

Description: 16–22 mm (0.6–0.9 in). The upperside of the forewing is essentially pale orange, but it is commonly so heavily clouded with brown that the wing appears brown with bands of orange or yellow spots. The hindwing is typically dark brown, sometimes with three bands of orange or yellow spots but often with almost no spots at all. The underside of the forewing is orange with a pale border and usually with some conspicuous black spots just beyond the cell. The underside of the hindwing is yellowish brown or orange with white spots near the base and a broad white band through the centre. The outer edge bears an arc of large, white marginal lunules and a clear yellow line edged with black on both sides.

Similar species: Heath, Nickerl's, and Assmann's fritillaries all resemble some of the less heavily dusted specimens of False Heath Fritillary, from which they are very difficult to separate in the field.

Flight: May to September in one or two broods, usually keeping close to the ground. Flight is a mixture of weak flapping and graceful gliding. The butterflies are often to be seen feeding at valerian flowers.

Habitat: Flowery grassland, especially in damp areas with scattered trees, from sea level to about 2,000 m (6,550 ft). The major larval foodplants are valerians, but plantains, cow-wheats, speedwells, bistorts, and several other low-growing plants have all been listed as foodplants.

Life-cycle: The pale-green or yellowish eggs are laid in small clusters on the undersides of the leaves, and they hatch in two or three weeks. The caterpillars live gregariously in flimsy silken webs during the early part of their lives and probably separate during the final instar. The mature caterpillar is 25–30 mm (1.0–1.2 in) long; it is pale brown, heavily marked with black, and has a black head and bristly orange spines. Pupation takes place low down on the vegetation and the chrysalis is white or pale

grey with black spots and stripes.
Caterpillars of the final brood hibernate in a
sturdy communal web while still quite
small and separate to complete their
growth in the spring.

Range: Most of Europe, from northern Iberia to
southern Finland, and on through
temperate Asia to China. Absent from the
British Isles.

The species is declining rapidly in some
areas, especially in Scandinavia.

p.164 **Heath Fritillary** *Mellicta athalia*

Description: 15–25 mm (0.6–1.0 in). The ground colour
of the upperside is a rich orange-brown,
overlaid with a black or dark-brown
network formed by the dark veins and wavy
cross-lines. This pattern varies considerably
in its density, but there are usually two
well-marked chains or arcs of orange spots
near the outer edge of the hindwing. These
spots do not contain dark centres. The
underside of the forewing is orange with
black spots and pale yellow lunules around
the margin. These lunules are edged with
black on the inside, and there is usually a
very heavy inner border to the marginal
lunule in space 2, and sometimes in space 3
as well. The underside of the hindwing has
a prominent cream or silvery-white band
through the centre, while the basal area
contains an irregular orange band and
several large pale spots. Beyond the central
or discal band there is an arc of orange
lunules, followed by an arc of cream or
white ones and then a pale-yellow marginal
band. All the bands and spots are edged
with black, which, together with the dark
veins, produces a distinctly chequered
appearance. The fringes of all wings are
clearly chequered on both surfaces.

Similar species: Glanville Fritillary, the only similar species
in Britain, has dark spots near the outer
edge of the hindwing, and the ranges of the
two species do not overlap. The Heath
Fritillary can usually be distinguished from

other Continental *Mellicta* species by the heavy black borders to the marginal lunules under the forewing, especially in spaces 2 and 3.

Flight: April to October in one or two broods. The butterflies flit and glide daintily over the vegetation, usually keeping close to the ground and visiting a wide range of flowers to take nectar.

Habitat: Open woods, especially coppiced woodlands, and woodland margins: also on heathland and flower-rich grassland, including roadside verges. It ranges from sea level to about 2,000 m (6,550 ft). The larval foodplants include Common Cow-wheat – probably the only plant used by woodland populations – Ribwort Plantain, and Germander Speedwell.

Life-cycle: The ribbed, thimble-shaped, pale-yellow eggs are laid in large batches, some on the foodplants but mostly under the leaves of surrounding plants. They hatch in two or three weeks and the young larvae make their own way to the foodplants. They live in small groups at first, with each group spinning a silken web around itself, but they gradually separate after the second moult. The mature caterpillar is up to 25 mm (1.0 in) long; it is mainly black with white freckles. The spines or tubercles are orange with black bristles. Pupation takes place close to the ground, usually under a leaf, and the chrysalis is mottled brown and white and rather smooth.

chrysalis

Caterpillars of the final generation go into hibernation during the third instar. They may hibernate in small groups, protected by a tent of silk and dead leaves, but more often hibernate singly in rolled-up leaves.

Range: Most of Europe, from the North Cape to the Mediterranean, and on through temperate Asia to Japan. Absent from southern Iberia and most of the British Isles, where the butterfly is single-brooded and confined to a few small colonies in southern England. Although some of these colonies are very strong, the Heath Fritillary is one of Britain's rarest butterflies and is strictly protected.

The Heath Fritillary is very variable. The uppersides are often very bright in southwest Europe, where yellow bands may replace the orange in the outer part of each wing. Arctic specimens (*M. a. norvegica*) are small and dark, while in the Balkans the hindwing may be almost entirely brown.

p.165 **Provençal Fritillary** *Mellicta deione*

Description: 15–25 mm (0.6–1.0 in). The ground colour of the male's upperside is orange, but it is not always uniform and the submarginal band is commonly brighter or darker than the rest of the wing. The veins and wavy cross-lines are dark brown and of varying thickness, being particularly heavy in mountainous areas. There is commonly a dumb-bell-shaped mark near the centre of the hind edge of the forewing. The female upperside often exhibits alternating orange and yellow bands, resulting from variation in the ground colour. The underside of the forewing is orange with sooty-black spots and yellowish marginal lunules, but there is not normally a heavy black mark in space 3. The underside of the hindwing is banded with cream or white and orange and is very like that of the Heath Fritillary.

Similar species: Heath Fritillary has a strong black inner border to the marginal lunule in space 3 under the forewing.

Flight: May to September in one or two broods.

Habitat: Rough fields and stony hillsides with plenty of flowers, from sea level to about 1,500 m (4,925 ft) but most common in upland areas. The larval foodplants are toadflaxes and antirrhinums, and also foxgloves.

Life-cycle: The pale-cream eggs are laid in small groups and the caterpillars live in small groups in their early stages. They are very like those of the Heath Fritillary — largely black with small white spots and bristly orange spines. The mature caterpillar is about 25 mm (1.0 in) long. It pupates close to the ground and the chrysalis is dark brown with orange spots and spines.

Final-brood caterpillars hibernate when half-grown in silken tents under leaves and stones.

Range: Southwest Europe, from Portugal to the western Alps, and North Africa.

p.165 **Grison's Fritillary** *Mellicta varia*

Description: 16 mm (0.6 in). The ground colour of the male upperside is rich orange, overlaid with the usual dark-brown pattern although often less heavily marked than in other *Mellicta* species. The female generally has a paler ground colour – quite yellow in some specimens – but is often heavily dusted with brown or grey scales, especially on the hindwing. Both sexes often have a dark, dumb-bell-shaped mark on the hind edge of the forewing, and this mark has a vertical outer edge. The underside of the forewing is orange with a few black spots and a yellow margin, and the rear edge – usually hidden in life – has a black streak sometimes shaped like a key. The underside of the hindwing bears orange and white or cream bands. The central pale band is of a fairly even width throughout.

Similar species: Nickerl's and Meadow fritillaries are both very similar and very difficult to distinguish in the field. Nickerl's Fritillary is usually more heavily marked above and the central band under the hindwing is usually more irregular. Meadow Fritillary usually has an oblique dash instead of a dumb-bell at the rear of the forewing.

Flight: June to August, usually keeping close to the ground and feeding from thymes and other low-growing flowers. It often drinks from seepages.

Habitat: Montane grassland, usually between 1,800 and 2,500 m (5,900 and 8,200 ft), although sometimes as low as 1,000 m (3,275 ft). The larval foodplants include plantains and gentians.

Life-cycle: The pale-yellow eggs are oval and shiny and are usually laid in small clusters. The caterpillars live together for a time, but

probably separate before going into
hibernation in the autumn. The mature
caterpillar is about 18 mm (0.7 in) long; it
is black with bristly orange spines and lots
of tiny white dots. It pupates low down
amongst the vegetation, and the chrysalis is
sooty black with numerous white streaks.

Range: Alps and Apennines.

---

p.166 **Meadow Fritillary** *Mellicta parthenoides*

Description: 15–20 mm (0.6–0.8 in). The ground colour
of the male upperside is bright orange, with
dark-brown veins. The discal line on the
forewing is generally rather heavy and
terminates in a prominent oblique dash at
the rear of the wing. The dash may extend
towards the base of the wing to form a
dumb-bell-shaped spot. The post-discal line
is often faint and broken. The discal area of
the hindwing is often paler than the rest of
the wing. The female's ground colour is paler,
and frequently quite yellow, although the
submarginal band may stand out in orange.
She is often heavily dusted with grey scales.
The underside of the forewing is pale orange,
with a yellowish outer margin and scattered
black markings. The underside of the
hindwing has a broad and rather wavy pale
band through the centre, with an orange or
yellowish band on each side of it. The outer
band usually contains red spots.

Similar species: Heath, Grison's, and Provençal fritillaries
are all difficult to separate, but generally
lack the bold oblique dash at the rear of the
forewing. Nickerl's Fritillary is more
obviously chequered.

Flight: May to September in one or two broods,
usually floating delicately low over the
vegetation.

Habitat: Flowery upland slopes, generally between
500 and 2,100 m (1,650 and 6,900 ft), in
both dry and wet habitats. The larval
foodplants include Ribwort Plantain,
Hoary Plantain, Common Cow-wheat,
Greater Knapweed, and scabious species.

Life-cycle: The eggs are pale yellow and thimble-
shaped with numerous ribs and they are

laid in clusters on the undersides of the leaves. The caterpillars live communally in silken tents for the first part of their lives, but separate before pupating. The mature caterpillar is about 18 mm (0.7 in) long; it is mainly black with numerous white dots and very bristly yellowish spines. It pupates low down in the vegetation, often surrounding itself with a few strands of silk. The chrysalis is dark brown with white stripes and spots. Caterpillars of the final brood hibernate in a silken tent and complete their growth in the spring.

Range: Western Europe, from Iberia and Brittany to the western Alps and Bavaria.

---

p.166 **Nickerl's Fritillary** *Mellicta aurelia*

Description: 15 mm (0.6 in). The ground colour of the male's upperside is bright orange, with dark-brown veins and cross-lines giving a bold, chequered or reticulate pattern. The female has a similar pattern, but her ground colour is often a little paler. Both sexes are often heavily dusted with dark-brown scales. The underside of the forewing is orange with variable black spots – sometimes virtually absent – and a yellowish margin. The underside of the hindwing resembles that of other *Mellicta* species, but the central band is rather irregular. The orange band outside it contains a row of distinctly red spots. The marginal band, enclosed in two thin black lines, is often noticeably darker than the neighbouring lunules.

Similar species: Heath and Provençal fritillaries are usually a little larger; Meadow and Grison's fritillaries have less obvious reticulation. But all these *Mellicta* species are rather variable and accurate identification can be extremely difficult without looking at the genitalia.

Flight: June to August.

Habitat: Flowery grassland, heaths, and moors, from sea level to about 1,500 m (4,925 ft). The main larval foodplant is Ribwort Plantain, but cow-wheats, speedwells, and foxgloves may also be used.

Life-cycle: The pale-yellow eggs are small, spherical and only lightly ribbed, and they are laid in batches on the undersides of the leaves. The caterpillars spend most of their lives together in silken nests. They hibernate in the nests when about half-grown, and complete their growth in the spring. The mature caterpillar is about 18 mm (0.7 in) long; it is black with numerous white spots and bristly orange spines. It pupates low down in the vegetation, and the chrysalis is white with conspicuous black streaks and spots.

Range: Southern and central Europe and on to central Asia, but absent from the British Isles, Iberia, and most of the Mediterranean region.

---

p.167 **Assmann's Fritillary** *Mellicta britomartis*

Description: 15–18 mm (0.6–0.7 in). The ground colour of the upperside is orange-brown, with a heavy pattern of dark-brown cross-lines. The brown margins vary a lot in width, and Scandinavian specimens tend to be rather dark all over. The fringes are chequered dark and light brown in most specimens, instead of brown and cream as in related fritillaries. The underside of the forewing is dark orange with black spots and a border of well-marked yellow lunules. The underside of the hindwing is banded with cream and dark orange and the marginal band, enclosed in two thin black lines, is dirty yellow and noticeably darker than the adjacent lunules.

Similar species: Nickerl's Fritillary may have a whiter discal band under the hindwing, but it is otherwise *very* similar in appearance. Meadow Fritillary has a pale marginal line under the hindwing

Flight: May to August in one or two broods, floating gracefully and low over the vegetation and often sipping water from the ground. The butterfly regularly visits scabious flowers.

Habitat: Lush, flower-rich grassland and heathland, from sea level to about 1,000 m (3,275 ft); generally near trees. The larval foodplants are mainly plantains and speedwells, but the caterpillars also eat toadflax and possibly cow-wheat.

Life-cycle: The shiny, pale-yellow eggs are laid in clusters on the leaves, and the caterpillars spend their early lives in communal silk webs. As winter approaches, they reinforce their webs and settle down to hibernate. They separate and complete their growth in the spring. The mature caterpillar is black with white spots and short, pale-yellow spines, and it is about 18 mm (0.7 in) long. It pupates low down in the vegetation, and the chrysalis is brown with pale stripes and spots.

Range: Eastern Europe, from southern Sweden and northern Germany to the Black Sea, and on to central Asia and Korea. There is also a small population in northern Italy.

p.167 **Little Fritillary** *Mellicta asteria*

Description: 15 mm (0.6 in). This tiny fritillary, the smallest in Europe, is very variable on the upperside. It is sometimes orange with dark-brown veins and cross-lines, and two heavy smudges at the front of the forewing, but it is usually so heavily dusted with dark brown or sooty-black scales that both wings appear brown, with small orange and yellow spots in the outer region. The underside of the forewing is orange with dark-brown spots and a white or yellow margin. The underside of the hindwing is essentially cream with two orange bands, the inner of which is highly convoluted – as in most *Mellicta* and *Melitaea* species. There is just a single black marginal line beyond the lunules.

Similar species: Other *Mellicta* species and False Heath Fritillary may be superficially similar, but they are usually noticeably larger and have two black marginal lines under the hindwing. Weaver's Fritillary is similar in size but much brighter and more clearly spotted on the upperside.

Flight: June to August, usually keeping very close to the ground with a fast and almost buzzing action. Because of its two-year life-cycle (*see* below), the butterfly appears only every two years in some places.

Habitat: Exposed mountain slopes, above the tree-line between 2,000 and 3,000 m (6,550 and 9,850 ft). The larval foodplant is Alpine Plantain.

Life-cycle: The pale-yellow eggs are laid in clumps on the foodplant, and the caterpillars probably live communally for much of their lives. They take nearly two years to mature, hibernating the first time while still very small and the second time when in the penultimate instar. The mature caterpillar is about 18 mm (0.7 in) long, and is black with pale-orange spines. It pupates on the stunted vegetation or on the surrounding stones, and the chrysalis is white with extensive black spots and streaks.

Range: Confined to the eastern Alps, in small and scattered populations.

p.168 **Scarce Fritillary** *Hypodryas maturna*

Description: 20–25 mm (0.8–1.0 in). The ground colour of the upperside is deep reddish brown, making this a very bright fritillary despite the broad brown bands. The post-discal area of each wing is particularly red, and there are two large reddish spots in the cell of the forewing. There are also numerous pale spots, including some very pale and conspicuous ones just beyond the cell in the forewing. The upperside of the hindwing has a red patch near the base, an arc of cream or white discal spots and an orange post-discal band. The underside of the forewing is basically orange with yellow spots. The underside of the hindwing is bright orange with yellow or cream spots and bands and an orange marginal line. The female may be a little paler, with less contrast than the male, but the sexes are otherwise alike.

Similar species: Asian Fritillary is somewhat duller and the pale spots beyond the forewing cell are less conspicuous. The two species do not overlap. Female Cynthia's Fritillary usually has small black spots in the post-discal band of the hindwing.

Flight: May to July, generally gliding slowly but with a good turn of speed when required. It feeds at a range of herbs and shrubs, including Privet, and often basks high in the trees.

Habitat: Light woodland, especially in river valleys, from sea level to about 1,000 m (3,275 ft). The larval foodplants include Ash and Aspen in summer, and plantains and other low-growing plants in spring.

Life-cycle: The pale-green, ribbed eggs are laid in batches on the leaves and twigs of the trees, where the young caterpillars feed communally in nests of silk and leaves. They hibernate in the webs while still quite small and the nests often fall to the ground in the autumn. In the spring the caterpillars scatter to complete their growth on plantains and other herbaceous plants. The mature caterpillar is up to 35 mm (1.4 in) long; it is black with rows of yellow spots and very bristly black spines. It pupates on rocks and tree-trunks, and the chrysalis is white with black and yellow spots. It is possible that some insects take two years to mature, passing the first winter as caterpillars and the second as pupae.

Range: From northern France eastwards to the Balkans and the Baltic, including southern Sweden and Finland, and on through Asia to Mongolia. A very local species living up to its English name, with small populations scattered over a wide area and regarded as in danger of extinction in Europe.

---

p.168 **Asian Fritillary** *Hypodryas intermedia*

Description: 20–25 mm (0.8–1.0 in). The upperside is largely dark brown with orange and yellow or cream spots. The cell of the forewing contains two large orange spots on a pale background. The hindwing is dark brown with a broad orange band near the margin and a sometimes ill-defined row of paler spots just inside it. The underside of the forewing is orange and yellow with yellow submarginal lunules of more or less even size. The underside of the hindwing is banded with bright orange and pale yellow and the central yellow band encloses a thin black line. Both wings have an orange marginal line.

Similar species: Scarce Fritillary has paler spots beyond the forewing cell, contrasting strongly with the rest of the spots, and the submarginal lunules under the forewing are very unequal and sometimes absent. Female Cynthia's Fritillary usually has black spots in the post-discal band on both surfaces of the hindwing.

Flight: June to August, often taking nectar from Wood Crane's-bill and Adenostyles.

Habitat: Open woodland in the mountains, usually above 1,000 m (3,275 ft) and sometimes reaching 2,500 m (8,200 ft). The larval foodplant is Blue-berried Honeysuckle.

Life-cycle: The eggs are golden yellow at first, but become brownish before hatching. They are laid in clumps and the caterpillars live in communal webs on the leaves. They take two years to mature, hibernating twice amongst leaves bound together with silk. They separate before completing their growth after the second hibernation. The mature caterpillar is black with rows of yellow spots and very bristly black spines; it is up to 25 mm (1.0 in) long. It pupates on the stems of the foodplant or on adjacent rocks, and the chrysalis is white with black and yellow spots.

Range: Confined to the Alps, but not overlapping with the rather similar Scarce Fritillary.

This butterfly is given the name *Hypodryas wolfensbergeri* in some recent literature.

---

p.169 **Cynthia's Fritillary** *Hypodryas cynthia*

Description: 20 mm (0.8 in). The male is easily recognized by the largely white basal half of the upperside. The outer part of the forewing is typically orange and there are two orange patches in the cell. Three broad, sooty-brown bands cross the forewing. The hindwing has an orange patch near the base and a broad orange post-discal band. This band usually contains small black dots and is followed by a narrow band of white lunules. At high levels, mainly in the western Alps, the orange is nearly all replaced by sooty brown or black, producing a startling black-and-white pattern. The female upperside is largely orange with brown bands, although the post-discal band is usually brighter than the rest. That of the hindwing usually contains black dots. The underside is a mixture of yellow and orange bands in both sexes. Both wings have a clear orange marginal line, and the orange post-discal band of the hindwing usually contains small black dots.

Similar species: The male cannot be confused with any other species. The female is very like the Asian Fritillary, but the latter has no black dots in the post-discal band of the hindwing.

Flight: May to August, flying restlessly close to the ground in the sunshine and pausing here and there to drink from saxifrages and other low-growing flowers and also from moist ground.

Habitat: Montane scrub and grassland, generally between 1,500 and 3,000 m (4,925 and 9,850 ft) although much lower in some areas. The larval foodplants include plantains and pansies.

Life-cycle: The eggs are rounded with little sculpturing, and they are laid in irregular clumps under the leaves. They are pale yellow at first, but become dark pink before hatching. The caterpillars take two years to mature and live communally in silken webs for the first year. They hibernate together during their first winter, but they gradually separate during the next summer and the fourth instar caterpillars hibernate separately under stones and clumps of grass. Growth is completed in the second spring, when the caterpillar is about 25 mm (1.0 in) long. It is black with narrow

yellow bands and very densely branched black spines. It pupates amongst the stones or vegetation, and the chrysalis is black with yellow and white spots.

Range: The Alps and the mountains of Bulgaria.

p.169 **Lapland Fritillary** *Hypodryas iduna*

Description: 17–20 mm (0.7–0.8 in). The ground colour of the upperside is pale yellow, with smoky-black or dark-brown cross-lines and a deep orange or brick-red post-discal band on each wing. There are also two red or orange patches in the forewing cell. The wings are often heavily dusted with grey scales, especially in the male, and the butterfly takes on a very smoky appearance. The underside is similar to the upperside, but less grey, and the hindwing is more strongly banded with cream. There is a conspicuous brick-red margin to both wings.

Similar species: There is no similar butterfly in the far north. Some races of Marsh Fritillary may be confused with Lapland Fritillary, but the Marsh Fritillary's hindwing has a yellowish margin underneath and black spots in the post-discal band.

Flight: June to July, emerging very soon after the snow has gone: one of the first Arctic species to appear each year. It flies rapidly, keeping close to the ground and drinking from Trailing Azalea and other ground-hugging plants.

Habitat: Damp moors and open birch forest, usually between 300 and 700 m (975 and 2,300 ft). The larval foodplants include plantains, speedwells, and *Vaccinium* species.

Life-cycle: The eggs are yellowish green and rather conical, and they are laid in small batches. The caterpillars live communally in small silken webs, hibernating there and pupating in the spring with little or no further feeding. The mature caterpillar is up to 20 mm (0.8 in) long; it is black with bristly spines and pale-yellow spots. The chrysalis is cream with black spots and very difficult to spot among the lichens.

Range: Arctic Europe, above about 64°N, and on through northern Asia to the mountains of Mongolia. Also in the Caucasian mountains.

pp.170 & 171   **Marsh Fritillary** *Eurodryas aurinia*

Description: 15–25 mm (0.6–1.0 in). This is a very variable species, with the ground colour of the upperside ranging from dirty yellow to bright orange or brick-red. It is always heavily marked with pale-yellow spots and sooty-black cross-lines. There is usually a clear orange-red post-discal band on both wings: that of the forewing usually contains small yellow spots while that of the hindwing always encloses an arc of black spots. The basal half of the hindwing is often heavily dusted with black. The underside of the forewing is orange with pale spots and a few faint black lines, but never with black spots at the tip. The underside of the hindwing is usually brighter, with broad cream and orange bands. The orange post-discal band contains a row of black spots just as on the upperside, and the margin is dull yellow. Females tend to be a little larger and slightly less bright than males, but otherwise the sexes are alike.

Similar species: Spanish Fritillary is usually brighter, with clear yellow marginal lunules on the upperside of both wings, and prominent black spots under the forewing.

Flight: April to July, skimming low over the vegetation. Populations fluctuate greatly from year to year.

Habitat: Open grassland – in dry areas as well as wet ones – and also on bogs and moorland, from sea level to about 2,000 m (6,550 ft). The larval foodplants include scabious – especially the Devil's-bit Scabious, which is the main one in the British Isles – gentians, honeysuckles, and possibly knapweeds.

Life-cycle: The rounded, lightly ribbed eggs are yellow when they are laid but gradually turn brown or grey before hatching. They are laid in large clumps under the leaves, and they hatch after three to four weeks. First-instar caterpillars are quite pale, and they live in groups between two leaves fixed together with silk. Older caterpillars are much darker and they spin communal webs over their foodplants. They feed under the webs but also spend a lot of time sunbathing on the outside. In late summer or autumn, immediately after the third moult, the caterpillars go into hibernation, clustered together in silken balls fixed low down in the vegetation. They become active again quite early in the spring and gradually separate into smaller groups, each of which makes its own silken shelter. The caterpillars regularly bask on their shelters in the spring, thereby raising their body temperature and speeding up their development. The mature caterpillar feeds alone. It is black with white speckles and bristly black spines, and it reaches a length of about 30 mm (1.2 in). It pupates on leaves and stems. The chrysalis is white or pale grey with black and yellow spots.

Range: Most of Europe except the far north, and on across temperate Asia to Korea. Absent from the eastern side of Britain. Although widely distributed, the butterfly is very local and usually exists in scattered colonies. Some colonies can produce several thousand butterflies in some years, but most colonies are small and this once-common species is declining in most areas as a result of land-drainage.

Several distinct races or subspecies of the Marsh Fritillary occur in Europe. The Iberian race (*E. a. beckeri*) is larger and brighter than most, sometimes lacking the yellow spots, and has a very broad orange post-discal band on the hindwing. *E. a. hibernica* from Ireland is darker than most races, with dense black markings and noticeably dark margins. *E. a. debilis* from high levels in the Alps and Pyrenees is smaller and mainly sooty brown with yellow and orange spots. It used to be treated as a separate species – *E. debilis* – and known as the Alpine Fritillary.

p.171 **Spanish Fritillary** *Eurodryas desfontainii*

Description: 20–25 mm (0.8–1.0 in). The ground
colour of the upperside is bright orange or
brick-red, with a yellowish discal area on
both wings and conspicuous black-edged
yellow lunules around the margins. Black
spots link up to form an irregular discal
cross-line in the forewing, and there is an
arc of black spots in the orange post-discal
band of the hindwing. The underside is
largely orange with yellow spots and bands,
but there are large black spots near the
middle of the forewing. The yellow bands
on the hindwing are edged with black and
there is an arc of black dots towards the
margin. The margins of both wings are
dirty yellow.

Similar species: Marsh Fritillary is usually darker and has
no black spots under the forewing.

Flight: May to June.

Habitat: Sunny, flower-rich slopes, generally
between 600 and 1,200 m (1,975 and
3,925 ft). The larval foodplants are teasels,
scabious, and possibly knapweeds.

Life-cycle: The eggs are pale yellow at first but
gradually turn orange. They are laid in
batches and the young larvae feed in a
communal web on the foodplant. After
hibernation in the leaf-litter, the
caterpillars regularly warm themselves by
basking on the vegetation. The caterpillar
matures quickly; it is black with white
spots and about 30 mm (1.2 in) long. It
pupates on the foodplants and the chrysalis
is white with bold black and orange spots.

Range: Spain and North Africa. A rare butterfly in
Europe, flying mainly in small and well-
scattered colonies.

THE BROWNS (SATYRIDAE)

The butterflies in this worldwide family, especially those inhabiting the temperate regions, are predominantly brown, and they often have a distinctly velvety texture brought about by a coating of hairs. There are over 1,500 species and their wingspans range from about 25 mm to 130 mm (1.0–5.1 in), although the largest European species are only about 80 mm (3.2 in) across. A number of veins in the forewing are distinctly swollen near the base and, with a few exceptions, the outer parts of the wings carry a number of eye-spots on both upper and lower surfaces. These eye-spots, technically called ocelli, usually have white or cream pupils, but some lack pupils and are said to be blind. The apical eye-spots, close to the wingtip, are sometimes fused together to form a single spot containing two pupils, and these are then said to be twinned. The eye-spots probably serve mainly as decoys, drawing the attention of birds and other predators away from the body and towards the expendable wing-margins. It is quite common to find specimens with beak marks around the eye-spots.

The sexes do not usually differ a great deal, although females are often paler than males. The males of some species carry a dark sex-brand on the forewing. The scent-scales or androconia forming these brands are long and tapering and end in tufts of microscopic filaments that disperse the scent.

The antennal club is often poorly developed and only weakly separated from the antennal shaft. The front legs are reduced to short, hairy 'brushes', as in the Nymphalidae, and for this reason the browns are often treated as a subfamily of the Nymphalidae.

Flight is often weak and many of the butterflies spend a lot of time resting on the ground or the vegetation. Their undersides are generally very well camouflaged. On alighting, many species

Scotch Argus

Meadow Brown

Small Heath

Satyrid eggs.

Caterpillar of Grayling.

close their wings immediately and display the apical eye-spots for a few seconds. If not disturbed, they commonly pull the forewings down so that the eye-spots are completely concealed between the hindwings, and they are then very difficult to spot. Some boost their camouflage even more by keeling over towards the sun and eliminating virtually all shadow. Many species, including most of the heaths, never open their wings at rest.

Small red mites are often seen on the bodies of the browns, with the meadow browns and marbled whites apparently more susceptible than most. These mites are the young stages of various species, and they commonly cluster around the thorax near the wing-bases. They gorge themselves on the butterflies' body fluids, falling to the ground when full having done no obvious harm to their hosts.

The eggs are mostly barrel-shaped or thimble-shaped with light ribbing, but some are more or less spherical (*see* previous page). The caterpillars are all green or brown, and all feed on grasses and/or sedges. They are clothed with short hairs, giving many a velvety texture, and all have a short, forked 'tail' at the rear. Most species pass the winter in the larval stage. The pupae are generally smooth, with none of the spiny projections seen in the nymphalid pupae, and they are usually suspended from the foodplants or nearby objects, although some lie freely in or on the soil below the foodplants.

Mountain Ringlet

Meadow Brown

Small Heath

Satyrid chrysalises.

Just over 100 members of the Satyridae live in Europe, and 11 of them breed in the British Isles. The great majority are grassland butterflies, although some prefer shady forest rides and clearings to open grassland. Many *Erebia* species live on the Arctic tundra and high in the mountains. Several Alpine species are restricted to just a few neighbouring peaks and undoubtedly evolved there fairly recently, after their ancestors were stranded and isolated on the mountains when the ice-age glaciers retreated.

p.174 **Marbled White** *Melanargia galathea*

Description: 20–30 mm (0.8–1.2 in). The ground
colour of the upperside ranges from chalky
white to cream, overlaid with a chequered
black pattern of variable extent and
intensity, the densest and darkest patterns
being found in specimens from the south,
such as f. *magdalenae* from northern Italy.
There is a heavy black patch at the end of
the cell in the forewing, but there is never
a black bar through the centre of the cell.
Eye-spots are often visible around the edge
of the hindwing and there may be one near
the tip of the forewing. The underside of
the forewing resembles the upperside,
although usually a little paler, and it has a
small eye-spot near the tip. The underside
of the hindwing is white, often with a
strong yellowish tinge in the female, and
it is usually crossed by two irregular
greyish bands. The outer band contains
several eye-spots and has a conspicuous
break in space 4. The underside of the
female hindwing may be almost unmarked
in the far south.

Similar species: The other *Melanargia* species are all
superficially similar, but they usually have a
black bar across the cell in the forewing.

Flight: June to August. The butterflies flap rather
slowly from flower to flower and are very
fond of knapweeds and other composite
flowers.

Habitat: Rough, flower-rich grassland, including
roadsides, from sea level to about 2,000 m
(6,550 ft). The larvae will eat a wide range
of grasses, but Red Fescue and Sheep's-
Fescue are probably the main ones and may
even be essential, at least in the British
Isles.

Life-cycle: The spherical white eggs are scattered as
the females fly over or perch on the
vegetation. They hatch in about three
weeks. The caterpillars attach themselves
to grass-blades and go into hibernation
immediately after eating their eggshells.
Feeding begins early in the spring, but
growth is slow and the caterpillars are
rarely ready to pupate until late May. In

common with many other satyrid larvae, they feed at night. The mature caterpillar is nearly 30 mm (1.2 in) long and is either brown or bright green, with darker lines on the back and purplish 'tails' at the rear. It pupates in the soil, and the chrysalis is pale yellowish-brown with darker spots.

Range: Southern and central Europe, North Africa, and western Asia as far as Iran. Absent from Scotland and Ireland. Most British colonies occur on lime-rich soils.

M.g. lachesis, which replaces the typical race in Iberia and some neighbouring parts of southern France, has much less black in the basal half of the upper side and is sometimes treated as a separate species – the Iberian Marbled White.

p.175 **Esper's Marbled White** *Melanargia russiae*

Description: 25–30 mm (1.0–1.2 in). The upperside is chalky white with black markings, including a conspicuous zig-zag bar through the centre of the cell in the forewing. There is a black or greyish patch at the base of the hindwing and it always encloses a large white patch. There are two or three eye-spots in a dark smudge towards the rear of the hindwing. The ground colour of the underside varies from chalky white to cream. The underside of the forewing is a slightly paler version of the upperside but has an eye-spot near the tip. The underside of the hindwing is crossed by a pale-grey central band, which is strongly edged with black. There are five prominent eye-spots in the outer region of the wing, although these are not enclosed in a grey band.

Similar species: Marbled White is usually much darker and lacks the bar in the forewing cell, and the eye-spots under the hindwing are enclosed in a grey band. Balkan Marbled White has a basal black or grey patch on the upperside of each wing. Western Marbled White has brown veins under the hindwing. Italian

Marbled White has brownish eye-spots underneath.

Flight: July to August.

Habitat: Dry, stony grassland from 900 to 2,000 m (2,950–6,550 ft). The larval foodplants are various grasses.

Life-cycle: The white, almost spherical eggs are scattered freely from the air or from a perch. The caterpillars go into hibernation soon after hatching and complete their growth in the spring. The mature caterpillar is leaf-green with darker stripes, a brown head, and brownish tails. It is about 30 mm (1.2 in) long and it pupates in or on the ground.

Range: Southern Europe, in scattered upland colonies, and on across temperate Asia to Siberia. Specimens from peninsular Italy (*M. r. japygia*) are more heavily marked than those from elsewhere in Europe and often a little smaller. The species is at risk in Italy and the Balkans.

p.175 **Balkan Marbled White** *Melanargia larissa*

Description: 25–30 mm (1.0–1.2 in). The upperside is basically chalky white with black markings, including an extensive black or grey smudge at the base of each wing. There is a wavy black bar through the centre of the forewing cell, but this may be obscured by the basal smudge. The black markings are sometimes so extensive that the wings appear black with a white band through the middle. A small, blind eye-spot is usually visible near the tip of the forewing, and up to five eye-spots may be visible on the hindwing. The underside of the forewing is a more lightly marked version of the upperside, with little or no black at the base and with the black cell-bar clearly visible. The underside of the hindwing is dusty white with pale-grey clouding at the base, and often with a yellow tinge in the female. The basal half is crossed by two very irregular black lines, and there are five variable eye-spots in a grey band in the outer half.

Similar species: The other *Melanargia* species usually lack the large, dark basal patch on the upperside. Esper's Marbled White has a black patch at the base of the hindwing, but always with a large white spot in it.

Flight: June to August.

Habitat: Dry, stony grassland from sea level to about 2,200 m (7,225 ft). The larval foodplants are various grasses.

Life-cycle: The white eggs are scattered freely over the habitat. The caterpillars go into hibernation soon after hatching and complete their development in the spring. The mature caterpillar is about 25mm (1.0 in) long and ranges from yellowish-grey, often with a reddish or greenish cast, to ochre with darker yellow-edged stripes. It pupates on or in the ground.

Range: Southeastern Europe and western Asia. Specimens from the Adriatic region (*M. l. herta*) are less heavily marked than those from other areas, and the cell-bar in the forewing is clearly visible on the upperside.

---

p.176 **Western Marbled White**
Melanargia occitanica

Description: 25–30 mm (1.0–1.2 in). The upperside is chalky white with black markings, the latter occurring mainly on the outer parts of the wings. An irregular black bar crosses the forewing cell and often links up with the adjacent black spots. At the end of the cell there is a small black circle, and there are two small, indistinct eye-spots near the tip. There are usually five eye-spots, often with pale blue centres, near the margin of the hindwing, and beyond these are four or five black-edged white triangles. The underside of the forewing resembles the upperside but the markings near the tip are brown instead of black. The veins under the hindwing are lined with brown and the eye-spots have pale-blue centres.

Similar species: No other marbled white has brown veins on the underside.

Flight: May to July, visiting a wide range of composites and other flowers and often basking with wings wide open on the ground.

Habitat: Dry, rocky grassland from sea level to about 1,800 m (5,900 ft), but most common in hilly areas. The larval foodplants are various coarse grasses.

Life-cycle: The eggs are white and more or less spherical in shape and are scattered in flight or dropped when the females are perched. The caterpillars go into hibernation in the ground or low down in the grass soon after hatching. The mature caterpillar is green and very like that of the Marbled White and it pupates on or in the ground.

Range: Southwest Europe, from Portugal through to northwest Italy, and North Africa. Also found in Sicily, where the eye-spots are very small or lacking altogether. All Italian populations are declining and are considered to be at risk.

p.177 **Italian Marbled White** *Melanargia arge*

Description: 25 mm (1.0 in). The upperside is white with thin, black or dark-grey markings. These include a crescent-shaped bar in the forewing cell, although it does not occupy the full width of the cell. A black ring at the end of the cell may contain a few blue scales, and there are one or two small eye-spots near the wingtip. Black-edged white triangles are conspicuous on the outer wing-margins, especially on the forewing. The hindwing bears up to five variable blue-centred eye-spots. The underside of the forewing is a paler version of the upperside, although the eye-spots are ringed with brown. The underside of the hindwing has a few dark lines in the basal half and the five eye-spots are brown with small blue pupils.

Similar species: Spanish Marbled White, with a different distribution, is more heavily marked and the underside has striations on the front edge of both wings.

Flight: May to June.

Habitat: Rough grassland from sea level to about

1,500 m (4,925 ft). The larval foodplants are grasses.

Life-cycle: The eggs are scattered over the habitat. The life history is probably much the same as that of other *Melanargia* species, with the caterpillars going into hibernation soon after hatching.

Range: Confined to peninsular Italy and Sicily, where it occurs in scattered colonies and is considered to be at risk.

---

p.177   **Spanish Marbled White** *Melanargia ines*

Description: 25 mm (1.0 in). The upperside is chalky or creamy white with a chequered black pattern, including a strong black bar crossing the forewing cell. A black ring at the end of the cell may have a faint blue centre. The two eye-spots near the tip of the forewing and the five eye-spots on the hindwing all have blue centres. The underside of the forewing resembles the upperside but the eye-spots are strongly ringed with brown. The underside of the hindwing, which is often quite yellow in the female, has a few black cross-lines in the basal half, and five large brown eye-spots with blue pupils. The front margins of both wings are marked with fine stripes on the underside.

Similar species: Italian Marbled White is usually less heavily marked and the bar in the forewing cell is incomplete. No other *Melanargia* species has stripes under the front edges of the wings.

Flight: April to June.

Habitat: Rough, stony grassland, usually between 900 and 1,200 m (2,950 and 3,925 ft). The larval foodplants are coarse grasses.

Life-cycle: The eggs are scattered freely over the habitat and the caterpillars go into hibernation soon after hatching, but little else is known of the early stages of this butterfly.

Range: Southern and central Iberia, where it is quite common in upland areas, and North Africa.

p.178 **Woodland Grayling** *Hipparchia fagi*

Description: 33–40 mm (1.3–1.6 in). The male upperside is essentially dark brown with a broad, pale post-discal band on each wing. The band on the forewing is heavily dusted with brown and contains one or two eye-spots: that on the hindwing is whiter and more distinct, with a small eye-spot at the rear. Its inner margin is very gently curved or almost straight. The female is similar, but the post-discal band is better defined; that on the forewing is often yellowish, especially towards the tip, and it always contains two eye-spots. The uppersides are not often seen at rest, although the female displays them during courtship. The two sexes are very similar on the underside, where the forewing is dark brown with a broad white or yellowish band containing a large eye-spot near the tip and sometimes a much smaller one further back. The underside of the hindwing has a brown basal half, often tinged with grey. It is bounded by a conspicuous wavy black line, and beyond this there is a broad, pale band whose outer edge is indistinct and merges gradually into a brown area in the outer part of the wing. Black flecks are scattered all over the wing, and there may be a number of faint eye-spots near the outer margin.

Similar species: Rock Grayling is almost identical but usually smaller, the forewing very rarely more than 33 mm (1.3 in) long; the pale band on the upperside of the hindwing has a more strongly curved inner margin. Eastern Rock Grayling can be distinguished with certainty only by examining the genitalia. Great Banded Grayling looks similar in flight, but is blacker above and the white bands therefore show up more clearly. It also has more white on the underside.

Flight: June to September, floating lazily, and commonly resting on tree-trunks with its wings closed and only the underside of the hindwing visible. Buddleia blossom sometimes attract the insect, but otherwise it shows little interest in flowers.

Habitat: Light woodland and scrubby places, from sea level to about 1,200 m (3,925 ft). The larval foodplants are various coarse grasses.

Life-cycle: The eggs are white, barrel-shaped and lightly ribbed. They are laid singly on the grasses or on neighbouring plants or debris. The caterpillars go into hibernation in the leaf-litter during the fourth instar and complete their growth in the spring. The mature caterpillar is pale brown with a broken black or dark-brown stripe along the back; it is about 35 mm (1.4 in) long. It pupates in the leaf-litter. The chrysalis is orange-brown.

Range: South and central Europe and eastwards into southern Asia. Absent from the British Isles and from most of the Iberian peninsula.

Where the ranges of Woodland and Rock graylings coincide, the Rock Grayling usually lives at higher altitudes, but size is the best way of distinguishing the two species when caught: the male forewing is very rarely under 33 mm (1.3 in) long in the Woodland Grayling and very rarely more than this in the Rock Grayling, although females are often a little larger in both species.

p.178 **Rock Grayling** *Hipparchia alcyone*

Description: 28–33 mm (1.1–1.3 in). The male upperside is dark brown with a pale post-discal band, often heavily dusted with brown, on each wing. There are two eye-spots in the band on the forewing, although these are often indistinct in the male, and there are one or more eye-spots in the hindwing band. The inner margin of the hindwing band is quite sharply curved. The female is similar but the post-discal band is broader and whiter, although it may be yellowish at the front of the forewing. The underside of the forewing is very like the upperside. The underside of the hindwing is largely brown or greyish brown, with a pale post-discal band of varying width that merges gradually with the brown marginal area. Black flecks are scattered over the wing-surface and there is sometimes a conspicuous black submarginal line. The female may reveal her upperside during courtship, but otherwise the upperside is rarely seen.

Similar species: Woodland Grayling is usually larger, but otherwise almost identical. Eastern Rock Grayling cannot be separated on external features, but does not inhabit the same area. Great Banded Grayling is similar in flight, but is blacker above and has more white patches underneath.

Flight: June to August, floating lazily, and commonly resting on the ground or on rocks with its wings closed and only the underside of the hindwing visible. It rarely visits flowers.

Habitat: Rocky slopes, moors, and light woodland, from low levels in the north of its range to about 1,800 m (5,900 ft) in the south, where it usually flies at higher levels than the very similar Woodland Grayling. The larval foodplants are various grasses, especially species of *Holcus* and *Brachypodium*.

Life-cycle: The white eggs are barrel-shaped with faint ribbing, and they are laid singly on the grass or on neighbouring plants or leaf-litter. The caterpillars feed in late summer and go into hibernation during the third instar. Growth is completed in the spring and the mature caterpillar, up to 35 mm (1.4 in) long, is pale brown with a prominent black stripe along the middle of the back and two pale-brown stripes on each side. It blends well with the grass-stems. It pupates in leaf-litter or grass tufts and the chrysalis is orange-brown.

Range: Southern and central Europe and eastwards to Belarus and Ukraine, but absent from the British Isles and from southeast Europe, where it is replaced by Eastern Rock Grayling.

p.178 **Eastern Rock Grayling** *Hipparchia syriaca*

Description: 30–33 mm (1.2–1.3 in). The upperside is
dull brown with a broad, white post-discal
band on each wing. The bands are usually
heavily dusted with brown in the male. The
forewing band carries two eye-spots in the
female but only one in the male, while the
hindwing band has just one in both sexes.
The underside of the forewing resembles
the upperside, although the post-discal
band may be yellowish and has little or no
brown dusting. The underside of the
hindwing is brown and grey and just like
that of Rock Grayling.

Similar species: Formerly regarded as a subspecies of Rock
Grayling, this butterfly cannot really be
distinguished from it or from the
Woodland Grayling without examination
of the genitalia.

Flight: June to July: commonly rests on tree
trunks.

Habitat: Rough grassland and light woodland, in
hot, dry places from sea level to about
1,500 m (4,925 ft). The larval foodplants
are grasses.

Life-cycle: Little is known of the life-cycle of this
butterfly but it is likely to be very similar
to that of the Rock Grayling.

Range: The Balkans and eastwards to the Caucasus.

Corsican Grayling *Hipparchia neomiris*

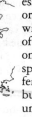

Description: 25 mm (1.0 in). The upperside is
essentially rich brown with a broad, bright
orange and yellow post-discal band on each
wing. There is a single eye-spot near the tip
of the forewing and usually a small blind
one further back. There is also a small eye-
spot at the rear of the hindwing. The
female may be a little paler than the male,
but otherwise the sexes are alike. The
underside of the forewing is largely orange
and yellow, but it has a brown base and a
mottled-brown tip enclosing the eye-spot.
The underside of the hindwing is largely
brown with a white post-discal band. The
inner edge of this band is clearly defined

and very wavy, but the outer edge is poorly defined and merges gradually with the brown borders.

Similar species: None.

Flight: June to July.

Habitat: Mountain slopes, usually between 900 and 1,800 m (2,950 and 5,900 ft) although lower down on Elba. The larval foodplants are not known but are undoubtedly grasses of some kind.

Life-cycle: Nothing is known of the early stages of this butterfly.

Range: Confined to Corsica, Sardinia and Elba, and rare throughout.

---

p.179 **Grayling** *Hipparchia semele*

Description: 20–30 mm (0.8–1.2 in). The upperside, hardly ever seen at rest, is basically brown with a yellow or orange post-discal band on each wing. The extent of these bands varies a good deal and they are often broken near the tip of the forewing, but the species can usually be distinguished from its numerous superficially similar relatives by the triangular orange patches in the post-discal band of the hindwing. There are two eye-spots on the forewing and a smaller one at the rear of the hindwing. The male has a dark, wedge-shaped sex-brand running through the centre of the forewing but otherwise the sexes are similar, although the female is usually larger and paler than the male. The underside of the forewing is largely orange or yellow, with two eye-spots and mottled-brown front and outer borders. The underside of the hindwing is mottled grey and brown, often with a dark zig-zag line separating a darker basal area from a greyer outer area. There is often a small and indistinct eye-spot at the rear.

Similar species: Southern Grayling usually has more orange on the upperside, but it is very like some southern races of the Grayling and accurate identification necessitates examination of the genitalia. Nevada Grayling has much paler post-discal bands.

Flight: May to October, keeping close to the ground and rarely flying far at any one time. The butterflies spend most of their time resting on the ground, with their wings tightly closed and only the underside of the hindwing visible. They blend beautifully with the ground and herbage, and make themselves even more difficult to spot by leaning towards the sun and therefore casting virtually no shadow. The butterflies sometimes visit Wild Thyme and other flowers, especially in dry weather, but probably feed largely on honeydew.

Habitat: Heaths and dry grassland, including coastal sand-dunes, from sea level to about 2,000 m (6,550 ft). The larval foodplants are a wide range of grasses, including the tough Marram Grass.

Life-cycle: The barrel-shaped eggs are white and finely ribbed, and they are laid singly on the grasses or on the surrounding leaf-litter. They hatch in two or three weeks and the caterpillars feed mainly at night. They go into hibernation in the soil or leaf-litter in the third instar, although they may wake to feed in mild weather. Growth is completed in the spring, and the mature caterpillar is up to 30 mm (1.2 in) long. It is straw-coloured with five longitudinal brown stripes. Pupation takes place in a small chamber in the soil or under the leaf-litter, and the chrysalis is reddish brown.

Range: Throughout Europe except the far north and possibly Greece, and eastwards into southern Asia. Populations in Ireland and northern Britain occur mainly in coastal regions.

The Grayling has several forms and races, differing in size and in density of colour: f. *cadmus* from the Alps and southern Europe is larger than most and often has a prominent white band across the underside of the hindwing. The Cretan Grayling (*H. cretica*), which was formerly regarded as a race of the Grayling, is identical to *H. s. cadmus* except in the structure of the male genitalia. It is confined to Crete.

p.179 Southern Grayling *Hipparchia aristaeus*

Description: 25–28 mm (1.0–1.1 in). The upperside, never seen at rest, is brown with a broad orange or yellow band on each wing. The bands contain two eye-spots on the forewing and a single eye-spot (often very small) on the hindwing. The male has a dark, wedge-shaped sex-brand on the forewing. The female is larger and often brighter, with broader orange bands that may extend inwards to cover much of the wings. In Greece the orange bands are often heavily dusted with brown. The underside of the forewing is largely orange, with brown borders. The female has two eye-spots but the male has only one. The underside of the hindwing is mottled brown and grey, usually with an irregular black line across the middle and a diffuse white band beyond it.

Similar species: Grayling is very similar, especially in southern areas: it usually has less orange, but cannot be reliably separated without examination of the genitalia. There is little or no overlap in range.

Flight: June to August, behaving in much the same way as the Grayling.

Habitat: Rough grassy places and maquis, from sea level to about 2,000 m (6,550 ft). The larval foodplants are grasses.

Life-cycle: Very little is known of the early stages of this butterfly but they are likely to be very similar to those of the Grayling.

Range: Corsica and Sardinia, Sicily, southern Balkans, and eastwards into southern Asia. Also in North Africa.

It seems likely that several very similar Mediterranean species are included under this name at present. Delattin's Grayling (*H. delattini*), which is confined to a few places in the southern Balkans, differs only in the detailed structure of the male genitalia and may be no more than a race of Southern Grayling, although it has recently been described as a subspecies of the Asiatic *H. volgensis*.

p.180 **Tree Grayling** *Neohipparchia statilinus*

Description:
23 mm (0.9 in). The male upperside is dark, sooty brown and more or less unmarked apart from two indistinct, blind eye-spots on the forewing and two small white spots between them. The female is a lighter brown, with a variably developed yellow or orange post-discal band on the forewing. Her eye-spots, larger than those of the male, may contain minute white pupils. There may also be traces of an orange submarginal band on the hindwing. The uppersides are rarely seen at rest in either sex. The underside of the forewing is brown, with a lighter post-discal band and a grey border; the two eye-spots are conspicuously ringed with yellow. The underside of the hindwing ranges from sooty brown to pale grey, often with little marking apart from a dark wavy line through the centre.

Similar species:
Freyer's Grayling has a similar pattern but is much larger.

Flight:
July to October, often resting on tree-trunks.

Habitat:
Light woodland, heaths, and scrub, from sea level to about 1,500 m (4,925 ft). The larval foodplants are various coarse grasses.

Life-cycle:
The white eggs are barrel-shaped and marked with widely spaced ribs. They are laid singly, usually on dry grass-stems and leaves, and the caterpillars go into hibernation in the first instar. In their early stages, the caterpillars are grass-green with white and dark-green longitudinal stripes, but in the penultimate instar the ground colour changes to yellowish-brown and the green stripes become dark brown. The mature caterpillar is about 30 mm (1.2 in) long. It pupates in a silk-lined chamber in the soil or leaf-litter, and the chrysalis is reddish-brown.

Range:
Southern and central Europe, North Africa, and eastwards into Turkey, but uncommon and probably at risk in the northern parts of its range. Absent from the British Isles.

p.180 **Freyer's Grayling** *Neohipparchia fatua*

Description: 30–35 mm (1.2–1.4 in). The male upperside is dull brown, sometimes with a paler tinge towards the outside. There are two small eye-spots on the forewing and one on the hindwing, and there is a dark, wavy line around the edge of the hindwing. The female upperside is brighter, with a yellowish post-discal patch on the forewing containing two conspicuous eye-spots and two other white spots. There is an arc of small white post-discal spots on the hindwing and the wavy line around the edge is very noticeable. The margin of the hindwing is clearly scalloped in both sexes. The undersides of both sexes are largely brown – darker in the male than in the female – with two large, yellow-ringed eye-spots on the forewing; between these there are two white spots, and there is a white blaze just beyond the cell. The hindwing is mottled brown, with two irregular black cross-lines.

Similar species: Tree Grayling is similar but much smaller, and greyer under the hindwing.

Flight: June to September, often resting on tree trunks.

Habitat: Light woodland, from sea level to about 1,000 m (3,275 ft) but most common in hot, dry upland areas. The larval foodplants are various grasses.

Life-cycle: The life history is probably similar to that of Tree Grayling, with the larvae hibernating in an early instar. The caterpillar, at least in its early stages, is grass-green with darker stripes.

Range: The Balkans and eastwards through Turkey and Syria.

p.180 **Striped Grayling** *Pseudotergumia fidia*

Description: 28–33 mm (1.1–1.3 in). The uppersides of both sexes, rarely seen at rest, are sooty brown with chequered grey fringes on the forewing. The latter has two very dark eye-spots, separated by two white dots, and a faint submarginal line parallel to the outer margin. The female also has two or three pale patches near the centre of the wing. The hindwing has a faint submarginal line and a small eye-spot near the rear, and the female may have a row of small white post-discal spots. The underside is grey and brown, with large yellow-ringed eye-spots on the forewing. Both wings are variably flecked with white and bear conspicuous black lines.

Similar species: The bold zig-zag stripes under the hindwing distinguish this species from all other graylings.

Flight: July to August.

Habitat: Rocky slopes and light woodland, from sea level to about 2,000 m (6,550 ft) but most common in upland areas above 1,000 m (3,275 ft). The larval foodplants are various grasses, especially fescues and *Brachypodium* species.

Life-cycle: The oval, white eggs are laid on or near the foodplants, usually on dry grass-stems or leaves, and the caterpillars go into hibernation in the first instar. Growth is completed in the spring, when the caterpillar reaches a length of about 30 mm (1.2 in). It is light brown with darker brown or olive-green stripes and a straw-coloured underside. The head is yellow with faint brown stripes.

Range: Southwest Europe, as far as northern Italy (where it is rare), and North Africa.

p.181 **The Hermit** *Chazara briseis*

Description: 20–35 mm (0.8–1.4 in). The uppersides of both sexes are sooty brown with a broad cream or white post-discal band on each wing. The forewing band, which is composed of several oval spots separated by dark veins, encloses two eye-spots, with or without pupils. The front edge of the forewing is white or yellowish. The underside of the forewing is greyish-brown with a wide cream post-discal band and a pale cell with a dark bar through the middle. The underside of the hindwing is mottled grey or brown, with a white band through the middle in the male and no obvious pattern in the female.

Similar species: Southern Hermit has dark V-shaped lines on the underside of the hindwing.

Flight: June to September, usually resting on rocks or on the ground with wings closed.

Habitat: Dry, stony grassland, from sea level to 2,000 m (6,550 ft). The larval foodplants are various grasses, especially the finer-leaved fescues and Blue Moor-grass.

Life-cycle: The barrel-shaped, white eggs have a few widely spaced ribs, and they are laid singly on dry grass close to the ground. The caterpillars go into hibernation while still quite small – in the first or second instar. The mature caterpillar is up to 30 mm (1.2 in) long; it is basically grey, with several broken sooty-brown stripes and dense, brown freckles. It pupates amongst the grass-roots, and the chrysalis is orange-brown.

Range: Southern and central Europe and eastwards to Mongolia. Also in North Africa. Absent from the British Isles.

In southern Europe, females may have pale-brown or buff bands. Southern specimens of both sexes are often much larger than those from elsewhere.

Southern Hermit *Chazara prieuri*

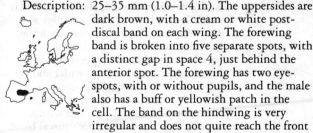

Description: 25–35 mm (1.0–1.4 in). The uppersides are dark brown, with a cream or white post-discal band on each wing. The forewing band is broken into five separate spots, with a distinct gap in space 4, just behind the anterior spot. The forewing has two eye-spots, with or without pupils, and the male also has a buff or yellowish patch in the cell. The band on the hindwing is very irregular and does not quite reach the front edge of the wing. The underside of the forewing is largely white, with conspicuous eye-spots and a large dark triangle or crescent in the cell. The underside of the hindwing is mottled-brown, with prominent pale veins, a variable white post-discal band, and an arc of dark V-shaped markings towards the margin. Females are often a good deal larger than males, and the cream or white markings are frequently replaced by orange-brown or buff (f. *uhagonis*).

Similar species: Hermit lacks the pale veins and dark V-shaped marks under the hindwing.

Flight: July to August.

Habitat: Rocky mountain slopes at about 1,000 m (3,275 ft). The larval foodplants are grasses.

Life-cycle: The caterpillar, up to 30 mm (1.2 in) long, is pinkish-brown with broken black or dark-brown stripes. Little else has been discovered of the life-cycle of this species, but it is likely to be much the same as that of the Hermit.

Range: There are scattered populations in eastern Spain and the Balearic Islands, but otherwise the butterfly is confined to North Africa.

---

p.181 White-banded Grayling
Pseudochazara anthelea

Description: 25–30 mm (1.0–1.2 in). The male upperside is dark brown, with a white post-discal band on each wing. The forewing band is very irregular and contains two large eye-spots, with or without white centres. There is a narrow, black sex-brand in the cell. The hindwing band gets wider towards the rear, where it is clouded with orange and encloses a small eye-spot, but it does not reach the inner margin. The underside of the forewing resembles the upperside except that the post-discal band is wider and the cell is pale with dark streaks crossing it. The underside of the hindwing is mottled-brown, flecked with white, and with a variably developed white post-discal band. The female is noticeably larger and paler than the male and has two very different patterns. *P. a. amalthea,* from the Balkan mainland, resembles the male except for her size, although her post-discal bands may be yellowish. *P. a. anthelea*, from the Aegean islands, has bright-orange post-discal bands and that of the forewing extends inwards to cover much of the wing.

Similar species: None.

Flight: June to July.

Habitat: Stony hillsides, from sea level to about 1,800 m (5,900 ft). The larval foodplants are grasses.

Life-cycle: Nothing is known of the life-cycle of this butterfly.

Range: The Balkans and eastwards into western Asia, where only *P. a. anthelea* is known.

Nevada Grayling *Pseudochazara hippolyte*

Description: 25 mm (1.0 in). The upperside is light brown with a broad, yellow post-discal band of fairly uniform width on both wings. The yellow sometimes gets deeper towards the outside of the band. There are two eye-spots in the band on the forewing and one near the rear of the hindwing. The underside of the forewing resembles the upperside but the yellow band is broader and the cell is pale with dark streaks across it. Both surfaces have brown and white chequered fringes. The underside of the hindwing is brown, with a paler post-discal band and three black cross-lines.

Similar species: Grayling has less uniform post-discal bands. Grecian Grayling, found only in Greece, lacks chequered fringes.

Flight: June to July.

Habitat: Sparsely vegetated montane slopes, usually between 2,000 and 3,000 m (6,550 and 9,850 ft) but sometimes as low as 1,400 m (4,600 ft). The larvae feed on Sheep's Fescue and possibly on other grasses.

Life-cycle: Winter is probably passed in the larval stage, but little else is known of the life-cycle of this butterfly.

Range: Confined to the Sierra Nevada in Europe, but also in Turkey and eastwards to the Caspian and western China.

Brown's Grayling *Pseudochazara mamurra*

Description: 26–27 mm (1.0–1.1 in). The upperside is light brown, with a broad orange post-discal band on the forewing and an extensive orange patch covering the outer half of the hindwing except for a narrow brown border. The forewing has two eye-spots that are usually blind. Two small white spots lie between the eye-spots and the orange band is interrupted by a smudge of brown ground colour in this area. The underside of the forewing resembles the upperside, although it is much paler. The underside of the hindwing has a greyish-brown basal half and a paler outer half, flecked with reddish brown and with a conspicuous brown border.

Similar species: Grecian Grayling has less orange on the upperside of the hindwing and no white spots between the eye-spots.

Flight: July to August.

Habitat: Rough grassland, usually between 200 and 700 m (650 and 2,300 ft). The larval foodplants are undoubtedly grasses, but it is not known which species the caterpillars prefer.

Life-cycle: Nothing is known of the life-cycle of this butterfly.

Range: Known in Europe only from northwest Greece, where it was discovered in 1975. Also in Turkey.

p.181 **Grecian Grayling** *Pseudochazara graeca*

Description: 25 mm (1.0 in). The uppersides are brown, with a broad orange or buff post-discal band on each wing and a conspicuous brown border with unchequered fringes. There are two eye-spots on the forewing, with or without pupils, and a streak of brown ground colour cuts across the post-discal band on vein 4, just behind the front eye-spot. The undersides resemble the uppersides, although they are somewhat paler and greyer, and the hindwings are speckled with black.

Similar species: Brown's and Macedonian graylings have white spots between the eye-spots. Nevada Grayling has chequered fringes.

Flight: July and August.

Habitat: Montane scree slopes between about 1,000 and 2,100 m (3,275 and 6,900 ft). The larval foodplants are grasses, although the preferred species is unknown.

Life-cycle: The egg is chalky white and barrel-shaped, with a pimply pattern on the top. The caterpillar is light brown with a darker dorsal stripe that is often broken by lighter patches. It hibernates in the second or third instar. Up to 40 mm (1.6 in) long when mature, it pupates in the soil.

Range: Confined to Greece and Macedonia.

---

p.182 **Dil's Grayling** *Pseudochazara orestes*

Description: 28–34 mm (1.1–1.4 in). The uppersides are essentially rich brown, with an orange or buff post-discal band on each wing. The bands become darker towards the outside and that of the forewing contains two eye-spots separated by two very small white spots. The underside of the forewing is a paler version of the upperside, but the underside of the hindwing is greyish brown with a white post-discal line and dark submarginal triangles. The forewings are lightly chequered on both surfaces.

Similar species: Brown's, Grecian and Macedonian graylings are all closely related, but all have the post-discal band of the forewing more or less broken at vein 4, just behind the front eye-spot. Grecian Grayling has unchequered fringes and no white spots on the forewing.

Flight: June to July.

Habitat: Montane grassland and scree, usually above 800 m (2,625 ft). The larval foodplants are grasses.

Life-cycle: The ribbed eggs range from dirty white to grey. The mature caterpillar is about 38 mm (1.5 in) long and is greyish brown with darker brown blotches and tiny white spots. It pupates in the leaf-litter, surrounded by a few strands of silk. The chrysalis, which overwinters, is brown with paler wingcases.

Range: Known only from Bulgaria and northern Greece.

Like Brown's Grayling and Macedonian Grayling, this species was discovered only in the 1970s. These three are closely related to each other and to the Grecian Grayling, but their taxonomic status is not fully understood at present.

Macedonian Grayling
Pseudochazara cingovskii

Description: 25–30 mm (1.0–1.2 in). The uppersides are dark brown with a broad yellowish or pale-orange post-discal band on each wing. There are two white-centred eye-spots on the forewing, with a streak of brown breaking the orange band between them. Two white spots lie between the eye-spots. The post-discal band of the hindwing encloses two or three small eye-spots. The underside of the forewing is greyish brown at the base and yellow or pale orange in the outer region, with a brown outer border and eye-spots as on the upperside. The underside of the hindwing is mottled brown, with a faint white post-discal band and often with a small white eye-spot.

Similar species: Grecian Grayling lacks white spots between the eye-spots. Brown's Grayling and Dark Grayling have brighter orange bands.

Flight: July to August.

Habitat: Montane scree slopes above 1,000 m (3,275 ft). The larval foodplants are grasses, but it is not known which species are preferred.

Life-cycle: The dirty-white eggs are barrel-shaped with a pimply pattern on the top. The mature caterpillar is light brown, mottled with white, and with darker stripes. It is up to 45 mm (1.8 in.) long and it pupates in the soil. Winter is passed in the larval stage.

Range: Confined to Macedonia, but local and never common.

p.182 Grey Asian Grayling *Pseudochazara geyeri*

Description: 25 mm (1.0 in). The uppersides are
yellowish grey with a broad pale-buff post-
discal band on each wing. The forewing
band encloses two large round eye-spots,
with or without white pupils, and its inner
edge is marked with an angular brown line.
The fringes are strongly chequered with
grey and brown. The pale band on the
hindwing has a deeply toothed outer
margin. The underside of the forewing is a
paler version of the upperside, with several
dark lines in the basal region. The
underside of the hindwing is mottled
brown, with an irregular, white post-discal
band bounded on the outside by an arc of
dark V-shaped marks.

Similar species: None.

Flight: July and August.

Habitat: Dry, rocky slopes between about 1,200 and
2,000 m (3,925 and 6,550 ft). The larval
foodplants are grasses, although the exact
species is unknown.

Life-cycle: The eggs are yellowish and the caterpillars
are pale brown with a dark stripe bounded
by white lines on each side. Little else
seems to be known of the life-cycle of this
butterfly.

Range: Known in Europe only from a small area
where Greece, Albania, and Macedonia
meet. Also in Turkey and eastwards to the
Caspian.

p.183 Dark Grayling *Pseudochazara mniszechii*

Description: 25–30 mm (1.0–1.2 in). The uppersides are
dark brown, with rich-orange post-discal
bands on both wings. The forewing band
contains two eye-spots and is clearly broken
by the brown ground colour just behind the
anterior eye-spot. Two conspicuous white
spots sit astride the broken area between
the eye-spots. The outer margins are clearly
chequered with grey and brown. The
hindwing often has two eye-spots towards
the rear. The underside of the forewing is
greyish brown at the base, and orange or

sand-coloured in the outer half, with eye-spots as on the upperside. The underside of the hindwing is mottled brown with no obvious markings, but the outer margin is distinctly scalloped.

Similar species: Macedonian Grayling has a similar pattern but the post-discal bands are much paler and the underside of the hindwing is much greyer.

Flight: July to August.

Habitat: Rough, stony grassland at about 1,200 m (3,925 ft). The larval foodplant is unknown, but it is undoubtedly some kind of grass.

Life-cycle: Little is known of the life-cycle of this recently discovered butterfly.

Range: The only known European locality is in northwest Greece, but the butterfly is widely distributed from Turkey to the Caspian Sea.

p.183   **Norse Grayling** *Oeneis norna*

Description: 25–28 mm (1.0–1.1 in). The uppersides, hardly ever seen at rest, lack the swollen basal veins seen in most other satyrids. They range from yellowish brown to a dull greyish brown, with a broad, pale post-discal band carrying a variable number of eye-spots – usually more in females than in males. The male also has a dark sex-brand in the middle of the forewing. The underside of the forewing resembles the upperside, while the underside of the hindwing is mottled-brown, often becoming sandy towards the outside. There is an irregular white post-discal band and a pale patch at the front of the wing near the base. The fringes of both wings are chequered on both surfaces.

Similar species: Baltic Grayling is very much darker, with narrower post-discal bands.

Flight: June and July, almost as soon as the snow melts, flying with a fast zig-zag motion but rarely travelling far and usually staying close to the ground. With its wings closed on the ground or on tree-trunks, it is very difficult to spot.

Habitat:	Northern birchwoods, moors, and tundra, from sea level to about 900 m (2,950 ft). The larval foodplants are various grasses and sedges.
Life-cycle:	The pale-brown, barrel-shaped eggs are laid singly on the foodplants and the caterpillars hibernate twice before maturing. The caterpillar is a dirty yellow with reddish-brown stripes, and it is 25–30 mm (1.0–1.2 in) long when mature.
Range:	Northern Scandinavia and in scattered localities through northern Asia. Specimens from the Arctic coasts of Europe are usually much yellower than those from the mountains further south.

The genitalia of the Norse Grayling are very similar to those of the Alpine Grayling and it is possible that the two butterflies are geographical races of a single species.

---

p.183 **Arctic Grayling** *Oeneis bore*

Description:	20–25 mm (0.8–1.0 in). The uppersides are pale greyish or yellowish brown, with no eye-spots and without the swollen veins typical of most satyrids. The outer areas are sometimes yellowish in the female and almost white in the male, and occasional males are chalky white all over. The male has a diagonal, dark sex-brand just behind the forewing cell. The hindwing usually has a dark band across the middle, but there is no other obvious pattern. The undersides resemble the uppersides, although the hindwing is a little darker and has a well-defined discal band. The fringes of both wings are strongly chequered on both surfaces. All surfaces are thinly and loosely scaled and often become translucent as the scales fall with age.
Similar species:	Norse Grayling has eye-spots, but otherwise its pattern is very similar.
Flight:	June to July, keeping close to the ground and spending much of its time resting with its wings closed.
Habitat:	Dry tundra slopes, from sea level to about 1,000 m (3,275 ft). The butterflies often

gather near the summits for mating, although the females move down to slightly moister areas to lay their eggs. The larval foodplants are various grasses, especially fescues.

Life-cycle: The eggs are white and almost spherical, and they are laid singly on the foodplants. The caterpillar is pale brown with darker stripes, including a broken one along the middle of the back. It hibernates twice before maturing at about 30 mm (1.2 in) long and it pupates in the leaf-litter. The chrysalis is green and yellow with brown markings.

Range: Northern Scandinavia and all other Arctic regions, extending southwards to Hudson's Bay in Canada.

---

p.184 **Baltic Grayling** *Oeneis jutta*

Description: 25–30 mm (1.0–1.2 in). The uppersides, rarely seen at rest, range from light brown to sooty brown, with a yellow post-discal band on each wing. The bands are often broken into a number of distinct yellow patches and they enclose a number of blind eye-spots – usually three or four on the forewing and two on the hindwing. The bands are often quite broad and sometimes extend almost to the wing-margin. The male, sometimes a little paler than the female, has a dark sex-brand running diagonally across the forewing. The underside of the forewing resembles the upperside, but the underside of the hindwing is mottled grey and brown, with a darker discal band and only very small eye-spots. The fringes are strongly chequered on both surfaces, especially on the forewing.

Similar species: The butterfly cannot be confused with any other northern species.

Flight: May to August, flying strongly in sunshine and perching – usually with wings closed – on the ground or on fallen timber or, less often, on tree-trunks.

Habitat: Lowland moors and open pine forests, especially in damp areas. The larval foodplants include Purple Moor-grass and other coarse, tussock-forming grasses.

Life-cycle: The eggs are cream and barrel-shaped. The caterpillar, which hibernates twice before reaching maturity, is pale brown with darker stripes and tapers strongly towards the rear. It is about 35 mm (1.4 in) long when mature, and it pupates on the ground. The chrysalis is yellowish green or sand-coloured, with brown stripes and fine black spots. The chrysalis may overwinter on occasion, giving the butterfly a three-year lifespan.

Range: Scandinavia and the Baltic area, and eastwards across the cooler parts of Asia. Also in North America, where it is called the Jutta Arctic. The butterfly varies in size from place to place, with the largest and darkest European specimens occurring in Norway.

---

p.184 **Alpine Grayling** *Oeneis glacialis*

Description: 25–30 mm (1.0–1.2 in). The male upperside is mid-brown, with a yellowish or pale-orange post-discal band on each wing and, usually, several small eye-spots that may or may not be blind. A dark sex-brand runs diagonally across the forewing just behind the cell. The female upperside is largely orange-brown with brown outer margins and a variable number of eye-spots. As in other *Oeneis* species, there is little or no swelling of the basal veins in either sex. Both sexes have strongly chequered fringes on both surfaces. In both sexes, the underside of the forewing is orange, with brown smudges and two or three eye-spots. The underside of the hindwing is mottled brown in both sexes and the veins are strongly lined with white.

Similar species: Norse Grayling resembles male, but lacks white lines under the hindwing.

Flight: May to August, often feeding at Wild Thyme, Moss Campion, and other low-growing plants, and basking with wings wide open on the ground or on rocks.

Habitat: Rough montane grassland, from about 1,400 m (4,600 ft) upwards and usually above the tree-line. The larval foodplants are Sheep's-fescue and other fine-leaved grasses.

Life-cycle: The white, barrel-shaped eggs are strongly ribbed, and they are laid singly – usually on the lowest parts of the grasses. The caterpillar, which hibernates twice before reaching maturity, is pale brown with darker stripes on the sides and a very dark one along the middle of the back. It is about 35 mm (1.4 in) long when mature, and it pupates in leaf-litter or other debris on the ground.

Range: Confined to the Alps, from southeast France to Bavaria and Austria.

p.185 **Black Satyr** *Satyrus actaea*

Description: 25–30 mm (1.0–1.2 in). The male upperside is sooty brown or black, with a single eye-spot near the tip of the forewing and sometimes a very faint one further back. The female upperside is dark brown, with one or two eye-spots in a dirty yellow post-discal band on the forewing. There may be one or two small white spots just behind the front eye-spot. The post-discal band of the hindwing is often almost obliterated by brown scales. The undersides of both sexes are brown, with one or two white bands in the outer part of the hindwing and a dull orange post-discal band on the female forewing. The forewing underside bears a large apical eye-spot and sometimes a very faint one further back, often associated with smaller white spots.

Similar species: Great Sooty Satyr has two large eye-spots in both sexes. Dryad has two blue-centred eye-spots on the forewing.

Flight: June to August, floating relatively slowly over the vegetation and visiting a wide range of flowers for nectar.

Habitat: Dry, stony grassland up to about 2,000 m (6,550 ft). The larval foodplants are various grasses, especially *Bromus* species.

Life-cycle: The barrel-shaped white eggs have widely spaced ribs and are laid singly on the grasses. In all but the coldest areas the caterpillar feeds throughout the winter. It is straw-coloured with several broad brown stripes running the length of the body. It is

about 30 mm (1.2 in) long when mature,
and it pupates in the soil. The chrysalis is
orange-brown.

Range: Southwest Europe, from Portugal to
northwest Italy.

p.185 **Great Sooty Satyr** *Satyrus ferula*

Description: 25–30 mm (1.0–1.2 in). The male
upperside is sooty brown or black, the only
markings being two conspicuous eye-spots
on the forewing and occasionally two
smaller white spots between them. The
female upperside is mid-brown, with an
orange post-discal patch around the eye-
spots on the forewing. The post-discal band
of the hindwing is often heavily dusted
with brown and there may be one or two
small eye-spots near the rear margin. The
underside of the male is dark brown with
grey or white marbling, including a fairly
prominent band across the middle of the
hindwing; the anterior of the two eye-spots
on the forewing is clearly ringed with
orange. The underside of the female
forewing is largely orange, with two heavy
eye-spots; the underside of the hindwing is
light brown, densely mottled with grey and
with a pale central band like the male. Both
sexes usually have small eye-spots near the
rear of the hindwing, although these are
often obscured by the dark ground colour
in the male.

Similar species: Black Satyr male has only one eye-spot, and
the underside of the female forewing is
largely brown. Dryad has blue-centred eye-
spots.

Flight: June to August, floating over the ground
and vegetation, and feeding from a wide
variety of flowers.

Habitat: Dry, rocky grassland from sea level to about
2,000 m (6,550 ft). The larval foodplants
are fescues and other fine-leaved grasses.

Life-cycle: The eggs are white and barrel-shaped, with
widely separated ribs, and they are laid singly
on the lower parts of the grasses. The
caterpillar is straw-coloured with several
dark-brown stripes along its length and, like

that of the Black Satyr, it is extremely well camouflaged. It is active throughout much of the winter. About 30 mm (1.2 in) long when mature, it pupates in the debris under the foodplants. The chrysalis is orange-brown.

Range: Southern Europe, from the Pyrenees to the Black Sea (including southern Austria) and on through southern Asia to the Himalayas. Also in North Africa.

---

p.186 **Dryad** *Minois dryas*

Description: 25–35 mm (1.0–1.4 in). The male upperside is sooty brown or black, with two blue-centred eye-spots on the forewing and, usually, a smaller eye-spot near the rear of the hindwing. There are no other obvious markings. The female upperside is light brown with blue-centred eye-spots like those of the male except that they are ringed with yellow or orange and usually sit on a dirty yellow post-discal patch. The undersides are paler versions of the uppersides, with the blue-centred eye-spots prominent on the forewing. The hindwing, usually densely speckled with dark brown, may have one or two greyish bands in the female. The outer margin of the hindwing is clearly scalloped in both sexes.

Similar species: The blue-centred eye-spots will distinguish this species from all other satyrids.

Flight: July to September, drifting slowly over the vegetation with a bouncy motion and feeding from a wide range of flowers.

Habitat: Rough grassland, scrub, and open woodland, from sea level to about 1,600 m (5,250 ft). Although the species prefers dry habitats it will occupy damp grassland. The larval foodplants are a wide variety of grasses.

Life-cycle: The eggs are almost spherical and have a pearly appearance. They are laid singly on the foodplant. The caterpillar feeds for a while and then goes into hibernation, in either the first or second instar, before completing its growth in the spring. The mature caterpillar is greyish brown with a broken brown stripe along the middle of the back and other brown stripes on the sides. It is 30–35 mm (1.2–1.4 in) long when mature, and it pupates amongst the grass tussocks. The chrysalis is orange-brown. It is possible that there are two generations in some southern parts of the range.

Range: Southern and central Europe, and across central Asia to Japan. Absent from most of Iberia and the Mediterranean region and from the British Isles.

p.187 **Great Banded Grayling** *Kanetisa circe*

Description: 30–40 mm (1.2–1.6 in). The uppersides are sooty brown or black in both sexes, with a broad white post-discal band on each wing. The band is more or less broken into separate patches on the forewing and the anterior patch contains an eye-spot which is often blind. The undersides are brownish grey with post-discal bands like those on the upperside. There are also two white patches in the forewing cell, and an incomplete white band in the basal half of the hindwing. The apical eye-spot on the forewing usually has a white pupil on the underside.

Similar species: Woodland Grayling and Rock Grayling are similar in flight, but the pale band is less clean-cut and there is just a single white band under the hindwing. White Admiral is also similar in flight, but the underside is very different.

Flight: June to September. Long graceful glides alternate with more active flight, and the butterfly frequently basks on rocks and tree-trunks, and also on sunny road surfaces. At rest with its wings closed, it is not at all easy to spot. The butterfly rarely visits flowers, although it occasionally drinks from Bramble blossom and garden buddleias.

Habitat: Rough grassland, scrub, and open woodland, from sea level to about 1,800 m (5,900 ft). The larval foodplants are bromes and other grasses.

Life-cycle: The eggs are pearly and more or less spherical, and they are laid singly on the grass or scattered in flight. They hatch in about two weeks and the caterpillars go

into hibernation when they are about half-grown. The caterpillar is greyish brown with several dark-brown longitudinal stripes. Growth is completed in the spring, when the caterpillar reaches a length of about 35 mm (1.4 in), and it pupates in a flimsy cocoon in the soil. The chrysalis is bright orange-brown.

Range: Southern and central Europe, and eastwards through Asia to the Himalayas. Absent from the British Isles and neighbouring parts of the Continent.

p.186 **False Grayling** *Arethusana arethusa*

Description: 20–25 mm (0.8–1.0 in). The uppersides of this rather variable butterfly are brown with a broken yellowish or brick-coloured post-discal band on each wing. In the southwest, these bands are broad and very bright, but they are often narrower elsewhere and may be virtually absent from the hindwing. There is usually just one blind eye-spot at the front of the forewing, although some females have a smaller one further back, and there is a very small one at the rear of the hindwing. The underside of the forewing is largely orange, with mottled-brown borders and a prominent, pupillate eye-spot. The underside of the hindwing is mottled-brown, often with a greyish-white or fawn post-discal band. The veins are prominent and often lined with white. Females are usually paler than the males on both surfaces, but otherwise the sexes are alike. The fringes of all wings are clearly chequered on both surfaces.

Similar species: Grayling and Southern Grayling have two pupillate eye-spots on the upperside of the forewing and are generally much greyer under the hindwing.

Flight: July to September, usually keeping low over the vegetation with a fast, bouncy motion. It feeds from a wide range of flowers, and males seem to have a strong liking for human sweat. Although the uppersides are often displayed for a few seconds after landing, the butterfly normally rests with its wings closed.

Habitat: Dry grassland and heaths, from sea level to about 1,500 m (4,925 ft). The larval foodplants are fescues and other fine-leaved grasses.

Life-cycle: The pearly-grey eggs are almost spherical, and they are simply dropped in the herbage. The caterpillar goes into hibernation in the first instar and completes its growth in late spring. The mature caterpillar is about 25 mm (1.0 in) long; it is straw-coloured with dark-brown lines running along the body. It pupates in grass tufts or amongst the debris on the ground. The chrysalis is orange-brown.

Range: Southern and central Europe, but absent from the British Isles and neighbouring parts of the Continent.

Erebia

The *Erebia* species, of which there are about 45 in Europe, occur mainly in the Alps and other montane regions, although there are some in the far north. Some of the montane species are restricted to just a few neighbouring peaks, to which their ancestors retreated at the end of the ice age and where they have since evolved along separate paths. All are some shade of brown on the upperside, with a greater or lesser amount of orange, and nearly all have conspicuous eye-spots, especially in spaces 4 and 5 near the tip of the forewing. Many of the species are very similar because they have evolved relatively recently, and separation of some of them is difficult without examination of the genitalia.

p.188 **Arran Brown** *Erebia ligea*

Description: 20–28 mm (0.8–1.1 in). The ground colour of the upperside is dark chocolate brown to almost black, with a broad brick-red post-discal band on each wing. There are three or four eye-spots on the forewing and three on the hindwing, usually all with white pupils. The sexes are alike, although the female is usually a little paler than the male. The underside of the forewing resembles the upperside, but on the underside of the hindwing the orange is reduced to narrow rings around the eye-spots, which sit on a pale-brown or greyish band. A conspicuous white streak runs back from the front edge of the hindwing, sometimes reaching the rear margin but often ending in the middle of the wing. The fringes are strongly chequered with brown and white on both surfaces.

Similar species: Large Ringlet is smaller, often with blind eye-spots in the male, but, although there may be a greyish post-discal band under the hindwing, there is no clear white streak.

Flight: June to August, feeding at scabious, crane's-bills, and a wide range of composite flowers.

Habitat: Rough grassland, heaths, and light woodland, from sea level to about 1,500 m (4,925 ft) although usually above 500 m (1,650 ft) in the southern parts of its range. The larval foodplants include various grasses and sedges.

Life-cycle: The eggs are pearly grey and almost spherical, with shallow, vertical grooves. They are laid singly on the lower parts of the foodplant and they often do not hatch until the following spring, although the caterpillars are fully formed inside the eggs before winter sets in. The caterpillars may complete their development and produce adults in their first summer, but in northern areas they go into hibernation during the third instar and do not complete their growth until the following spring – nearly two years after the eggs were laid. The mature caterpillar is straw-coloured, with darker lines along the back and sides, and is rather hairy. It is up to 35 mm (1.4 in) long, and it pupates on the ground or in the leaf-litter at the base of the foodplant. The chrysalis is flesh-coloured with dark brown streaks and spots.

Range: Most of Europe from the North Cape to the Alps and northern Greece, and on across Asia to Japan: absent from Iberia and

western France. Although the butterfly takes its name from the Isle of Arran in Scotland, only occasional specimens have been taken in the British Isles and there is no concrete evidence that the butterfly was ever a British resident.

Scandinavian specimens (*E. l. dovrensis*) are smaller than those from further south and the white streak under the hindwing may be reduced to a small spot.

p.188 **Large Ringlet** *Erebia euryale*

Description: 20–23 mm (0.8–0.9 in). The uppersides are dark brown to black in both sexes, with a brick-red or orange post-discal band of variable width on each wing. In some races the bands are reduced to little more than rings around the eye-spots. There are three or four relatively small eye-spots on each wing, often blind but sometimes with white pupils. The underside of the forewing resembles the upperside, although the orange band may extend inwards to cover much of the wing. The underside of the male hindwing is typically brown with orange-ringed eye-spots, although the latter are often indistinct. The underside of the female hindwing has a grey or yellowish post-discal band enclosing a variable number of eye-spots. The fringes of both sexes are strongly chequered on both surfaces.

Similar species: Arran Brown is larger and, where it overlaps with Large Ringlet, it has a bold white streak or spot under the hindwing.

Flight: June to August.

Habitat: Open woodland and grassland, rarely far from trees and usually between 1,000 and 2,000 m (3,275 and 6,550 ft). The larval foodplants include various grasses and small sedges.

Life-cycle: The pearly-grey eggs are more or less barrel-shaped with a few widely spaced ribs, and they are laid singly near the bases of the foodplants or neighbouring plants. They do not hatch until the following spring, although the caterpillars are fully

formed in the autumn. The caterpillars feed
during the summer and then go into
hibernation before completing their growth
in their second spring – nearly two years
after the eggs were laid. The mature
caterpillar is up to 30 mm (1.2 in) long and
is pinkish brown with dark-brown
longitudinal stripes. It pupates at the base
of the turf, and the chrysalis is flesh-
coloured or yellowish brown.

Range: Mountainous regions of southern and central
Europe, from northern Spain to Germany
and on through eastern Europe to the Black
Sea. Also widely distributed in Asia.

---

p.189 **Eriphyle Ringlet** *Erebia eriphyle*

Description: 15–20 mm (0.6–0.8 in). The uppersides are
dark, sooty brown with variable orange
markings. In the western parts of the range
they are marked only by a hint of orange near
the tip of the forewing, but in the eastern
Alps the forewing has a bright-orange post-
discal band, containing several small black
dots, and the hindwing has one or more
orange spots. The underside of the forewing
is largely orange, with a broad brown outer
border, and the underside of the hindwing is
deep brown with three or four orange spots,
one noticeably larger than the rest.

Similar species: Mountain Ringlet has larger black dots on
the upperside and there are usually black
dots under the hindwing. Lesser Mountain
Ringlet also has black dots under the
hindwing.

Flight: July to August.

Habitat: Rough mountain slopes, usually between
1,400 and 2,100 m (4,600 and 6,900 ft)
although sometimes a little lower. The
larval foodplants are various grasses,
including Sweet Vernal Grass.

Life-cycle: The pearly, barrel-shaped eggs have a number
of widely spaced ribs, and they are laid near
the base of the foodplant. The fully developed
caterpillars remain in the eggs until the
spring, feed during the summer, and then go
into hibernation for a second winter before
maturing in late spring. The mature

caterpillar, which is about 20 mm (0.8 in) long and rather hairy, is light brown with darker longitudinal stripes. It pupates in the litter at the base of the foodplant. The chrysalis is flesh-coloured with brown stripes.

Range: Confined to the Alps.

---

p.191 **Yellow-spotted Ringlet** *Erebia manto*

Description: 17–22 mm (0.7–0.9 in). This butterfly is named for the pattern on the underside of the female hindwing, but the species is very variable and many individuals bear no sign of yellow spots. In its typical form, the uppersides are dark brown in both sexes, with orange post-discal markings on all wings. The marks on the forewing form a more or less triangular patch which is widest at the front, but on the hindwing they are reduced to a few small spots. Many of these orange marks contain tiny black dots. The male underside is just like the upperside, but the underside of the female hindwing has a post-discal band of yellow spots and another group of yellow spots at the base. At high levels in the Alps and Pyrenees, both sexes are sooty black and often unmarked on both surfaces, although there may be a few faint orange spots in the post-discal area. In some areas, a proportion of the females have the yellow spots replaced by white spots on a greenish-yellow background.

Similar species: The yellow-spotted female cannot be confused with any other butterfly. The male can usually be distinguished from other superficially similar *Erebia* species by the orange band on the forewing – it is noticeably wider at the front than in the middle – but unmarked specimens from high altitudes are not easily distinguished from similar forms of the Mountain Ringlet or from Sooty Ringlet.

Flight: June to September, feeding from a wide range of flowers.

Habitat: Montane grassland from about 900 to 2,500 m (2,950–8,200 ft), especially in damp areas with lush vegetation. The larval foodplants are various grasses and sedges.

Life-cycle: The eggs are pearly white and almost spherical, with shallow ribs and grooves. The fully formed caterpillars normally remain in the eggs through the winter and hatch out in late spring. They feed through the summer and then go into hibernation in the penultimate (fourth) instar. Growth is completed during the second spring, nearly two years after the eggs were laid, although in some southern localities it is possible that development is completed in one year. The mature caterpillar is straw-coloured, with faint brown lines and sparse, bristly black hairs. It is about 20 mm (0.8 in) long, and it pupates in the litter at the base of the foodplant. The chrysalis is yellowish with dark-brown streaks.

Range: Confined to the mountains of southern and central Europe, from northern Spain to Romania.

---

p.190 **White-speck Ringlet** *Erebia claudina*

Description: 18 mm (0.7 in). The uppersides are chocolate-brown in both sexes, with an orange-red post-discal band containing two tiny eye-spots on the forewing. The submarginal area of the hindwing bears two or three tiny white dots in the male and four in the female, and there may also be a faint orange post-discal band. The underside of the male resembles the upperside except that there are six small white specks on the hindwing: there may also be more orange on the forewing. The underside of the female forewing is largely orange, with two eye-spots and greyish-brown borders. The underside of the female hindwing is yellowish grey with six white submarginal specks.

Similar species: Several other *Erebia* species are superficially similar, but none has the white specks.

Flight: July.

Habitat: Montane grassland above about 1,800 m (5,900 ft). The larval foodplants are various grasses, especially Alpine Hair-grass.

Life-cycle: Little is known of the life history of this

butterfly, but it probably takes two years to complete its development.

Range: Confined to a few places in the Austrian Alps.

---

p.191 **Mountain Ringlet** *Erebia epiphron*

Description: 16–22 mm (0.6–0.9 in). This is an extremely variable butterfly, with several races or subspecies scattered over the mountains of Europe. The upperside is essentially dull brown, and there is usually a rather shiny, brick-red or orange post-discal band on each wing – although this varies a great deal in extent and is often broken into small blotches, especially on the hindwing. It is absent altogether in some high-altitude specimens. The bands contain a number of small black eye-spots, usually blind although in some females they have tiny white pupils. The number of eye-spots varies, but there are commonly four on the forewing and three on the hindwing. The underside of the forewing generally resembles the upperside, although in some races it is largely orange. The underside of the hindwing is plain brown, either completely unmarked or else with three or four small black dots – with or without small orange rings around them.

Similar species: Several other *Erebia* species are superficially very similar but the underside of the hindwing is usually less uniform.

Flight: June to August, fluttering weakly just above the grass and basking with wings wide open in the sunshine. The butterflies hide away in the grass when the sun is not shining.

Habitat: Damp montane grassland and moorland, usually between 500 and 3,000 m (1,650 and 9,850 ft), but lower in Scotland. Mat Grass is the main larval foodplant, and the only one used in Britain, but other grasses are readily eaten in captivity and probably in the wild as well.

Life-cycle: The barrel-shaped, strongly ribbed eggs are yellow with orange blotches, and they are laid singly near the base of the foodplant. The caterpillars are grass-green with light and dark longitudinal stripes. They feed for a few weeks in the autumn, but when they reach the third instar they hide deep in the grass-bases and go into hibernation until the spring. Growth is completed by mid-summer, when the caterpillar is about 20 mm (0.8 in) long, and pupation takes place in a flimsy cocoon at the base of the foodplant. The chrysalis is bright green with brown flecks and spots. The species has a two-year life-cycle in the higher parts of Alps.

Range: The mountains of southern and central Europe, from northern Spain to Bulgaria, and also in Scotland and the English Lake District. The butterfly possibly existed in Ireland until late in the 19th century.

The species was once called the Small Mountain Ringlet and is still referred to by this name in some recent literature, but there is no justification for this name. The Bulgarian race (*E. e. orientalis*), in which the eye-spots are much more conspicuous, is sometimes regarded as a separate species. Descimon's Ringlet (*E. serotina*), known only from a few males collected in the Pyrenees, figures in some books but has now been shown to be a hybrid between the Mountain Ringlet and the Yellow-spotted Ringlet.

p.192 **Yellow-banded Ringlet** *Erebia flavofasciata*

Description: 18 mm (0.7 in). The male uppersides are sooty brown and each wing has a narrow orange post-discal band that is more or less broken into a number of distinct blotches. The blotches contain several small black spots, those of the forewing forming an almost straight line. The female's post-discal blotches are often larger and yellower than those of the male. The undersides are largely brown, although the forewing has a strong reddish tinge. Each wing has a broad yellowish post-discal band containing a number of conspicuous black dots, which is diagnostic for the species.

Similar species: None.

Flight: June to August, keeping close to the ground and basking with wings open in the sunshine. The butterflies gather to drink from Wild Thyme and other low-growing flowers.

Habitat: Montane grassland above about 2,000 m (6,550 ft). The larval foodplants are fescues and other fine-leaved grasses.

Life-cycle: The eggs are barrel-shaped with faint ribs, and they are laid singly on the foodplants. They change from pale yellow to orange as they mature. The caterpillars hibernate twice and complete their growth in the second spring, nearly two years after the eggs were laid. The mature caterpillar is yellowish green, with a pale brown head and faint brown lines along the body. It is about 20 mm (0.8 in) long, and it pupates on the ground. The chrysalis is largely green with dark streaks, especially on the wingcases.

Range: Confined to the Alps on the Swiss/Italian border and officially classed as at risk.

p.192 **Blind Ringlet** *Erebia pharte*

Description: 15–20 mm (0.6–0.8 in). This species owes its name to the complete lack of eye-spots on either surface. The uppersides are chocolate-brown with orange-red post-discal spots on each wing. The spots on the forewing are rectangular and more or less linked up to form a continuous band which narrows towards the front. The spots on the hindwing are more rounded and well separated. Females are a little paler than males and the spots are sometimes yellowish, but otherwise the sexes are alike. The undersides are paler than the uppersides, but the pattern is the same.

Similar species: Mountain Ringlet may look similar but is never entirely devoid of eye-spots.

Flight: July to August, staying close to the ground and feeding from a wide range of low-growing flowers.

Habitat: Damp montane grassland, between 1,400 and 2,400 m (4,600 and 7,875 ft). The larval foodplants are various fescues, Mat Grass, and some of the smaller sedges.

Life-cycle:

The eggs are barrel-shaped and yellow with red splashes. The caterpillar goes into hibernation while still quite small and completes its growth in the spring. When mature it is about 20 mm (0.8 in) long and is bright green with a number of dark-edged white stripes. It pupates on the ground, surrounded by a few grass-blades drawn together with silk. The chrysalis is yellowish green with dark streaks.

Range: Confined to the Alps and the Tatra Mountains.

E. p. phartina from high in the central Alps is small and has only the faintest trace of orange markings.

Rätzer's Ringlet *Erebia christi*

Description: 20 mm (0.8 in). The uppersides are dark brown and the forewing has a red post-discal band of more or less uniform width. The post-discal band on the hindwing is usually broken into several distinct blotches. The bands and blotches contain several small, distinctly elongated, black spots. The underside of the forewing is largely orange, with greyish-brown borders and three or four small black spots near the tip. The underside of the hindwing is light brown, slightly paler in the outer half than at the base, and carries just a few, small, black submarginal dots. The female may have slightly wider and paler post-discal bands on the upperside, but otherwise the sexes are alike.

Similar species: Some races of Mountain Ringlet are similar, but they usually have more obvious eye-spots and the post-discal band on the forewing is constricted near the middle.

Flight: June to August, basking on the rocks with its wings wide open and feeding at a variety of low-growing flowers.

Habitat: Rocky and grassy montane slopes, especially in the vicinity of larchwoods, between about 1,300 and 2,100 m (4,275 and 6,900 ft). The primary larval foodplant is Sheep's-fescue.

Life-cycle: The barrel-shaped and lightly ribbed eggs are yellow with dense pink or red spotting. They are laid singly on the lower parts of the foodplant. The caterpillars take nearly two years to mature, usually going into hibernation in the first instar and again in the final instar. The mature caterpillar is a rather dirty green with white lines along the body, and it is about 20 mm (0.8 in) long. It pupates at ground level in a little chamber of silk strands and grass-blades and the chrysalis is green with brown streaks and spots.

Range: Confined to a small area on the Swiss/Italian border. In order to protect this vulnerable species, all butterfly collecting is banned in the Lagginal area of Switzerland, where it is an offence even to carry a butterfly net.

---

p.193 **Lesser Mountain Ringlet** *Erebia melampus*

Description: 15–20 mm (0.6–0.8 in). The uppersides are dark brown with a red post-discal band on each wing. Although the forewing band is crossed by dark veins, it appears more or less complete and it contains two or three small black spots near the front. The band on the hindwing is broken into three or four rounded spots, each containing a black dot. The undersides resemble the uppersides, although the post-discal markings may be yellower in the female.

Similar species: Eriphyle Ringlet has no black dots in the orange spots under the hindwing. Mountain Ringlet has more distinct eye-spots on the upperside and generally less obvious orange spotting under the hindwing. Sudeten Ringlet has six orange post-discal spots under the hindwing.

Flight: June to September.

Habitat: Montane grassland, between about 800 and 2,000 m (2,625 and 6,550 ft). The larval foodplants are fine-leaved grasses, including Sweet Vernal Grass, Sheep's-fescue, and various meadow-grasses (*Poa* species).

Life-cycle: The eggs are shaped like slender barrels and are cream with red blotches. The caterpillar, which is grass-green and rather hairy, goes into hibernation in the second instar and completes its growth in the spring. Up to 20 mm (0.8 in) when mature, it pupates on the ground. The chrysalis is more or less white with black spots and streaks.

Range: Confined to the Alps, from southern France to Austria.

Sudeten Ringlet *Erebia sudetica*

Description: 17 mm (0.7 in). The ground colour of the uppersides is dull brown in both sexes, although slightly paler in the female than in the male. There is a narrow, orange or red post-discal band on the forewing and a smoothly curved row of four or five similarly coloured spots on the hindwing. The forewing bands enclose four or five small black dots, and each spot on the hindwing also usually contains a black dot. The underside resembles the upperside, although it is a little paler and has six reddish spots on the hindwing: there may be a reddish flush under the forewing.

Similar species: Lesser Mountain Ringlet has two to four post-discal spots under the hindwing.

Flight: June to August, feeding from a wide range of flowers.

Habitat: Montane grassland and woodland clearings, usually between 1,200 and 2,000 m (3,925 and 6,550 ft). The larval foodplants are grasses, especially Sweet Vernal Grass.

Life-cycle: The lightly ribbed eggs are more or less oval and are pearly white with red spotting. They are usually laid singly. The caterpillar is grass-green with short hairs and faint longitudinal lines. It hibernates while still quite small and completes its growth in the spring. It is up to 20 mm (0.8 in) long when mature, and it pupates at the base of the turf. The chrysalis is creamy white with brown spots and streaks.

Range: Confined to the European mountains, from the Massif Central of France to the Carpathians.

p.194 **Scotch Argus** *Erebia aethiops*

Description: 20–26 mm (0.8–1.0 in). The ground colour of the uppersides ranges from chocolate-brown to sooty black, with the females usually a little paler than the males. There is a deep-orange or rust-coloured post-discal band on each wing, although this is often divided into separate spots on the hindwing. There are three or four white-centred eye-spots in the band on each wing. The underside of the forewing is a paler version of the upperside, but the underside of the hindwing has no orange: it is brown with a greyish or pale brown post-discal band containing small white spots. The female may also have a pale basal area.

Similar species: Autumn Ringlet and Water Ringlet have similar uppersides, but no white spots in the post-discal band under the hindwing.

Flight: July to September, usually flying only in sunshine and low over the vegetation, although the female does not fly much at all.

Habitat: Damp grassland, moorland, and open woodland, usually between 300 and 1,500 m (975 and 4,925 ft) but reaching 2,000 m (6,550 ft) in the Alps: sometimes found on coastal dunes. The larval foodplants are various grasses, including Purple Moor-grass and Blue Moor-grass.

Life-cycle: The globular eggs are cream with reddish spots and numerous ribs, and they are laid singly low down on the grasses or in the surrounding leaf-litter. The caterpillars hibernate in the second or third instar, while still very small, and complete their growth in the spring. The mature caterpillar is pale brown with darker stripes. It is tinged with green and clothed with brown-tipped hairs. It is 25–30 mm (1.0–1.2 in) long, and it pupates in a flimsy cocoon in the moss or leaf-litter. The chrysalis is pinkish brown with darker stripes.

Range: Central Europe and a few mountains further south, and eastwards into central Asia. British populations are confined to Scotland and the English Lake District.

p.195 **de Prunner's Ringlet** *Erebia triaria*

Description: 25 mm (1.0 in). The ground colour of the
upperside is chocolate-brown with a bright-
orange post-discal band on each wing. That
on the forewing tapers sharply towards the
rear and may be almost triangular. It contains
five or six white-centred eye-spots of varying
sizes. The three anterior spots lie almost in a
straight line and are often linked together.
The post-discal band on the hindwing is
often broken into four round spots, each
containing an eye-spot. The underside of the
forewing resembles the upperside. The
underside of the hindwing is entirely brown,
with the outer part paler than the rest –
especially in the female – and enclosing a
number of small, white-centred eye-spots.

Similar species: Piedmont Ringlet is very similar above, but
the small eye-spot at the tip of the forewing
is usually absent: only two eye-spots are
ever linked together.

Flight: April to July.

Habitat: Stony montane grassland, from about 400
to 2,100 m (1,300–6,900 ft), but usually
above 1,000 m (3,275 ft). The larval
foodplants are fescues and other grasses.

Life-cycle: The barrel-shaped eggs have numerous ribs
and are white with reddish spots. The
caterpillar goes into hibernation, probably
in the fourth instar, and completes its
development in early spring. The mature
caterpillar is grass-green with pale-edged
dark stripes. It is about 25 mm (1.0 in)
long, and it pupates at the base of the
foodplant. The chrysalis is yellow with
bright-green wingcases streaked with black.

Range: The Alps and other southern mountains.
Spanish race (*E. t. hispanica*) has yellowish
post-discal bands.

p.195 **Lapland Ringlet** *Erebia embla*

Description: 25 mm (1.0 in). The ground colour of the
upperside is chocolate-brown, and generally
has four yellow-ringed eye-spots on each
wing. The front two eye-spots on the
forewing are joined together and may have

small white pupils, but the other eye-spots are usually all blind. The underside of the forewing resembles the upperside. The underside of the hindwing is usually plain brown, although the outer part may be greyish. There are some small black dots, sometimes faintly ringed with orange, in the outer part. There may be a short zig-zag white band near the middle of the wing.

Similar species: Arctic Ringlet is similar below but has no eye-spots on the upperside of the hindwing.

Flight: May to July, keeping close to the ground. Although flight is quite powerful, it spends most of the time resting on the ground or vegetation.

Habitat: Moors and marshes, and in and around light conifer and birch forests, from sea level to about 500 m (1,650 ft). The larval foodplants are various sedges and coarse grasses, including Tufted Hair-grass.

Life-cycle: The thimble-shaped eggs are yellow with brown marbling. The caterpillar is straw-coloured with brown hairs and greenish-brown stripes, and it takes nearly two years to mature. The chrysalis is unknown.

Range: Scattered through Scandinavia – mainly Finland and northern Sweden – and northern Asia.

---

p.196 **Arctic Ringlet** *Erebia disa*

Description: 25 mm (1.0 in). The ground colour of the upperside is dark brown. The forewing has a narrow orange band with four or five blind eye-spots. The two anterior eye-spots do not touch. The hindwing is unmarked. The underside of the forewing resembles the upperside. The underside of the hindwing is greyish brown with a contrasting brown discal band. The fringes are conspicuously chequered grey and brown on both surfaces.

Similar species: Lapland Ringlet is similar underneath, although the base of the hindwing is brown instead of grey: upperside of hindwing has eye-spots.

Flight: June to July, with a rather jerky movement, as soon as the birches come into leaf.

Habitat: Moors and damp grassland, in and around the northern birch forests, usually above 350 m (1,150 ft). The larval foodplants are various grasses.

Life-cycle: The eggs are almost spherical and are straw-coloured with brownish specks. The caterpillar is brownish or greenish yellow, lighter on the back and with a dark stripe along the middle. It hibernates twice and is about 33 mm (1.3 in) long when mature. Pupation takes place on the ground, where the pale-brown chrysalis lies almost naked. The species fails to appear in some years in certain areas – perhaps the result of its two-year life-cycle.

Range: Northern Scandinavia and throughout the Arctic region. In North America it is known as the Spruce Bog Alpine.

p.196   **Woodland Ringlet** *Erebia medusa*

Description: 20–25 mm (0.8–1.0 in). The male upperside is dark brown and the forewing has up to five pupillate eye-spots on an orange post-discal band that is clearly broken in the region of vein 3. The second and third eye-spots are usually linked together. The hindwing has five eye-spots, each ringed with orange. Females are paler than males, with yellower and slightly more extensive markings. The underside is virtually identical to the upperside in both sexes. There are several forms and subspecies, differing in the size and number of the eye-spots. At high levels in the Alps, f. *hippomedusa* is small, with very little orange and often only two eye-spots on the forewing. *E. m. psodea* of eastern Europe has paler post-discal bands and much brighter eye-spots.

Similar species: Bright-eyed Ringlet resembles f. *hippomedusa*, but it has very bright pupils. Arctic Woodland Ringlet has less orange on both surfaces and occurs only in the far north.

Flight: May to July.

Habitat: Moorland, bogs, damp grassland, and open woodland, from sea level (in the north) to about 2,000 m (6,550 ft). The larvae feed on a wide range of grasses, including Red Fescue, Upright Brome, and Wood Millet.

Life-cycle: The eggs are globular with numerous ribs. They are white or pale green and densely speckled with reddish brown. The caterpillars take either one or two years to mature, depending on the altitude. The mature caterpillar is about 25 mm (1.0 in) long and grass-green with a dark stripe along the back. It pupates amongst the leaf-litter. The chrysalis is pale brown with darker streaks.

Range: Central and southeast Europe, from central France eastwards, and on into central Asia.

p.197 Arctic Woodland Ringlet *Erebia polaris*

Description: 18–22 mm (0.7–0.9 in). The upperside is dark brown in both sexes. The forewing has two small, orange-ringed eye-spots near the tip, and there may be one or two smaller ones further back, although these are often absent in the male or represented only by orange spots. The hindwing has up to four small orange-ringed eye-spots. The undersides resemble the uppersides, but the underside of the hindwing usually has a pale-brown or greyish post-discal band enclosing the rather faint eye-spots.

Similar species: None in the far north. Woodland Ringlet lacks the pale band under the hindwing. Bright-eyed Ringlet has much brighter eye-spots, especially under the hindwing.

Flight: June to July.

Habitat: Rough grassland in and around birch forests, from sea level to about 300 m (975 ft); often common in coastal areas. The larval foodplants are Wood Millet and other grasses.

Life-cycle: The mottled yellow and brown eggs are almost spherical, and they are laid singly on the foodplant. The caterpillar ranges from green to straw-coloured, with a dark line along the middle and others along the sides. It takes two years to mature, by which time it is about 25 mm (1.0 in) long.

It pupates in a flimsy cocoon on the ground, and the chrysalis is pale brown with darker streaks on the wing-sheaths.

Range: Arctic Scandinavia (beyond 86°N) and eastwards to Arctic Siberia.

This butterfly is sometimes treated as a subspecies of the Woodland Ringlet.

---

p.197 **Almond-eyed Ringlet** *Erebia alberganus*

Description: 20–25 mm (0.8–1.0 in). The ground colour of the upperside is dark brown, and the orange post-discal bands are usually broken into a number of oval or almond-shaped spots, most of which enclose a small eye-spot. The sizes of the ovals vary a good deal and they are often very small in high-altitude populations. The underside is almost identical to the upperside, although the female ground colour is a little paler. Some females also have yellowish ovals instead of orange.

Similar species: Small-spotted forms can be confused with some forms of Woodland Ringlet, but the latter's orange spots are always round on the hindwing. Bright-eyed Ringlet has brighter eye-spots, with very little orange around them.

Flight: June to August, feeding from a wide range of flowers but especially thistles and other composites.

Habitat: Montane grassland, usually between 1,000 and 2,000 m (3,275 and 6,550 ft). The larval foodplants are various fine-leaved grasses, including fescues and *Poa* species.

Life-cycle: The barrel-shaped eggs are yellow, with reddish-brown spots and numerous ribs, and they are laid singly or in small groups. The young caterpillars are light brown with darker stripes. They go into hibernation in the third instar and become bright green with black bristles as they complete their growth in the spring. Mature larvae are about 25 mm (1.0 in) long, and they pupate in flimsy cocoons on the ground. The chrysalis is pale green with a brown abdomen.

Range: The Alps and a few other mountainous areas from northern Spain to Bulgaria.

---

p.198 **Sooty Ringlet** *Erebia pluto*

Description: 20–25 mm (0.8–1.0 in). This very variable butterfly got its name because many of the males are sooty black on both surfaces, although there is usually a faint red or orange flush under the forewing. Females are sooty brown on both surfaces, with an orange flush on the underside of the forewing. Both sexes may have small eye-spots on the upperside, but the underside of the hindwing is completely unmarked in most races. *E. p. oreas* from the Swiss Alps is dark brown in both sexes, with no trace of eye-spots. The male has a broad orange post-discal band on both surfaces of the forewing and the female has similar bands on her forewings and hindwings.

Similar species: The unmarked underside of the hindwing distinguishes this from most other *Erebia* species. Black Ringlet and Lefèbvre's Ringlet have similar males, but they usually have more obvious eye-spots and they live in different areas.

Flight: June to August.

Habitat: Montane scree from 1,600 to 3,200 m (5,250–10,500 ft), reaching higher levels than most other European butterflies. The larval foodplants are fescues and other fine-leaved grasses.

Life-cycle: The barrel-shaped eggs are white with reddish-brown freckles and numerous ribs. They are laid singly or in small groups, often on stones some distance from the foodplants. Larval development normally takes two years, with hibernation taking place in the first or second instar and again in the final instar. Some larvae may take three years to mature. Mature caterpillars, about 25 mm (1.0 in) long, are bluish green with darker stripes. They pupate on the ground. The chrysalis is largely green, becoming brown towards the rear.

Range: Found only in the Alps and Apennines.

p.198 **Silky Ringlet** *Erebia gorge*

Description: 15–20 mm (0.6–0.8 in). The ground colour of the upperside is chocolate-brown and quite shiny, with a gleaming brick-red band on each wing. The forewing band typically contains two eye-spots near the tip, but some forms have additional eye-spots on both wings and some have no eye-spots at all. The underside of the forewing is brick-red with a narrow brown border, and eye-spots as on the upperside. The underside of the hindwing is mottled brown and grey and often has a wavy-edged, dark band across the middle: eye-spots are present near the outer margin in some forms.

Similar species: Mnestra's Ringlet has smaller eye-spots or none at all and the underside of the hindwing is almost unmarked. False Mnestra Ringlet has narrower orange bands on the upperside and broader brown borders under the hindwing. Gavarnie Ringlet is darker, especially on the underside.

Flight: June to August, gliding elegantly over the ground but rarely visiting flowers.

Habitat: Stony montane slopes between 1,500 and 3,000 m (4,925 and 9,850 ft). The larval foodplants are fescues and other grasses.

Life-cycle: The cream or pearly-coloured eggs are barrel-shaped with strong ribs. The caterpillar takes two years to mature, hibernating in the first instar and again in the penultimate instar. The mature caterpillar is green or brown with dark-brown and white stripes, and it is 20–25 mm (0.8–1.0 in) long. It pupates among the stones, and the chrysalis is green and brown.

Range: Confined to the mountains of southern and eastern Europe, from northern Spain to Greece and the Carpathians. Many butterflies from the southwestern Alps (f. *erynnis*) lack eye-spots, but f. *triopes* from the Swiss Alps has several conspicuous eye-spots on each wing.

p.199 **Mnestra's Ringlet** *Erebia mnestra*

Description: 18 mm (0.7 in). The uppersides are chocolate-brown with a brick-red post-discal band on each wing. The forewing band is rather broad, especially at the front, but the hindwing band is rarely more than an elongated spot in the middle of the wing. The female usually has two small, but conspicuous eye-spots on the forewing and may have two or three tiny eye-spots on the hindwing; the male usually lacks eye-spots, although there may be two very small ones on the forewing. The underside of the forewing is brick-red with a wide brown border in both sexes. The underside of the male hindwing is plain brown, sometimes with a slightly paler post-discal band. The underside of the female hindwing is paler and has a more marked post-discal band.

Similar species: False Mnestra Ringlet has a more complete post-discal band on the upperside of the hindwing and a more obvious pale band on the underside. Silky Ringlet has much more pattern under the hindwing.

Flight: July to August.

Habitat: Montane grassland between about 1,400 and 2,600 m (4,600 and 8,525 ft). The larval foodplants are mainly fescue grasses.

Life-cycle: The barrel-shaped eggs have numerous ribs and are usually flesh-coloured with reddish spots. The caterpillar is bright green with a brown head and is up to 25 mm (1.0 in) long. It takes one or two years to mature. It pupates on the ground, and the chrysalis is orange-brown.

Range: Confined to the Alps, where it is local and generally rare.

p.199 **False Mnestra Ringlet** *Erebia aethiopella*

Description: 20 mm (0.8 in). The ground colour of the uppersides is chocolate-brown in both sexes. There is a bright brick-red post-discal band on each wing, sometimes reaching inwards to the end of the cell in the forewing. Two small eye-spots — generally larger in the female than in the

male – are usually present near the tip of the forewing. The hindwing band usually tapers markedly towards the rear. The underside of the forewing is largely brick-red, with a wide brown border and two apical eye-spots, and sometimes it has a brown smudge at the base. The underside of the hindwing is mainly brown, with a greyish or pale-brown post-discal band.

Similar species: Mnestra's Ringlet has a shorter post-discal band on the upperside of the hindwing. The underside of the hindwing is less clearly banded. Silky Ringlet usually has broader orange bands.

Flight: June to August.

Habitat: Montane grassland, usually above 1,800 m (5,900 ft). The larval foodplants are fine-leaved grasses.

Life-cycle: Little is known of the life-cycle.

Range: Confined to the Alps and the Balkan mountains, and very local in both regions.

Balkan specimens (*E. a. rhodopensis*) have additional eye-spots and are sometimes regarded as a separate species – Nicholl's Ringlet.

---

p.200 Gavarnie Ringlet *Erebia gorgone*

Description: 20 mm (0.8 in). The ground colour of the upperside is sooty brown in the male and a little paler in the female. Both sexes have an orange post-discal band on each wing, although this is sometimes almost obliterated by a dusting of brown scales in the male. There are three or four eye-spots on each wing. The underside of the forewing is a slightly paler version of the upperside in both sexes, although the post-discal band may be somewhat expanded. The underside of the hindwing is dark brown in the male and mottled greyish brown in the female. Both sexes have pale veins and a pale brown or greyish post-discal band: eye-spots, if present, are small and indistinct.

Similar species: Silky Ringlet in the Pyrenees (f. *ramondi*) has larger and more obvious eye-spots on both surfaces of the hindwing.

Flight: July to August.
Habitat: Montane grassland, between about 1,500 and 2,500 m (4,925 and 8,200 ft). The larval foodplants are various grasses, especially meadow-grasses (*Poa* species).
Life-cycle: Nothing is known of the life-cycle of this butterfly.
Range: Confined to the Pyrenees.

---

p.201 **Spring Ringlet** *Erebia epistygne*

Description: 20–25 mm (0.8–1.0 in). The ground colour of the upperside is chocolate-brown and the forewing has a broad, yellowish or buff post-discal band and a small patch of the same colour in the cell. Three apical eye-spots are linked together and are very conspicuous, and there may be other smaller eye-spots further back. The post-discal band of the hindwing is orange or brick-red and carries four or five eye-spots, but it may be broken up into individual red-ringed eye-spots. The underside of the forewing usually resembles the upperside, except that the markings are more orange. The three linked eye-spots are always present. The underside of the hindwing is mottled brown, with a dark discal band and indistinct eye-spots. The veins are quite pale, especially in the female.
Similar species: The upperside coloration is unique. Dalmatian Ringlet from southeast Europe is superficially similar but has no pale patch in the cell and only two eye-spots are linked together near the wingtip.
Flight: March to June – earlier than any other *Erebia* species.
Habitat: Rough grassland and woodland clearings and edges, mainly between 400 and 2,300 m (1,300 and 7,550 ft). The larval foodplants are fescues and other fine-leaved grasses.
Life-cycle: Little is known of the life-cycle of this butterfly.
Range: Confined to southwest Europe, from central Spain to Provence.

Brassy Ringlets

The following six species belong to a fairly
distinct group known as the brassy ringlets,
so named because the males usually have a
metallic-green sheen on the upperside.
They are all similar in appearance, with the
males all largely grey under the hindwings.
Identification of species without data is not
easy without examining the genitalia, but
identification in the field is fairly simple
because no two species fly in exactly the
same place: where their ranges overlap, the
species are restricted to different altitudes.
European brassy ringlets fly at high altitude
in southern and central Europe and, with
the exception of the Ottoman Brassy
Ringlet, they are all confined to Europe.

---

p.201   **Swiss Brassy Ringlet** *Erebia tyndarus*

Description: 18 mm (0.7 in). The male upperside is
chocolate-brown, with a metallic-green
sheen, and the forewing has an almost
triangular, brick-red post-discal band that
narrows towards the rear and is often
broken into several rectangular patches.
There are two small eye-spots, often
touching and sometimes blind, near the
wingtip. The female upperside is paler and
lacks the green sheen, but is otherwise
similar to the male. Both sexes usually have
unmarked hindwings, although there may
be a faint orange band. In both sexes the
underside of the forewing is brick-red with
a broad, greyish-brown border, and it
usually has two apical eye-spots. The
underside of the hindwing is shiny greyish
brown with a darker discal band and dark
smudges near the outer margin.

Similar species: Lorkovic's Brassy Ringlet is less heavily
marked under the hindwing. Other brassy
ringlets have eye-spots on the upperside of
the hindwing.

Flight: July to September, often basking with
wings wide open on the ground.

Habitat: Montane grassland, between about 1,200
and 2,700 m (3,925 and 8,850 ft) but

usually above 1,800 m (5,900 ft). The larval foodplants include Mat Grass and various fescues.

Life-cycle: The pearly-white eggs are barrel-shaped with strong ribs. They are laid singly or in small groups on the foodplant, and the caterpillars go into hibernation in the first or second instar before completing their growth in the spring. The mature caterpillar is olive-green or greyish brown with light and dark stripes; it is 20–25 mm (0.8–1.0 in) long. It pupates in the turf or leaf-litter, and the chrysalis is orange-brown.

Range: Confined to the central Alps from France to Austria.

---

p.202 **Common Brassy Ringlet** *Erebia cassioides*

Description: 15–20 mm (0.6–0.8 in). The male upperside is chocolate-brown, with a metallic-green tinge. The forewing has an orange or brick-red post-discal patch that is rounded or rectangular and rarely extends back beyond the middle of the wing. It encloses two touching eye-spots near the wingtip. The hindwing has three or four eye-spots in a narrow orange or red band. The female upperside is a little paler and the reddish patch on the forewing may extend further back; she lacks the green sheen, but otherwise resembles the male. The underside of the forewing is reddish brown or orange with a greyish border. Both sexes have twin apical eye-spots. The underside of the hindwing is grey, often with a yellowish tinge. There is a slightly darker wavy band through the centre and there may be dark smudges near the outer margin.

Similar species: Swiss Brassy Ringlet has a tapering post-discal band on the forewing and rarely has eye-spots on the hindwing. De Lesse's Brassy Ringlet has a broader post-discal band on the forewing, extending inwards to the cell, and the apical eye-spots do not touch. The apical eye-spots of Lorkovic's Brassy Ringlet do not touch.

Flight: June to September.

Habitat: Montane grassland, usually between 1,600 and 2,400 m (5,250 and 7,875 ft). The main larval foodplants are various fescues, but the larvae probably eat Mat Grass as well.

Life-cycle: The eggs are pearly white and almost globular, with numerous ribs. They are laid singly on the foodplant and the caterpillars go into hibernation in the first or second instar. Growth is completed in the spring, when the caterpillar is either green with faint darker stripes, or greyish brown with light and dark stripes; it is up to 25 mm (1.0 in) long. It pupates in the turf or leaf-litter, and the chrysalis is orange-brown with a strong green tinge at the front.

Range: The Alps and other montane areas of southern and central Europe from northern Spain to the Black Sea. The populations are widely scattered and exhibit many minor variations.

---

p.202 **Spanish Brassy Ringlet** *Erebia hispania*

Description: 17–21 mm (0.7–0.8 in). The uppersides are chocolate-brown in both sexes, although slightly paler in the female. A pale-orange, triangular post-discal band on the forewing encloses twin apical eye-spots in a strongly oblique black patch. The post-discal band on the hindwing is commonly broken into three separate spots. It encloses three tiny eye-spots that are often no more than black dots. The underside of the forewing is orange-brown, with a brown border and a pale-orange post-discal band containing the large twin eye-spots. The underside of the male hindwing is grey and that of the female is yellowish brown. Both sexes have a slightly paler post-discal band.

Similar species: Other brassy ringlets have redder post-discal patches or bands on the forewing and their apical eye-spots are usually smaller.

Flight: June to August.

Habitat: Stony montane grassland from about 1,500 to 2,500 m (4,925–8,200 ft). The larval foodplants are fescues and other fine-leaved grasses.

Life-cycle: Nothing is known of the life-cycle of this butterfly.

Range: Confined to the Pyrenees and the mountains of southern Spain.

---

p.203 **de Lesse's Brassy Ringlet** *Erebia nivalis*

Description: 15–17 mm (0.6–0.7 in). The uppersides are chocolate-brown in both sexes, with bright-green reflections in the male. There is a brick-red, more or less triangular post-discal patch that extends to the apex of the cell in the forewing. It contains two small, well-separated eye-spots. The hindwing is often unmarked, although there may be a faint orange band with or without black dots. The underside of the forewing is brick-red with greyish-brown front and outer borders and two small eye-spots. The underside of the hindwing is silvery grey with a bluish sheen in the male, but much browner in the female. Both sexes have pale veins, a darker discal area, and dark smudges around the outer margin.

Similar species: The orange patch on the forewing of other brassy ringlets does not normally reach the cell.

Flight: June to August.

Habitat: Stony montane grassland, usually above 2,000 m (6,550 ft) and a good 300 m (975 ft) higher than the Common Brassy Ringlet in areas where the two species overlap. The larval foodplants include Mat Grass and fescues.

Life-cycle: The eggs are pale green or pearly white and almost round, with numerous ribs, and they are laid singly or in small groups. The caterpillars take two years to mature, usually hibernating in the first instar and again in the final instar. The mature caterpillar is greyish brown with light and dark stripes; it is about 20 mm (0.8 in) long. It pupates amongst the stones or turf, and the chrysalis is brown with green wingcases.

Range: Confined to the Alps.

p.203 **Lorkovic's Brassy Ringlet** *Erebia calcaria*

Description: 18–20 mm (0.7–0.8 in). The ground colour of the uppersides is chocolate-brown in both sexes, although slightly paler in the female. The male shows the usual green reflections when viewed from certain angles. The post-discal bands are orange but often poorly developed, especially on the hindwing. There are two small, well-separated apical eye-spots on the forewing and there may be two or three on the hindwing. The underside of the forewing is dark orange with grey or brown borders and two small eye-spots. The underside of the hindwing is silvery grey in both sexes, but with a yellow tinge in the female. The post-discal area is noticeably paler than the rest of the wing.

Similar species: Other brassy ringlets have larger eye-spots and/or larger orange patches on the upperside, but none overlaps with this species.

Flight: July to August.

Habitat: Montane grassland, above about 1,500 m (4,925 ft). The larval foodplants are fescues and other grasses.

Life-cycle: Nothing is known of the life-cycle of this butterfly.

Range: Confined to the southeastern Alps, in Italy and Slovenia.

---

p.204 **Ottoman Brassy Ringlet** *Erebia ottomana*

Description: 17–22 mm (0.7–0.9 in). The uppersides are chocolate-brown in both sexes – slightly paler in the female – with bright-orange post-discal bands of variable extent. Those on the hindwing are often broken into separate orange spots. The forewing has two conspicuous, touching eye-spots and the hindwing has three or four eye-spots. The male has a relatively weak green tinge. The underside of the male forewing is deep orange with a brown border; in the female it is paler and sometimes almost yellow. The two eye-spots are always prominent. The underside of the male hindwing is silvery grey with a slightly darker discal band; the female hindwing is much yellower. Small eye-spots may be present, although they are absent in most Balkan populations.

Similar species: Common Brassy Ringlet is very similar and difficult to distinguish in eastern areas, but it generally flies somewhat higher than Ottoman Brassy Ringlet in areas where their ranges overlap.

Flight: July to August.

Habitat: Montane grassland, generally between 1,500 and 2,000 m (4,925 and 6,550 ft) but occasionally much lower. The larval foodplants are fescues and other fine-leaved grasses.

Life-cycle: The eggs are green. The caterpillar probably goes into hibernation while still quite small. When mature, it is about 20 mm (0.8 in) long. It is greyish with a pink stripe on each side just above the legs and white stripes higher up.

Range: Southern France, northern Italy, and the Balkans, and eastwards into western Asia.

Several races or subspecies are recognized. The French race (*E. o. tardenota*), which is confined to the Massif Central, has a very small post-discal patch on the forewing – little more than a circular patch around the eye-spots. *E. o. balcanica*, the most widely distributed of the Balkan races, has no eye-spots under the hindwing.

p.204 **Water Ringlet** *Erebia pronoe*

Description: 20–25 mm (0.8–1.0 in). The male uppersides of this rather variable species range from sooty brown to black. A brick-red or orange post-discal band of variable width usually runs across the forewing, but is sometimes greatly reduced. There are two eye-spots, often touching, near the tip of the forewing and there may be one or two smaller ones further back. The hindwing has two or three small eye-spots and the post-discal band is often broken into discrete spots. The underside of the forewing is largely brown with greyish margins and an orange post-discal band and eye-spots like those on the upperside. The underside of the hindwing is mottled brown and grey with a darker discal band and outer border, but silvery scales give it a distinct violet tinge. The female is paler than the male on both surfaces, but otherwise similar.

Similar species: The violet tinge under the hindwing will usually distinguish this from other *Erebia* species with similar uppersides.

Flight: July to October.

Habitat: Grassy and lightly wooded mountainsides, thriving in both damp and dry habitats, from about 1,000 to 3,000 m (3,275–9,850 ft). The larval foodplants are fescues and meadow grasses (*Poa* species).

Life-cycle: The barrel-shaped eggs are pearly white with brown spots. The caterpillars go into hibernation in the first instar, and almost all growth takes place in the spring. The mature caterpillar is pinkish brown with greyer sides and a dark stripe along the middle of the back. It is up to 25 mm (1.0 in) long, and it pupates amongst the stones and turf. The chrysalis is light brown or flesh-coloured.

Range: The mountains of southern and central Europe, from the Pyrenees to the Black Sea and southern Poland.

In specimens from the western Alps (*E. p. vergy*), the orange markings are much reduced in both sexes and the male is sooty black with little or no trace of eye-spots.

---

p.205 **Black Ringlet** *Erebia melas*

Description: 20–25 mm (0.8–1.0 in). The male is sooty brown or black on both surfaces, with little or no trace of orange around the eye-spots, of which there are two or three on each wing. The two apical eye-spots are often twinned in a single black spot. The female is sooty brown above and may have an orange patch around the eye-spots on the forewing. The underside of the female forewing resembles the upperside, although the post-discal area may be lighter; the underside of her hindwing is mottled brown and grey. Small eye-spots can be seen on both surfaces of the hindwing in both sexes.

Similar species: None in southeast Europe. Some races of Sooty Ringlet and Lefèbvre's Ringlet are similar, but their ranges do not overlap.

Flight: July to September.

Habitat: Montane slopes, usually on limestone, up to about 2,500 m (8,200 ft). The larval foodplants are grasses, but the exact species are not known.

Life-cycle: Little is known of the life history of this butterfly.

Range: Southeast Europe, from the Dinaric Alps to the Carpathians and northern Greece.

---

p.205 **Lefèbvre's Ringlet** *Erebia lefebvrei*

Description: 20–25 mm (0.8–1.0 in). The male is sooty brown or black on both surfaces, with or without a faint brick-red post-discal band on the forewing. Eye-spots, somewhat closer to the wing-margin than in other ringlets, are usually prominent on both surfaces although they are very small or absent on the hindwing of *E. l. astur*. The female upperside is chocolate-brown, with larger eye-spots than the male and orange bands on both wings. The female underside resembles the upperside except that the eye-spots of the hindwing are enclosed in a greyish-brown band.

Similar species: The marginal position of the eye-spots should distinguish this from most similar ringlets. Black Ringlet and some races of Sooty Ringlet resemble *E. l. astur*, but do not inhabit the same area.

Flight: June to August.

Habitat: Montane slopes, usually above about 1,800 m (5,900 ft). The larval foodplants are fescues and other fine-leaved grasses.

Life-cycle: The caterpillar hibernates, but little else is known of the life-cycle of this butterfly.

Range: Confined to the Pyrenees and the Cantabrian Mountains of northern Spain.

p.206   **Larche Ringlet** *Erebia scipio*

Description: 25 mm (1.0 in). The male upperside is
chocolate-brown with an orange post-discal
band on each wing, although this is often
rather narrow and clearly broken by the
veins in the hindwing. There are two apical
eye-spots on the forewing, sometimes with
one or two smaller ones further back, but
the hindwing rarely has eye-spots at all.
The female is a little paler, with chequered
grey fringes and sometimes with eye-spots
on the hindwing. In both sexes the
underside of the forewing is orange with
prominent apical eye-spots. The borders are
brown in the male and greyish in the
female. The underside of the hindwing is
dark brown in the male, pale greyish brown
in the female, and unmarked apart from a
slightly paler post-discal band.

Similar species: The orange underside of the forewing and
the plain underside of the hindwing
distinguish this from all superficially
similar species.

Flight: June to August.

Habitat: Stony mountainsides, usually in lime-rich
areas, from about 1,500 to 2,500 m
(4,925–8,200 ft). The larvae feed on the
grass *Helictotrichon sedenense*.

Life-cycle: The caterpillar is pale grey at first,
becoming browner with age. It is rather
bristly, and even the head is clothed with
hair. It is about 25 mm (1.0 in) long when
mature. The chrysalis is largely beige, with
a pale-green thorax and wingcases and a
faint greyish-green line along the centre of
the abdomen.

Range: The mountains of Provence and
neighbouring parts of Italy. This is a very
local species and apparently becoming rarer.

---

p.207   **Styrian Ringlet** *Erebia stirius*

Description: 25 mm (1.0 in). The ground colour of the
upperside is chocolate-brown, often with a
dusting of sooty-black scales in the male.
There is a rather dull, brick-red post-discal
band on each wing and that on the male

forewing tapers and fades away well before the rear margin. There are usually just two, touching apical eye-spots on the forewing. The hindwing, on which the red band is often broken into separate spots, normally has three conspicuous eye-spots. The underside of the forewing is largely orange, although the basal half is darker than the rest and often quite brown; there are two eye-spots, as on the upperside, and the brown border tapers away towards the rear corner of the wing. The underside of the hindwing is dark brown in the male, with three eye-spots in a slightly paler post-discal area. The underside of the female hindwing is grey, becoming paler in the outer half, and has three or more eye-spots in the post-discal area.

Similar species: Stygian Ringlet is very similar but the brown outer border under the forewing does not taper away and female hindwing is much browner underneath.

Flight: July to September.

Habitat: Stony mountainsides from about 700 to 1,800 m (2,300–5,900 ft). The larval foodplants are grasses, especially Blue Moor-grass and meadow-grasses (*Poa* species).

Life-cycle: Little is known of the life history of this butterfly, but the early stages are unlikely to be much different from those of the Stygian Ringlet.

Range: Confined to the southeastern Alps.

At the highest altitudes the red markings are much reduced and all surfaces are sooty brown.

p.208 **Stygian Ringlet** *Erebia styx*

Description: 25 mm (1.0 in). The ground colour of the upperside is chocolate-brown in both sexes. There is a brick-red post-discal band on each wing, but it varies in extent, and in the male it is often heavily dusted with brown. The eye-spots vary in number and the large apical eye-spots on the forewing are often twinned. There are three or four eye-spots on the hindwing. The underside of the male forewing is orange, heavily dusted with brown in the basal half and with a brown border. The latter has a prominent 'tooth' projecting into the orange band near the rear edge of the wing. The underside of the female forewing is largely orange and the tooth on the border is less obvious. The underside of the male hindwing is dark brown, sometimes with a paler outer region. The underside of the female hindwing is mottled greyish brown, usually darker in the basal half. Both sexes may have indistinct eye-spots, although these are usually missing in the northern parts of the range.

Similar species: In Styrian Ringlet the brown border under the forewing tapers away towards the rear margin. Marbled Ringlet has more contrast under the hindwing, usually with white-edged veins, and no tooth on the border under the forewing. Water Ringlet has a clear grey post-discal band under the hindwing.

Flight: July to August.

Habitat: Rocky slopes, usually in the mountains between about 800 and 2,000 m (2,625 and 6,550 ft). The larval foodplants are various grasses, especially Blue Moor-grass.

Life-cycle: The barrel-shaped eggs are greyish brown with brown spots and prominent ribs. The caterpillar is greyish brown with light and dark stripes, and it takes two years to mature – at least in the higher and more northerly parts of the range: hibernation takes place in the first instar and again in the penultimate instar. The mature caterpillar is 20–25 mm (0.8–1.0 in) long, and it pupates amongst the stones and turf. The chrysalis is green and brown.

Range: Confined to the central and eastern Alps.

---

p.208   **Marbled Ringlet** *Erebia montana*

Description: 22–25 mm (0.9–1.0 in). The ground colour of the upperside is chocolate-brown in both sexes, with a brick-red post-discal band crossing almost the full width of each wing. The bands, noticeably wider in the female forewing than in the male, contain a number of relatively small eye-spots, with the two apical eye-spots often twinned. The fringes are clearly chequered in the female. The underside of the forewing is brick-red with a brown suffusion in the basal half and a brown border tapering slightly towards the rear. The eye-spots resemble those of the upperside. The underside of the hindwing is mottled grey and brown in both sexes, with white edged veins and a wavy white discal stripe.

Similar species: Stygian Ringlet is less brightly marked under the hindwing and the border under the forewing has an inward-pointing 'tooth' near the rear. Female fringes are not strongly chequered.

Flight: July to September.

Habitat: Stony grassland in the mountains, from about 1,000 to 2,500 m (3,275–8,200 ft). The larval foodplants are grasses, including Mat Grass and various fescues.

Life-cycle: The eggs are greyish brown and barrel-shaped with strong ribs. The caterpillars hibernate in the first instar, when still very small, and complete their growth in early summer. The mature caterpillar is pale brown with darker stripes and is up to 25 mm (1.0 in) long. It pupates on the ground, and the chrysalis is largely green with dark stripes on the wingcases.

Range: Confined to the Alps and the Apennines.

Zapater's Ringlet *Erebia zapateri*

Description: 20 mm (0.8 in). The uppersides are dark brown in both sexes, with a very bright, pale orange or yellowish post-discal band on the forewing. The band tapers strongly towards the rear and contains two apical eye-spots, which are sometimes joined. The female may have other smaller spots further back. The male hindwing has no more than a smudge of orange and is generally unmarked, but the female hindwing has a more obvious band which often contains eye-spots. The underside of the forewing resembles the upperside, but in the female it has slight orange flush in the basal region. The underside of the hindwing is dark brown in the male and light brown in the female, both sexes having a greyish post-discal band.

Similar species: Autumn Ringlet has similar pattern, but is much duller.

Flight: July to August.

Habitat: Open pinewoods and scrub, between 1,000 and 2,000 m (3,275 and 6,550 ft). The larval foodplants are fescues and other fine-leaved grasses.

Life-cycle: Winter is passed in the larval stage, but little else seems to be known of the early stages of this butterfly.

Range: Confined to a small area of eastern Spain.

---

p.209 **Autumn Ringlet** *Erebia neoridas*

Description: 18–25 mm (0.7–1.0 in). The male upperside is sooty brown, with a brick-red post-discal band usually enclosing three eye-spots on each wing. The band on the forewing tapers very strongly towards the rear and is clearly pear-shaped or triangular. The band on the hindwing is often broken into separate spots, but these are always clearly truncated on the outer edge. The female is similarly marked, but somewhat paler. The underside of the forewing resembles the upperside. The underside of the hindwing is brown with a well-marked greyish post-discal band and no obvious eye-spots.

Similar species: The truncated spots on the upperside of the hindwing distinguish this from most other *Erebia* species. Zapater's Ringlet is much brighter.

Flight: August to September.

Habitat: Rough grassland and open woodland, usually in the hills between 300 and 1,500 m (975 and 4,925 ft). The larval foodplants include Hairy Finger-grass and various meadow-grasses (*Poa* species).

Life-cycle: Little seems to be known of the early stages of this butterfly.

Range: Southwest Europe, from the eastern Pyrenees through southern France to central Italy.

p.209 **Bright-eyed Ringlet** *Erebia oeme*

Description: 20–22 mm (0.8–0.9 in). The uppersides are sooty brown in both sexes, with very variable amounts of red or orange in the post-discal area: some specimens show almost no colour, while others have almost complete bands. The eye-spots vary in number and are quite small, but the white pupils are very bright, especially in the female and particularly those of the two apical eye-spots. The undersides are very similar to the uppersides, although the eye-spots are usually larger and more conspicuous and those of the female hindwing sit on a yellowish band or are individually ringed with yellow.

Similar species: The less brightly marked forms of this species are easily confused with some forms of Woodland Ringlet, but the latter has brown-tipped antennae rather than black-tipped as in the Bright-eyed Ringlet. Piedmont Ringlet has no red under the hindwing.

Flight: June to August.

Habitat: Upland grassland and light woodland, usually in damp situations, from about 900 to 2,300 m (2,950–7,550 ft). The larval foodplants include a wide range of grasses, small sedges, and woodrushes (*Luzula* species).

Life-cycle: The eggs are dirty yellow and almost globular and, unlike those of other *Erebia* species, they have no ribbing. The caterpillars are straw-coloured with darker stripes and, at least in the northern parts of the range, they take two years to mature. The second hibernation occurs when the caterpillars are fully grown, at about 25 mm (1.0 in) long, and pupation takes place on the ground as soon as the snows melt in the spring. The chrysalis is cream with dark-brown streaks.

Range: Southern and central Europe, from the Pyrenees and central France to Austria, northern Italy, and the Balkans.

p.210 **Piedmont Ringlet** *Erebia meolans*

Description: 20 mm (0.8 mm). The ground colour of the uppersides ranges from dark or sooty brown in the male to light brown in the female. There is usually a well-defined brick-red post-discal band on the forewing, enclosing two conspicuous apical eye-spots and often some smaller ones as well. The band on the hindwing is often narrower and contains three or four eye-spots. It is often broken into separate pear-shaped spots. The underside of the forewing resembles the upperside, with a well-defined brick-red post-discal band and prominent apical eye-spots. The underside of the male hindwing is plain brown with a slightly paler outer region containing small eye-spots. The underside of the female hindwing is paler, with a more obvious arc of eye-spots. The outer region is noticeably paler than the basal area and usually separated from it by an irregular white stripe.

Similar species: The conspicuous red post-discal band on the otherwise plain brown underside of the forewing distinguishes this from most superficially similar species. De Prunner's Ringlet has three touching apical eye-spots, virtually in a straight line, on both surfaces of the forewing.

Flight: May to August, spending a good deal of time basking on the ground with wings wide open.

Habitat: Mountain slopes, between about 600 and 2,300 m (1,975 and 7,550 ft) but usually between 1,000 and 1,500 m (3,275 and 4,925 ft). The larval foodplants include Mat Grass, fescues, and other fine-leaved grasses.

Life-cycle: The eggs are greyish brown and barrel-shaped with prominent ribs. The young caterpillar is generally green with light and dark stripes, and it goes into hibernation while still quite small. Growth is completed in the spring. The mature caterpillar is greyish brown and is about 20 mm (0.8 in) long. It pupates amongst the stones, and the chrysalis is pale orange with a strong green tinge to the wingcases.

Range: Southern and central Europe, from central
Spain to Italy and southern Germany.

Chapman's Ringlet *Erebia palarica*

Description: 25–30 mm (1.0–1.2 in). The male
upperside is dark or sooty brown with a
conspicuous orange or brick-red post-discal
band containing large eye-spots on each
wing. The female upperside is slightly paler
but otherwise similar. The underside of the
forewing resembles the upperside in both
sexes. The underside of the male hindwing
is dark greyish brown with a slightly darker
discal area. The underside of the female
hindwing is paler, but otherwise similar.
Both sexes have indistinct eye-spots in the
outer region and there may be a thin white
line on the outer edge of the discal band.

Similar species: The large size should distinguish this from
all other *Erebia* species.

Flight: June to July.

Habitat: Rough grassland and scrub, from about
1,000 to 1,800 m (3,275–5,900 ft). The
larval foodplants are fescue grasses.

Life-cycle: Nothing is known of the early stages of this
butterfly.

Range: Confined to the Cantabrian Mountains of
northern Spain.

---

p.210 **Dewy Ringlet** *Erebia pandrose*

Description: 20–25 mm (0.8–1.0 in). The uppersides are
smoky brown in both sexes. The upperside
of the forewing has a broad brick-red post-
discal band which is often shiny and often
extends well into the centre of the wing. It
encloses up to four small, blind eye-spots
and is crossed by or bounded internally by a
conspicuous dark line. The upperside of the
hindwing has up to four blind, orange-
ringed eye-spots, but is sometimes
unmarked. The underside of the forewing is
orange, with greyish-brown borders and up
to four blind eye-spots as on the upperside.
The underside of the hindwing is silvery
grey in the male and yellowish grey in the

female. Two dark wavy lines enclose the discal area, which may be a little darker than the rest of the wing, especially in the female. Specimens from the far north may be browner under the hindwings.

Similar species: The greyish underside of the hindwing, together with the four blind eye-spots on both sides of the forewing, distinguish this from almost all other *Erebia* species. False Dewy Ringlet lacks the dark lines across the forewing and the eye-spots are much closer to the outer margin.

Flight: June to August, with a jerky or bouncy motion, often flying almost as soon as the snow as melted.

Habitat: Mountain slopes and tundra, especially on damp ground, from sea level in the north to 3,000 m or more (9,850 ft) in the Alps. The larval foodplants are Blue Moor-grass, fescues, and other fine-leaved grasses.

Life-cycle: The eggs are flesh-coloured and more or less round. The caterpillar is usually grass-green, with or without a dark stripe along the back, but there is also a brown form. The life-cycle may be completed in a single year in some areas, with hibernation in the last larval instar, but in the far north and in most Alpine areas the butterfly takes two years to mature. The mature caterpillar is about 25 mm (1.0 in) long, and it pupates on the ground in early spring, often before the snows have melted. The chrysalis is yellowish brown with green wingcases heavily streaked with black.

Range: Scandinavia, right up to the North Cape, and the high mountains of southern and central Europe. Also in the mountains of western and central Asia.

p.211 **False Dewy Ringlet** *Erebia sthennyo*

Description: 20–22 mm (0.8–0.9 in). The uppersides are smoky brown in both sexes. The forewing carries a brick-red post-discal band, enclosing four or five blind eye-spots close to its outer edge. The hindwing has three or four orange-ringed eye-spots. The underside of the forewing

is orange or brick-red with greyish-brown borders: there are two blind eye-spots in the male and four in the female. The underside of the hindwing is pale grey in the male and light brown in the female, with very little marking apart from a slightly darker discal area bounded by wavy lines.

Similar species: Dewy Ringlet has a dark line through or bordering the red patch on the forewing, and the eye-spots are much further from the outer margin.

Flight: June to July.

Habitat: Montane pastures above about 1,800 m (5,900 ft). The larval foodplants are fescues and other fine-leaved grasses.

Life-cycle: Nothing is known of the early stages of this butterfly.

Range: A local and rare butterfly, confined to the Pyrenees and rarely, if ever, overlapping with Dewy Ringlet.

Dalmatian Ringlet *Proterebia afra*

Description: 22–25 mm (0.9–1.0 in). The uppersides are chocolate-brown in both sexes, with a yellowish-grey tip and outer border to the forewing. The post-discal band is orange in the male and yellowish in the female, with eye-spots in every forewing space, including twin spots near the tip. The hindwing has a full arc of eye-spots, ringed with orange or yellow. The underside of the forewing is chestnut-brown with a grey apical area and eye-spots as on the upperside. The underside of the hindwing is sooty brown or black with pale veins and a full set of eye-spots, but these have very little yellow around them and they are not always very obvious.

Similar species: None.

Flight: May to June.

Habitat: Rough grassland, mainly on the coast and rarely much above sea level, but occasionally reaching 1,000 m (3,275 ft). The main larval foodplant is Sheep's Fescue Grass.

Life-cycle: The eggs are often dropped into the grass while the female is in flight. Caterpillars are brown, sometimes tinged with green.

Range: Eastern coastal areas of the Adriatic and northern Greece, where the species seems in real danger of extinction: also in Turkey and southern Russia.

p.212 **Meadow Brown** *Maniola jurtina*

Description: 20–27 mm (0.8–1.1 in). The male upperside is smoky brown, with a fairly obvious black sex-brand in the rear half of the forewing and a single, orange-ringed apical eye-spot. There is usually no more than a faint orange smudge around and below the eye-spot, but the species is very variable and in some specimens there is a well-developed orange post-discal band. The hindwing is unmarked, although the post-discal region may be a little paler than the rest of the wing. The female upperside is slightly paler than that of the male, with a broad orange post-discal band and usually an extensive orange flush in the centre of the forewing as well. The apical eye-spot is often much larger than that of the male and occasionally contains two pupils, and the upperside of the hindwing has a pale brown or orange post-discal band. In both sexes, the underside of the forewing has an orange basal half, a slightly paler post-discal band, brown borders, and a very conspicuous eye-spot. The underside of the hindwing is light brown, often speckled with darker scales, and has a paler post-discal band which is often greyish or yellowish. The outer edge of the hindwing is noticeably scalloped, especially in the female.

Similar species: Sardinian Meadow Brown is generally smaller, with much more orange on the uppersides. Dusky Meadow Brown has blind eye-spots on the upperside and the female always has two. Oriental Meadow Brown is much plainer under the hindwing and the female has two eye-spots on the forewing. Gatekeeper is brighter on both surfaces and the apical eye-spot always has two pupils.

Flight: May to October in a single brood, feeding at a wide range of flowers and often basking with wings wide open in weak sunshine. The butterflies aestivate during the summer in southern Europe.

Habitat: Grassy places of all kinds, including open woodland, from sea level to about 2,000 m (6,550 ft). The larval foodplants are a wide range of grasses, but the caterpillars avoid coarse and hairy species and also those with very fine leaves.

Life-cycle: The barrel-shaped eggs have numerous ribs and are flesh-coloured with darker blotches. They are laid singly on the grass or surrounding plants, or merely dropped amongst the grass-blades when the female lands. The caterpillar is grass-green, with a darker stripe along the back and a pale stripe on each side. It is clothed with relatively long white hairs. Caterpillars become quiescent in the autumn, but may feed on warm winter days. Growth is completed in the spring and the mature caterpillar is about 25 mm (1.0 in) long. It pupates suspended low down in the vegetation, and the chrysalis ranges from green to chestnut, with a variable amount of dark brown or black streaking.

Range: Throughout Europe apart from the far north, and eastwards to Iran. Also in North Africa. Several subspecies are recognized at present, and some may eventually be proved to be separate species.

The Meadow Brown has always been one of the commonest European butterflies, but agricultural set-aside has increased the available habitat in recent years and populations have increased dramatically in some areas.

p.212 **Sardinian Meadow Brown** *Maniola nurag*

Description: 20–22 mm (0.8–0.9 in). The ground colour of the uppersides is dull brown, but the forewing has an extensive pale-orange or yellowish patch that may cover much of the wing. The male has a conspicuous black sex-brand near the rear of the wing, while the female has two short brown bars

running back from the front margin. There is just a single apical eye-spot, larger in the female than in the male. The outer part of the hindwing has a broad orange patch, more extensive in females than in males. The underside of the forewing is orange with brown borders and an apical eye-spot. The underside of the hindwing is yellowish brown, almost unmarked in the male but with a paler post-discal band in the female.

Similar species: Meadow Brown is generally larger, with much less orange on the upperside. Dusky and Oriental meadow browns have little or no orange on the hindwing and females have two eye-spots on the forewing. Gatekeeper has a much deeper orange on the upperside, and the eye-spot has two pupils.

Flight: May to July, usually keeping low over the ground.

Habitat: Rough grassland and scrub, from sea level to about 1,500 m (4,925 ft). The larval foodplants are grasses.

Life-cycle: Nothing is known of the early stages of this butterfly.

Range: Confined to Sardinia, where it is rare.

---

p.212 **Dusky Meadow Brown** *Hyponephele lycaon*

Description: 20–25 mm (0.8–1.0 in). The male upperside is dusky brown. The forewing has a variable orange flush, which is heavily dusted with brown, and one or two small, blind eye-spots. There is also a dark, curving sex-brand near the rear of the wing. The hindwing is unmarked. The upperside of the female forewing is largely orange, sometimes heavily dusted with brown at the base, and it has broad brown borders and two large, blind eye-spots. The upperside of the hindwing is dusky brown with a pale-brown or orange post-discal band. In both sexes the underside of the forewing is orange with greyish brown borders: it has one pupillate eye-spot in the male and two in the female. The underside of the hindwing is brown with a dusting of grey scales and is noticeably darker at the base than in the outer region. Both sexes have scalloped hindwings.

Similar species: Oriental Meadow Brown has more strongly scalloped hindwings and has less orange on the female upperside. Meadow Brown has only one eye-spot, always pupillate, on the upperside.

Flight: June to October.

Habitat: Rough, dry grassland, from sea level to about 2,000 m (6,550 ft). The larval foodplants include fescues and other fine-leaved grasses.

Life-cycle: The pale-brown or pink eggs are barrel-shaped with prominent ribs, and they are usually laid singly on the foodplants. The caterpillar goes into hibernation in the first instar and almost all of its growth occurs in the spring. The mature caterpillar is grass-green with pale stripes and it is about 25 mm (1.0 in) long. It pupates suspended from the grasses, and the chrysalis is bright green.

Range: Southwest Europe and the Alps, and then northwards to the Baltic and eastwards to the Balkans and on to Central Asia.

---

p.213 **Oriental Meadow Brown**
Hyponephele lupina

Description: 20–25 mm (0.8–1.0 in). The male upperside is sooty brown, sometimes with a slight orange flush on the forewing. There is also a broad, dark sex-brand and a small blind, eye-spot. The hindwing is virtually unmarked, although it may have a pale dusting in the outer region and, sometimes, a golden tinge at the base. The female upperside has a similar colour, but both wings have a pale post-discal band and the forewing has two large, blind eye-spots each surrounded by a broad yellowish ring. In both sexes the underside of the forewing is orange with brown borders. It has a single pupillate eye-spot in the male and two in the female. The underside of the hindwing is plain brown with a dusting of grey scales. The hindwings are strongly scalloped in both sexes.

Similar species: Dusky Meadow Brown has less strongly scalloped hindwings and more orange on the female upperside. Meadow Brown has only one eye-spot, always pupillate, on the forewing, and it is usually patterned under the hindwing.

Flight: May to August.

Habitat: Dry, rocky grassland from sea level to about 1,200 m (3,925 ft). The larval foodplants are various grasses.

Life-cycle: The eggs are pale yellow. The caterpillar is bright green with yellow stripes on the sides and two conspicuous brown horns on the head. The caterpillars hibernate and pupate in the spring. The chrysalis is green.

Range: Southern Europe, from Portugal to Greece, and eastwards into central Asia. Also in North Africa.

p.213 **Ringlet** *Aphantopus hyperantus*

Description: 20–25 mm (0.8–1.0 in). The male upperside is velvety black when fresh, fading to sooty brown as it ages. It usually has two eye-spots on each wing but these are often so indistinct that the wing appears unmarked. The female upperside is always sooty brown and always has two or three eye-spots, although these are not always easy to see. In both sexes the underside is brown, often with a yellowish sheen, and has a variable number of yellow-ringed eye-spots on the outer half of each wing.

Similar species: False Ringlet, which rarely rests with its wings open, has a much paler underside, with a silvery submarginal line on the hindwing.

Flight: June to August, feeding regularly at Bramble blossom and many other flowers. Adults may bask with their wings wide open in cool weather, but are most often seen with their wings closed. They often fly in overcast weather, when most butterflies hide away, and are sometimes on the wing in light drizzle.

Habitat: Damp grassy places, including hedgerows and woodland rides and clearings, from sea level to about 1,500 m (4,925 ft). The larvae feed on numerous grasses, including the very tough Tufted Hair-grass, and sedges.

Life-cycle: The eggs are like miniature, thimble-shaped pearls and are scattered freely in flight. The young caterpillar is cream with brown stripes, but it becomes darker with age. It goes into hibernation in the penultimate instar, and completes its growth in the spring, when it reaches about 20 mm (0.8 in) long. The mature caterpillar is light brown with a dark stripe along the back and a white one on each side; it is clothed with short, dark hairs. Pupation takes place at the base of the foodplant, and the chrysalis, wrapped in a few strands of silk, is pinkish brown.

Range: All of Europe – except the far north and south – and across Asia to Manchuria.

p.214 **Gatekeeper** *Pyronia tithonus*

Description: 17–25 mm (0.7–1.0 in). The upperside of the forewing is bright orange with broad, dark-brown borders and a twin (double-pupillate) apical eye-spot. The male, which is generally much smaller than the female, has a broad brown sex-brand running diagonally through the centre of the wing. In both sexes the hindwing is dark brown with an orange post-discal band that sometimes extends inwards to cover much of the wing. There may be one or two small eye-spots near the rear corner. The underside of the forewing resembles the upperside, although the male sex-brand is not visible. The underside of the hindwing is dark brown, mottled with yellow or grey in the outer region. The latter contains a variable number of small eye-spots, often reduced to white dots.

Similar species: Southern Gatekeeper has a fragmented sex-brand in the male, and a greyer underside to the hindwing with no eye-spots. Sardinian Meadow Brown has paler-orange areas on the upperside and a single pupil in the apical eye-spot.

Flight: June to September, feeding at a wide range
          of flowers, including ragwort, Marjoram,
          and Bramble.

Habitat: Hedgerows, woodland rides and clearings,
          and scrubby grassland – in keeping with
          the butterfly's alternative name of Hedge
          Brown – from sea level to about 1,500 m
          (4,925 ft). The larval foodplants include a
          wide range of grasses.

Life-cycle: The ribbed, barrel-shaped eggs are flesh-
          coloured with rusty patches. They may be
          laid singly on or near the foodplants, but
          are usually dropped in flight. The
          caterpillar hibernates in the first or second
          instar, while still very small, and completes
          its growth in the spring. The young
          caterpillar is green with a greyish-brown
          head and pale stripes on the flanks, but in
          the final instar the green often turns to
          greyish brown. The mature caterpillar is up
          to 25 mm (1.0 in) long, and it pupates
          suspended low down in the vegetation. The
          chrysalis is dirty white with dark-brown
          streaks and blotches.

Range: Southern and central Europe, and eastwards
          to the Caspian region. Absent from
          Scotland and the northern half of Ireland.

p.214   **Southern Gatekeeper** *Pyronia cecilia*

Description: 15–20 mm (0.6–0.8 in). The uppersides are
          bright orange with dark-brown borders on
          both wings. There is a twin-pupillate eye-
          spot on the forewing, and the male has a
          large brown sex-brand clearly broken up by
          orange veins. The hindwing has no eye-
          spots. The underside of the forewing is a
          paler version of the upperside, apart from
          the absence of the male's sex-brand, but the
          eye-spot is clearly ringed with yellow and
          there may be a pale streak near the centre of
          the wing. The underside of the hindwing is
          marbled brown and grey and has no eye-
          spots.

Similar species: Gatekeeper has eye-spots under the
          hindwing and the male sex-brand is not
          obviously fragmented. Spanish Gatekeeper
          has eye-spots on both surfaces of the

hindwing and a bright-yellow or cream stripe on the underside. Sardinian Meadow Brown is less bright and has only one pupil in the eye-spot.

Flight: May to August.

Habitat: Dry, scrubby grassland, from sea level to about 1,200 m (3,925 ft). The larval foodplants are various grasses.

Life-cycle: The caterpillar is pale brown with dark spots on the sides and a dark stripe along the back. Winter is passed in the larval stage, but it is not known if the caterpillar hibernates or remains active. It is about 20 mm (0.8 in) long when mature, and it pupates suspended low down in the vegetation. The chrysalis is greyish brown with black spots.

Range: Southern Europe, southwest Asia and North Africa.

p.215 **Spanish Gatekeeper** *Pyronia bathseba*

Description: 18–23 mm (0.7–0.9 in). The uppersides are essentially bright orange-red with dark-brown borders. There is a dark-brown dusting at the base of each wing, sometimes extending half-way across the wing in the male although less extensive in the female. The forewing has a large twin apical eye-spot, and there are three smaller eye-spots on the hindwing. The underside of the forewing resembles the upperside but has little or no brown dusting and the eye-spot is often ringed with yellow. The underside of the hindwing is dark brown and crossed by a prominent yellow or cream band. There are five yellow-ringed eye-spots just outside the band.

Similar species: Gatekeeper has a similar upperside but the underside of the hindwing rarely has a prominent pale band; if there is one, it is broken in the middle. Southern Gatekeeper has no eye-spots on the hindwing.

Flight: April to August.

Habitat: Dry grassland, scrub, and light woodland, from sea level to about 1,500 m (4,925 ft). The larval foodplants are various grasses, especially *Brachypodium* species.

Life-cycle: Winter is passed in the larval stage, but little else seems to be known of the early stages of this butterfly.

Range: Iberia and southern France, and also North Africa.

p.215 **Large Heath** *Coenonympha tullia*

Description: 15–22 mm (0.6–0.9 in). The uppersides, never seen at rest, are light brown or orange, often with a strong greyish tinge. Borders are rarely obvious. The species is very variable and some races are completely unmarked on the upperside, although most have a few yellow-ringed, blind eye-spots. The underside of the forewing is orange, often with a wide grey border and often heavily dusted with grey elsewhere. There are one or two eye-spots, with or without pupils, and there is often a diagonal yellow or white post-discal streak. The underside of the hindwing is essentially grey, sometimes with a greenish tinge, and an irregular pale streak, often broken in the middle, crosses the central region. A full arc of yellow-ringed eye-spots is present in some races, but others may have just one or two eye-spots; *C. t. scotica* from northern Scotland often has none at all.

Similar species: Balkan Heath is more orange above and has less white underneath. Small Heath is smaller and has inconspicuous eye-spots under the hindwing.

Flight: June to August, keeping low over the vegetation and rarely travelling far at a time.

Habitat: Bogs, moors, and damp grassland, from sea level to about 1,500 m (4,925 ft). The larval foodplants include cotton-grasses and other sedges and possibly various grasses.

Life-cycle: The eggs are more or less spherical and are yellowish green with rusty patches. They are laid singly on the foodplants. The caterpillar is grass-green with light and dark longitudinal stripes. It hibernates in the third instar and normally completes its growth in the following spring, although in some northern areas it takes two years to mature. The mature caterpillar is about 25 mm (1.0 in) long, and it pupates suspended low down in the vegetation. The chrysalis is bright green, with dark streaks on the wingcases.

Range: Northern and central Europe, and mountains in the southeast, but absent from all of southern England and much of France. The species is found right across temperate Asia, and very similar butterflies occur in the northern and western parts of North America. Some of these may be races of the Large Heath, but they are generally double-brooded and probably represent different species.

---

p.215 **Balkan Heath** *Coenonympha rhodopensis*

Description: 17 mm (0.7 in). The upperside, never seen at rest, is plain orange, with a slight greyish tinge around the edges and a dark dusting at the base of the hindwing. There may be some small eye-spots at the rear of the hindwing, and spots may also show through from the underside. The underside of the forewing is orange in both sexes, with a greyish or brownish apex and one or two eye-spots. The underside of the hindwing is greyish brown, with a pale patch near the centre and a post-discal arc of eye-spots beyond it.

Similar species: Large Heath is browner above and has more white on the underside.

Flight: June to July.

Habitat: Montane grassland, usually between 1,500 and 2,100 m (4,925 and 6,900 ft). The larval foodplants are grasses and sedges.

Life-cycle: Nothing seems to be known of the life-cycle of this butterfly.

Range: Central Italy and the northern Balkan mountains, from the Adriatic to the Black Sea.

The species is also known as the Eastern Large Heath.

p.216 **Small Heath** *Coenonympha pamphilus*

Description: 12–18 mm (0.5–0.7 in). The uppersides, never seen at rest, are bright orange with narrow grey borders and a small eye-spot near the tip of the forewing. Dusky patches may show through from the underside of the hindwing. The underside of the forewing is orange with grey borders, a yellow-ringed eye-spot, and sometimes a yellowish post-discal streak. The underside of the hindwing has a greyish-brown basal area and a paler outer region, separated by an irregular, pale post-discal streak. There are usually some very small and indistinct eye-spots in the outer region.

Similar species: Large Heath is generally larger and usually has conspicuous eye-spots under the hindwing; if these are absent, the eye-spot under the forewing has no white pupil.

Flight: April to October in one, two, or three broods. Flight is rather erratic and rarely far from the ground. The butterfly rarely visits flowers.

Habitat: Heathland and grassy places of all kinds, including roadsides, woodland clearings, and coastal dunes, from sea level to about 2,000 m (6,550 ft). The larval foodplants are various grasses, especially the fine-leaved fescues and bents although Mat Grass and other tough species are also eaten.

Life-cycle: The almost spherical eggs are laid singly on the foodplants. They are pale green at first, but become flesh-coloured and speckled with brown as they mature. Caterpillars in each of the early broods follow one of two pathways: some feed up quickly and produce another adult brood in the same year, but others develop more slowly and go into hibernation as large larvae before completing their development and producing adults in early spring. Caterpillars of the final brood hibernate while still quite small and produce adults later in the spring or in early summer. Caterpillars of northern and high-altitude populations, with just one brood each year, all develop at the same rate and hibernate in the normal way. The mature caterpillar is about 20 mm (0.8 in) long. It is grass-green with darker stripes and may be tinged with chestnut. It pupates suspended from the foodplant, and the chrysalis is bright green with brown or black streaks on the wingcases.

Range: All Europe except the Arctic. Also in North Africa and much of western and central Asia. One of Europe's commonest butterflies.

Summer broods in the far south are often brighter and more strongly marked. *C. p. thyrsis* from Crete is rather small and very heavily marked and is often regarded as a distinct species.

---

p.216 **Corsican Heath** *Coenonympha corinna*

Description: 15 mm (0.6 in). The uppersides, never seen at rest, are bright orange, with an irregular brown border on the forewing and on the front half of the hindwing. There is a single eye-spot at the tip of the forewing, and the female has two or three very small ones on the hindwing. The underside of the forewing is orange, with a slightly darker border and a conspicuous apical eye-spot in a yellow patch. The underside of the hindwing is orange-brown, heavily dusted with grey at the base and with a very irregular cream or yellow post-discal stripe. There is a yellow-ringed eye-spot on the front edge and there may be three more forming a straight line just outside the pale stripe.

Similar species: Elban Heath has a greyish submarginal band on the underside of each wing and larger eye-spots under the hindwing, but the two butterflies may prove to be races of the same species.

Flight: May to October in two or three broods.

Habitat: Open grassland, usually at around 1,000 m (3,275 ft). The larval foodplants include various grasses and sedges.

Life-cycle: The caterpillar hibernates and the chrysalis is reddish grey with white markings, but

otherwise little is known of the life history
of this butterfly.

Range: Restricted to Corsica and Sardinia, unless it
proves to be conspecific with the Elban
Heath – in which case it also occurs on the
neighbouring mainland of Italy.

---

p.216   **Elban Heath** *Coenonympha elbana*

Description: 12 15 mm (0.5 0.6 in). The uppersides,
never seen at rest, are bright orange with
dark brown borders, especially on the
forewing. The undersides are orange-
brown, heavily dusted with grey at the base
and with a well-marked, greyish
submarginal line on each wing. The
forewing has a conspicuous apical eye-spot,
and the hindwing has several eye-spots
together with a fairly straight, pale post-
discal stripe.

Similar species: Corsican Heath has less obvious eye-spots
under the hindwing and the submarginal
lines are less well developed.

Flight: May to September in two or three broods.

Habitat: Open grassland. The larval foodplants are
grasses, but the species are unknown.

Life-cycle: Nothing is known of the life-cycle of this
butterfly.

Range: Confined to the island of Elba and
neighbouring parts of the Italian mainland.

The Elban and Corsican Heaths are very
similar and, although commonly treated as
separate species, they may turn out to be
conspecific.

---

p.216   **Dusky Heath** *Coenonympha dorus*

Description: 15–17 mm (0.6–0.7 in). The uppersides,
never seen at rest, are essentially orange
with broad brown borders, but the male
forewing is heavily dusted with brown
scales and often appears completely brown.
In both sexes the basal half of the hindwing
is dusted with brown. The forewing has a
large apical eye-spot, with or without a
pupil, and the hindwing has an arc of blind

eye-spots curving inwards towards the centre of the wing. The underside of the forewing is orange with a pale post-discal stripe and a large apical eye-spot, and there is a silvery submarginal line. The underside of the hindwing is yellowish brown at the base, with an irregular, white post-discal stripe. Beyond this, the wing is yellowish with an inwardly curving arc of pupillate eye-spots and a silvery submarginal line. The anterior eye-spot, on the front edge of the wing, lies to the inside of the white stripe.

Similar species: Although the Dusky Heath is quite variable in colour and pattern, it can be recognized immediately by the inwardly curving arc of eye-spots on the hindwing. No other heath has such a curve.

Flight: June to August.

Habitat: Rough, dry grassland from sea level to about 2,000 m (6,550 ft). The larval foodplants are fescues and other fine-leaved grasses.

Life-cycle: The smooth, barrel-shaped eggs are pale green or pearly with red spots, and they are laid singly on the foodplant. The caterpillar is bluish green with light and dark longitudinal stripes. It hibernates before completing its growth in the spring; when mature it is about 25 mm (1.0 in) long. It pupates suspended on the foodplant.

Range: Southwest Europe, from Portugal to Italy. Also in North Africa.

---

p.216 **Pearly Heath** *Coenonympha arcania*

Description: 17–20 mm (0.7–0.8 in). The upperside of the forewing, never seen at rest, is bright orange with a broad brown border. The upperside of the hindwing is greyish brown, with a paler post-discal band. A very narrow, orange submarginal line is usually visible near the rear, and traces of eye-spots may show through from the underside. The underside of the forewing is orange with a brown border and a small apical eye-spot. The underside of the hindwing is golden brown with a broad white or cream post-discal stripe and prominent eye-spots just beyond it. With rare exceptions, there is also a large eye-spot on the front margin – on the inner edge of the pale band but not enclosed by it. There is a silvery-grey submarginal line.

Similar species: In Darwin's Heath the anterior eye-spot under the hindwing is enclosed in the pale band. Alpine Heath is greyer under the hindwing and the anterior eye-spot is smaller and enclosed in the pale band.

Flight: May to September, usually in a single brood but there may be a partial second brood in some southern areas.

Habitat: Grassland, scrub, and light woodland, from sea level to about 2,000 m (6,550 ft): especially common in hilly areas with well-drained slopes. The larval foodplants are various grasses, especially melicks.

Life-cycle: The barrel-shaped eggs are almost smooth and pearl-like with brown spots. They are laid singly on the foodplant. The caterpillars are grass-green with light and dark longitudinal stripes and, apart from those that mature quickly to produce a second generation in the summer, they go into hibernation before maturing in the spring. The mature caterpillar is about 25 mm (1.0 in) long. It pupates suspended on the foodplant, and the chrysalis is white or green with dark stripes.

Range: Southern and central Europe, including southern Sweden but not the British Isles, and eastwards into western Asia.

---

p.217 **Alpine Heath** *Coenonympha gardetta*

Description: 15 mm (0.6 in). The uppersides, never seen at rest, are dusky brown, with a variable orange or brick-red flush on the forewing and a faint indication of eye-spots showing through from the underside of the hindwing. Both wings may have a narrow orange outer border. The underside of the forewing is brick red in both sexes with a variable grey border. There may be a small apical eye-spot. The underside of the hindwing is dusky brown or grey with a conspicuous pale post-discal band containing eye-spots of varying size and intensity. The eye-spots are not ringed with yellow and the anterior spot, on the front edge of the wing, is enclosed in the pale band. Beyond the band, there is usually a silvery-grey submarginal line and an orange or yellow marginal line.

Similar species: In Pearly Heath the anterior eye-spot under the hindwing is not enclosed in the pale band. Darwin's Heath has yellow rings around the eye-spots.

Flight: June to September.

Habitat: Montane grassland between 800 and 3,000 m (2,625 and 9,850 ft), but usually between about 1,400 and 2,400 m (4,575 and 7,875 ft). The larval foodplants are various grasses.

Life-cycle: The eggs are barrel-shaped and bright green, becoming speckled with brown before hatching. They are laid singly on the foodplant. The caterpillar is bright green with pale stripes, and it hibernates before completing its growth in spring; the mature caterpillar is 20–25 mm (0.8–1.0 in) long. It pupates suspended on the foodplant. The chrysalis is bright green with a bluish tinge on the front end.

Range: Confined to the Alps.

p.217 **Darwin's Heath** *Coenonympha darwiniana*

Description: 17 mm (0.7 in). The upperside of the forewing is orange with a wide brown border; the upperside of the hindwing is dull brown, sometimes with a pale post-discal band and a small arc of orange at the rear corner. The uppersides are never seen at rest. The underside of the forewing is orange with a narrow brown border and usually a small apical eye-spot. The underside of the hindwing is largely brown, with a narrow white or cream post-discal band and an arc of yellow-ringed eye-spots. The anterior eye-spot is enclosed in the white band and the rest lie on its outer margin. There is a silvery sub-marginal band and an orange marginal band.

Similar species: In Pearly Heath the anterior eye-spot under the hindwing is not enclosed in the pale band. Alpine Heath has no yellow rings around the eye-spots.

Flight: June to August.

Habitat: Alpine meadows, from about 800 m to 1,800 m (2,625–5,900 ft). The larval foodplants are various grasses.

Life-cycle: The eggs are barrel-shaped and pale green, usually with brown spots in the later stages. The caterpillar is grass-green with light and dark stripes, and it goes into a long hibernation before completing its growth in the spring; the mature caterpillar is 20–25 mm (0.8–1.0 in) long. It pupates suspended low down on the foodplant. The chrysalis is green, with a bluish tinge on the front end.

Range: Confined to the Alps.

Darwin's Heath, also known as the Simplon Heath, was described as a distinct species in 1871. It has sometimes been treated as a high-altitude race of the Pearly Heath, but recent observations suggest that it may be a hybrid between Pearly and Alpine Heaths.

p.217 **Russian Heath** *Coenonympha leander*

Description: 17 mm (0.7 in). The upperside of the forewing is orange with a diffuse brown border that may extend over much of the wing in the male. There is usually a small apical eye-spot. The upperside of the hindwing is brown with an orange or yellow band near the edge, although the latter is often reduced to a small patch at the rear corner, and there may be two or three blind eye-spots. The uppersides are never seen at rest. The underside of the forewing is orange, often with a paler border, but there is no grey patch at the tip. There are one or two eye-spots near the tip. The underside of the hindwing is orange-brown, often with a grey basal area. There is a full arc of yellow-ringed eye-spots, bounded on the outer edge by a bright-orange band. There is also a silvery submarginal band.

Similar species:	Chestnut Heath has a grey apical patch under the forewing. Spanish Heath also has a grey apical patch, and the orange band under the hindwing is marginal rather than submarginal – not touching the eye-spots.
Flight:	May to July, sometimes abundant at the flowers of Wild Thyme although the species is generally rare.
Habitat:	Rough grassland from sea level to about 2,000 m (6,550 ft). The larval foodplants are grasses, including Annual Meadow Grass.
Life-cycle:	The eggs are light green. The caterpillar is greyish green with white stripes and is about 20 mm (0.8 in) long when mature. It hibernates among the grass bases.
Range:	Southeast Europe, from the Carpathians to Albania and northern Greece, and eastwards to Iran.
	C. l. orientalis, from western parts of the range, has a broad cream post-discal band just inside the arc of eye-spots.

p.217 Chestnut Heath *Coenonympha glycerion*

Description:	17 mm (0.7 in). The male upperside is dark brown and usually unmarked apart from a variable orange flush on the forewing. The female forewing is orange with an indistinct brown submarginal band, while the hindwing is brown with two or three small eye-spots and an orange marginal line. The uppersides are never seen at rest. In both sexes the underside of the forewing is orange with a greyish apical patch and outer border, but the female also has a small apical eye-spot. The underside of the hindwing is greyish brown with an arc of shining, yellow-ringed eye-spots and sometimes a few small white marks near the middle. There is usually an orange submarginal line, although this may be restricted to the rear part of the wing in the male, and there is also a narrow metallic line just inside the orange.
Similar species:	Russian Heath has no grey patch under the forewing. Large Heath is usually greyer and

lacks the orange submarginal line under the hindwing.

Flight: May to August.

Habitat: Grassland and moorland from sea level to about 2,000 m (6,550 ft). The larval foodplants are various grasses, including False Brome, melicks, and Quaking Grass.

Life-cycle: The barrel-shaped eggs are grass-green with reddish spots, and they are laid singly on the foodplants. The caterpillar hibernates before completing its growth in the spring. The mature caterpillar is grass-green with lighter and darker stripes; it is about 20 mm (0.8 in) long. It pupates suspended from the foodplant and the chrysalis is bright green with a dark stripe on each side.

Range: Much of Europe, east and northeast, from central France to the Black Sea and southern Finland, and on through Asia to Siberia. (*See* Spanish Heath below.)

Spanish Heath *Coenonympha iphioides*

Description: 17–20 mm (0.7–0.8 in). The male upperside is dark brown, with an orange flush on the basal half of the forewing and a thin orange marginal line in the rear half of the hindwing. The female has a light orange forewing with a greyish brown submarginal line and a bright-orange marginal line, while the hindwing is pale brown with an orange marginal line. Both sexes may have a number of small, blind eye-spots on the hindwing. In both sexes the underside of the forewing is orange, with a grey apical patch and outer border, and one or two small apical eye-spots. The underside of the hindwing is grey or greyish brown, with a bright arc of uniform, yellow-ringed eye-spots, a silvery sub-marginal line, and a clear orange marginal line.

Similar species: Chestnut Heath is very similar, although less brightly marked underneath, but their ranges do not overlap.

Flight: June to August.

Habitat: Rough, damp grassland from sea level to about 1,700 m (5,575 ft). The larval foodplants are grasses, but the preferred species are unknown.

Life-cycle: Little is known of the life-cycle of this butterfly, but it must be very similar to that of the Chestnut Heath.

Range: Confined to northern and central Spain.

This species is sometimes regarded as a race of the Chestnut Heath. At high altitudes in the Pyrenees the insects are relatively small and the eye-spots under the hindwing are often less well developed; the butterfly is then difficult to distinguish from the Chestnut Heath.

p.218 **False Ringlet** *Coenonympha oedippus*

Description: 17–22 mm (0.7–0.9 in). The uppersides, rarely seen at rest, are sooty brown in both sexes. Yellow-ringed eye-spots are conspicuous on the female hindwing and sometimes on the forewing as well, but they are very faint in the male and confined to the hindwing. The underside of the male is chocolate-brown with a heavy dusting of yellow scales. The hindwing carries five or six conspicuous, yellow-ringed eye-spots, and there may be two or three blind eye-spots on the forewing. The female underside is golden brown, with better-developed, pupillate eye-spots on the forewing. Both sexes have a silvery submarginal line, although this is rather weak on the male forewing. A conspicuous white flash usually crosses the female hindwing just inside the eye-spots, but this is weakly developed or absent in the male.

Similar species: Ringlet eye-spots are less bright and there is no white flash or silvery submarginal line. Scarce Heath has orange-ringed eye-spots on the upperside of the hindwing and the eye-spots under the hindwing are enclosed in a bright-orange band.

Flight: June to July, flying weakly when disturbed but spending much of the time at rest with wings closed. Unlike other *Coenonympha* species, the butterfly occasionally basks with wings open in dull weather.

Habitat: Damp grassland and other poorly drained
places, including heaths and light
woodland, from sea level to about 1,000 m
(3,275 ft). The larval foodplants include
various meadow-grasses (*Poa* species) and
possibly other grasses and sedges.

Life-cycle: The eggs are bright green and almost
spherical, and they are laid singly or in
short rows on the foodplant. The
caterpillar hibernates before completing its
growth in the spring. The mature
caterpillar is grass-green with darker
stripes; it is about 20 mm (0.8 in) long. It
pupates suspended low down in the
vegetation. The chrysalis is bright green
with pale stripes.

Range: Central Europe, in widely scattered
populations from the Atlantic coast of
France to Hungary, and on through Asia to
Japan.

The False Ringlet is one of Europe's most
threatened butterflies because, although it
is still quite numerous in some of its
localities, its habitats are rapidly being
reduced by drainage schemes.

p.219 **Scarce Heath** *Coenonympha hero*

Description: 15–18 mm (0.6–0.7 in). The uppersides,
rarely seen at rest, are sooty brown in
both sexes with three or four orange-
ringed eye-spots and traces of an orange
marginal line on the hindwing. The
forewing is generally unmarked apart
from a small apical eye-spot in the
female. The undersides range from sooty
brown to golden brown, with an apical
eye-spot and a narrow orange border on
the forewing. The hindwing has a wavy,
white or cream post-discal stripe and a
broad orange band containing six
pupillate eye-spots. Both wings have a
thin silvery submarginal line.

Similar species: False Ringlet is usually larger and lacks the
orange band under the hindwing, although
there may be a slight orange tinge beyond
the eye-spots.

Flight: May to July, keeping close to the ground and rarely flying far at a time.

Habitat: Moors and grassland, including coastal dunes, and also in open woodland, from sea level to about 1,000 m (3,275 ft). Most populations are in damp habitats, but some flourish in dry woods and grassland, especially in the northern parts of the range. The larval foodplants are various grasses, including hair-grasses and Wood Barley, and possibly sedges.

Life-cycle: The bluish-green eggs are barrel-shaped, with numerous faint ribs, and they are laid singly on the foodplant. The caterpillar goes into hibernation before completing its growth in the spring. It is grass-green with light and dark stripes, and it is 20–25 mm (0.8–1.0 in) long when mature. It pupates suspended on the foodplant, and the chrysalis is bright green with a black stripe along the rear edge of each wingcase.

Range: Central Europe and southern Scandinavia and across temperate Asia to Japan. Absent from the British Isles, and generally rare and declining elsewhere in Europe as a result of habitat destruction.

p.219 **Speckled Wood** *Pararge aegeria*

Description: 20–25 mm (0.8–1.0 in). This butterfly exists as two very different races: *P. a. aegeria* south and west of a line from Brittany to southern Greece, and *P. a. tircis* to the north and east of that line, although the two races grade into each other where they meet. The ground colour of the uppersides is dark brown in both races, but *aegeria* has a pattern of orange blotches and *tircis* has cream blotches. The blotches vary in size and are often partly obliterated by dark scales, especially in *tircis*. The forewing has a single apical eye-spot, although this is not always very clear, and the hindwing has an arc of three or four more obvious eye-spots ringed with orange or cream. The only other markings on the hindwing are a pale patch near the centre and one on the front edge, and these often link up to form a single patch. The underside of the forewing resembles the upperside, although the pale patches are more extensive. The underside of the hindwing is mottled-brown with yellow spots, a darker border, and an arc of rusty-brown eye-spots with yellow pupils. The outer edge of the hindwing is strongly scalloped.

Similar species: The pale-spotted *P. a. tircis* cannot be confused with any other butterfly. *P. a. aegeria* is often confused with Wall Brown, but the latter has more orange on the upperside and is often much greyer under the hindwing, with more obvious eye-spots.

Flight: March to October, with a single brood in the north and two or three overlapping broods further south. The butterflies get most of their nourishment from honeydew, but occasionally drink from Bramble blossom and often visit ragwort later in the year. Males establish small territories in patches of sunlight and defend them against all comers.

Habitat: Woodland rides and clearings and shady lanes in wooded areas, often in quite dense shade, from sea level to about 1,500 m (4,925 ft). The larval foodplants are a wide range of grasses, including Cock's-foot and False Brome.

Life-cycle: The pearly, thimble-shaped eggs are almost smooth and are laid singly on the grasses. In the first-instar the caterpillar is cream with a glossy black head, but it then becomes yellowish green with light and dark stripes. When mature it is 25–30 mm (1.0–1.2 in) long, and it pupates suspended low down in the vegetation or surrounding debris. The chrysalis is green or brown, with dark streaks on the wingcases. Single-brooded populations in the north pass the winter in the pupal stage, as do some of the montane populations further south, although these are double-brooded. Elsewhere, winter is passed either as a caterpillar or as a chrysalis. In the British Isles, for example, caterpillars hatching in late summer may develop quickly and pupate in the autumn or they may grow more slowly and pass the winter in the third larval instar, feeding from time to time if the weather is not too cold. This is the only British butterfly known to pass the winter in two different stages. Temperature and day-length both seem to play a part in determining the rate of larval development. Butterflies that have passed the winter in the larval stage tend to be larger than those that have overwintered as pupae. They also have smaller spots and therefore look darker.

Range: Throughout Europe, apart from the far north, and eastwards into central Asia.

The Speckled Wood has been increasing its range and numbers in Britain in recent years, especially in areas where new forestry plantations are maturing and providing the shady conditions enjoyed by this butterfly.

p.220 **Wall Brown** *Lasiommata megera*

Description: 17–25 mm (0.7–1.0 in). The upperside of the forewing is golden orange with a brown border and a network of other brown markings. Three dark bars cross the cell, and the two outer ones commonly continue on an irregular course to the rear margin, although in the male they are obscured by the broad brown sex-brand that runs diagonally through the centre of the wing. There is a single apical eye-spot. The veins in the outer part of the wing are strongly lined with brown, giving it a slight resemblance to a section of brick wall – although the butterfly was named for its habit of settling on walls. The basal half of the hindwing is brown, with a narrow orange band outside it and then a broader orange band containing three or four eye-spots. The two bands are usually separated by a narrow brown streak, but this is sometimes very faint and the two bands merge together. The wing is lightly clothed with golden hair, especially at the base. The underside of the forewing is a slightly paler version of the upperside. The underside of the hindwing is mottled brown and pearly grey and often has a strong golden sheen. It is crossed by narrow, wavy, dark lines and there are six eye-spots in the outer region. The hindmost eye-spot usually contains two pupils.

Similar species: The southwestern race of Speckled Wood (*P. a. aegeria*) has similar colours, but usually has less orange and the hindwing is strongly scalloped. Large Wall Brown and Northern Wall Brown are similar underneath, but the upperside of the hindwing is largely brown. Some fritillaries look similar in flight, but they have no eye-spots.

Flight: March to October in two or three broods, flying strongly but usually keeping close to the ground. The butterfly commonly basks with wings wide open on rocks, walls, and bare earth.

Habitat: Rough, dry grassland, including roadside verges, heaths, and waste ground, from sea level to over 2,000 m (6,550 ft). The larval foodplants are a wide range of coarse grasses, including Tor Grass and Yorkshire Fog.

Life-cycle: The pearly-green eggs are almost spherical, and they are laid singly or in small groups at the bases of the foodplants. Winter is normally passed in the larval stage; the caterpillars feed sporadically in milder weather, although some individuals feed up and pupate in the autumn or early winter. The mature caterpillar is bluish green and rather hairy, with indistinct white stripes; it is about 25 mm (1.0 in) long. It pupates suspended low down in the vegetation. The chrysalis is usually green with white streaks on the wingcases, but it is sometimes brown or purplish black. Winter pupae are usually quite dark.

Range: Throughout Europe, apart from the far north, and eastwards to the Caspian region. Also in North Africa.

---

p.220 **Large Wall Brown** *Lasiommata maera*

Description: 20–30 mm (0.8–1.2 in). The male upperside is brown, with a dark sex-brand running diagonally through the forewing. Both wings normally have a well-marked orange post-discal band, containing a large apical eye-spot on the forewing and two or three smaller eye-spots on the hindwing. In Scandinavia, the orange is reduced to small rings around the eye-spots and perhaps a faint orange sheen elsewhere. The female upperside is also basically brown, but the post-discal area of the forewing is always orange, even in the far north. In most areas, the orange also extends towards the base of the wing. The apical eye-spot commonly has two pupils. The hindwing is brown with three or four orange-ringed eye-spots. The fringes are clearly chequered brown and white in both sexes. The underside of the forewing is orange with broad greyish-brown borders, while the underside of the hindwing is mottled grey and brown with six yellow-ringed eye-spots.

Similar species: Wall Brown is usually smaller, with browner fringes and more orange on the hindwing. Northern Wall Brown is smaller and darker. Some *Erebia* species have similar uppersides, but are very different under the hindwing.

Flight: May to September in one or two broods, flying rapidly close to the ground and can regularly be seen basking on the ground.

Habitat: Rough grassland, including roadsides and open woodland, with plenty of rocks and bare ground, from sea level to about 2,000 m (6,550 ft). The larvae feed on a wide range of grasses.

Life-cycle: The shiny, pale-green eggs are round or thimble-shaped, and they are laid singly or in small groups. Caterpillars of the second brood go into hibernation in the penultimate instar before completing their growth in the spring. The mature caterpillar is grass-green with pale stripes, and it is 25–35 mm (1.0–1.4 in) long. It pupates suspended from the vegetation or rocks. The chrysalis is green or brown with rows of yellow dots.

Range: Most of Europe, apart from the British Isles and the Arctic, and eastwards to the Himalayas. Also in North Africa.

In the far south, both sexes have wider orange bands on the forewing (f. *adrasta*), and the female forewing may be almost entirely orange with faint brown markings

p.221   **Northern Wall Brown**
Lasiommata petropolitana

Description: 20 mm (0.8 in). The uppersides are sooty brown in both sexes, with a variably developed orange post-discal band on each wing. The band is usually bright and clear in the female, but often no more than a smudge in the male. There is a large apical eye-spot, sometimes with two pupils, on the forewing, while the hindwing bears three or four smaller ones. Two dark bars cross the forewing cell and a dark, wavy line runs across the centre of the hindwing, although these are not always easily seen. The underside of the forewing is greyish brown with a large apical eye-spot and often with an extensive orange flush below it, although this may be much reduced in the male. The underside of the hindwing is mottled greyish brown with six yellow-ringed eye-spots.

Similar species: Large Wall Brown is usually larger and brighter. Some *Erebia* species have similar uppersides, but are very different under the hindwing.

Flight: April to September in one or two broods, but mostly flying in a single emergence from May to July. Flight is low over the ground and rather jerky, and the butterfly spends a lot of time basking on the ground.

Habitat: Rough, grassy places, including roadsides and open woodland, usually on well-drained sites from sea level to about 2,000 m (6,550 ft). The larval foodplants are mainly fescue grasses.

Life-cycle: The globular, pearly-white eggs are laid singly or in small groups. The caterpillar is grass-green and rather hairy, with longitudinal white stripes. It is 25–30 mm (1.0–1.2 in) long when mature, and it

pupates suspended low down in the
vegetation. The chrysalis is green with
white spots and streaks. Southern
populations overwinter in the final larval
instar, but in Scandinavia and other
northern areas the winter is passed in the
pupal stage.

Range: Northern Europe, the Alps and other
mountains in southern and central
Europe, and probably throughout
temperate Asia.

---

p.222 **Woodland Brown** *Lopinga achine*

Description: 25–30 mm (1.0–1.2 in). The uppersides are
sooty brown, with an arc of large, yellow-
ringed, blind eye-spots on each wing. The
undersides, a little paler than the
uppersides, have similar eye-spots,
although some of these may have white
pupils. An irregular cream streak crosses
the forewing just inside the arc of eye-spots,
and there is a similar white streak on the
hindwing. Each wing has two pale
submarginal lines just beyond the eye-
spots.

Similar species: None.

Flight: May to August, flying quite slowly and
often basking on sunny patches of
vegetation like the Speckled Wood.

Habitat: Open woodland, from sea level to about
1,500 m (4,925 ft). The larval foodplants
are various grasses, including Tor Grass and
False Brome.

Life-cycle: The thimble-shaped eggs are greyish green
and very smooth, and are scattered as the
female flies over the vegetation. It goes into
hibernation while still very small and
completes its growth in the spring or early
summer. The caterpillar is green, with
darker stripes on the back and paler ones on
the sides. It is up to 35 mm (1.4 in) long
when mature. It pupates suspended low
down in the herbage, and the chrysalis is
bright green with white streaks.

Range: Central Europe, including southern Sweden
and southern Finland, with a few outlying
populations further south. Absent from the

British Isles. This is a very local butterfly with widely scattered populations.

p.223 **Lattice Brown** *Kirinia roxelana*

Description: 30 mm (1.2 in). The uppersides, rarely seen at rest, are dull brown with a fiery-orange flush and a small apical eye-spot on the forewing. The male has a dark sex-brand in the cell, and the veins are rather distorted at the base. The female has a few pale-yellow or cream spots in the apical region. The hindwing is unmarked apart from the faint eye-spots showing through from the underside. The underside of the forewing is orange with greyish-brown borders and a more obvious eye-spot than on the upperside. The female has pale apical spots as on the upperside. The underside of the hindwing is greyish brown, with wavy cross-lines and an arc of seven yellow-ringed post-discal eye-spots. The spots in spaces 4 and 5 (the third and fourth spots from the front) are much smaller than the rest, and the hindmost spot is usually twinned. The outer edge of the hindwing is strongly scalloped, and streaked with white.

Similar species: Lesser Lattice Brown is smaller, with smaller eye-spots under the hindwing. Large Wall Brown is smaller, with large eye-spots on the forewing and more equal ones under the hindwing.

Flight: May to September, often feeding at the flowers of Christ's-thorn bushes but most often seen resting on tree-trunks, where it may drink oozing sap. The butterfly seems reluctant to fly and rarely moves far even when disturbed. It may open its wings momentarily when it alights, but quickly closes them again.

Habitat: Scrubby hillsides and light woodland, including orchards and olive-groves, from sea level to about 1,500 m (4,925 ft). The larval foodplants are various grasses.

Life-cycle: The eggs are pale and rounded, and they are laid in small batches in bark-crevices. The caterpillars feed mainly in autumn and winter. They are light green with darker stripes and there are two conspicuous, white-streaked horns on the head. Mature caterpillars are 35–40 mm (1.4–1.6 in) long. The chrysalis is green or brown with white streaks and it is suspended from plants or rocks in the spring.

Range: Southeast Europe and eastwards to the Caspian region.

---

p.223 **Lesser Lattice Brown** *Kirinia climene*

Description: 22–25 mm (0.9–1.0 in). The uppersides of both sexes are dull brown, with a fiery-orange flush and an obscure blind eye-spot on the forewing. The female also has a few pale spots near the wingtip. The hindwing may have a short orange post-discal band containing two or three small eye-spots, but it is often unmarked. The underside of the forewing is bright orange with broad, brown borders and a small apical eye-spot. The underside of the hindwing is greyish brown, often tinged with yellow, and it has an arc of small eye-spots. The outer margin of the hindwing is strongly scalloped in both sexes.

Similar species: Lattice Brown is larger, with stronger markings and larger eye-spots under the hindwing.

Flight: June to July.

Habitat: Rough grassland and woodland clearings up to about 1,500 m (4,925 ft). The larvae feed on coarse grasses.

Life-cycle: The eggs are yellow and globular and are probably dropped by the female in flight. The mature caterpillar is about 30 mm (1.2 in) long and is pale green with white or cream stripes. Winter is probably passed in the caterpillar stage.

Range: Until recently, this butterfly had rarely been seen in Europe, and the scattered individuals that appeared here and there in southeast Europe were thought to be vagrants from Asia – where it occurs from Turkey to the Caspian region – but the species now appears to be resident in several parts of the Balkans.

THE SKIPPERS (HESPERIIDAE)

These butterflies owe their common name
to their darting and dancing flight, which
often involves abrupt changes of direction.
Coupled with their rapid wingbeats, their
characteristic flight is very different from
that of other butterflies. Their wingspans
range from about 20 to 90 mm (0.8–
3.5 in), although the great majority –
including all 40 or so European species –
are under about 35 mm (1.4 in) across. The
head is relatively wide, and the antennae are
often pointed and sometimes hooked at the
tip. All the wing-veins arise from the wing-
base, or from the large cell, and do not
branch. All six legs are fully functional.

Essex Skipper

Brown, black, and grey are the dominant
colours among the European skippers, many
of which look more like moths, although
there are some brightly coloured skippers in
the tropics. The males of many species carry
their detachable scent-scales in a groove at
the front of the forewing, while others –
including the 'golden skippers' of the
subfamily Hesperiinae – bear them in dark
streaks near the middle of the wings. Most
skippers sunbathe with their wings more or
less flat; but the golden skippers adopt an
unusual attitude, with their hindwings
almost flat and the forewings partly closed
above them. At other times, the skippers
nearly all close their wings above their backs
like other butterflies, although the Dingy
Skipper (*see* p.619) rests with its wings
wrapped around its body like a moth.

Silver-spotted
Skipper

Dingy Skipper

Hesperid eggs.

The eggs are either lozenge-shaped, with
a marked central depression, or dome-
shaped, and sometimes they are elegantly
sculptured. Skipper caterpillars are
cylindrical or shuttle-shaped, tapering at
both ends, with a rather conspicuous **head**
which is often coloured differently from the
rest of the body. Those of the golden
skippers feed on grasses, but the rest use a
variety of low-growing plants. They
normally live in shelters made by spinning
leaves together, and several species feed
mainly at night. A comb-like fringe

*Caterpillar of
Large Skipper.*

*Anal comb of
skipper
caterpillar used
for ejecting frass.*

Small Skipper

Grizzled Skipper

Hesperid chrysalises.

overhanging the anus is used to hold the caterpillar's droppings and to flick them away from the shelter. Pupation takes place in flimsy cocoons, commonly inside the larval shelters. The pupa often has a pointed head, but otherwise has a smooth outline. This is a cosmopolitan family, with over 3,000 species. About 40 live in Europe, but only eight occur in the British Isles and only the Dingy Skipper occurs in Ireland. Anatomically, the skippers are rather different from the other butterflies and they are placed in their own superfamily.

p.226 **Grizzled Skipper** *Pyrgus malvae*

Description: 10–15 mm (0.4–0.6 in). The ground colour of the upperside is black, with a dusting of greyish scales near the wing-bases and strongly chequered with white on the fringes. Both wings carry conspicuous white spots, and the outer part of the hindwing usually has a clear arc of white dots. There is also a fairly large, somewhat rectangular white spot near the centre. The underside is brownish or yellowish grey, often darker on the forewing than on the hindwing, with white spots similar to those of the upperside.

Similar species: Several other *Pyrgus* species have similar patterns, but most of these are larger. The clear arc of white dots and the large central spot on the upperside of the hindwing should distinguish the Grizzled Skipper from others with brownish undersides.

Flight: April to August: usually in two broods in the southern half of Europe, although there is normally only one brood in the north and at high altitudes. The British population is normally single-brooded and on the wing in May and June, but there is sometimes a partial second brood in August. The butterfly keeps close to the ground and likes to bask in the sunshine with its wings wide open.

Habitat: Open grassland, heaths, and woodland edges and clearings, especially where there are patches of bare ground on which the butterfly can bask; from sea-level to 2,000 m (6,550 ft). The larval foodplants include Wild Strawberry, cinquefoils, and other low-growing members of the rose family.

Life-cycle: The ribbed, dome-shaped eggs are pale green at first, but gradually assume a creamy colour. They are laid singly on the foodplants, usually on the undersides of the leaves. The caterpillar is yellow at first, but then becomes green with brown stripes and a black head. The young caterpillar feeds under a sheet of silk spun on a leaf, but after the second moult it draws the edges of a leaf together with silk to form a tubular retreat. Feeding takes place either inside or outside the retreat and the caterpillar is fully grown when it is about eight weeks old and 18 mm (0.7 in) long. It pupates in a flimsy cocoon at the base of the foodplant, and the chrysalis is reddish brown with white or pale-green wingcases. Winter is passed in the pupal stage.

Range: Most of Europe, but absent from northern Scandinavia, Scotland, Ireland, and the Mediterranean islands. Also in much of temperate Asia, from the Black Sea to northern China.

p.227 **Large Grizzled Skipper** *Pyrgus alveus*

Description: 11–16 mm (0.4–0.6 in). The ground colour of the uppersides is grey-brown to black, often with a yellowish or rusty tinge and with a variable pattern of white spots on the forewing. The upperside of the hindwing has a pale central band, often confined to the front half, with some indistinct white spots beyond it. The underside of the forewing is mainly grey, while that of the hindwing is brownish green with large white spots. As in all *Pyrgus* species, the wing-margins are chequered with black and white.

Similar species: Oberthür's Grizzled Skipper has more obvious white spots on the upperside of the hindwing, and the underside of the hindwing is usually browner, but the two species rarely fly together. Foulquier's

Grizzled Skipper has yellower markings on the underside of the hindwing. Safflower Skipper is yellower on the underside of the hindwing and has an almost complete white border.

Flight: June to August in a single brood with an extended emergence. A very alert and quick-flying species, it enjoys basking on the ground and drinking from wet mud.

Habitat: Open, flowery places, especially on stony ground in the uplands and often close to streams, from 100 to 1,800 m (325–5,900 ft), but rarely found below 1,000m (3,275 ft) except in Scandinavia. The larval foodplants include Bramble, Agrimony, cinquefoils, milkworts, and rock-roses.

Life-cycle: The eggs are green and hemispherical, with longitudinal ribs, and they are laid singly on the foodplants. In Scandinavia they do not hatch until the spring, but elsewhere they hatch quite quickly and winter is passed in the larval stage. The caterpillar, up to 25 mm (1.0 in) long, is brown with a darker back stripe and feeds mainly at night. It pupates in a flimsy cocoon amongst the leaves or leaf-litter. The chrysalis is dark brown.

Range: Most of Europe, but absent from the British Isles and northern Scandinavia. Also across Asia to Mongolia and China.

This is a rather variable butterfly and sometimes only an examination of the genitalia can separate it with certainty from several similar species. Specimens from Scandinavia are usually rather small, while those from southern Europe often have extra-large markings on both surfaces of the hindwing.

---

p.227 **Oberthür's Grizzled Skipper**
Pyrgus armoricanus

Description: 12–14 mm (0.5–0.6 in). The ground colour of the upperside is greyish brown to black, with conspicuous white spots on the forewings. The hindwing markings are fainter and greyer, but there is a clear row of pale spots near the margin and a central grey band that extends across most of the wing. The underside of the forewing is grey and white with a brownish tip, while the underside of the hindwing is yellowish brown with white bands and spots.

Similar species: Large Grizzled Skipper is usually greener on the underside, and in most regions it has less obvious spots on the upperside of the hindwing. The grey band on the upperside of the hindwing is often confined to the front half. Foulquier's Grizzled Skipper usually has less distinct white markings on the upperside of the hindwing.

Flight: May to September, usually in two broods, but single-brooded in northern parts of the range and possibly with three broods in the far south.

Habitat: Dry, flowery places with plenty of scrub, from sea level to about 1,900 m (6,225 ft) but most frequent in lowlands. The larval foodplants are Wild Strawberry, cinquefoils, and rock-roses.

Life-cycle: The eggs are pale-green hemispheres with longitudinal ribs, and they are laid singly on the foodplants. The young caterpillar spins a silken tent on the upperside of a leaf, but after the first moult it fixes two or more leaves together to form a shelter. It makes new shelters from time to time when it has eaten the surrounding leaves. The caterpillar is brownish green with a black head and three dark back-stripes, and it is about 22 mm (0.9 in) long when mature. It pupates amongst the leaves at the base of the foodplant, and the chrysalis is speckly brown with pale wing-sheaths. Winter is passed in the larval stage.

Range: Throughout southern and central Europe, and just creeping into Denmark and southern Sweden. Absent from the British Isles. Also in North Africa and Western Asia.

Northern specimens, especially those from Sweden, tend to be rather small with poorly developed markings. In most parts of

Europe Oberthür's Grizzled Skipper flies in early and late summer, either side of the main emergence of the very similar Large Grizzled Skipper. The latter is also more of an upland butterfly.

p.228 **Foulquier's Grizzled Skipper**
Pyrgus foulquieri

Description: 12–15 mm (0.5–0.6 in). The ground colour of the uppersides is sooty brown, often with a red or yellowish suffusion, and the wings are noticeably hairy at the base. The white markings are quite variable in extent and density, but there is usually a prominent pale band across the hindwing. The underside of the forewing resembles the upperside, but the underside of the hindwing is largely green with three more or less complete white bands.

Similar species: Large Grizzled Skipper and Oberthür's Grizzled Skipper generally have less white on the underside, but examination of the genitalia is often necessary for positive identification.

Flight: July to August.

Habitat: Flowery mountain slopes up to 2,000 m (6,550 ft). The larval foodplants are cinquefoils.

Life-cycle: Very little is known of the early stages of this butterfly.

Range: Northeast Spain, the mountains of southern France, and very locally in central Italy. The Italian race (*P. f. picenus*) is smaller and much yellower than the typical race, especially on the underside.

Warren's Grizzled Skipper
Pyrgus warrenensis

Description: 10–12 mm (0.4–0.5 in). The uppersides are very dark brown with scattered, small, white markings and, in the female, a good deal of yellowish hair at the base. The undersides are greyish brown with extensive white markings, including an almost complete band across the middle of the hindwing.

Similar species: The pattern resembles that of some forms of Large Grizzled Skipper, but the small size should distinguish this species from any similar skipper in the Alps.

Flight: July to August.

Habitat: Montane grassland above about 1,800 m (5,900 ft), where it often flies with Large Grizzled Skipper. The larval foodplant is unknown.

Life-cycle: Nothing seems to be known of the early stages of this butterfly.

Range: French, Swiss, and Austrian Alps. A very local butterfly.

---

p.229 **Olive Skipper** *Pyrgus serratulae*

Description: 12–16 mm (0.5–0.6 in). The ground colour of the uppersides is dark brown, with a variable amount of white spotting on the forewing. The hindwing may have some obscure pale patches, but is often unmarked. The underside of the forewing resembles the upperside, although it is greyer, but the underside of the hindwing is olive-green or yellowish green with white markings. The central white band is broken near the middle. The sexes are alike, but the female is browner and often has a yellowish tinge over the whole upper surface.

Similar species: Large Grizzled Skipper has a brighter-green underside, usually with a complete central white band on the hindwing.

Flight: May to August in a single brood, commonly basking on bare ground.

Habitat: Flowery slopes, usually in the mountains, up to about 2,500 m (8,200 ft) although *P. s. major*, which has darker and more clearly spotted undersides, flies at lower levels in southwest France and in southeast Europe. The larval foodplants are cinquefoils and lady's-mantles.

Life-cycle: The eggs are laid on the foodplants during the summer, and they hatch within a few weeks. The caterpillars hibernate while still quite small and complete their growth in the spring. They are bright green at first, but they darken as they get older. They are about 25 mm (1.0 in) long when mature. Pupation takes place at the base of the foodplant.

Range: Most of southern and central Europe, but absent from the British Isles and neighbouring parts of the Continent. Small and vulnerable populations exist in the Baltic States and the species reaches far into central Asia.

---

p.228 **Carline Skipper** *Pyrgus carlinae*

Description: 13–14 mm (0.5–0.6 in). The ground colour of the uppersides is sooty brown or black, with variable amounts of white spotting. *P. c. carlinae* has rather small spots, especially in the female, and the spot at the end of the forewing cell is C-shaped. The upperside of the hindwing is poorly marked. *P. c. cirsii* is more heavily patterned and has a rectangular spot at the end of the forewing cell. The underside of the hindwing in both subspecies is largely reddish brown, with a large white patch on the outer margin in *carlinae*.

Similar species: Olive Skipper has a similar pattern, but the underside of the hindwing is olive-green. Rosy Grizzled Skipper is paler on both surfaces.

Flight: June to August in a single brood, often gathering in large numbers to drink from wet ground.

Habitat: Flower-rich slopes up to about 2,500 m (8,200 ft), with *P. c. carlinae* most abundant above 1,500 m (4,925 ft) and *P. c. cirsii* rarely found above 1,300 m (4,275 ft). The larval foodplants are various cinquefoils.

Life-cycle: The caterpillars go into hibernation soon after hatching and may stay dormant for as long as nine months before waking to complete their growth in late spring. Pupation takes place at the base of the foodplant.

Range: *P. c. carlinae* is confined to the western Alps, but *P. c. cirsii* occurs locally throughout southwest Europe, from Portugal to southern Germany and Hungary.

Although the two subspecies interbreed in places where they overlap, they are often treated as distinct species – the Carline Skipper (*P. carlinae*) and the Cinquefoil Skipper (*P. cirsii*).

p.230 **Rosy Grizzled Skipper** *Pyrgus onopordi*

Description: 11–14 mm (0.4–0.6 in). The ground colour of the uppersides is sooty brown, often with a yellowish flush. The white spots are well developed on the forewing, but on the hindwing they are yellowish grey and much less clear, although there is a prominent spot on the front margin. The underside of the forewing is grey with white spots, and the underside of the hindwing is yellowish brown with white spots, the most characteristic being an anvil-shaped one in the middle of the central band. Some specimens have a faint pink tinge to the upperside, but the species does not seem to be well-named.

Similar species: Carline Skipper is darker above and much browner underneath.

Flight: April to October in two or three broods.

Habitat: Flower-rich grassland from sea level to about 1,500 m (4,925 ft). The larval foodplants are cinquefoils and Dwarf Mallow.

Life-cycle: The eggs are laid on the foodplant. Autumn caterpillars hibernate and complete their growth in the spring.

Range: Iberia, southern France, and Italy. Also in North Africa.

p.230 **Sandy Grizzled Skipper** *Pyrgus cinarae*

Description: 15–16 mm (0.6 in). The ground colour of the male upperside is almost black, with large white spots. The conspicuous spot at the end of the forewing cell is either rectangular or dumb-bell-shaped. The hindwing bears a clear white band near the centre. The female is browner and less well marked. In both sexes the underside of the forewing is blackish brown with white spots and a green tinge. Except in Spain (*see* below), the underside of the hindwing is olive-green and white. The central white band is usually complete.

Similar species: Female Large Grizzled Skipper is quite similar, but underside of forewing is paler and has smaller white spots.

Flight: June to July.

Habitat: Dry, grassy and stony hillsides up to about 1,500 m (4,925 ft). The larval foodplants are probably cinquefoils.

Life-cycle: Little is known of the early stages of this butterfly.

Range: The Balkans, where it usually flies at around 1,000 m (3,275 ft), and on through southern Russia to Central Asia. Also in the mountains of central Spain.

The Spanish race (*P. c. clorinda*) has a yellow tinge on the upperside, and the ground colour of the underside of the hindwing is distinctly yellow.

---

p.231 **Yellow-banded Skipper** *Pyrgus sidae*

Description: 13–18 mm (0.5–0.7 in). The uppersides of both sexes are sooty brown, with greyish hair at the base and a variable amount of white spotting, including a large, more or less rectangular spot at the end of the forewing cell. The undersides have white margins, but the most obvious and characteristic features are the two broad yellow bands on the hindwing. These are usually bright yellow, but may be paler in Italy and southern France.

Similar species: No other skipper has the yellow bands.

Flight: April to July in a single brood: males often gather to drink from muddy ground.

Habitat: Flower-rich grassland from sea level to 1,800 m (5,900 ft). The larval foodplants are cinquefoils and possibly various mallows, especially Abutilon.

Life-cycle: The eggs hatch soon after they are laid and the caterpillars hibernate before completing their growth in the spring.

Range: Central Spain and the Mediterranean region, from France to the Black Sea coasts, and on through Asia to western China.

p.232 **Safflower Skipper** *Pyrgus carthami*

Description: 15–17 mm (0.6–0.7 in). The uppersides
are brownish grey, with dense grey hair at
the wing-bases in the male. The white
spots on the forewing are well developed,
and there is usually a well-marked row of
spots towards the outer margin of the
hindwing. The undersides are yellowish
grey and the white marginal spots link up
to produce an almost complete pale
border. The spots on the hindwing are
edged with grey. The central band on the
underside of the hindwing is often
incomplete.

Similar species: The pale borders of the undersides
distinguish this from all but the Yellow-
Banded Skipper.

Flight: June to September in a single brood with a
prolonged emergence.

Habitat: Open, flower-rich grassland up to about
2,000 m (6,550 ft). The larval foodplants
are cinquefoils, mallows, and possibly
Safflower.

Life-cycle: The eggs are laid singly on the foodplants,
and the caterpillars hibernate before
completing their growth in the spring.

Range: Most of southern and central Europe, but
absent from the British Isles and from most
of Europe's Atlantic seaboard.

p.232 **Alpine Grizzled Skipper**
Pyrgus andromedae

Description: 12–15 mm (0.5–0.6 in). The ground
colour of the uppersides is dark brown to
almost black, with abundant pale hairs,
especially on the hindwing. The forewing
has numerous well-defined white spots, but
is characterized by three small ones in a
line just below the end of the cell. The
hindwing has no more than a few
indistinct blotches. The underside of the
forewing resembles the upperside,
although it is paler and has larger spots.
The underside of the hindwing is olive-
brown or yellowish, with a large central
white patch, and a prominent white streak

and a round spot – looking like a horizontal exclamation mark – close to the inner (lower) margin. The inner margin is usually greyer than the rest of the wing.

Similar species: Dusky Grizzled Skipper has smaller white spots on the upperside, and the underside markings are much fainter.

Flight: June to July in a single brood. It keeps close to the ground and often settles to bask on stones and bare earth.

Habitat: Mountain slopes, usually above 1,500 m (4,925 ft), in the Alps and Pyrenees. At much lower altitudes in Scandinavia, where it inhabits stony heaths and moors dotted with saxifrages and Moss Campion. The larval foodplants are mallows, cinquefoils, and lady's-mantles, especially *Alchemilla glomerulans*.

Life-cycle: Little is known of the early stages of this butterfly.

Range: Pyrenees, Alps, and Balkan mountains, and also in northern Scandinavia, especially within the Arctic Circle.

---

p.233 **Dusky Grizzled Skipper** *Pyrgus cacaliae*

Description: 12–15 mm (0.5–0.6 in). The ground colour of the uppersides is sooty or greyish brown, with relatively small spots on the forewing (except in Romania) and an almost unmarked hindwing. The undersides are paler, with fairly large and rather 'blurred' white spots on the hindwing, including two quite large ones on the outer edge.

Similar species: Alpine Grizzled Skipper has three small white spots below the end of the forewing cell, and darker undersides with more distinct spotting.

Flight: June to August.

Habitat: Montane grassland, usually above 1,600 m (5,250 ft). The larval foodplants include cinquefoils and Sibbaldia.

Life-cycle: Nothing is known of the early stages of this butterfly.

Range: Confined mainly to the Alps, with additional colonies in Bulgaria and Romania and possibly in the Pyrenees.

p.233 **Northern Grizzled Skipper**
Pyrgus centaureae

Description: 12–15 mm (0.5–0.6 in). The ground
colour of the uppersides ranges from dark
greyish brown to almost black, with a
liberal coating of pale hairs that gives them
a paler look. There are two fairly
prominent white spots just below the
forewing cell, and the hindwing has a well-
defined arc of white spots in the outer half
and a conspicuous rectangular spot on the
front margin. The undersides are grey and
white, with bold white lines along the
veins of the hindwing, and sometimes
appear almost entirely white.

Similar species: Alpine Grizzled Skipper has no clear white
spotting on the upperside of the hindwing,
and no white lines on the veins of the
underside.

Flight: June to July, often basking on low-growing
vegetation.

Habitat: Moorland and marsh, especially among the
dwarf birch and sallow scrub around the
tree-line – up to 1,000 m (3,275 ft). The
larval foodplant is Cloudberry.

Life-cycle: The hemispherical, ribbed eggs are pale
green, and they are laid singly on the
foodplant. The caterpillars are pale brown
with a dark back-stripe, and the chrysalis is
brown with darker spots on each side of the
abdomen. Nothing is known of the life-
cycle in the wild.

Range: Northern Scandinavia and a large area of
northern Asia. Also widely distributed in
the Arctic and montane regions of North
America, where it is known as the Alpine
Checkered Skipper.

p.234 **Red-underwing Skipper** *Spialia sertorius*

Description: 9–14 mm (0.4–0.6 in). The uppersides are
dark brown to black with the usual
scattering of white spots, including a
complete row of small, but conspicuous
submarginal spots on each wing. The
underside of the forewing is largely grey
with brick-red patches at the base and the

tip, while the underside of the hindwing is brick-red with large white spots.

Similar species: No other skipper combines the dark uppersides with the brick-red underside of the hindwing.

Flight: April to September, usually in two broods although there may be only one brood at high altitudes. Insects of the second brood are noticeably smaller than those of the first.

Habitat: Dry, scrubby places from sea level to about 2,200 m (7,225 ft). The larval foodplants include cinquefoils, Bramble, Raspberry, Salad Burnet, and various other rosaceous plants.

Life-cycle: The eggs are laid singly on the foodplants and they hatch within two weeks. The caterpillar is dark brown and rather hairy, with a broad, pale back-stripe. It feeds mainly at night and spends the daytime in a tent of silk and leaves. Autumn caterpillars hibernate and complete their growth in the spring. Pupation takes place in the leaf-litter beneath the foodplants.

Range: Much of south and central Europe, but absent from the British Isles. Also found over a large area of temperate Asia and in North Africa.

S. s. therapne is a very small race – the smallest of all European skippers – with forewings only 9–10 mm long (0.4 in); it is confined to Corsica and Sardinia.

---

p.234 **Hungarian Skipper** *Spialia orbifer*

Description: 11–14 mm (0.4–0.6 in). The uppersides are dark brown to black, with scattered white spots and a uniform row of submarginal spots on each wing, although these spots may be quite small. The underside of the forewing is brownish grey, and the underside of the hindwing is olive-green with a conspicuous round white spot on the front edge. There is also a markedly rounded spot in the centre of the underside of the hindwing.

Similar species: Red-Underwing Skipper is very similar on the upperside, but has brick-red undersides. Carline Skipper has no submarginal spots on the forewing and lacks the round spot in the centre of the underside of the hindwing.

Flight: April to September in two broods.

Habitat: Scrubby grassland with plenty of flowers, usually in upland areas from 600 to 2,000 m (1,975–6,550 ft) and most frequent on limestone. The larval foodplants are Salad Burnet, Great Burnet, and cinquefoils.

Life-cycle: The caterpillars are black with a yellow stripe on each side. They hibernate in the leaf-litter and pupate in rolled-up leaves of the foodplant.

Range: Eastern Europe, from the eastern shores of the Adriatic and on through southern Asia to Iran. Also in Sicily, but overlapping with Red-Underwing Skipper only in Hungary and Austria.

This species, which was once treated as a subspecies of the Red-Underwing Skipper, is also known as the Orbed Red-Underwing Skipper.

p.234 **Persian Skipper** *Spialia phlomidis*

Description: 14–15 mm (0.6 in). The uppersides are almost black, usually with a complete series of submarginal spots and with a pale smudge at the base of the forewing. There is a large rectangular white spot in the centre of the hindwing. The underside of the forewing is greyish brown with relatively large white spots. The underside of the hindwing is olive-green or grey, with a white streak along the front margin and a prominent white band across the centre. The white submarginal spots are triangular and often contain dark spots.

Similar species: Hungarian Skipper is smaller, with no white streak on the underside of the hindwing and no pale smudge on the upperside of the forewing.

Flight: June to July.

Habitat: Flower-rich scrubby grassland up to about 1,700 m (5,575 ft). *Phlomis* species have often been quoted as foodplants, but there is no proof of this; *Convolvulus* species have also been suggested as likely foodplants.

Life-cycle: Nothing is known of the early stages of this butterfly.

Range: Southern Balkans and across southern Asia to Iran. A very local species.

---

p.235 **Tessellated Skipper** *Muschampia tessellum*

Description: 16–18 mm (0.6–0.7 in). The uppersides are dark grey – often somewhat paler than other similar skippers – with well-developed white spots, including two or three pairs in the space just in front of the rear margin of the forewing and three elongated spots just before the wing-tip. There is a conspicuous oval white spot on the front edge of the hindwing. The underside of the forewing is largely dark grey but the underside of the hindwing is olive-green and white, and sometimes has a broad white outer margin.

Similar species: Spinose Skipper is slightly smaller and has a larger amount of white.

Flight: May to June. In common with other *Muschampia* species this butterfly often basks with its forewings swept back, largely concealing the hindwings.

Habitat: Flower-rich grassland, from sea level to about 1,000 m (3,275 ft). The larval foodplants are *Phlomis samia* and possibly other *Phlomis* species.

Life-cycle: Winter is passed as a small caterpillar.

Range: Southern Balkans and on through Asia to Mongolia.

Spinose Skipper *Muschampia cribrellum*

Description: 13–16 mm (0.5–0.6 in). The ground colour of the uppersides is dark grey, heavily marked with white spots, including three pairs strung out in the space just in front of the rear edge of the forewing and a full set of submarginal spots. There is usually a large square white spot in the middle of the hindwing, with a somewhat elongated oval spot on the front margin. The undersides are yellowish grey or greenish with large white markings on both wings. The sub-marginal spots on the hindwing usually link up to form a white border.

Similar species: Tessellated Skipper is a little larger and the three elongated spots near the tip of the forewing are isolated and more obvious.

Flight: May to June.

Habitat: Dry, open grassland (steppes). The larval foodplants are unknown but are possibly cinquefoils.

Life-cycle: Little or nothing is known of the early stages of this butterfly.

Range: Small populations occur in Hungary and western Romania. Outside Europe, the butterfly extends right across Asia from the northern shores of the Black Sea to Mongolia and northern China.

---

p.235 **Sage Skipper** *Muschampia proto*

Description: 14–15 mm (0.6 in). The ground colour of the uppersides is dark grey, often appearing yellowish in the male because of a coating of fine yellowish hair. The pattern is rather variable, but the submarginal spots are reduced to narrow and often obscure lunules, which generally link to form slender, wavy lines. There are usually two, more or less rectangular spots near the centre of the forewing. The undersides are yellowish grey or reddish brown, with white veins and a dark, eye-like spot on the forewing. The white spots of the hindwing usually link up to form three rather faint and narrow cross-lines.

Similar species: The white veins on the underside of the forewing should distinguish this butterfly from the other skippers.

Flight: April to September, in a single brood with a prolonged emergence period. Butterflies emerging late in the season tend to have more red on the underside.

Habitat: Dry, grassy places and waste ground from sea level to about 1,500 m (4,925 ft), but usually in upland areas. The larval foodplants include sages, *Phlomis* species, and other labiates.

Life-cycle: Eggs are laid throughout the summer and often do not hatch until the following spring. Caterpillars that do hatch in the summer go into hibernation at various stages of development before completing growth in the following spring. Mature caterpillars are dark grey with darker markings.

Range: The Iberian peninsula and the Mediterranean region, and on through southern Asia to the Caspian Sea. Also in North Africa. Rare in southern France and absent from northern Italy.

---

p.236 **Mallow Skipper** *Carcharodus alceae*

Description: 12–17 mm (0.5–0.7 in). The uppersides are brown with a variable amount of dark mottling and often a slight pink or purplish tinge on all four wings. The forewing has a few small, pale spots, including a more or less transparent one at the end of the cell. The undersides are greyish brown, with white spots on both wings. The outer edge of the hindwing is strongly toothed or scalloped.

Similar species: Tufted Marbled Skipper has larger white spots, including one or more in the middle of the upperside of the hindwing, a tuft of dark hair near the base of the underside of the male forewing, and white streaks on the underside of the hindwing.

Flight: April to September in one, two, or three broods. Summer butterflies are usually paler than first-brood insects, but in the far south the third-brood insects are quite dark and small.

Habitat: Dry grassland, from sea level to about 1,600 m (5,250 ft) but most common in upland areas. The larval foodplants are mallows and related plants.

Life-cycle: The eggs are laid singly on the foodplants and they hatch in a week or two. The caterpillar is greyish green with a blue tinge and black-ringed yellow spiracles. The head is black. It lives in a shelter made by spinning leaves together with silk and it is about 22 mm (0.9 in) long when mature. Autumn caterpillars hibernate in their shelters when they are more or less fully grown and they pupate in the same place in the spring.

Range: Southern and central Europe, but absent from the British Isles. Also in North Africa and eastwards into central Asia.

C. a tripolinus – a rather small race from the southwestern part of the Iberian peninsula – is sometimes treated as a separate species (*Carcharodus tripolinus*) and called the False Mallow Skipper.

---

p.236 **Marbled Skipper** *Carcharodus lavatherae*

Description: 14–17 mm (0.6–0.7 in). The upperside of the forewing is olive-brown, often with a greenish tinge, and marked with white spots and darker smudges. There is a conspicuous, more or less transparent spot in the cell, and there are triangular white spots or streaks around the outer margin. The upperside of the hindwing is darker, with a conspicuous row of white spots across the centre, and an arc of white chevrons beyond it. The outer margin appears scalloped, but this is really just a pattern of light and dark tooth-like markings. The undersides are greenish grey with pale borders and indistinct white bands.

Similar species: The pattern of the upperside, combined with the pale borders to the underside, distinguish this butterfly from all other skippers.

Flight: May to August, usually in a single brood, but second broods have occasionally been reported,

Habitat: Dry, flower-rich places from sea level to about 1,800 m (5,900 ft): usually in limestone uplands. The larval foodplants are woundworts.

Life-cycle: Eggs are laid during the summer and hatch within a couple of weeks. The caterpillars live in silken webs spun on the foodplants, and they hibernate there before completing their growth in the spring. The chrysalis is brown with a bluish bloom.

Range: Most of southern and central Europe, but rare north of the Alps. Also in North Africa and western Asia. Absent from the British Isles and most of western France.

---

p.236 **Southern Marbled Skipper**
Carcharodus boeticus

Description: 13–14 mm (0.5–0.6 in). The ground colour of the uppersides is greyish brown, heavily marbled with brown, especially on the hindwing. The forewing has a few white spots; the hindwing has two fairly distinct white bands, the outer one being formed from linked lunules and therefore very wavy. The undersides are pale brown or yellowish grey, with a characteristic network of white bands and veins on the hindwing. The male has a dark hair-tuft on the inner margin of the underside of the forewing.

Similar species: Sage Skipper has white veins on the underside of the forewing, but not on the hindwing, and also has much darker uppersides. Tufted and Oriental marbled skippers have similar uppersides, but lack the network on the underside of the hindwing.

Flight: May to October in one, two or three broods. Second- and third-brood insects tend to be paler than spring ones, and the male's hair-tuft is also paler in summer butterflies.

Habitat: Dry, sunny, flower-rich places from sea level to about 1,500 m (4,925 ft), but most common in hilly areas. The larval foodplants are horehounds and other labiates.

Life-cycle: Eggs are laid throughout the summer. Autumn larvae hibernate before completing their growth in the spring.

Range: Iberia and southern France, extending into the Italian and Swiss Alps where it is rare and single-brooded. Also in central Italy, Sicily, North Africa, and across southern Asia to Iran.

p.237 **Tufted Marbled Skipper**
Carcharodus flocciferus

Description: 14–16 mm (0.6 in). The uppersides are dark greyish brown, with a black patch and three conspicuous white spots near the middle of the forewing – that in the cell being rather glassy. The hindwing is a little browner, with two or more white spots near the middle and, as in all *Carcharodus* species, the outer margin has a distinctly toothed or scalloped appearance. The underside of the forewing is greyish brown, with white streaks on the margins; the male has a dark hair-tuft. The underside of the hindwing is greyish, with white streaks and chequered margins.

Similar species: Mallow Skipper has smaller white spots on both surfaces – often none on the upperside of the hindwing – and the male has no hair-tuft. Southern Marbled Skipper has a network of white veins on the underside of the hindwing. Oriental Marbled Skipper is paler underneath and hindwing has more obvious white banding.

Flight: May to August in one or two broods.

Habitat: Rough, flower-rich grassland from sea level to 2,000 m (6,550 ft), but most often in upland areas. The larval foodplants are various woundworts and other labiates, especially White Horehound.

Life-cycle: Winter is passed in the larval stage.

Range: Southern and central Europe, and possibly across southern Asia to Afghanistan, but the eastern boundary is not really known because of the species' confusion with the very similar Oriental Marbled Skipper. Absent from the British Isles and northern and western France.

p.237 **Oriental Marbled Skipper**
Carcharodus orientalis

Description: 14–15 mm (0.6 in). The ground colour of the uppersides ranges from greenish grey to brown, with the hindwing a little darker than the forewing. The forewing has a dark band near the middle and a few slender white spots, while the hindwing usually has an arc of white spots in the centre. The undersides are pale greyish brown with indistinct white markings. The male has a prominent, dark hair-tuft on the underside of the forewing.

Similar species: Southern Marbled Skipper has a distinct reticulate pattern on the underside of the hindwing. Tufted Marbled Skipper has a darker underside with conspicuous white streaks on the hindwing.

Flight: April to September in two or three broods.

Habitat: Dry grasslands from sea level to about 1,800 m (5,900 ft), but most common in upland areas. The larval foodplant is probably some kind of woundwort.

Life-cycle: Winter is passed in the larval stage.

Range: The Balkans and Hungary, flying at much lower altitudes than the Tufted Marbled Skipper in areas where the two species overlap.

This butterfly was once regarded as an eastern race or subspecies of the Tufted Marbled Skipper.

---

p.238 **Dingy Skipper** *Erynnis tages*

Description: 12–15 mm (0.5–0.6 in). The uppersides are dark greyish brown, with a full set of white dots around the outer margin of each wing. The forewing has two rather indistinct darker bands, which often enclose a paler and somewhat shiny grey area. This is particularly noticeable in the Irish race *(E. t. baynesi)*, while specimens from southern Europe are almost uniformly brown. The undersides are pale brown, with a full set of small white dots around the outer margins and sometimes a few other small white spots as well.

Similar species: The combination of dark-brown uppersides and pale-brown undersides makes this butterfly unmistakable.

Flight: April to August in one or two broods: usually single-brooded in the British Isles and other more northerly regions. Adults rarely visit flowers and like to bask on the ground with their wings wide open, often pressed tightly against the earth. When truly at rest – at night or in dull weather – the wings are wrapped around the body like those of many moths.

Habitat: Flower-rich grassland from sea level to 2,000 m (6,550 ft), especially on lime-rich soils. Rough areas, including sand-dunes and old gravel pits, with short turf and bare patches are particularly favoured. The larval foodplants include Bird's-foot Trefoil, Crown Vetch, and other low-growing legumes. Field Eryngo is said to be eaten in some areas.

Life-cycle: The eggs are acorn-shaped with several studded ribs; they are pale yellow at first but gradually turn to orange. They are laid singly on the foodplants and hatch within a week or two. The downy caterpillar is bright green, with a purple back-stripe, a dark-brown or black head, and a yellow stripe along each side; it is about 17 mm (0.7 in) long when mature. It feeds in a shelter made by spinning leaves together low down on the foodplant. When fully grown, autumn caterpillars hibernate in similar shelters, and in spring they pupate in them without further feeding. The chrysalis has a shiny brown abdomen, but the rest of it is dark green. In parts of Scandinavia, where the species is single-brooded, hibernation may occur in the pupal stage.

Range: Throughout southern and central Europe and southern Scandinavia, and on through Asia to China. In Wales and much of northern Britain it is confined largely to coastal regions, but in Ireland – where it is the only skipper – it occurs mainly in inland areas. It is absent from the Mediterranean islands.

p.238 **Inky Skipper** *Erynnis marloyi*

Description: 14–16 mm (0.6 in). The uppersides are chocolate-brown without obvious marginal white dots. The forewings are heavily dusted with grey towards the outer margin and are crossed by two narrow black bands. There are up to three white dots at the front of the outer band. The undersides are plain brown and unmarked except for a white streak or a few dots near the tip of the forewing.

Similar species: Dingy Skipper has paler undersides and white marginal dots on both surfaces.

Flight: May to August, usually in a single brood but possibly with two broods in some places.

Habitat: Montane scree and grassland, up to 2,000 m (6,550 ft) or more. The larval foodplant is not known.

Life-cycle: Nothing is known of the life-cycle and early stages of this butterfly.

Range: Southern Balkans and on through Asia to the Himalayas.

p.239 **Chequered Skipper**
Carterocephalus palaemon

Description: 14–16 mm (0.6 in). The upperside is dark brown with yellow or orange patches. The latter vary in size, but the forewing cell is always pale with a brown spot in the centre. There is a distinct arc of yellow or orange spots close to the outer margin of the hindwing. The underside of the forewing is yellow with brown spots, and the underside of the hindwing is brown with pale spots similar to those on the upperside. The sexes are alike, although the female is slightly larger and a little paler.

Similar species: Northern Chequered Skipper has a similar pattern but has much less brown on the upperside. Duke of Burgundy Fritillary has deeper orange spots, and those near the edge of the hindwing have black centres; it also has a conspicuous white stripe on the underside of the hindwing.

Flight: May to July in a single brood. Adults are especially fond of the flowers of Bugle and Marsh Thistle, and in sunny weather they like to bask on the vegetation with their wings wide open.

Habitat: Scrubby grassland, including woodland margins and clearings, from sea level to 1,500 m (4,925 ft). The caterpillars feed on various grasses, with Purple Moor-grass being the main foodplant in Scotland.

Life-cycle: The domed, white or creamy eggs are laid singly on the grass-blades. The young caterpillar is pale green with darker stripes, but in its final instar it becomes yellowish with brown stripes. It lives in a tubular retreat made by drawing the edges of a grass-blade together, and it eats the rest of the blade right down to the midrib before moving to another blade and constructing another retreat. When fully fed in the autumn, the caterpillar is about 25 mm (1.0 in) long; it then binds several grass-blades together to form a snug chamber in which it spends the winter. Reappearing in the spring, the caterpillar makes a new chamber from dead leaves and pupates without further feeding. The chrysalis is pale brown with darker lines and a long point at the front.

Range: Most of Europe apart from the far south: absent from Iberia except Pyrenees. Also in Asia and North America, where it is called the Arctic Skipper.

The Chequered Skipper used to be widely distributed in the southern half of England, but it declined rapidly during the 19th and 20th centuries. The last English specimen was seen in 1976, but plans are now underway to re-introduce the butterfly into England. The species still flourishes in western Scotland and seems to be in no danger there.

---

p.239 **Northern Chequered Skipper**
Carterocephalus silvicolus

Description: 12–15 mm (0.5–0.6 in). The upperside of the forewing is yellow or orange with black or dark-brown spots, while the upperside of the hindwing is brown with yellow spots, including a prominent one close to the front margin. The underside has slightly more brown, but otherwise resembles the upperside. The sexes are alike, although females have more brown on the upperside.

Similar species: Chequered Skipper has a rich brown and orange pattern on the upperside and appears altogether darker, although the underside is much yellower.

Flight: May to July in a single brood.

Habitat: Sheltered valleys and light woodland, especially in damp areas, from sea level to about 500 m (1,650 ft). The larval foodplants are various grasses, especially Wood False Brome and Crested Dog's-tail.

Life-cycle: The shiny yellow, hemispherical eggs are laid singly on grasses. The caterpillar is straw-coloured with a reddish back-stripe and a dark-brown head. It lives in a tubular shelter made of grass; it hibernates there and completes its growth in the spring. It is about 25 mm (1.0 in) long when mature. The chrysalis is greenish yellow with narrow red stripes and is attached to the grass-stems.

Range: From Norway and the Baltic region, across northern Asia to Japan.

p.238 **Large Chequered Skipper**
Heteropterus morpheus

Description: 15–18 mm (0.6–0.7 in). The uppersides are dark chocolate-brown, with a few small yellow spots on the forewing. The underside of the forewing is brown with yellow markings near the tip, and the underside of the hindwing is largely yellow with large, black-ringed white spots. The sexes are alike except that the female has chequered fringes on the upperside: the male has no more than a faint chequering towards the front of the forewing.

Similar species: No other European butterfly has a similar pattern.

Flight: June to August in a single brood, keeping low over the vegetation with a very characteristic bouncing flight. It normally rests with its wings closed – the pattern on the underside of the hindwing providing surprisingly good camouflage on sun-dappled vegetation – but it will occasionally open its wings rather hesitatingly and bask for short periods.

Habitat: Damp heaths and meadows, including woodland clearings, from sea level to about 1,000 m (3,275 ft). The larval foodplants are various grasses, including Purple Moor-grass and Common Reed. A very local species, occurring in small and widely scattered colonies.

Life-cycle: The more or less spherical, ribbed, white eggs are laid singly on the grass-blades, and they hatch in two to three weeks. The caterpillar is grey with a brown head and a white stripe on each side. It feeds in a tubular retreat made of grass-blades or else right inside the hollow grass-stems. After passing the winter in a dormant state in its shelter, it completes its growth in the spring, reaching a length of about 25 mm (1.0 in). It then pupates at the base of the foodplant. The chrysalis is pale green and very slim.

Range: From northern Spain and the Atlantic coast of France, through central Europe and Asia, to Korea, but absent from central and eastern France and most of Germany.

The Large Chequered Skipper has been established in Jersey since 1946, possibly having been introduced with hay from France during the Second World War, but it has only a precarious hold and may have died out there at the end of the 1980s. The butterfly is threatened with extinction in many areas of Europe because the damp habitats that it requires are being drained.

---

p.241 **Small Skipper** *Thymelicus sylvestris*

Description: 12–16 mm (0.5–0.6 in). The uppersides are a bright golden orange with black margins; in the male there is a conspicuous black streak – the sex-brand – in the centre of the forewing. The undersides are also golden orange, but with a heavy dusting of greyish-green scales at the tip of the forewing and over much of the hindwing. The underside of the antennal club is orange.

Similar species: Essex Skipper is almost identical, but the underside of the antennal club is black. Lulworth Skipper is browner, with a faint arc of yellow spots near the tip of the forewing.

Flight: May to August, in a single brood but emerging over a long period. One of the golden skippers, it basks with its forewings partly raised.

Habitat: Rough, grassy places of all kinds, including roadsides, from sea level to about 2,000 m (6,550 ft). The larval foodplants are various grasses, but especially Yorkshire Fog in Britain. Creeping Soft-grass and Timothy are commonly used elsewhere.

Life-cycle: The cream-coloured eggs are lozenge-shaped, and they are laid in short rows inside the leaf-sheaths of the grass-stems. They hatch in about three weeks. The caterpillars eat their eggshells, but then immediately surround themselves with silk and go into hibernation without leaving the leaf-sheaths. Upon waking in the spring they separate, and each constructs a tubular retreat by fixing grass-blades together with silk. The young caterpillars feed inside their shelters, but older ones feed outside and leave characteristic V-shaped notches in the grass-blades. The mature caterpillar is pale green with lighter stripes on the sides and a darker one on the back; it is about 25 mm (1.0 in) long. It pupates inside a flimsy cocoon loosely wrapped in grass-blades, and the chrysalis is pale green with a brownish point at each end.

Range: Most of Europe, but absent from Ireland, Scotland and Scandinavia. Also in North Africa and on through southern Asia to Iran.

p.240 **Essex Skipper** *Thymelicus lineola*

Description: 12–15 mm (0.5–0.6 in). The uppersides are bright orange with black margins; in the male there is a conspicuous black streak – the sex-brand – in the centre of the forewing, although it is shorter and straighter than that of the Small Skipper.

The underside of the forewing is orange with a greyish tip, while that of the hindwing is orange with a heavy dusting of greyish scales, especially in the male. The underside of the antennal club is black.

Similar species: Small Skipper is almost identical, but can be distinguished by the orange underside of the antennal club. Lulworth Skipper is browner, with a faint arc of yellow spots near the tip of the forewing.

Flight: May to August in a single brood. One of the golden skippers, it basks with its forewings partly raised.

Habitat: Grassy places of all kinds, including roadsides and coastal salt-marshes, from sea level to about 2,000 m (6,550 ft). The larval foodplants are various coarse grasses, but mainly Cock's-foot and Creeping Soft-grass in Britain.

Life-cycle: The pale-yellow, lozenge-shaped eggs are laid in short rows in the leaf-sheaths of the foodplants; they remain there throughout the winter, although the caterpillars are fully formed inside the eggs long before the winter sets in. The eggs hatch in the spring and each young caterpillar feeds openly on the grasses for a few days before making a tubular retreat by rolling a grass-blade and binding it with silk. The fully grown caterpillar is about 25 mm (1.0 in) long; it is pale green with a dark stripe along the back, pale stripes on the sides, and three brown stripes on the head. It feeds mainly at the tips of the leaves, carving out V-shaped notches like those of Small Skipper. Pupation takes place in a silken net among folded grass-blades at the base of the foodplant. The chrysalis is green with a white point at each end.

Range: Throughout southern and central Europe and extending to southern Sweden and Finland. Also in North Africa and across central Asia to the Pacific. Introduced into North America, where it is known as the European Skipper, it has become something of a pest of hay-crops, especially Timothy grass.

The English name, given because the butterfly was first caught in Essex, is somewhat misleading because the insect is in no way restricted to Essex. It is widely distributed south of a line joining the Wash to the Bristol Channel.

p.240 **Lulworth Skipper** *Thymelicus acteon*

Description: 10–13 mm (0.4–0.5 in). The uppersides are brown with a dusting of golden scales, the latter usually more obvious in males than in females. There is an arc of golden or yellowish spots towards the tip of the forewing, usually quite conspicuous in the female, but very faint in the male. The male has a slightly wavy, black sex-brand in the centre of the forewing. The undersides are orange with a variable amount of grey scaling: the gold spots are faintly visible on the female forewing.

Similar species: Small Skipper and Essex Skipper are mainly orange and lack the golden spots on the forewing.

Flight: May to August in a single brood. In common with other golden skippers, it basks with its forewings partly raised.

Habitat: Rough, grassy places from sea level to about 1,700 m (5,575 ft). The caterpillars feed on Tor Grass and other coarse grasses.

Life-cycle: The yellow, lozenge-shaped eggs are laid in neat rows in the old flower-sheaths of the foodplants. They hatch in about three weeks, but the young caterpillars immediately spin silken hibernation chambers among the eggshells and do not feed until fresh leaves are available in the spring. On emerging from hibernation, each caterpillar makes a tubular shelter by drawing the edges of a grass-blade together with silk; it remains in the shelter by day, coming out to feed in the evenings. Like the Small Skipper, it carves out wedge-shaped notches from the grass-blades, although these tend to be broader and less V-shaped than those of the Small Skipper. The fully grown caterpillar is about 25 mm (1.0 in) long; it is pale green with cream stripes and a darker stripe along the back. Pupation takes place close to the ground in a flimsy cocoon of silk and grass. The chrysalis is pale green with a darker thorax and an unusually long 'beak' at the front.

Range: Throughout southern and central Europe, and through the Middle East to Iran. Also in the Canary Islands and North Africa.

The species is close to its northern limit in the British Isles and confined to the south coast from Dorset to Cornwall, but where it does exist it is often very abundant. Rarely found more than a few miles from the sea, it is especially common around Lulworth Cove.

p.241 **Silver-spotted Skipper** *Hesperia comma*

Description: 14–15 mm (0.6 in). The upperside of the male forewing is largely orange, with wide brown borders containing a few pale spots near the tip. There is a conspicuous black sex-brand near the middle of the wing. The upperside of the hindwing is largely brown with an orange flush and paler spots that often run together. The upperside of the female is a warm brown, with pale spots and an orange flush. The undersides of both sexes are largely olive-green with silvery-white spots, the spots on the hindwing forming a strongly curved and often V-shaped row towards the outer margin.

Similar species: Large Skipper has more orange on both surfaces and the underside spots are dull yellow.

Flight: June to September in a single brood. One of the golden skippers, it basks with its forewings partly raised.

Habitat: Grassy and stony slopes on lime-rich soils, from sea level to about 2,500 m (8,200 ft). The species generally requires heavily grazed areas with patches of bare soil, although it inhabits sand-dunes in parts of Scandinavia. The adults visit a wide range of flowers, including scabious and knapweeds. The caterpillars are confined to Sheep's-fescue grass in Britain, but also eat some other fine-leaved grasses, especially *Poa* species, elsewhere in Europe.

Life-cycle: The eggs, looking like miniature volcanoes complete with dimples in the top, are white at first, but soon become peach-coloured. They are laid singly, usually on small tufts of grass close to bare areas of soil. The caterpillar is dirty green in colour and heavily spotted with black. It lives in a shelter made by spinning grass-blades together and usually comes out to feed at night. It is about 25 mm (1.0 in) long when mature, and it pupates close to the ground in a cocoon of silk and grass-blades. The chrysalis is yellowish or greenish brown with violet-green wing-sheaths. Winter is passed in the egg stage or as a first-instar larva in northern and central Europe, but as a fully grown caterpillar in some southern areas.

Range: Most of Europe, but absent from most of northern Scandinavia. It is one of the rarest British butterflies, now confined to the south of England. The butterfly also occurs in North Africa, throughout temperate Asia, and over a large area of North America – where it is called the Common Branded Skipper.

p.242 **Large Skipper** *Ochlodes venata*

Description: 12–18 mm (0.5–0.7 in). The male upperside is bright orange-brown, becoming browner towards the outer margins, and studded with orange spots near the tip. There is a large black scent-brand in the centre of the forewing. The female tends to be a little darker than the male and more obviously spotted. The underside of the forewing is orange, while that of the hindwing is greenish yellow, both wings having faint yellow spots.

Similar species: Silver-spotted Skipper is superficially similar, but the upperside is generally browner and the underside has silvery spots on a greener background.

Flight: May to September in one or two broods. Single-brooded in the British Isles and other northern areas. One of the golden skippers, it basks with its forewings partly raised.

Habitat: Grassy places of all kinds, including open hillsides, forest clearings, roadsides, and hedgerows, from sea level to 2,500 m (8,200 ft), although it is absent from most upland areas of Britain. The adults visit a wide range of flowers, including Bramble and knapweeds. The larval foodplants are a range of broad-leaved grasses, but especially Cock's-foot grass and the larger fescues.

Life-cycle: The eggs are more or less hemispherical, pearly white at first but soon becoming yellow. They are laid singly under the grass-blades, most commonly on exposed plants at about 30 cm (1 ft) above the ground. The caterpillar, up to 30 mm (1.2 in) long, is dark green above, becoming bluish green below the yellow spiracular stripe. It has a prominent black head. It lives in a slender retreat made by rolling a single grass-blade into a tube, although as the caterpillar matures it may need to spin two or more blades together. Winter is passed in the larval stage, securely wrapped up in a sturdy tube of grass. Single-brooded populations can spend as much as ten months in the larval stage. Pupation takes place in a loose cocoon spun between several grass-blades. The chrysalis is slender and grey and covered with a waxy grey bloom.

Range: Most of Europe, but absent from northern Scotland and northern Scandinavia and from Ireland and most Mediterranean Islands. The species also ranges right across temperate Asia to Japan. Specimens from the northern areas tend to be smaller and darker than those from elsewhere.

p.243   **Mediterranean Skipper**
Gegenes nostrodamus

Description: 15–16 mm (0.6 in). The outer edges of the forewing are almost straight and the hindwings are distinctly angular. Male uppersides are uniformly pale brown, almost the colour of milk chocolate. The female is a little larger and has an arc of irregular white spots on the forewing. The undersides resemble the uppersides but are much paler and often almost grey: both sexes may have a few white spots on the forewing.

Similar species: The pointed wingtips and uniform colour distinguish this from almost all other European butterflies. Pigmy Skipper is smaller and darker – more like plain chocolate. Zeller's Skipper has translucent spots on the forewing.

Flight: May to October in two broods; most abundant from August to September. Basks on the ground in full sun.

Habitat: Dry, rocky places, especially around the coast and near dry riverbeds, from sea level to about 900 m (2,950 ft). The larval foodplants are undoubtedly grasses, but the exact species are unknown.

Life-cycle: Little is known of the early stages of this local and generally rare butterfly.

Range: From southern Portugal and the Mediterranean region, through much of Africa and the Middle East to the Himalayas. The butterfly occurs in central Spain, but is absent from France.

---

p.243 **Pigmy Skipper** *Gegenes pumilio*

Description: 12–15 mm (0.5–0.6 in). The forewings are fairly pointed and the hindwings are distinctly angular. The ground colour of the male upperside is dark chocolate-brown, with no markings. The female is slightly paler, with dirty-white spots on the forewing. The undersides are paler and greyer in both sexes, with indistinct white spots on both wings.

Similar species: Mediterranean Skipper has similarly pointed forewings, but it is lighter brown and has no spots on the underside of the hindwing. Zeller's Skipper has translucent spots on the forewing. Inky Skipper has more rounded forewings, with dark bands on the upperside and a white streak or row of spots on the underside.

Flight: April to October in two or three broods. It keeps close to the ground and often basks in full sun on stones and bare soil.

Habitat: Dry, rocky places, usually near the coast, from sea level to about 1,500 m (4,925 ft). The larval foodplants are undoubtedly grasses, but the exact species are not known.

Life-cycle: The caterpillar is up to 30 mm (1.2 in) long and it passes the winter in this stage, but little else is known of the early stages of this rather rare and local butterfly.

Range: Rarely far from the Mediterranean coastline in Europe, but widely distributed in Africa, and on through the Middle East to the Himalayas.

Zeller's Skipper *Borbo borbonica*

Description: 14–15 mm (0.6 in). The forewings have almost straight outer edges. All wings are dark brown on both surfaces, with translucent spots on the strongly pointed forewings. There are often small, dark-ringed white spots on the underside of the hindwing.

Similar species: Mediterranean and Pigmy skippers are of similar shape and colour but have no translucent spots on the wings.

Flight: August to October.

Habitat: Coastal cliffs and scrub. The larval foodplants are probably a variety of grasses.

Life-cycle: Little is known of the early stages of this butterfly.

Range: Widely distributed in Africa and also on some of the islands in the Indian Ocean. European records are only from Gibraltar and Spain where the species is probably just an occasional visitor from North Africa.

THE CONSERVATION OF BUTTERFLIES

People often say there are not as many
butterflies around today as there were 50
years ago. There are some good spots where
large numbers of butterflies can still be
seen but, in general, the observation is only
too true; the populations of most European
butterfly species have been declining for
many years. The main cause is the
exploding human population, with its
ever-increasing demands for houses, roads,
factories, and agricultural land, leading to
the destruction of all kinds of natural
habitat. In their wake, urbanization,
industry, and intensive farming bring
widespread pollution of air, soil, and water,
causing further problems for butterflies
and other wildlife. Conifer plantations are
insidiously taking over from what were
once butterfly-rich deciduous or mixed
woodlands, and they are also spreading
into previously open habitats to satisfy the
need for timber. Even the remaining
natural woodlands have lost a lot of their
butterflies as a result of changing
management regimes. There are just not as
many suitable places for butterflies as there
were 50 years ago.

Butterfly collectors have often been
blamed for the reduction in butterfly
numbers, but their effect has usually been
grossly overstated. Butterflies tend to get
on with the important business of
reproducing as soon as they have emerged
from their pupae, and most of the
butterflies that we see flying around have

probably already mated and the females have probably laid some if not all of their eggs. Collecting a few of these specimens will not harm a healthy butterfly population. It is unlikely that any butterfly has been driven to extinction, or even threatened, by collecting alone, but collecting can be a threat to species whose populations have already been diminished by other factors. Collectors may well have been responsible for the final demise of the English race of the Large Copper in the 1850s, although the drainage of the fens to make way for agriculture was already whittling away the butterfly's habitat more than a century earlier. Only a few small areas of fenland remained by the early part of the 19th century, and the decline of reed-cutting and peat-digging in these areas further reduced the habitat available for the butterfly. Collectors homing in on the remaining populations probably reduced them to levels from which they were unable to recover.

Whether or not normal collecting has a detrimental effect on butterfly populations, there is certainly no reason to fill cabinets with pinned specimens today. Our museums have extensive collections of preserved insects, which any interested person can examine and admire if they wish, and we are unlikely to add much to our knowledge of the anatomy of the adult insects by catching and killing more of them. This is not to say that no butterflies should be caught; it is often necessary to examine a specimen at close quarters to be sure of its identity, but there is no reason to keep it once its identity has been confirmed. Living insects are inestimably more interesting than dead ones, and modern photographic equipment and materials enable the butterfly hunter to get superb pictures of the insects in their natural surroundings without harming them in any way, as the photographs in this book demonstrate.

At the present time, about a dozen butterfly species are classified as endangered in Europe, which means that they are in real danger of extinction in the near future. They are not the rarest species, but those whose habitats are under the greatest threat. There are several much rarer butterflies, but they are relatively safe because they are mostly upland species and their habitats are not under threat. Most of the endangered butterflies favour damp, low-lying habitats where land-drainage is a constant threat. A further 50 or so species, which is about an eighth of all European butterflies, are classified as vulnerable, meaning that they are not in immediate danger, but could well become endangered if habitat destruction continues at its present rate. Some of them are already endangered in particular countries.

A great deal of effort, by both statutory and voluntary organizations, is now being devoted to wildlife conservation in Europe and, although few of these bodies are primarily concerned with butterflies, the insects are beginning to get the recognition they deserve. The loss of butterflies might not cause too much hardship, although they play a not unimportant role in pollinating various flowers, but the world would be a much less attractive place without them. This alone is a sufficient reason to conserve butterflies; it would be a sad indictment of today's society if our descendants had to grow up without knowing these delightful and attractive creatures.

Legislation to protect certain butterflies by preventing their collection is in force in many European countries. Apart from a few common species, such as the cabbage whites, all butterflies are legally protected in Germany and Luxembourg and in most parts of Austria. The French Département Alpes de Haute-Provence, a favourite collecting ground for many years, bans all collecting of butterflies and moths other than by children under 12 years old using nets no more than 20 cm (8 in) in diameter. The Wildlife and Countryside Act gives total protection to the Large Blue, Heath Fritillary, High Brown Fritillary, and

Swallowtail in Great Britain. Capturing any of these species is illegal, even if the insects are released immediately. The Act also gives limited protection to a further 22 species, including the Purple Emperor, Adonis Blue, Glanville Fritillary, and Silver-spotted Skipper. While it is not illegal to capture these butterflies, it is illegal to trade in them in Britain, even if the specimens were obtained elsewhere. Separate legislation gives total protection to the Brimstone, Large Heath, Small Blue, Holly Blue, Purple Hairstreak, Marsh Fritillary, and Dingy Skipper in Northern Ireland and the Isle of Man. Similar laws are designed to protect various threatened and vulnerable species elsewhere in Europe, but enforcing these laws is never easy and protection of the habitat must always be the prime aim of butterfly conservation.

Nature reserves are playing an increasingly important rôle in the conservation of butterflies and other forms of wildlife, by protecting and conserving a wide range of habitats. It has been estimated that a fifth of Britain's butterfly species will soon be confined to nature reserves. It might be thought that fencing a piece of land and sticking up a 'Nature Reserve' sign is all that is necessary for conserving the local wildlife, but there is much more to it than that. Nature does not stand still; any neglected land is quickly covered with scrub, and trees soon follow. This is fine if a dense woodland habitat is what is wanted, but it is no good for butterflies. Regular management must be carried out to maintain suitable butterfly habitats, but before this can be done the precise conditions that are required by each species at each stage of its life cycle must be discovered. Several butterfly species have been lost from nature reserves simply because their requirements were not fully understood.

The Heath Fritillary thrives in various grassy habitats in southern Europe, but many of its more northerly populations, including those in southeast England, require open woodland of the type that was continually being created by coppicing in earlier times. With the decline in coppicing, the butterfly became progressively rarer in Britain and in 1980 it was regarded as our most endangered species. In an early attempt to conserve the species, two woods with healthy populations were acquired as reserves, but the butterfly died out in both places because its dependence on the earliest stages of woodland was not appreciated at the time. Research by Martin Warren, now Head of Conservation at Butterfly Conservation, later uncovered the precise requirements of the butterfly and its larvae, and appropriate management of the insect's remaining woodland habitats has led to a marked increase in numbers in recent years. The butterfly has now been successfully re-established to some of its old haunts.

The Large Blue has also suffered through lack of understanding of its requirements. In common with many other British grassland butterflies, it declined rapidly during the 1950s, when the myxomatosis outbreak wiped out most of the rabbit population and many hillsides became covered with coarse grass and scrub as a consequence. The remaining Large Blue colonies, all in southwest England, were carefully guarded, but populations continued to shrink. It was then realized that the ant (*Myrmica sabuleti*) that plays such a vital rôle in the butterfly's life cycle (*see* pp.349–50) cannot survive when the turf is more than about 4 cm (1.6 in) high, but this discovery came too late to the butterfly in Britain and it was declared extinct in 1979. Since then, thanks to Jeremy Thomas and his colleagues at the Institute of Terrestrial Ecology, the Large Blue has been re-established in a few carefully managed sites and early indications are that it is doing well.

Many attempts have been made to re-establish butterflies in their former haunts in various parts of Britain and they have met with varying degrees of success. Apart from the Heath Fritillary and Large Blue mentioned above, the Black Hairstreak and the Adonis Blue have done well in their new homes. The Adonis Blue population on one reserve was estimated at 4,500 individuals just two years after the release of 65 adults. But the habitats and management regimes must be right if such re-establishments are to have any chance of success. There have been several attempts to re-establish the Swallowtail at Wicken Fen in Cambridgeshire, but they have failed because, despite massive scrub-clearance operations, the habitat still does not seem to be able to support enough large milk parsley plants.

Re-establishment can be an exciting and constructive aspect of butterfly conservation. Some naturalists disapprove of such interference, but where the original extinction was simply due to loss of habitat, brought about by human activity, it seems perfectly good conservation practice, as long as a suitable habitat can be re-created and maintained in a state capable of sustaining a viable population of butterflies. However, it must be done under professional guidance and only after consultation with local conservation organizations. Indiscriminate release of butterflies can upset monitoring schemes that may be in existence and even damage existing butterfly populations. As well as ensuring that the receiving site is suitable, great care must be taken in choosing the stock for re-establishment. It must be healthy stock of the correct race. Normally, it should be taken from the nearest available locality, but only if the donor population is vigorous enough to survive the removal of a dozen or more adult females.

Gardens cover many thousands of hectares of Europe, and their millions of nectar-filled flowers attract huge numbers of butterflies. Apart from some of the high-altitude species, every species probably visits a garden somewhere or other, but not many of them actually breed in our gardens. With a few well-known exceptions, butterfly caterpillars do not like our cultivated plants and the adults go elsewhere to lay their eggs. Nevertheless, our flower gardens are important filling stations for the adults: they provide them with energy for seeking out their foodplants elsewhere, and the butterflies give us a lot of pleasure at the same time. Moths, bees, and various other insects also enjoy the feast and add to the interest of the garden. However, it is possible to encourage butterflies to breed in the garden by growing certain flowers. Honesty and Sweet Rocket, for example, will encourage the Orange-tip to settle down, and Bird's-foot Trefoil may bring in some of the blues. A little untidiness can also help: leaving long grass at the base of walls and hedges may persuade the Gatekeeper and other browns, and some of the skippers to lay their eggs there. Gardeners are often urged to leave a patch of stinging nettles as breeding grounds for the Peacock, Small Tortoiseshell, and other vanessids. This is an excellent idea in theory, but don't expect the butterflies to come flocking to a small patch behind the potting shed. They like to lay their eggs in the sunshine, so the nettles must be in the sun for at least part of the day – and to be really successful you need quite a large patch. If the butterflies don't come, you can always eat the nettles yourself.

The organizations involved in the conservation of butterflies include big international bodies, such as the Worldwide Fund for Nature (WWF) and The International Union for Conservation of Nature and Natural Resources (IUCN), governmental organizations, such as English Nature, national societies, such as Butterfly Conservation, and numerous local natural history societies. The latter might simply tend a few butterfly gardens or monitor the butterflies on their local roadside verges, but they still play a very important rôle in conservation. WWF is essentially a fund-raising organization and is particularly concerned with endangered species. IUCN is primarily a monitoring and advisory organization, working closely with governments and other official bodies to initiate scientifically based conservation programmes. Butterfly Conservation was founded in 1968 as the British Butterfly Conservation Society and has as its stated aim the restoration of a healthy and balanced environment, with butterflies and wildlife returned as far as possible to their former glories. Supported by a vigorous network of local branches, it creates and manages reserves, advises landowners and others on various aspects of butterfly conservation, and carries out a great deal of the monitoring work necessary to keep track of what is happening to butterfly populations all over the country. Many other European countries have similar organizations and are actively assessing their butterfly populations and taking steps to ensure their future survival.

The United Kingdom also has a flourishing network of county-based Wildlife Trusts, which have played an invaluable rôle in nature conservation for many years. The Trusts own or manage hundreds of reserves, ranging from a few hundred square metres to hundreds of hectares, and between them they look after almost all of Britain's butterfly species. With members all over the country, the Trusts quickly learn of new threats to wildlife and are often able to take swift remedial action. As well as managing reserves, the Trusts and Butterfly Conservation are heavily involved with education, which is arguably their most important function. If the conservation message does not get across to our descendants, what has been achieved so far will ultimately count for nothing. But if interest can be stimulated in the young people of the next generation at an early age, they are likely to maintain that interest and carry on the good work, and if they keep the butterflies in good shape the rest of the environment is likely to remain in good condition as well.

GLOSSARY

aestivation A period of inactivity or dormancy during the summer.

anal angle The rear corner of the hindwing.

androconia The scent-releasing scales on a male butterfly's wing.

antennae The two sensory appendages (feelers) on an insect's head.

basal region The region of a wing closest to the body (see p.13).

cell Any area of an insect wing bounded by veins, but in butterflies it refers particularly to the discal cell – the generally closed and more or less oval area near the middle of the wing.

chrysalis See pupa.

cocoon A silken bag or shelter bag spun by some caterpillars, especially those of moths, in which they then pupate.

compound eye An eye composed of numerous separate lenses. Butterflies and most other insects have eyes of this kind.

costa The front margin of a wing.

discal cell See cell.

discal region The central region of a wing (see p.13)

dorsum The rear or inner margin of the wing.

ecdysis Moulting or skin-changing.

hibernation A period of inactivity or dormancy during the winter.

instar A stage in an insect's life between any two moults, although a newly hatched insect that has not yet moulted is said to be in its first instar. After the first moult, it enters the second instar. The final instar is the adult insect.

larva The scientific name for a caterpillar or any other young insect that has to pass through a pupal stage before reaching maturity.

lunule A crescent-shaped spot, especially one in an arc close to the wing margin.

migration The regular to-and-fro movement of animals between different areas. In the northern hemisphere, migratory butterflies move northwards in spring and southwards in autumn.

palps Short sensory appendages, attached to the mouth-parts and playing a major rôle in detecting food and foodplants (see p.11).

pheromone   A chemical 'messenger' released by an animal and stimulating a particular response, such as mating behaviour, in another creature of the same kind.

post-discal region   An area in the outer part of a wing, between the discal and submarginal areas (*see* p.13).

proboscis   The tongue of a butterfly or moth.

prolegs   The thick, fleshy legs on the rear half of a caterpillar's body.

pupa   The third major stage in the life of a butterfly or moth, between the larva (caterpillar) and the adult stage. Also known as the chrysalis.

pupation   The change from a caterpillar to a pupa or chrysalis.

scent brand   A patch of scent-emitting scales (androconia) on the wing of a male butterfly. Also called a sex brand.

sex brand   *See* scent brand.

space   Any of the areas of wing membrane partly or completely enclosed by veins (*see* p.12).

sphragis   The horny pouch secreted by male Apollo butterflies during mating and attached to the females as a sort of 'chastity belt' to prevent further mating (*see* p.23).

submarginal region   An area in the outer part of a wing, beyond the post-discal region but not quite reaching the margin (*see* p.13).

succinct pupa   A pupa or chrysalis fixed in a head-up position and held in place by a silken girdle (*see* pp.20–1).

suspended pupa   A pupa or chrysalis hanging in a head-down position from a small pad of silk (*see* pp.20–1).

tarsi   The feet of an insect, made up of one or more small segments.

termen   The outer margin of the wing.

tornus   The outer angle at the rear of the wings, especially the forewing.

venation   The arrangement of veins in a wing.

PICTURE CREDITS

All pictures have been researched and supplied via The Frank Lane Picture Agency Ltd. FLPA would like to thank Jean and David Hosking; Rosemary Foulger; Marcus Webb; the contributing photographers; and the following agencies for all their help with this project: Panda Foto Library, Natural Image, Natural Science Photos. Special thanks to Ted Benton.

Cover photograph: Swallowtail, *Papilio machaon*, Hans Dieter Brandl.

t = top; um = upper middle; m = middle; lm = lower middle; b = bottom

Balint: 69t; Barnham: 52b, 81b4, 5, 83b3, 105m2, 122b2, 128b, 162m, 196b1; Bebbington: 100b; Benton: 43b, 44t1, 2, 44m1, 44b3, 45m, 45b, 50t1, 2, 50b1, 2, 51t, 53t1, 2, 53m3, 4, 53b1, 2, 54t, 54m2, 3, 54b4, 5, 55t, 56b, 57b2, 58t2, 58m, 59m, 59b, 60t, 60m, 60b, 61m, 61b, 62um, 62lm, 62b4, 5, 64b, 65m1, 2, 66b, 69b1, 2, 72b3, 73b, 74t, 74b1, 2, 75t, 75m, 75b1, 2, 76t, 76m, 76b, 77t, 77m3, 78um, 78b, 79t2, 4, 80t, 80m, 81t, 82t1, 2, 3, 82b1, 2, 3, 83t, 83m, 84b, 85t, 85m, 85b, 86t, 86m, 86b, 87m1, 2, 87b, 88m, 89t2, 89b1, 2, 3, 90b2, 91t, 91b, 92t, 92b, 93t2, 93b1, 2, 94b3, 95t2, 96t1, 2, 96m3, 96b1, 2, 97t1, 2, 97m1, 2, 97b, 98m, 98b4, 99t, 99b3, 100t, 100m, 101t, 101m, 101b, 102t, 102m, 102b, 103t2, 103lm, 103b, 104t1, 2, 105t1, 105b1, 2, 106t, 106b, 107t1, 2, 108b, 109b, 110t2, 110m, 110b1, 2, 111t2, 113t, 113m, 114t, 114m, 114b, 115m2, 115b, 116t2, 3, 116b1, 3, 117b, 118b, 119t1, 2, 119b1, 2, 120t, 121t, 121m, 121b3, 4, 122t, 122lm, 124m, 128t, 128lm, 135t, 135b, 136t2, 137b, 141t, 142t, 142b, 143t1, 143m, 144b, 145m3, 145b1, 2, 147t, 148t2, 148um, 149t1, 2, 149b3, 150t, 150m, 151t1, 3, 151b1, 2, 152t2, 152b1, 2, 153t1, 2, 153lm, 154t2, 3, 154lm, 155m3, 156um, 157t1, 2, 157lm, 158lm1, 2, 159b1, 2, 160t1, 2, 161t1, 3, 161b1, 2, 3, 163t1, 2, 163b1, 3, 164t1, 2, 165t1, 2, 165lm, 167b1, 2, 168t1, 2, 168b, 169um2, 3, 169b1, 2, 170t, 170b3, 171t, 171b1, 2, 174t, 174m, 175b1, 2, 176t, 176b, 177b1, 2, 179t, 180b, 181t, 181m, 181b, 183b1, 185um, 185lm2, 188um, 188b, 189t, 189b, 190t, 190m, 190b, 191t1, 2, 191m, 191b, 192t1, 2, 192b2, 193t, 193b, 194t, 194b, 196um, 196l2, 198b1, 2, 199t1, 2, 199lm, 200t, 200m, 200b, 201b1, 2, 202um, 202lm, 203t1, 2, 203b1, 2, 204b1, 2, 205t1, 2, 205b1, 2, 3, 207t, 207m, 207b, 208t1, 2, 208b, 209b1, 2, 210b1, 2, 211t1, 2, 212um, 212lm, 214t, 214m3, 215m3, 215b2, 216t, 216b2, 217t2, 219lm, 219b3, 220t1, 220um, 220lm2, 223t, 226b, 227um, 227lm, 229t, 229b, 230m, 230b1, 2, 231t, 231b, 232lm, 232b, 233um3, 233b1, 2, 234t2, 234m1, 2, 234b1, 2, 235t1, 2, 235b1, 2, 236t1, 2, 236m, 237um, 237b1, 2, 238t2, 238m, 240t, 240m, 241um, 241b1, 242t, 242m, 243m, 243b;

Bird: 213lm; Brandl: 42t, 42m, 47m; Borrell: 129lm;
Chinery: 69m1, 79b1, 2, 3, 4, 87t, 96m4, 123t, 137t, 146t, 147b,
148t1, 155b, 170b4, 213b, 217m1, 218t, 218m, 238b1, 240b,
243t; Ferrari: 51b, 57t1, 2, 57b1, 63um, 136m, 139t, 139b,
171um, 177t1, 2, 198t, 216m1, 2; Goodden: 43t1, 2; Gore: 45t;
Harmer: 66t, 215bl; Heard: 145t; Hosking: 42b, 129b;
Hyde: 104b1, 2; Kreutzer: 47t, 55b, 63t1, 2, 63b1, 2, 3, 64t,
67t1, 2, 3, 67b1, 2, 3, 88b, 111b1, 2, 113b, 115t, 117t, 135m,
138t, 138m, 153b, 160b1, 2, 167um, 174b, 178b, 180m, 182t,
182m, 182b, 183t, 183m, 196t, 211b1, 2, 217m2, 223b, 239b1, 2;
Natural Science Photos: 141b, 149h2, 158h, 167t, 175um, 229m;
Newton: 136b, 148lm; Ojalainen: 65t, 68t, 109t5, 6, 156b1, 2,
158t1, 2, 159t1, 2, 164b, 183b2, 184m, 184b, 195b1, 2, 197t1, 2;
Petretti: 65b; Rose: 61t, 72b1, 2, 78lm, 79t3, 140t, 145um2,
164lm, 238t1; Stella: 46m, 187t; Tinning: 143t2, 148b2, 166um,
179b; Watts: 95b1, 133m, 221b, 236b2; West: 129t1, 2;
Wharton: 72t1, 2, 146lm, 170m, 194m, 226t, 242b;
Wilmshurst: 52m, 77m2, 77b, 124b, 128um2, 3, 133b, 141m,
144t, 154b, 155m2, 241b3; Wilson: 125b; Yates-Smith: 43m,
44lm, 46t, 46b, 47b, 52t, 55m2, 3, 56t, 56m, 58t1, 58b1, 2, 59t,
62um, 64m, 66m, 68b1, 2, 3, 69m2, 73t, 73m, 74t, 78t, 79t1,
80b, 81m2, 3, 83b4, 84t1, 2, 3, 88t, 89t1, 90t1, 2, 90b1, 93t1,
94t1, 2, 3, 94b1, 2, 95t1, 95b2, 98t, 98b3, 99m, 99b2, 103t1, 3,
106m2, 3, 107b1, 2, 108t1, 2, 108m, 109m, 110t1, 111t1,
112t1, 2, 112b3, 4, 115m1, 116t1, 116b2, 118t, 118m, 120m,
120b, 121b4, 122um, 123m, 123b, 124t, 125t, 125m, 132t, 132b,
133t, 134t, 134m, 134b, 136t1, 140b, 143b, 146um, 146b, 147m,
148b1, 149lm, 150b1, 2, 151um2, 152t1, 154t1, 155t, 156t, 157b,
161t2, 162t, 162b, 163b2, 165um3, 165b, 166t, 166b1, 2, 3,
168lm, 169t, 175t, 178t, 178m, 180t, 184t, 185t, 185b1, 3,
186t1, 2, 186b1, 2, 187b, 188t, 188lm, 192lm, 195t1, 2,
197b1, 2, 198um, 199b, 201t1, 2, 202t, 202b, 204t1, 2, 206t,
206m, 206b, 208lm, 209t1, 2, 210t1, 2, 212t, 212b, 213t1, 2,
214m2, 214b1, 2, 215t, 215m2, 216b1, 217t1, 217b, 218b, 219t,
219um, 219b4, 220t2, 220b3, 4, 221t, 221m, 222t, 222b, 227t,
227b, 228t1, 2, 228b1, 2, 230t, 232t1, 2, 233t, 234t1, 236b1,
237t, 238b2, 239t1, 2, 241t, 241b2.

Ted Benton would like to thank Vic Barnham and John Kramer for
their company on many delightful European field trips; Ron
Leestmans, Joe Firmin, Peter Russell, John Coutsis, Stanislav
Abadjiev, and many others for indispensable help and advice; and
Shelley and the boys for putting up with some very eccentric
'holidays'.

Basil Yates-Smith would like to acknowledge the following for
their help in tracking down various butterflies for photography:
André Chauliac, Sylvain Cuvelier, Joe Firmin, the late Peter Cribb,
and the late Lt Col W. B. L. (Bill) Manley.

INDEX

Numbers in **bold** refer to colour plates. The circle preceding English names makes it easy for you to keep a record of the butterflies you see. Species marked by an asterisk (*) are not included in this book, although they are covered in some other books on European butterflies. Apart from one or two recently discovered species, they are mostly Asiatic butterflies that get no further into Europe than various islands in the Aegean Sea.

C